MW00534516

2004
COACH OF THE YEAR CLINICS
FOOTBALL MANUAL

Edited by Earl Browning

www.coacheschoice.com

ISBN: 1-58518-896-4

Library of Congress Control Number: 2004105091

Telecoach, Inc. Transcription: Kent Browning, Tom Cheaney, Joe Maupin

Diagrams: Steve Haag

Book layout and cover design: Bean Creek Studio

Front and back cover photos of Pete Carroll: courtesy of University of Southern California Sports Information

Front and back cover photos of Nick Saban: courtesy of Steve Franz/LSU Sports Information

Back cover photo of Barry Switzer: courtesy of the University of Oklahoma

Special thanks to the Nike clinic managers for having the lectures taped.

Coaches Choice
P.O. Box 1828
Monterey, CA 93942
www.coacheschoice.com

Contents

Contents

ESTABLISHING THE 3-4 DEFENSE

University of Kentucky

I came to this clinic a year ago at this time and sat in on the lectures with great interest. I did not know what I was getting into when I accepted the job as defensive coordinator at the University of Kentucky. At that time I announced we were going to play the 3-4 defensive alignment. I was questioned by a lot of football people all over the state. They wanted to know how we were going to play a 3-4 defensive alignment when we did not have any linebackers. I was undertaking the task of installing a defense that very few people knew anything about.

Believe me, we had our growing pains this past year. We learned a lot about our players, and we learned a lot about ourselves as coaches. One thing that I already knew, but it really was true for me last year, was this. It is what your players can do, and not what you know as a coach. All of you know a lot about football. It is not what you know, but it is what you can convey to your players and what they can execute in the game come Friday or Saturday night.

I had the good fortune of coaching in the NFL, where we got the best players in the world. I came to UK with realistic goals as to what we could accomplish. Halfway through the season, we had to sit down as a staff and make the decision that there were certain things we could not do. Instead we had to do what our players could handle. I will give our defensive staff a lot of credit. They were able to find out what we could handle as a defensive football team. They were able to determine what we could use in our coverage package. We made a lot of improvement from the first game to the last game of the season.

One thing we had to overcome was the confidence factor on defense. Defense has never been a big thing at the University of Kentucky. Defense had never been talked about at UK since Jerry Claiborne retired. When Coach Claiborne was at UK, I was at LSU. We hated to come to Lexington to play them. They played the wide tackle six defense and they were very physical. They got after the offense and made them work for everything they got. After Coach Claiborne left, the defense was placed on a back burner at UK.

So when we got to UK this past year, we had a very negative attitude to overcome with the defense. The big issue was the fact the defense had no respect. They did not have the respect of their teammates. They had to earn that respect. I can tell you, now, our defensive players have earned the respect of their teammates and the respect of their opponents. However, we did go through some trying times. It was easy for them to go into a tank and say, "That is just the way it is here at UK."

As I look at our players in the off-season conditioning program, I can tell you we are light-years ahead of where we were last year. We had players that could not finish the gassers last year. They could not finish the conditioning program last year. Now the players do not try to avoid hard work.

Why the 3-4 defensive alignment? If you looked at New England in the Super Bowl, you know they did some interesting things on defense.

A lot of people give Bill Coward a lot of credit for getting the 3-4 defensive alignment going in the pros. But Dick LeBeau is the coach that brought the defense to Pittsburgh. Bill Belichick of New England has been running the defense for years. When we played them, it was interesting to see some of the concepts they use on defense. It is difficult to play them because you never know which linebackers are going to come on the blitz. That is the flexibility that the 3-4 defense gives you.

Basically, what we see from the offense today is the spread offense. The game of football has changed. It has moved down the ladder from pro football to college football to high school football. You can get a high school tape today, and you will see the offense is a one back set with four wide outs. Football has become fast-break basketball on grass. So, you must put pressure on the quarterback. Today, the secondary must be able to play a lot of different coverages. You must be able to drop off defenders to cover the receivers before the quarterback can throw the ball on hot routes. The 3-4 defensive alignment gives us that flexibility. It gives you a lot of different variables that you can use. This is not the perfect defense, but it is something we believe in. We feel we have made a lot of improvement in the first year and hope to continue to improve next year.

Now, I want to cover a few of the reasons why we ran the 3-4 defensive alignment, and then cover some of the strengths and weaknesses of the defense.

The strength of our football team, besides the players, was our coaching staff. The one thing that comes across with our staff is the teaching of fundamentals. We are very fortunate in that we have a head coach that was a college assistant coach before, and he was an assistant in the NFL. We are lucky as a staff. Normally we get 30 minutes a day to work on individual fundamentals. Having been in the NFL, where you have only 10 minutes a day to work on individual fundamentals, it is nice to have 30 minutes to work with the players on individual fundamentals. Coach Brooks will cut the time down to 20 minutes as the week goes on. It is vital to teach fundamentals.

The game of football has changed in some aspects today because of what teams are doing on offense. But still, games are won and lost with fundamentals. It still comes down to blocking and tackling, catching the football, protecting the football, and forcing teams to turn the ball over. That aspect will never change.

After we get the practice schedule, we sit down as a staff and go over what we are going to do in our individual sessions. We meet with Coach Brooks in the morning. Then we decide what we need to work on for that particular practice. This is based on what we are going to face during the upcoming week. This focus may be on things we have not done well previously.

This year, we played against Ohio University, which ran the wishbone offense. I had not played against a team that ran this offense in years. We took advantage of Coach Ron McBride's expertise on this subject. Coach McBride has been the head coach at Utah, and had faced the Air Force Academy for several years. We took some of the old Utah practice plans and came up with a schedule for the week that gave us a chance to prepare for a team such as Ohio. We never used a football all week. Instead we used Nerf balls to simulate the snap. We did that so we could get the actual speed of the inside reads for the quarterback coming to the corner and then pitching the ball outside on the option. The Nerf balls were flying all over the place, but it gave us a true picture of what we were going to see in the game that week.

That game was our best as far as playing assignment football. You know, when you play teams that run the triple option, you must have someone that takes the dive, the quarterback, and the pitchman. The offense will gash you. If one man does not do his job, it results in a big play for the offense. Our players went out and executed the game plan very well. That was because we practiced on the game plan all week. We did not even do 7- on-7 drills. The scouting report showed they only threw the ball on third down. We took a chance and worked against the inside and outside veer plays.

These are the things as coaches we can do to help our players. As I said earlier, we all know a lot of football. But we must remember it is not what the coach knows, it is what the players know. What you see on the tapes is a reflection of what you teach. In the middle of the year, we had to make a decision on what we could and could not do on defense. That is when our players started to play good football. Schemes are all great. But the bottom line is this. Who can line up and play, execute the defense, and control their A-gap? That is who wins the game. That is the bottom line. You still must move around because the offense can block you if they know where you are going to line up.

Next, I want to get to the benefits of the 3-4 alignment. I am not saying it is the greatest defense in the world. However, I have been coaching for 28 years and I have coached the 3-4 for 24 years. I think you must base the defense on your personnel. When Rich Brooks hired me as defensive coordinator, he asked me what I wanted to run. I told him I was not sure and that I would like to look at the personnel. When I got to UK, I felt we had two noseguards that would force teams to double-team them. I did not know if we had any linebackers or not. I was on a radio show in Lexington and a caller told me I was an idiot because I did not have two linebackers on the team and I wanted to run a 3-4 defensive alignment. I wish that same person had called me at the end of the season because our two inside linebackers led the SEC in tackles.

In your 3-4 alignment, the two inside linebackers should be your leading tacklers. The strong safety should be the third-leading tackler. He is going to be the eighth defender in the box most of the time. The concept of the defense works. We just have to get a lot better, and we have to coach the players better. Also, we must recruit better football players. That is a part of the total picture.

We continue to use two words in implementing this defense. The first word is attitude. When we came into the program at UK, it was obvious we had to change the attitudes of the players. In our playbook we have a description of attitude and what attitude means in our life. You control your own attitude. You control your attitude each day as to what your attitude is going to be that day.

The second word we use a lot is trust. Coach Bill Coward of the Steelers used the word every day. Trust is a big word. It is a very powerful word. In sports, you will have to trust people. In football, you

must trust the player next to you is going to take care of the A gap or the B gap so you can do your job.

The third word we have in our playbook is confidence. Again, we stress attitude, trust, and confidence. We put the word confidence in the playbook because it was obviously that our players were not very confident. In the spring, we watched our offense go up and down the field with ease. Our defensive players came off the field after each drive, and it did not mean anything to them. To them, that was how it worked for them at UK. It was accepted at UK. So we had to change those attitudes. We had to learn to trust each other, and we had to develop confidence we could stop the opponents.

Let me talk about some of the ideas we stress in our game plan with our defense. Number one, we must play well on first down. We want to force the offense to give up the ball on downs. We want to hold the opponents to three yards or less on first down. In my opinion, first down is the most important down in football. Offensive coaches know the same thing. If the offense gains four yards on first down, it is difficult for the defense to anticipate what the offense is going to do on the next downs. Their tendencies change a great deal. When it is second-and-ten, it is much easier for the defense. The offense knows that we know what they will probably have to do on the next downs. So, first down is very important to us on defense.

We want to eliminate mental errors and big plays against our defense. As coaches, we must do a good job with our players in eliminating mental errors. Early in the season, mental errors really hurt us. Our players put forth the effort. It wasn't that they were not giving their best effort. If you are aggressive as hell and go in the wrong gap, we are going to get gashed. It is more important that you know what to do.

You must play team defense in this alignment. We have players on our team that are better players than others, but we try to treat all of our players the same. This is very important when you are playing a sport that is based on the team concept: that you treat the players the same. They continue to hear the three words we discussed earlier: attitude, trust, and confidence.

Our defense must learn to deal with adversity. If you are on the field for 14 straight plays, you get tired. You better trust the player that is playing inside of you, that he will do a good job so you can get off the field. You must play as a team.

We have team goals, and we have defensive goals. We want to force a turnover. To do this you must talk about it and you must drill it. It is the one thing we stress as a team. We had 16 interceptions and 11 fumbles on turnovers this past year. We need to get more turnovers. That is not good enough. We must work on it, and we must drill it.

We want to pressure the quarterback to throw early. We must be able to cover receivers. We were not a good football team against the run this past year. But we were second in the SEC in sacks this past year. We had 38 sacks. I do not think we are a good pass rushing football team in our base defense or in our dime package. But with the multiplicity of the 3-4 alignment and with the things we added during the year, it was difficult to prepare for us in one week of practice.

Let me discuss the run defense. This is something we must get better at. Our players must get mentally tougher. We are working on that in our morning workouts. We must drill into the players' heads that they do not ever give in. In talking about the defense against the run, we stress several key points.

First, using your eyes is the most important thing in playing football, whether playing offense or defense. I had the good fortune to work with Bill Arnsparger. This is the one thing he learned from Blanton Collier. Coach Arnsparger talked about the eyes all of the time. You must use your eyes when you are on offense or defense to be effective. You play the game of football with your eyes, your hands, and your feet no matter what position you play.

On defense, you must see the blocker, you must neutralize him, and you must keep your feet moving.

You must locate the ball and shed the blocker. Next, you must attack the ballcarrier and knock him back. The key is the eyes, the hands, and the feet.

Our pass defense did improve this past year. We were 26th in the country in pass defense. However, we were not very good against the run. Teams did not think they had to throw the ball against us to be successful. We did everything out of a two shell. We made people have to read the defense on the run. We played two cover, and we played three cover, and we played three cover different ways. We played man-to-man and we played it as well as any defensive coverage we played. We were able to run the different blitzes in our packages. Because of the different things we did, it allowed us to put pressure on the quarterback as the season went on with our blitz packages.

Our pass defense this year was good. I think the reason for that was because of the different things we did in our secondary. We made great strides with the secondary and with the underneath coverage. It was a team concept, with the front line and our linebackers doing a good job.

I have talked about team defense. We must eliminate the mental mistakes. I coached for the Pittsburgh Steelers the last seven years. Every day we wrote down any mental mistakes. That was one of my jobs as the linebacker coach. We kept a folder on all the mental mistakes made each day. It went into a folder, and we reviewed this folder. At the end of the year we were able to go to this folder and let the players know where they stood on defense. Mental mistakes will kill you. If a player knows what to do and still gets beat, that is different. But if he does not know what to do, it will kill you.

We were in different forms of a three-deep zone look most of the time this past year. We found this was our best coverage. We played that defense the best last year. We had to pick and choose to get to that defense.

When we say three deep, we have different ways in playing the three deep. We have strongside rotation. We can run sky or cloud rotation. We can go weakside rotation. We can bring a safety down, and play zone coverage to the X side. We can go down and play the tilt, or we can go down to a particular receiver, all based on what we have in for that game plan. We do not just play a simple cover 3 sky coverage. We could run the 3 backer, where we buzz the outside backer, and the safety to the tilt is coming down to play the hook. We are bringing one of our inside linebackers (see Diagram 1). There are a lot of different ways the 3-4 alignment give you.

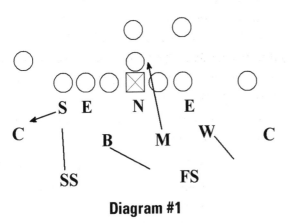

Diagram #1

We played some man-to-man coverage this year. We played different forms of man-to-man coverage. We played that defense 218 snaps. It was, by far, our best defense against the run and the pass. We used several versions of the coverage. We played two deep zone with five-under man. We could bring any combination of five defenders. We could play what we call special seven coverage. That is where we bring the strong safety down in the box to become the eighth defender. That was a big defense for us.

When we blitzed, we brought at least five rushers. This was in our dog coverages or our fire zone coverages, or in our zero coverages. We are not a big zero cover team. We had 885 snaps this past year, and played zero coverage only seven times. We are not selling out very much. We are not going to take away that centerfield player very many times. We pressured 165 times out of those 885 plays. That is roughly twenty percent of the time. It is all based on different down-and-distance. That includes our base okie, dime, nickel, and goal line defenses.

We played two deep zone 113 times of the 885 plays. That is 12 percent of the time. You have to play two deep in the SEC because the receivers are so good that you can not set out there and play them one-on-one all of the time. Our corners played very well this year. Going into the season, all we heard was how bad they were. They were well coached, and the scheme we used helped them. As in any coverage, there are weaknesses in two deep Coverage.

We played quarter-quarter-half coverage. We played it 72 snaps, or eight percent of the time. We also played our quarter coverage. We played 30 snaps in the quarter coverage, for five percent of the time. There may be about two percent missing, which consisted of other coverages we used a few times. This gives you an idea of some of the things we did this past year.

Coming into the season, I thought we could play a lot of different defenses. I found out there were a lot of things we just could not play very well.

If you watched the Super Bowl recently, you saw what New England did on defense in the 3-4 alignment. They do a great job of jamming and disrupting pass routes. In the NFL, that is hard to do because you have to do it within five yards. It is not like college football, where you can jam the receivers all the way down the field as long as the ball is not in the air. They will walk the corners up tight on the outside receivers and jam them and take them out of the game. The quarterback sits back in the pocket, waiting for someone to come open, and then the pressure gets to the quarterback. Their scheme fits with what they do very well. They do not have great rush linemen, but they get the job done and that is why they are successful. They do a great job of disguising the defense.

We are going to do everything out of our "two shell" look. We have the ability to bring any of four linebackers. We can bring a lot of different combinations with the four linebackers. We did not bring all four of them at one time, but we do have different combinations that we run. We can bring the two outside linebackers. We can bring the two inside linebackers. We can bring both linebackers on the open side, or two on the closed side. We can bring two from the closed side and one from the open side.

We are trying to make the quarterback read the defense on the run. As the year went on, we found quarterbacks would come to the line of scrimmage and give a hard count on the cadence to see if they could get our defense to jump. They wanted to see if we would give our rush away, or see if they could force us to declare our safety one way or the other. That has become the in-thing now in college football. You can see this in the NFL as well. Quarterbacks come to the line and give a hard count to see if they can figure out which safetyman is coming down in the box. You can see Indianapolis do this when the get into their two tight ends and two wide receivers set. They come to the line and give the hard count to see where the strong safety is going to be, and then he runs away from him. They read the box and determine if they are going to run the ball or if they are going to throw it.

It is no different with us at our level. It is true for any team that runs the 3-4 alignment on defense. All the offense is trying to do is to find out who the rushers are and where they are coming from. Disguise is the most important thing we are trying to do. We try to make the quarterback read our safeties in 1.5 seconds. We must make sure our players are not giving our coverage away. We are trying to make everything look like two cover.

The other thing we can do with this defense is to go to a five under-three deep look. We can still do the same things. We can go 3 cloud, 3 sky, 3 buzz, 3 weak, and we can go 3 cloud weak. It ends up as a five under – three deep. Against teams that threw the ball on a three-step drop, we knew we were not going to get to the quarterback if he three on that third step. So, we started dropping eight defenders to try to give them a different look.

The other defense we play was our man-to-man. There are different ways to play this defense.

We are still trying to show the cover two. We still must be able to stop the run. Based on personnel, all teams have certain tendencies. If the regular players are in the lineup, it is usually heavier loaded toward the running game. When regular personnel are in the game against us, we are going to try to get the eighth defender in the box somehow, some way. One of the ways we do that is by playing man-to-man (see Diagram 2).

We cover the outside receivers man-to-man and bring the safety down to the tilt. If the strongside is to the tight end side, we bring the safety down to that side. You can rush the outside backer or the inside backer. Now, you get the eighth defender in the box. He is the safety, and he is going to play the back man-to-man.

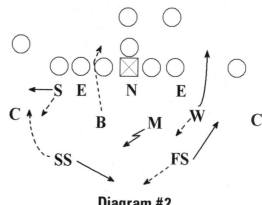

Diagram #2

If the defense tries to change the tilt, we can switch the defense with the offense. We just reverse the safeties and bring the opposite man down to the tilt. We always want to get that extra defender to that side. Because we are in man to man, we must hold up the receivers outside. We thought our corners did a great job this year. One of the three linebackers is going to be the "hole" player. You can design the game plan to have him double on the tight end, or you can have him double on a receiver (see Diagram 3).

If it is a back that is hurting us, we can have the backer double on the back. There are different ways to use that extra player. It is all sound against the run, and you can be effective against a good receiver.

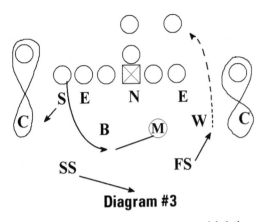

Diagram #3

We will play some cover one, which is a single safetyman. Depending on what the formation is, you can predetermine where you want the safeties to lock down. It can be based on tilt, on who you want to cover, and what your match-ups are. For example, we would bring both outside linebackers. That puts the strong safety on the tight end and the free safety in the deep middle. We can press it or we can play off (see Diagram 4). We can play a catch technique. Against some of the teams we play, we have to play off. We know we have to be able to step up and take away the quick pass. If we play off, they are going to hit the out routes and the slant routes on us. We have to mix it up.

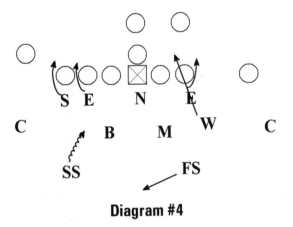

Diagram #4

We have different games that we can use on the defense. There are different ways in which we can play cover one. You can blitz any combination of linebackers. There are different combinations that you can do on this. We only did a few things with this last year because our players were not ready to handle a lot of this. We finally decided what we could do and what we could not do on defense. The more we ran the defenses, the better we became. We went back to the KISS theory, Keep It Simple Stupid. We became more productive by cutting down on the different stunts we used on the defense. We did a better job of coaching it and we did more reps on it in practice. That is our job. We must look at the tapes to see if we covered the things in practice that we see in the game. If we did not cover those things in practice, it is the fault of the coaches and not the players.

I see my time is up. Let me finish up with this. Our staff really appreciates the job the high school coaches do in working with the kids today. It is not an easy job. Having been out of recruiting for seven years now, I can see the job the high school coaches are doing with our young players today. Coaches are trying to get the players to do the right things. It is like Chan Gailey said, "Integrity and loyalty are words that are forgotten in our society."

The game of football is very much a disciplined game played by unselfish people. We live in a very selfish society. Coaches are teaching our young men to be unselfish and to be disciplined. It is not an easy job. The things players learn from you at a young age will help them when they get to be 24 or 30 years of age when they have to make tough decisions that will affect the rest of their life.

TACKLING TECHNIQUES AND DRILLS

University of North Carolina

It is a pleasure to be here. You may wonder why I am going to talk about tackling today. In the past two years, the Carolina defense has been ranked almost last in the country in defense. In 2001, my first year at North Carolina, we beat Florida State and Clemson in the regular season and beat Auburn in the Peach Bowl. During that year, we were ranked number one in the ACC and number 12 in the country on defense. We have not been in the top 100 the past two years.

We are not very happy with that fact. When you have failure on defense, it comes down to tackling. That is the topic I am going to discuss with you today. One thing I know from my 13 years of playing professional football is you have to tackle in line and in space.

I spoke at a clinic in Minnesota yesterday. That is Big Ten country, where they like to run the ball. In the ACC and this town, they like to throw the football. They want to spread you out, throw the football, and force your defenders to make tackles in space.

In 1999, I coached the defense in St. Louis for the Rams. Mike Jones made perhaps the biggest tackle ever made in Super Bowl history. He made a tackle at the one-yard line, on the last play of the game, to keep Kevin Dyson out of the end zone and save the game for St. Louis.

In my mind there is no such thing as a bad tackle. If the tackler can get the ballcarrier on the ground, it is a good tackle. That is especially true in the game that so many people are playing today. The spread offenses spread the defense out and force defenders to make tackles in space.

Too many times on the football field, we allow players to be in an improper football position. I drive the players nuts emphasizing proper football position. It is a particularly important point with linebackers and defensive backs.

Whenever you have the opportunity work with your players on fundamental positions, take advantage of it. Make your players better athletes. They have God's gift, but they can get better in this great game of football. In football, every inch counts. Practice the fundamentals of tackling to get better at that skill.

When you get in a fundamental position, the player should bend at the ankles and not at the waist. His head should be up, and his chest, out over his knees. The stance should be balanced, with his feet shoulder-width apart. When a tackler tries to tackle and his feet are too wide apart, he will not maintain that tackle. The stance should be narrower at the point of attack and widen as he makes contact.

The arm should be loose and the elbows slightly bent. His hands should be down in what I call a hostler position. He has to be prepared to draw his guns. I want the arms to shoot out from the hostler position. I do not want a big windup with the arms going into the tackle.

To tackle, the feet have to be on the ground. As the tackler approaches the ballcarrier, he wants his feet skimming the grass with his cleats in the ground. Too many times the player misses the tackle because he has one foot up in the air. The linebackers and safeties have to practice that skill because they spend so much time inside the box shuffling around.

There are some critical elements to the skill of tackling. In spring practice, I am guilty of trying to find out who the men on the team are in the first drill. I put them in a goal line tackling drill and have not taught them a thing about tackling. All we want to find out is who the tough guys are on the squad. Sometimes you will get the attitude you are looking for in a tackler. You have to have a good attitude to tackle and that will come as the defender gains confidence. Make your defenders confident they can tackle by doing drills that improve their technique. I want to practice tackling every single day. There will be days we do not practice in pads, but we are still going to practice tackling. If you want to be a good defense, you have to tackle.

If the defense wants to stop the run and stop big plays, you have to tackle. Most big plays come from a defender missing a tackle. You have to have your eyes on the target. To be a good tackler, you have to see what you are going to hit. The coach has to watch what the tackler is seeing. He has to get into a position to see the tackler's eyes. In tackling, where the eyes go is where the body goes.

Too many times, the tackler leaves his feet too soon and dives when there is no need. We want the tackler to step to contact. We want the tackler to take the extra step to put him closer to the ballcarrier. We emphasize getting as close as possible, and then taking another step.

When the tackler gets into position to tackle, we want him to shoot his guns. That is in reference to the position of the hands before attempting to tackle a ballcarrier. The arms are cocked at his hips so he can club up and through the ballcarrier. Make sure that as he shoots his guns he does not wind up with his arms. That is wasted motion, and it takes time to do it.

In blocking or tackling, the finish is tremendously important. The tackler clubs up and through the ballcarrier, grabs cloth, and finishes with his feet. We talk about a two-step redirect in the skill of tackling. That is simply stepping into the contact and closing the gate with the second step. The second step comes as the arms are shot from the hips. On the second step, the tackle has to accelerate his feet.

Any tackle is a good tackle, whether it is a high tackle or low tackle. I do not teach tackling low, although there will be times the tackler will have to execute that kind of tackle. I do not want the corners, safeties, or linebackers to tackle low. There are too many injuries that occur when the tackler hits the ballcarrier low. If they tackle low, the head is going down and something bad is going to happen. Most concussions come from low tackling with the head hitting the thigh board.

When players miss tackles, it is generally because of some common errors. When the tackler tries to tackle with his head down, it generally results in a missed tackle. It increases the chance for injury; in addition, the tackler cannot tackle what he cannot see.

The second common error a tackler can commit is lunging at the ballcarrier. When a tackler leaves his feet, he will either miss or slide off the ballcarrier. To correct this error the coach has to emphasize body control and footwork. Footwork drills will help the athlete to improve his change of direction and skill.

The third error in tackling is winding up with the arms. When a players runs, he does not let his hands extend behind his hips. That is an unnatural movement that should not be done in tackling. The hands are carried about the hip. That is the position from which the hands are shot.

There are all kinds of footwork problems that relate to common errors in tackling. If the tackler overstrides, has his feet off the ground at contact, or loses his base while trying to tackle, he is prone to miss tackles. He has to have closing speed and come into balance as he approaches in the tackle. We do not want the players to break down, but to continue to move when making a tackle in line or in space.

The last error that tacklers make is not pursuing. The tackler has to trust his buddies. He must not assume the tackle will be made and keep coming to the ball. On every defensive play, someone has to force the play, someone must fill, and somebody has to pursue. If the force man stops and breaks down, everyone else stops and slows down. If the force man does not turn the ballcarrier in, the fill man doesn't know where to fill, and the pursuer do not know what angle to take. Even if the force man does not make the tackle, he has to force the ball inside. If he forces the ball carrier inside, the fill man is there with the rest of the pursuit.

An important coaching point in football is teaching players judgment. Teaching judgment is basically learning to play the game. As you watch the tape you will see some good tackles and some bad tackles. I am going to show you some drills that I think teach proper judgment.

A tip I think you should follow is to keep track of your good tackles. You can study them yourself or use them to study with your players. In our opening game against Florida State last year, our opponents had a great game plan. They used their strength, which was speed, and had a simple game plan. They threw bubble screens and flare passes and forced us to make tackles on the perimeter.

When a tackler breaks down 5-6 yards from the ballcarrier, he allows the ballcarrier to continue to run and makes everyone on the defense break down. They have to break down because they do not know where the ballcarrier is going. The tackler has to continue to run and trust his buddies that are pursuing. He may miss the tackle, but if he uses proper technique, he will force the ballcarrier into the pursuit.

One drill we do is called the tamp drill (see Diagram #1). It is a simple straight-line drill. You can set cones or use five-yard line markers. The players run in a straight line, and as they approach each cone or yard mark they tamp their feet. The tamp drill is a quick foot movement with the cleats close to the ground. After they tamp their feet, they accelerate out to the next cone and repeat the exercise. The coaching points are to make sure they keep their base sound but not too wide. They need to keep the cleats close to the ground and accelerate out of the tamp drill.

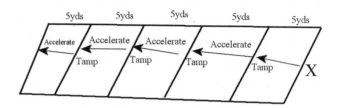

Diagram #1. Tamp drill

You can do a variation of this drill (see Diagram #2). It is the same tamp drill, except as we get to the second cone, we tamp the feet, cross over with the foot opposite the direction we are going to redirect, and accelerate to the coach.

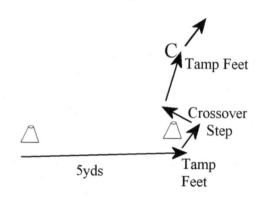

Diagram #2. Tamp crossover

Another variation of the tamp drill is the angle tamp and redirect drill (see Diagram #3). The players start at the cone. The coach gives the player a movement signal. He runs to the coach and tamps his feet. The coach gives him a direction, and he sprints to the second coach, tamps his feet, and is given another redirection.

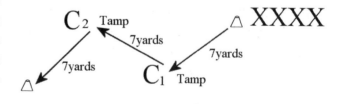

Diagram #3. Angle tamp

There are all kinds of bag drills that help players with body control and foot movement. We use a shuffle drill with four blocking dummies (see Diagram #4). The players run up the first bag, shuffle over to the second lane, and backward run through that lane. They shuffle over to the third lane, run up through the lane, shuffle over to the last lane, and backward run. They shuffle over on the last dummy and accelerate forward and execute a form tackle.

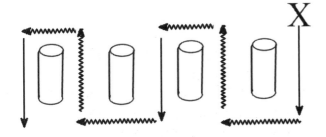

Diagram #4. Shuffle drill

In this drill you work on the proper base, cleats close to the ground, acceleration, and change of direction. This is a combination drill where you can work on several fundamentals at once.

I do not believe in high knee drills for linebackers. I want them to keep their feet close to the ground. We work ladder drills instead of stepping over bags. When I use bags in the agility drills, we run in and out of them, not over. At the end of each drill, we try to incorporate a tackle or a change of direction movement.

We do a shed drill to teach how to engage a blocker and make the tackle (see diagram #5). It is a one-on-one drill with an offensive blocker and tackler. The tackler starts at linebacker depth. As the ball is snapped, the linebacker works downhill at the blocker, gaining ground as the back gains ground toward the line of scrimmage. He engages the blocker with his hands, locks out his arm, and moves across the blocker's face. He proceeds to the ballcarrier and makes a form tackle on the ballcarrier. This is a form drill in the beginning. What we are working on is footwork, proper hand placement, the rip through, and finally the form tackle.

The next drill is an angle bag drill. We have a series of six bags aligned at an angle to the player (see Diagram #6). The player on movement does an up/down in the middle lane. He pops to his feet, then steps over three bags, moving back at an angle.

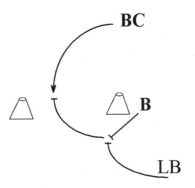

Diagram #5. Shed drill

When the tackler gets to the last bag, a runner with a hand shield runs a lane around two cones. The tackle shuffles to the outside and makes a cross-the-bow hit on the hand shield.

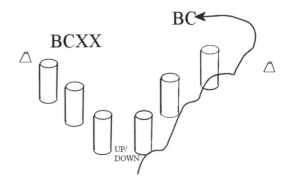

Diagram #6. Angle bag drill

Defenders have to learn to play low blocks to stay on their feet. These next two drills involve using the hands to punch down on the blocker to keep them from getting into the defender's knees and feet (see Diagram #7). In this drill, there will be a series of long tube dummies to simulate the low block. The defender shuffles down in front of the dummies. As he moves down the dummy line, a player on the other end of the dummy pushes the dummies toward his feet. The linebacker must maintain good fundamental position and punch down with his hands to stop the dummies. When he reaches the end of the dummy line, a ballcarrier is coming forward and he executes a tackle. During the tackling part of the drill, the defender is running his feet, attacking with his eyes, and exploding up through the ballcarrier. He grabs cloth and drives the ballcarrier back but does not take him to the ground.

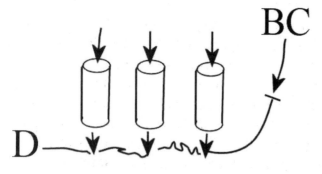

Diagram #7. Low block drill

The ball drill is similar to the last drill as it makes the defender play a low block at the beginning. The defender begins in a good football position (see Diagram #8). The big ball is rolled at him to start the drill; the defender reacts up and punches the ball to keep it from getting into his feet. A series of four dummies are lying on the ground, and they form three lanes for a ballcarrier to run into. It is the old eye-opener drill. The ballcarrier turns into the first lane. The defender meets the ballcarrier in the lane and delivers an explosion and extension blow on him. We have the ball carrier use hand shields for protection against the strike of the tackler. They retreat out of the first lane and enter the second lane, where the next explosion occurs. They continue through the third lane and repeat the explosion. As the ballcarrier comes out of the last lane, the defender executes the entire tackle and drives the ballcarrier back.

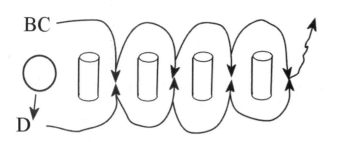

Diagram #8. Low block eye opener

There are any numbers of drills that can be used to practice tackling. We use the W-drill as one that involves change of direction, footwork, and tackling (see Diagram # 9). In this drill, the defender backpedals five yards to a line, plants, and sprints forward at a 45-degree angle to the next line. He

plants at that line and side shuffles back at a 45-degree angle to the line, and then accelerates forward on a 45-degree angle, tamps, and makes a cross the bow tackle.

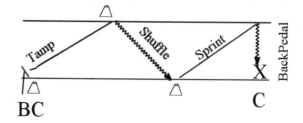

Diagram #9. W-drill

We want to create habits in every skill the tackler does that help with tackling. He has to see the target with his eyes, bend his knees, shoot his guns, and accelerate his feet.

In the pass drop drill, we incorporate the linebacker drop into his zone and react back up for a flare pass (see Diagram #10. We work this drill off the hash marks. The coach pulls the ball up to show pass. The linebacker drops into his hook area. The ballcarrier flares, with the ball turning upfield. The linebacker breaks on the throw and reacts back to the line of scrimmage. He uses the sideline, tamps, and makes a form tackle across the bow. In this drill, let the ballcarrier use a move to try to get back inside on the tackler. The tackler wants to keep his position and use the sideline as another defender.

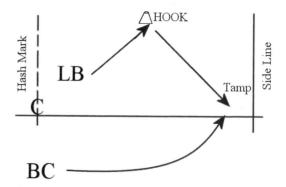

Diagram #10. Pass drop drill

Another drill that requires low block protection, footwork, change of direction, rip, and form tackle is the gauntlet drill (see Diagram #11). The defender begins the drill with a big ball punch on a low blocker. He has three dummies to shuffle through, changing direction but not crossing his feet. As he comes out of the last dummy, he rips through a dummy holder. He faces up on a ballcarrier that moves one way or the other. The defender tamps his feet, centers himself, and uses proper technique on a form tackle.

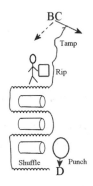

Diagram #11. Gauntlet drill

This next drill is a pursuit drill we use at North Carolina (see Diagram #12). It is a good drill to get everyone involved and conditioned. We align in our base defense. On the snap of the ball, everyone goes to his initial responsibility. After the first movement, they turn and get into a prescribed pursuit. There are two coaches 40 yards from the line of scrimmage on each hash mark. In their pursuit pattern, the players have to do three up/downs on the way to the coaches. Once they get to the coaches, they chop their feet in a good football position. When everyone reaches the coach, he releases them. They do another up/down and sprint off the field.

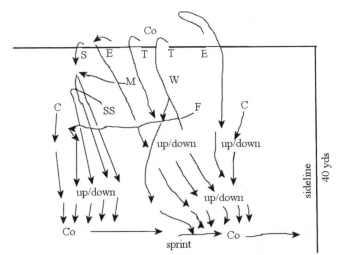

Diagram #12. Team pursuit

I brought this next drill from the St. Louis Rams when I was coaching the defense. It is called the ram drill (see Diagram #13). We have three different groups going rapid fire in a full-speed contact drill. It is good for both the offense and defense. It benefits the defense more because they, in most cases, have an extra defender. In three years of using this drill, I have never had an injury. Nobody gets tangled up in a mass of bodies. We keep the groups in close proximity so we can use one camera to film the entire drill. We run our offensive play, which fits each grouping. We go one group at a time, but go in rapid succession. The advantage of the drill is the tempo and security against injury.

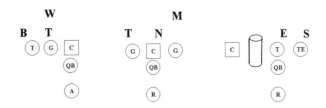

Diagram #13. Ram drill

We are trying to come up with new ideas to help with our off-season program. The coaches are not allowed to be on the field with our players in any organized way. This is called a discretionary period. The only people that can work with the players are the strength and conditioning staff. That is a concern of the NCAA. We meet with our strength and conditioning staff and suggest things we should do with the running program. We are not allowed to have balls in these drills. We use a towel taped together instead of the ball. We have to coach the strength staff so they will know what we want taught in these drills. This drill is called the piano drill. We set up five cones, five yards apart. The offense takes the towel and runs into the cone area. The defender mirrors his movement as he runs. The runner has to choose a lane to run into. Once he turns into the lane, he can use any move to elude the defender. The defender tags the runner below the waist by bring his hands from underneath and up through the runner. The emphasis in this drill is not to reach or get over extended.

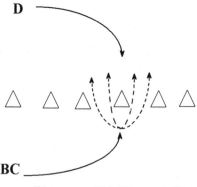

Diagram #14. Piano drill

This next drill is called the leverage cutback drill (see Diagram #15). The runner is running down a yard line on the field. The defender is offset inside of the ballcarrier on the next yard line. The ballcarrier comes down the line, and the defender moves up and over to the line. The ballcarrier tries to make a move and cut back on the defender. The defender has to use good technique to make the tag.

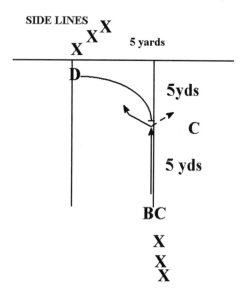

Diagram #15. Leverage cutback drill

The purpose of shuffle tackling drill is to develop the timing of the hit (see Diagram #16). Doing this drill is similar to a baseball team taking batting practice prior to each game. The ballcarrier will align on a line facing the tackler, about three to five yards from the tackler. The tackler will be offset on a cone three yards perpendicular to the line. On the command, the ballcarrier will run down the line toward the tackler. The tackler will shuffle to get in the proper body position to make the tackle.

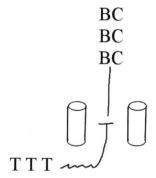

Diagram #16. Shuffle tackling drill

With this drill, the tackler must do several things. He must shuffle, not cross over, and have his head up with his eyes on the target. As he steps to contact, he narrows his base and extends his ankles, knees, and hips together to time the punch on the tackle. He must remember that on contact his base will widen. He clubs with his arm and does not encircle the body. He grabs cloth and accelerates his feet on contact to work the finish of the tackle. Make sure to have the ballcarriers and tacklers switch lines and work the drill from the right and left sides. You can let the ballcarrier use a hand shield in the chest area for protection.

In the goal line tackling drill, we want to develop the head-across- the-bow tackle (see diagram #17). The tackler has to have an all-out mentality and has to run his feet through the contact. The ballcarrier and tackler align on the five- yard line back to back. The coach is standing between them and the sideline, seven yards from the sideline. The ballcarrier wheels, runs around the coach, and tries to score. The tackler wheels, and when he feels the ballcarrier move, he runs around the coach and tries to keep the ballcarrier from scoring. The tackler wants to get his head across the ballcarrier and have great extension to keep the ballcarrier from falling forward. The most important thing is to finish hard by accelerating the feet.

The goal line tackling drill is competitive in nature and is a great tempo setter for the practice. You also get tremendous overall tackling benefits because you cannot win the drill without getting your head and shoulder across the bow and keeping the feet moving on contact.

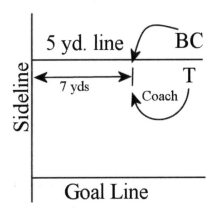

Diagram #17. Goal line tackling drill

This spring we are going to do a two-whistle drill. I got this drill from another coach. I have never done it before, but it sounds like a good drill. It is a defensive pursuit drill. The ball is snapped, and the ballcarrier runs with the ball. When he is stopped, the first whistle is blown. All the defenders on the defense who are not on the tackle continue to come hard to a coach positioned up the sideline from the tackle. Everyone continues to run hard until the second whistle is blown. The first whistle kills the ballcarrier and the rest of the offense. The defense continues to pursue until the second whistle.

The secret is to practice it right and not allow your players to get away from sound fundamentals. Make sure you emphasize the details of each point of tackling. To be a good tackler, the athlete has to develop confidence. The only way to develop that confidence is to practice the proper techniques daily.

We can improve our defense by pursuing the football and not missing tackles. That amounts to a tremendous chunk of hidden yardage given up by your defense. If the defense does not give up the extra yardage after contact, they can improve drastically. We have to have the proper angles by the force man and fill defender. They have to keep coming and stop breakdown. If a force defender can make a runner turn inside, the fill man knows where it has to fit. Improvement goes back to attention to detail and proper techniques in tackling.

Guys, it has been a pleasure being here with you. You are welcome to come and visit us at any time. It is a great place to come visit; in addition, we have a lot of great golf courses in the area. Our facilities and offices are always open to any of you. Thank you very much.

DEVELOPING A DEFENSIVE PHILOSOPHY

University of Southern California

I want to thank Nike for giving me the chance to attend this clinic and talk football. After spending so many years in the NFL, I did not have a chance to do this.

We had a wonderful year at Southern California. We did not know what to expect. We had a bunch of question marks on both sides of the football. We lost our top running backs, and we lost our quarterback, Carson Palmer, who was the top pick in the NFL draft. We took major hits on defense, and we were in a transition in our offense.

Obviously, we still had some excellent football players, and we were fortunate to have them. We had to depend on a lot of young guys to come into our program. We started a sophomore quarterback who had never thrown a football in a college game. He had to replace the Heisman Trophy winner, Carson Palmer, who had thrown for 39 touchdown passes the year before. We had some running backs and receivers that came through for us this year, and we were very fortunate.

During the season, we witnessed the rise and fall of a small institution called the BCS. The system that was in place got blown out of the water this year because it did not work. At the end of the season, we had to play through the controversy that existed within the system. I hope that they can iron out the problems and come up with a better system next year.

The whole situation worked out pretty well for us because we got to play in the Rose Bowl, for the national championship, and it was a home game. The Rose Bowl was a great game for us, and it speaks to our ability to recruit. We have a wonderful place to sell to our recruits. We are in Southern California, which has great weather. We have an excellent academic program, which is one of the top-ranked universities in America. We get to play our home games in the Coliseum, which is one of the premier sports venues in the United States. With all of those things working for us, we have a great chance to have an outstanding program.

I am excited about the future of the Southern California football program. We were really young this year, and next year we will have to replace one guy on offense. That means there will be high expectations for us next year. We are going to take those expectations and match them with what I expect and go for that national championship again.

If you have watched the news, you are aware of what is happening with underclassman becoming eligible for the NFL draft. It looks as if that is going to be the trend for the near future. We are right in the middle of that bit of controversy also. We have a wide receiver by the name of Mike Williams who has announced he will forego the remainder of his college career and announce his eligibility for the NFL draft. That is a difficult situation for our school and coaching staff to work through. I only hope we handle the situation properly to set the stage for other athletes who have these aspirations.

I am going to talk about two things in my lecture. The first thing I am going to address is our philosophy. The second thing is what we are doing in our secondary coverage. I hope at the end we can have a question-and-answer period where I can answer any questions that you might have.

I want to talk about discovering your own philosophy. I got the opportunity to be the head coach of the New York Jets. It was a blast for one year, but it did not last, and I got the axe after one year at the helm. I was not prepared for, nor did I anticipate being a head coach in the NFL. it just kind of happened. I had the opportunity so I took it to see how it would go. It did not work out.

After that, I had a chance to go to San Francisco, which was great because I am from the West Coast. George Seaford had been tremendously successful with the 49ers, and George Walsh was coming back in some capacity with the team. I saw this as a great opportunity to learn from these legendary coaches whom I had admired ever since I was a young coach. I was going to get a chance to get into the greatest offensive system known at that time. I wanted to absorb all I could and make it part of my philosophy. After my experience with the Jets, I knew I needed to work on developing a sound philosophy.

When the New England job came along, I thought I was ready for it. I had a short stint as a head coach and had worked in the 49ers' system. I had developed a philosophy and had a good base. I had solidified my thought and I felt I was ready.

As I look back at the New England job, I was not allowed to make the kind of decisions I do at Southern Cal today. I was not in complete control, and there were other people involved in the decision-making. It is really hard to get your philosophy over when you have to share your perspective with other people.

The New England situation worked for two years and then ended. It was a great experience, and I learned a lot from it. I took off for 10 months and really concentrated on getting my act together to prepare myself better for the next job.

I read a book written by John Wooden, the famed coach for UCLA. While I was reading that book, one statement hit me right between the eyes. Coach Wooden went to UCLA in 1948, and 17 years later he won his first national championship. He was head coach for 17 years before he won his first national championship. In his next 11 years as head coach he won 10 national championships, including

seven in a row. That accomplishment is unparalleled in any sport.

He was a great coach before he went to UCLA, but it took him 17 years to get it just right. Things came together for him at the right time. His recruiting, practices, tactics, approach, beliefs, delivery, and all the other attributes he possessed came together at the right time.

That story said something to me. If you get the chance, know exactly what you want, and know how you want it to happen within your program, you have to jump at the chance. Obviously, we do not get to stay for 17 years in a job trying to perfect a program. I had already done the flash-in-the-pan thing at the Jets and New England. I did not want that to happen again. I thought I had a strong belief system in what I was doing. From that moment I started to try to figure out what I thought about everything that affected my life. I started writing down in notebooks everything I could think of. I wrote down philosophies, stories, principles, and problems that I had. I wrote down discipline ideas, football ideas, and everything that came into my mind.

I was competing against myself, but I came to understand that I wanted to be a football coach and I did not have a job. When the Southern Cal job came open and I was being considered for it, I knew that was the job for me. I knew I was ready. We have had phenomenal success in such a short period of time, and it is clear to me why I am now more effective than I was before. In this program there is one voice, one man making all the decisions, and no one else to go to.

To develop your philosophy, you have to expedite the process by trying to come up with a belief about everything that you can think of. The next question is when you stop the process. You never do: you continue to question and think about your beliefs as long as you live.

An older coach can deal with these things better because of his experience. If you are an offensive or defensive coordinator sitting in this room and cannot write down your philosophy of offense or defense, you do not have one. You have to know where you stand on every aspect of that offense or defense. If you cannot do that, you are not committed and are not being the best coach you can possibly be.

If you cannot tell me what you think about every position on your team, there is no way you can teach a player so he can understand. Your message has to be so clear in your mind so there is no way the player you are teaching can miss the point. If you do not know how you feel about every position, how are the players going to learn? If you do not know, you are taking a shot in the dark when it comes to coaching.

The challenge is not as a head coach, receiver coach, or line coach; it is as a coach. We are teachers teaching the game of football. You must teach the information in different ways. You may not reach a player in one way, so try it another way. You have to try to make sense to every player on the team and not just the guy who is motivated because he is playing Friday night.

Our philosophy is all about the ball. If we are on offense, we have to do everything in our power to protect the football at all times. It is not just ball security when carrying the ball. It is catching the ball and putting it away. It is the exchange between the center and quarterback. It is protecting the quarterback on his backside. If the offense gives up the ball, they give up their chance to score. You cannot score without the football.

On defense, we do not play defense to stop someone. We do not play football to go three plays and out. We play defense to get possession of the football. That is our philosophy, and it is clear. The first year we were at USC, we were plus 14 in turnovers. The second year we were plus 18 in turnovers. The third year we were plus 21 in turnovers. That is plus 53 turnovers in three years, and there is no one in America that has done better than that.

That is the first thing our players hear when they come to Southern California. If you know that is your philosophy, if you sell it to the players, and you passionately believe it, the players will get the point.

I get carried away when I talk about philosophy. The second part of my lecture is about zone defense. The first thing I want to show you is what we call zone concepts. The first concept we have to know about zone coverage is this. Zones are areas of the field, not men. Therefore, the first concept is to know your drop into the area. It does not matter what defensive coverage you are playing, you have to know where you are going in that coverage.

After the defender finds the area he is going to defend, he has to know the formation. The defender wants to know the formation because that has to do with his ability to anticipate where the ball is going.

When he finds the formation, the next thing in progression is the flow of the play when the ball is snapped. The defender has to know if the flow is full or a split flow. He wants to know if the flow is toward the strength of the formation, or away form the strength of the formation.

When playing defense we have to know the quarterback's intention. This concept deals with where the quarterback is intending to throw the football. If the defender does not break on the ball until it is in the air, he does not stand a chance of getting to the ball. The defender has to break to where the quarterback intends to throw the ball. That means we have to read body position and action of the quarterback as to where he is going to throw the ball.

To get to the position where the quarterback intends to throw the ball, the defender has to anticipate where to go. To anticipate the delivery of the ball, the coach has to free up his defender. He cannot make the defenders robots.

Once the defender anticipates where the ball is going to be thrown, he has to break on the ball. Those are the concepts of zone coverage, which are commonly known to most coaches.

If we go back to the quarterback's intention, we can learn how to anticipate and break on the ball. If the quarterback drops into the pocket, the defenders can get a tip as to where the ball is going by the way the quarterback's hips are tilted. That does not mean he is going to throw the ball in that direction, but his attention is to that area. If he bounces and tilts his hip the other direction, the ball could possibly go that direction.

When the quarterback tilts his hip in one direction and the front hand comes off the ball, he is throwing in that direction. The quarterback is going to carry the ball in his drop in both hands. As he reaches his plant foot and steps to throw the ball, the first thing he will do is take the forward hand off the ball. When he does that, it allows the action of the throw to take place. For him to throw the ball, his hips have to be pointed at his target.

If there is a trips set to our defensive left side, and the quarterback comes out looking left with his hips opened left, the ball has a better than even chance of going to the left side of the defense. If the quarterback drops, and his hips are more squared toward the middle of the field, the quarterback is probably trying to look to the right or down the middle. If he comes out with his hip opened to the right, he is probably going to the right. That way the defensive backs can anticipate where the quarterback is going with the ball.

Once the quarterback passes three steps and takes the drop to five steps, the way he sets his hips is generally the way he is going to throw. He does not have the luxury of holding the ball and trying to fake the secondary. Passing offenses time their patterns so the quarterback can deliver the ball almost immediately after the quarterback hits the fifth steps.

If the quarterback sprints out with the ball, the secondary can squeeze the field to the side of the rollout. As long as the quarterback continues to run, the secondary continues to squeeze. If the quarterback stops, the secondary stops. The only way the quarterback can throw the ball away from the direction he is running is to stop.

When the quarterback half rolls, he is generally going to throw the ball away from his motion. If the defenders watch his hips, they can still get the jump on the throw. Every quarterback coach in the world tells his quarterback to square his shoulders and step toward his target. If the shoulders pop backside, the defender should get on his horse and locate the receivers going that way. On this type of roll, the defenders make up the width the quarterback gets in the half roll. Once he stops and sets, that is as wide as the defenders want to go in relationship to his drop.

The defenders have to understand the football is thrown on timing. The quarterback has only so much time to throw the ball. If the ball does not come out in a certain amount of time, a sack generally occurs. When the quarterback carries his drop to five or seven steps, the defender, in addition to watching the offhand come off the ball, should see the level of the quarterback's front shoulder. If the shoulder is level, the throw is going to be delivered on a line and probably not over 15 yards deep. If the level of the shoulder is up, the ball is generally coming out with a long throw.

In half field coverage, the safety away from the quarterback's tilt should get a bigger jump then the safety to the side of the tilt. If the safety has two receivers coming vertical down the field, he cannot break toward one or the other until he is sure of the quarterback's intent. The safety away from the tilt can squeeze until the quarterback stops and looks back.

If the quarterback is flushed out of the pocket, we react differently to the type of quarterback we are facing. If the quarterback is a dangerous runner, we want to try to keep him in the pocket. If the quarterback is no threat to run, we want to flush him and make him throw on the run or make him run.

Most quarterbacks will usually scramble toward their dominant formation or to the wideside of the field. They generally do not scramble into the boundary side of the field unless they have nowhere else to run. When the quarterback is flushed out of the pocket, we work hard on the wideside of the field to cover up zones.

QUESTION AND ANSWER SESSION

Question: What do you look for in recruiting an athlete?

We recruit our state from top to bottom. We see the kids as they are growing up in our area. We have 18 million people as our base from which to recruit. When we go out of state to recruit, we feel we have to get the top athlete from any given state. We are aware of national athletics, and we know who the high-profile athletes are in different areas. We check the profile of those players and see if there is something common about them and our program. We were able to get a good linebacker out of Orlando, Florida. He grew up in California but moved to Florida while he was in high school. We found out he liked California and wanted to come back. Our academic requirements are a big thing as far as recruiting goes with a lot of the athletes.

The thing that a lot of coaches do not realize is the number of schools through the country who are looking for scholarship athletes. In the northeast section of the United States, there are small colleges looking for good football players. They do not have the recruiting budget to go get players like the big universities. You can find those schools, and your players can take advantage of that situation. The only thing about going back east to school is the travel and getting homesick.

The reason pro football is against underclassmen coming out early is the time factor they have to evaluate the talent coming out. If a player stayed in college for three years, the scouts have time to compare his statistics and physical skills because they can watch him for three years. If a kid comes out after one year of college, the information and evaluation on that kid is lacking. They do not want to invest millions of dollars into a kid that cannot play at that level. In Mike Williams's case, he is the best receiver that is available in the draft, and may be the best player in the entire draft.

The problems I had as a head coach in the NFL were simple. The team never had any real dealings with me. They saw me before practice and after practice. They very seldom were around me before games, at halftime, or after the game. The only coaches they knew were the coordinators and their position coaches. I could have been the head coach and still coordinated the defense while I was at New England. I thought about that a lot. If I did that, at least half of the team would have known what I stood for.

Question: What happens if the quarterback fakes the pass and brings it down without throwing it?

We never get hurt with the quarterback raising the ball or faking with the ball. If you watch the motion of enough quarterbacks the defensive back knows when the quarterback intends to throw the ball and when he does not. There is an entirely different action from the actual throw to the faked. When the quarterback looks one way and tilts his hips that way, it is not a signal for us to jump the receiver.

He could bounce and face the other way. He may take the front hand off the ball in an attempt to pull the defensive back. We know what the action looks like when the front hand comes off and the throw is coming. If he takes the front hand off the ball and does not throw it, he has to start all over again. He has to put his front hand back on the ball and reload to throw. Our defensive backs know when the quarterback intends to throw the ball. Your backs will know if you work with them enough.

The key we look for is the evolvement of the lower body in the throw. The plant with the foot and the stride of the legs, plus the arm action, indicates to us the ball is coming out. If the quarterback waves the ball with his arm, he is not going to throw it.

Question: What about the quarterback running out of the pocket?

We do not worry about the quarterback running out of the pocket. That goes back to the part of the lecture which talks about formation and anticipation. If the wide side end has the formation into the field, he must anticipate action coming toward him. He must think before the ball is snapped that containment to the wide side is important. The quarterback is going to scramble to the receivers in the pattern if he has a choice. The defensive contain man has to think about all those things before the ball is snapped. That gives him an advantage when events within a play start to happen.

Question: How do you contain the sprint-out quarterback?

If the quarterback sprints out and as long as he is running, the defensive man does not have to worry about containment. As the quarterback runs, he is squeezing the field for the defense. He is giving himself less and less area to throw the ball. When the quarterback stops and starts to look for the receiver is when we bring heavy containment. Everyone in the secondary stops with the quarterback and plays the condensed field. As the quarterback finds a target he will slow his speed and start to balance for the set up and throw.

Question: How do you avoid the pick when you are on the goal line?

When we are in man-to-man coverage and we get motion from the outside going back to the formation, we think this is the setup for a rub pattern. The offensive receiver motions inside and cuts behind another receiver that comes off the line of scrimmage. The intent is to pick off the defender with the receiver or the other defensive man playing that receiver. We have learned to drop off the receiver as if we were in zone coverage to allow passage of the trash. That keeps the defensive back out of the traffic. All we do is to inject some zone principles into our man-to-man technique.

Question: Has recruiting become a big problem in college coaching?

Everyone seems to have an opinion about recruiting. However I do know this. Recruiting has gotten out of hand. You want your recruits to have a good time when they visit. They come to the campus and see the school and the facilities, and for the most part, are with the coaches during that entire period of time.

At night is when you seem to have the problems. You want them to meet your players. At night is when they are socializing with your players. That part is out of the control of the coaches. Some coaches may let those things happen. I feel like you must have control of those situations because things can happen fast. Then all the work you have put into a program can go out the window fast. If you do not keep your hands on those situations, things can end in disaster.

Question: How do you keep good assistant coaches from leaving?

I want my assistant coaches to be as successful as they can be. I hire the best football coaches I can find. I want the assistant coach who is the best at what he does. Norm Chou is a good example of that. I cannot imagine Norm going much longer and not being a head coach. That is why I hire them, and I know they are going to leave if the right opportunity comes along.

Being an organized person, I always look at our staff and know who is going to be the next guy to move up. If I lose an assistant, I am going to mold the other assistants and get them ready for that position.

If one of my coaches wants to leave, I am not going to fight it. That is what should happen when a coach is successful. He should get a chance to be a head coach and develop his own program. I will help my coaches all I can. I will make calls for them and do anything I can to help them get whatever job they are seeking. That is what they did when they worked for me. They helped me become successful and pushed my agenda, and I am going to help them.

Thank you for your attention.

THE HIGH PERCENTAGE PASSING GAME

University of Miami

In my career I have coached junior high athletics and women's basketball in Oklahoma. I have been where most of the coaches in this audience are today. I know you have to coach, teach, and do a lot of other things besides coach football. My goal is to give you something you can take back to your program.

I have been blessed to get the opportunity to coach at a major university at a later stage in life. I guess when you think about Coach Bowden and Coach Paterno, I am a young pup. I have been fortunate in what I have been able to do. I inherited an outstanding football team. Coach Butch Davis did a great job of recruiting, coaching, and disciplining the Miami team before I took over.

Before I get into our passing game, I want to share some of the things that we talk about as a staff. These are some things you might think about as you get ready to go through your off-season training.

We wanted to know what we had to do to win. We knew we had good talent, but so did the teams we play. We wanted to make sure talent was not an issue for us. We work extremely hard recruiting the type of people we get in our program.

I grew up in a small town in Oklahoma. We did not have cable TV, and if you wanted to change the channel, you had to get up and do it manually. That was no problem because we only had three channels that we could get anyway. Bud Wilkinson, the great legendary coach at Oklahoma, had a coach's show on TV in that area. He always said, "Put people in the X's and O's on the drawing board and do not ask them to do things they cannot do."

We have been blessed to have a great number of All-American tight ends at Miami. When you look at the things we do with our tight ends, you may not be able to do those things with the personnel you have. Do not ask a player to do something because that is the way they do it at Miami.

At Miami, we have a lot of high-profile players. The first thing we have to work on in our program is to develop an attitude of unselfishness. If a player comes into our program and wants to throw for all the yards or get all the carries, he is not going to be very happy. Individual statistics are not what is important in our program. We try to sell unselfishness to our players, and the idea that everyone contributes to have a winning program.

I asked our players if they knew how many Bowl games John Elway played in when he was in college. John Elway is one of the most outstanding quarterbacks to ever play in the NFL, but he never went to a Bowl game when he was at Stanford. His team never won enough games to qualify for a Bowl. He was a great player, but being a great player alone does not get the job done.

We do not want any excuses in our program. The first year I was head coach, we had a new offensive and defensive coordinator, and an unfriendly schedule. I had never won a game as a head coach, and we had to play Penn State and Florida State on the road. At that time Coach Bowden had not lost a game at home in ten years. We had all kinds of reasons for us not to be successful. We wanted to put all those things behind us and see how good we could be as a team.

To win games, you have to avoid losing games first. We lost two games this year to two very good teams. We lost to Tennessee, who only gained 176 yards of total offense. We had an outstanding defensive team this year. Tennessee's strategy for the game was brilliant. Their objective in the game was play mistake-free football. They wanted us to screw up and lose the game, and that is exactly what happened. We turned the ball over too many times to win the game. We had an opportunity to win the game late, but fumbled the ball at the nine-yard line.

More games are lost than are won in the game of football today. We want to pride ourselves as being one of the best-prepared teams in the country. We have some of the best video equipment available. With all the film breakdowns that are available for our players, it is hard not to be prepared. When our players play the game on Saturday, we want them relaxed and able to play without a lot of thinking. We want them prepared and confident in what they are doing.

We want our players to play fast. Confused players or players who have no confidence are slower players. If you have a 4.6 corner, you want him to play at that speed instead of playing at a 4.8 speed because he would be confused.

We want balance in our offense. Last year we played Florida in the Sugar Bowl. In that game we had 83 snaps for the line of scrimmage. We ran the ball 43 times and threw it 40 times. That is the type of balance we like to have in our game plan.

We encourage our players to take ownership in our program. When we were getting ready to play for the national championship in the Rose Bowl two years ago, we had four starters that were going to miss the game because of injuries. We had to use a third team running back at the fullback position. He had never played a down at that position. We personalized the challenge for him by telling what he had to do for us to win the game. We were very specific about the things he had to do. Be very specific in what you want your players to do, so that they will take ownership in the program.

I have a Players Counsel that is elected by the players. There are between six and eight players elected by the team to meet with me on a regular basis to discuss different issues about our football team. One of the big issues that just came up is the need for another couch in our locker room.

When the couch shows up in the locker room, the players will know we are listening to them. We have an entirely new locker room in our building. We have beautiful new lockers, and right in the middle of the room, on the floor, is a big logo with the "U" that we wear on our helmets. No one is allowed to step on the "U" in our locker room. That is not my policy. This is the policy of the team. We do not have the area roped off. It is an understood rule that no one steps on the "U." When our athletic director came into the locker room the other day the players guided him around the "U" to make sure he did not step on the logo. Those are things you like to see. That shows the players taking ownership of the football team.

We want to be focused in our program. We want to be as good as we can be. We have high expectations of our team at Miami. We want to be realistic about those expectations. We do not want the press or someone's mother or dad setting the expectations for the team.

I want to tell you about our passing philosophy we have at Miami. I am sure there are teams that pass the ball better than we do. I do not have anything that is revolutionary about passing the football.

In our passing game, we want to throw high-percentage passes and use a possession type of attack. We do not want to take risks in throwing the ball. We want to avoid beating ourselves.

We want to take our shot when we get the proper match ups between receiver and defender. If we get Kellen Winslow matched up on a linebacker, we consider that a mismatch. When we get our big receivers matched up on shorter defenders, we like to exploit that. When we get those situations, we are going to take a shot at the end zone.

We have basic reads for the quarterback. If he can't find a receiver as he completes his basic reads, we want him to get the ball to the outlet man. We have to force the quarterback to go the outlet man because quarterbacks feel if they do not throw the ball forty yards down the field, it is not a pass.

I coached the secondary at Ohio State, and we taught the defensive backs that you never got beat by the quarterback and receivers playing catch. You got beat with a blown coverage and missed tackles. How many times have you seen Jerry Rice catch a six-yard slant over the middle that goes for sixty yards? From an offense perspective, we want to get the ball into the hands of playmakers and let them make plays.

In the passing game, the offense needs to have an alert or deep-passing opportunity. In the off-season, we are studying our cut-ups from last year. We had a new quarterback who was learning the offense, and we did a poor job of completing the deep throw. We have some players that can run and get deep on any secondary. Getting deep in the secondary is something we have to improve upon next year. You always need a deep opportunity to go to at any time if the secondary is unsound.

On offense, the most important down is first down. You have to win on first down whether it is by the run or the pass. When I first came to Miami, we lost to Florida State four years in a row. Because they had better players and were a better team, it seemed we ended up on second and third down in long yardage almost every time. When you are in that situation against Florida State, you do not win many of those battles.

We throw in practice against air quite a bit. I want our quarterback to throw passes that are high-percentage passes. I want them to throw the ball correctly and throw balls the receivers can catch. I do not want a back swinging out of the backfield and have to stop or turn around to catch the ball. If the receiver has his momentum broken, he has trouble getting four yards on first down. I really stress properly thrown balls in the control-passing game. We have good backs at Miami. If we catch the ball in stride, we can turn that into good yardage.

The passing game is designed for the quarterback. We have a 20 practice hour rule in college football. You cannot spend more than 20 hours a week with your players. When Miami had that long run of outstanding quarterbacks, Gary Stevens was the quarterback coach. Gary spent almost 20 hours a day with his quarterbacks. He was a heavy smoker, and I am sure most of those quarterbacks have second-hand smoke damage to their lungs. Now, unless you cheat, you do not have that many hours to devote to your quarterback.

I think we all are guilty of what I call TV offense. We watched Louisville beat Florida State and decided we needed to integrate some of their passing game into ours. On Sunday, you watch some pro team do something that looks good and decide that could help our offense. If you keep adding things for the quarterback to do, you will not have an offense. We have to understand the passing game is designed for the quarterback, but we want to keep it as simple as we can.

We feel concepts of a play are more important than the particular play itself. We may have personnel changes or formation changes for a play, but the concepts and progressions of that play never change for the quarterback. The basic assignments and reads do not change for the quarterback when the formations and personnel grouping do. That is the big trend in college and pro football these days.

We want to make sure we have a multiple passing attack that takes advantage of moving pockets, throwing play action, using different types of passes, and using different types of screens. That is more of an individual thing we have built into the offense.

We want to make sure we emphasize to the quarterback the shutdown routes. There is no reason for the quarterback to eat the ball because he cannot find a receiver. He has to know that he is going to always have a shutdown pattern to throw. During practice, the quarterback wants to throw every pass downfield. When that happens, we load the secondary on the outside receivers and make the quarterback throw to the shutdown routes. We do not tell the quarterback we are doing it, but it forces him to use everyone in the offense.

We want to emphasize to our receivers that it is important to make yardage after the catch. The first thing the receiver has to do is secure the ball. The next thing we want him to do is make the first defender miss the tackle. If he can make the first defender miss, we have a big play potential.

We treat the high-percentage pass as a run. If the quarterback drops back five steps and hits the back on a swing pass, that is like a sweep for us. We feel if we can get our backs in the open field, that can be a good play for us. That is why the emphasis has to be placed on throwing on time and making the ball a catchable pass.

When we coach our quarterbacks and receivers we want them to think man coverage first on every play. That keeps the quarterbacks and receivers on the same page. If the coverage is a zone, we can react and find the holes.

You need a plan to handle a blitz package. I do not like to handle blitzes with double reads, play action passes, bootleg, and naked bootlegs. I think that is risky. You have to have a plan as to what you want to do. If you decide to keep additional blockers in to block or sight-adjust the pattern, work on that plan. It is hard to check out plays because the defense does such a good job of disguising what they are going to do.

An offense has to eliminate penalties and maintain tempo and rhythm. We want our quarterback to get under the center immediately. If the quarterback comes to the line, stands behind the center, and attempts to read the defense, he is not going to see what they are going to play. Defenses will not move until the quarterback gets under the center.

We have some plays I call the automatic game plan, which are available for the quarterback. If the quarterback is confused or the crowd has gotten into the game and he cannot hear, he has a few runs and passes to call. We could run these plays with 50,000 men playing on defense and execute them.

I do not like to see the quarterback under the center, coming out from under the center, pointing at the defense, checking off two or three times, and trying to run a play. All that does is break the rhythm of the offense. If we have checks, we call it and run the play. We want to maintain the rhythm in our offense.

When we spend time making a game plan, we should follow it. We shouldn't make things up as we go along. I do not think there are too many people that can change their game plan in the middle of a game. I think your players panic when you do things like that.

That has happened to us before. Two years ago, we were playing Virginia Tech. They had an excellent team and ended up playing for the national championship. In that game, we started to improvise and got away from the game plan. It did not work because we had not practiced those things. Our players lost confidence with what we were trying to do and we lost the game. You can adjust your game plan, but do not scrap the plan and go to something else.

When you establish a pass-protection scheme, make sure to always protect your quarterback's backside. Most quarterbacks in college are right-handed, and the position that is essential in the protection scheme is the left tackle. Our left tackle two years ago was our first player drafted in the NFL that year. He was the ninth pick in the draft and now plays for the Vikings. He was a huge, at 6-9 and 340 pounds. We did not worry about the backside with him in the game.

However, do not ask a left tackle to block the backside area without help if he cannot do it. There are a number of ways to help the left tackle. We bring a back to that side and chip on the rusher or set a tight end to that side. Whatever you have to do, make sure you protect the backside of the quarterback.

The key to running a successful offense play is communication. Make sure the calls are communicated to everyone on the team. Never leave the huddle without having everyone on the same page. It is amazing the number of times the huddle is broken and some players do not know the snap count. If you get to the line of scrimmage and everyone is not clear as to what went on in the huddle, the play is doomed. If everyone is on the same page leaving the huddle you have a chance to run a successful play.

We do not want the quarterback to check away from a good play to another good play. If the play is a good play, run it. We do not want to change the play unless we see a blitz we cannot protect. Do not check off just to be checking off.

I have talked about this before, but if you have a good match-up, take advantage of it. We move our tight ends around in our offense. We are looking for the mismatches that might occur as the defense adjusts to what we are doing. In the Sugar Bowl two years ago we hit our tight end on a wheel route for a touchdown. We lined him up at the fullback position to get the match-up we wanted.

Against blitzes, we like to use hitches, slants, and speed outs. In press coverage, we use the fade if we have a mismatch. We throw those patterns against the blitz or against off-man coverage. When we throw those passes, they have to be like a running play to us. The pass has to be a completion, and we want positive yardage from the play.

We do not like to throw sight-adjustment patterns. We build hot patterns into the scheme as part of the route. Too many times in a sight-adjustment situation, the quarterback and receiver are not seeing the same thing. When that happens, the quarterback throws the ball to a defensive back because he thought the receiver was going to be there, but the receiver went the other way.

We do not sight adjust our patterns, but we do throw hot patterns. When we see a player in the defensive scheme we cannot block, we have to have an answer. The things you can handle in your offensive schemes are things you are going to see a lot of. Defensive coaches are paid to know what the offense cannot do.

We have routes in our offense which we refer to as concept routes. Here is a passing concept we call Texas (see Diagram #1). We run the play from a pro set, which is a basic set for us. The pro set has two wide receivers, two backs, and a tight end. In this concept pattern, you always have an alert pattern, which is a deep opportunity. That pattern is a backside post pattern run by the split end, with a breaking point at 12 yards. The tailback is running a checkdown pattern, which is a backside route run at four yards deep and two yards outside the tackle box.

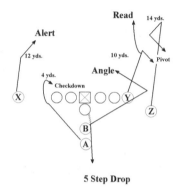

Diagram #1. Texas

To the strongside, we have an angle route run by the fullback. We run the fullback to the flat so much, it sets up the angle route. The fullback runs the pattern as if he were going to the flat. Once he gets three yards outside the alignment of the tight end, he plants and angles back inside behind the tight end's release. The tight end is running a read route. He is looking into the middle zone of the field. If he sees a middle safety, he runs a come-back route to the outside. He runs his pattern to 10 yards and comes back to eight yards. If the middle of the field is open with no safety in the middle, he runs a deep vertical route down the seam.

The flanker back or pro back runs a 14-yard pivot route. He is running to a depth of 14 yards, pivots back to the inside, and comes outside and back to 12 yards. The quarterback is taking a five-step drop and knows the concept patterns being run.

What we do from that pattern is change the formation and run the same concept (see Diagram #2). This formation is two tight ends, two wide receivers, and one back set. We shift the second tight end back, send him in motion across the set, and snap the ball as he gets to the tackle. The patterns are the same. The split end shifts up when the tight end shifts back to get on the line of scrimmage. He runs the alert route. The running back runs the check-down pattern. The motioning tight end runs the angle, and the strongside tight end runs the read pattern. The flanker runs his 14-yard pivot route.

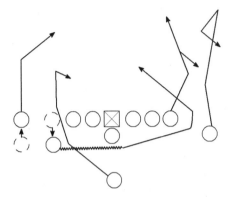

Diagram #2. Two tight end set

In the two tight end set, we could align the second tight end on the weakside, and trade him to the strongside in a wing set. We could align him in the wing set and have a trips formation. We could align him in the wing set, bring him in motion to the quarterback, and use return motion to get him back to his original position.

The protection we use with this play is a basic protection (see Diagram #3). To the strongside, the center, guard, and tackle are blocking the two down linemen. The frontside tackle is blocking the man on him or outside of him. The uncovered lineman double reads the Mike and Sam linebackers. If one linebacker blitzes, he blocks him. If both linebackers blitz, he blocks the nearest threat to the quarterback, and the quarterback throws hot off the second linebacker. The hot route will be the angle route. In Diagram #3, the center is the uncovered lineman and has the double read. If neither frontside linebacker comes, the uncovered man is a help blocker.

On the backside, the guard and tackle have the down linemen. The tailback does not have a free release. He is reading the Will linebacker. If the Will

linebacker retreats into coverage, the tailback runs his check downroute. If the Will linebacker blitzes, the tailback blocks him.

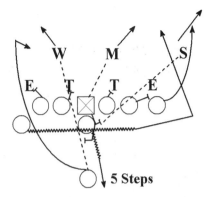

Diagram #3. Protection scheme

We can run the same play from three wide receivers, one tight end, and one back set (see Diagram #4). We align the formation in a two-by-two set and bring the weakside slot into motion to the strongside. The protection and routes are the same, with the slot wide receiver running the angle route. In Diagram #4, the frontside guard will be uncovered and has the double read on the Mike and Sam linebackers.

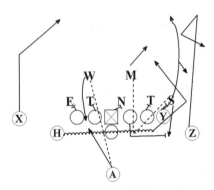

Diagram #4. Three wide receivers

Another possibility is a trips formation to the tight end side (see Diagram #5). The first inside receiver to the trip side is the angle route runner. His alignment is almost a wing set outside the tight end. If we have a good feel for what the defense is doing, we motion the tailback to the weakside and go empty in the backfield. The concept and the blocking are the same. The tailback has to be aware of the Will linebacker as he goes in motion.

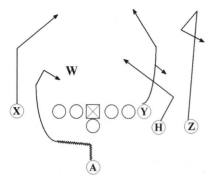

Diagram #5. Trips/empty

Our tight end is almost like a wide receiver for us (see Diagram #6). Instead of aligning him in tight, we put him in the slot to the flanker, with the flanker on the line of scrimmage. The formation looks like a twin set to the strongside and a split end set to the weakside. The fullback runs the angle route, and the tailback runs the check down.

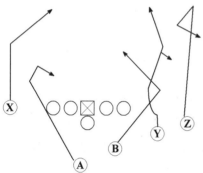

Diagram #6. Tight end twin set

The fullback can be in a number of different sets (see Diagram #7). He can be in the strong halfback position, or King set. We can set him in the weakside slot or the weakside halfback position, which is the Queen set, and motion him to the angle route. We could set him in the wing set outside the strong tackle and motion him in return-motion to that side. This makes the defense adjust, but does not change the offense.

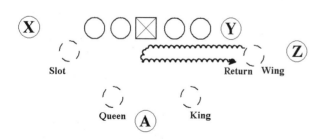

Diagram #7. King/Queen/slot/wing

The formation we like to run this play from is the twins look, with the flanker and split end on the same side, and the tight end to the other side (see Diagram #8) When we use this formation, we change the alert route. Since the tight end is tight, we adjust his pattern to a post-corner route. If he runs a post, it puts him too close to the read route if that X-receiver is running the seam. The post-corner gives us better spacing on the vertical routes.

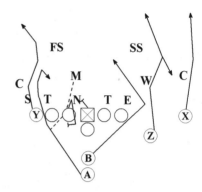

Diagram #8. Twins/post-corner

I think you can see what we are doing. I have showed you different formations, but we are still running the same concept. You have to evaluate your personnel and decide what the strengths of each back or tight end might be. If your tailback can play wide receiver, you can move him throughout your formations and give the defense more problems (see Diagram #9). Instead of using a fullback, you could use a second tight end at the fullback's position and move him throughout the formation. The combinations the offense can put on the field are endless in regard to formations.

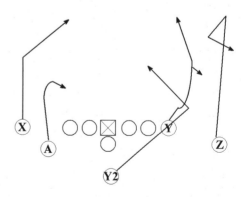

Diagram #9. Tailback wide receiver

Before I close I want to share with you an eight-point plan to help your players become better teammates. We do a lot at the University of Miami to stress team unity. I bring the entire team to my house for an outing each year to get them out of the school routine. I want to give them a family atmosphere. To be a better teammate, remember:

- The team is more important than the individual.
- Everyone's job is important.
- Treat everyone with respect.
- Share victories and defeats.
- Accept constructive criticism.
- Keep your coaches well informed.
- Focus on your work ethic. You can only control your contribution.
- Allow for differences in lifestyles. Not everyone likes the same kind of music or haircuts.

The reason I love football is because everyone's job is important. If someone fails to do his job, everyone on the team suffers. The year we won the national championship, against Florida State, we had a long snapper blow his knee out, and he did not play for the rest of the year. We had a backup come in and snap perfectly for the remainder of the year. Deep snappers are not that important unless you do not have one. He was ready to fill that position because his job as the backup snapper was important.

I was a walk-on football player when I played. Our walk-on players are just as important as anyone else. They may serve only on scout teams, but they are going to get a championship ring and they are going to be treated with respect.

When we win a game, we all win the game. When we lose a game, we all lose the game. We put a lot of effort into our Tennessee game because we had lost to Virginia Tech and looked bad doing it. When we lost the VPI game, we were at a point where a less mature team could have started to point fingers at one another. The defense was playing well, but the offense was turning the ball over.

The bottom line was the defense lost the game because we win and lose as a team. I think that helped us come back, win four games in a row, beat Florida State in the Orange Bowl.

When you talk about differences in lifestyles, it is mind boggling. Some players may have earrings or tattoos. Our starting running back is Gary Payton. He is Walter Payton's son. He has a tattoo of his father's face on his right shoulder, and it looks like a snapshot. It as authentic as anything I have seen. I do not particularly like those tattoos, but they are part of the lifestyles from which our players come. The only thing we try to do is make sure that everyone respects those differences. If we had hard and fast rules about hair, tattoos, earrings, and those kinds of things, we would not be able to recruit one-third of the people we sign. Whatever your philosophies are, I think you have to allow for the differences in lifestyle.

I want to tell you one story before I end my presentation. I had just gotten the job at Miami and had the opportunity to be at a coaching clinic with Lou Holtz. I was happy to get the Miami job because it was a great opportunity. Coach Holtz asked me if I was the best coach in America. I told him I was not the best coach in the room. He told me I should resign if I was not the best coach in America. I asked him what he meant by that. He told me the University of Miami hired me to be the best coach in America. I thought about that statement, and he was exactly right. They did not hire me as an "on-the-job-training coach," or to see how things would go." They hired me to be the best football coach in America.

That is the thought I want to leave with you today, because that is what you have been hired to do. You were hired to be the best you can be at whatever you do. Our players are just like your players, except they are a little older. They have the same immaturities and needs to develop and grow.

I wish all of you the best of luck next year.

Mark Dantonio

THE ZONE BLITZ PACKAGE

University of Cincinnati

It is a pleasure to be here today representing the University of Cincinnati. What I want to do today is talk about our base zone pressure philosophy and some of our zone pressure schemes. In the past three years at Ohio State, we used the zone pressure package quite a bit. In 2001, we had more of a pressure package, with man-to-man coverage on the outside and a free safety in the middle of the field. As we became a better and more experienced team, we became more of a zone pressure team.

I spent a lot of time talking to Bob and Mike Stoops at the University of Oklahoma. We patterned our defense at Ohio State after what the Oklahoma staff was doing with their zone pressure blitzes. We felt this type of scheme could make it easier for our players to understand the defense. This type of defense lets the players be more aggressive. They were not reading and reacting. They were reading on the run and playing fast. This type of scheme allowed the players to become more aggressive with less thinking. They knew where they were going, and they were getting there fast. Your team can play fast when they know what to do. They play faster when there is no hesitation and they go a hundred miles an hour.

It is difficult to be simple when the offensives are as varied as they are today. We had to stay comprehensive on defense to stay up-to-date with the things the offense was doing. You see so many things on offense that your defensive plan has to be well thought out and diversified, while at the same time, you must keep it simple so your players can play fast. You have to build a good foundation on defense. If you have a solid foundation, you can build up from there.

We had a theory that we built upon at Ohio State. The first thing we wanted was a penetrating defense that would disrupt what the offense was trying to do. At Ohio State, we led the nation in run defense this year. We wanted to disguise the blitz as much as possible and surprise the offense. We felt with a penetrating defense we could strip off the run blockers and make the tackle with our front seven. If they couldn't make the tackle, the secondary would. In every defense, everyone has a role to play. Our defensive line, linebackers, and secondary had responsibilities in the run defense for stopping the run.

In the passing game, we wanted to disrupt the timing of the play. At Ohio State, we kept statistics on how many times we hit the quarterback during the course of the game. Against Texas Tech, we hit the quarterback 24 times during the game. Against Washington, we hit the quarterback 26 times, with 14 coming in the first half. In our Michigan game this year, we hit the quarterback only twice. When we play well, we have an effect on the quarterback's performance. When we don't play well and the quarterback has time to throw the ball, he can have an effect on us.

When you blitz, your pursuit will be distorted. If the ball breaks the line of scrimmage, the defense has to react quickly to prevent big plays from occurring. That is a critical point. The defense can't allow big plays when they blitz. In 2002, we had eight running plays in 14 games that went for over 15 yards. This year, we were better than that. That all occurred because we put an emphasis on tackling. We work on tackling every day. We work extremely hard in our secondary on tackling. With the offenses we are seeing today, it is essential that the defense make tackles in space. The offense spreads the field with their formations. They run a wide variety of screens that are designed to get the ball on the perimeter. If you can't tackle in space, you are going to give up a large number of big plays.

There is a lot of technique involved in tackling. We are going to put our players in positions they would normally be in during a game situation to make those tackles. The corners are going to have six to seven drills a day that involve tackling in space. One of our best drills does not have to be performed in pads. When we are not in pads, we have the defenders tag the ballcarriers instead of tackling them. When the defenders get in position to tackle, we require them to buzz their feet, take a flat step, get their feet up under the body with a good bent-knee position, and tag the ball carrier by bringing their hands from below their waist. By bringing the hands from underneath, the tackler doesn't get overextended. If he simply reaches out and tags the ballcarrier, he gets overextended. We do a lot of different things to make us better tacklers. We want to do is have the eleven best tacklers on the field.

With our blitz package, we are going to put different zone pressures in categories and make them simple for our players. We used places to name our zone pressures. We gave our zone pressures names like Alaska, Florida, and Vegas. We went further to differentiate between the places. Our open front was called Arizona, and within that front, we had Tucson and Phoenix, which are cities in Arizona. Our nickel back in our defense is called our money-backer. Any nickel-based pressure that involved our money-backer became places in Nevada. We called those defensive pressures Reno, Tahoe, and Vegas. We tried to use systematic thinking to make it simple for our players.

Within our zone pressures we have five different coverages. We categorize them by using key words. Our MAGIC coverage stands for Missing A Guy In Coverage. That means we are playing a three-under and three-deep type of coverage. We are missing a man in our underneath coverage. In our fire-zone pressure we are bringing our safety down into the area from which the blitz is coming. We use the term Zorro coverage to get the safety coming down away from a certain position. We try to give our player some rhyme and reason as to what we are doing by using these names. The first year we used this scheme we called all the adjustments fire-zone calls, and the players had to know where they fit.

Our dog package is press coverage by the corners, with a safety in the middle of the field. Any time we blitzed a safety, we called it a snake. Any time the defense heard a snake name, they knew a safety was coming on a max blitz. An example of a snake was python or cobra. The six-man blitzes were named after birds. We designated a six-man blitz with names like hawks or eagles. Our key blitzes were named after act of nature. Those types of blitzes were given names like lightening or thunder.

In building a sound base within the defense, you should try to give your players and coaches ownership within the system. Coach Tressel gave me ownership within our defense as the defensive coordinator. I, in turn, gave ownership to the defensive position coaches who worked under me. They all played important roles in practice and on game day. They had a say-so in the decisions that were made in relationship to our defense. During time-outs and between series, we asked our players how they wanted to play the defense. We wanted to give them ownership and let them buy into who we were as coaches. When you give players ownership in the defense, the first thing they will do is see that their peers are accountable.

We broke down our game each week with a chart to indicate the number of times we blitzed. On the chart, we broke the field down from the 0 to the 50-yard line, 50 to the 20, and from the 20 to the goal line. We showed the down-and-distance, the number of times we blitzed in each zone, and a total for all zones. We showed our base defenses and our blitzes. Our blitzes are broken down into two categories. If we have a middle of the field safety, we call that a pressure. If there is no safety in the middle of the field, we called that a blitz. The totals on this particular chart for last year showed that we played base defense 441 times. We pressured 409 times during the course of the year. In those 409 times, we pressured 335 times and total blitzed 74 times. We were about 50/50 in our base defense to the pressure defense.

When we refer to our down-and-distance, we differentiate between first-and-ten and the first down of a series. We refer to the first play of a series as P-and-ten. We look at P-and-ten differently then first-and-ten. However, we do combine them at times in our statistics. On this chart, in the P-and-ten situations from the 0-yard line to the 50-yard line, we pressured 42 times, blitzed twice, and played 61 base defenses.

The first defensive pressure I want to show you is what we call Field Florida. This is America's play. Everyone in America runs this pressure defense. We have a progression that we use to teach it. We show players on the board, show them a film, use a walk-through in practice, and make adjustments during the walk-through. After the walk-through, we take the defense into some kind of individual drill work to practice the skills needed to run the pressure. From the individual drill, we advance to a group drill such as 7-on-7 to practice the individual skills. Next we take the skill to a team drill, practice it in a scrimmage, and finally use it in a game. That is the progression we use to install all of our pressures and blitzes.

We systematically teach our players in a progression. The progression for our players is stance, alignment, keys, and responsibility. We teach each player how to take a stance with regard to the pressure we are running. When we teach keying, we talk a lot about eye control. The eye control is what the player is looking at to tell him what to do. In teaching responsibility, it can be as complex as you want it to get, or as simple as you need it to be. As you go through the responsibilities, you need to keep in mind that we want the players to play fast.

When we teach, we use the unit method. We teach the entire defense first. We teach it very quick and brief. We give them a handout that shows the defense and adjustments, and has position, alignment, key, and responsibility for each player. We do not spend time talking about these things. Each player studies this sheet back at the dorm and files it in his notebook. Each time we cover something new, we issue another sheet, which the player places in his notebook. He will have a growing notebook of pressures and blitzes.

We don't give them a whole notebook of defenses. We give them the first chapter, which may have ten pages in it. At the end of two-a-day practices, we take back the notebooks from each player. They won't have a notebook because the bottom line is how well they tackle and how well they play, not what they read. With that in mind, I'll teach you the way we would teach our team.

In our field Florida, we have a bubble side into the wide side of the field (see Diagram #1). Our Sam linebacker is aligned in a 9 technique on the tight end's outside shoulder or walked off against a slot formation. The field side end is aligned in a heavy 6 technique on the outside shoulder of the offensive tackle. That technique is generally a 5 technique, but at Ohio State we called it a 6 technique. The field side tackle aligns in a shade technique on the center to the wide side of the field. The boundary side end alignment is what we call a crash 8 technique. The boundary tackle aligns in a 3 technique on the outside shoulder of the offensive guard. The Mac linebacker aligns in a 30 technique on the outside shoulder of the guard off the line of scrimmage. The Will linebacker aligns in a 30 technique on the boundary side guard.

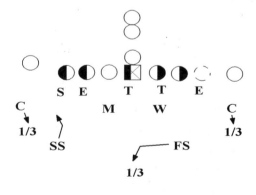

Diagram #1. Field Florida alignment

The boundary side end keys the ball and the tight end, if he has one (see Diagram #2). He keys the offensive tackle if there is no tight end to the near back in the backfield. His responsibility is to loop to a 9 technique against the run. Against the pass, he loops to the 9 technique and drops to the flat or walls off the number two receiver to his side.

The boundary side tackle keys the ball and the offensive guard. He loops into the B gap through the inside shoulder of the offensive tackle and has containment on passes.

The field side tackle keys the ball and the center. His movement is across the face of the center and into the weakside A gap. If the weakside guard blocks down on the field tackle, he plays across the guard's face.

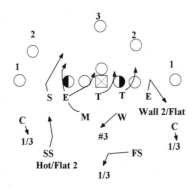

Diagram #2. Field Florida movement

The field side end keys the ball, the offensive tackle, and the near back. He runs a shallow stunt inside into the strongside A gap. This is what we call a big stick. It is not a loop. It is a shallow slant inside and a penetrating up move through the A gap. If the offensive guard turns out on him, he crosses the guard's face into the A gap. If he blocks down, he comes off his hip.

The Sam linebacker keys the tight end unless he is walked off. If he is walked off, he keys the triangle of the slot receiver, the tackle, and the near back. He is an edge blitz man coming from the outside. The Mac linebacker keys the ball and is in a scrape blitz position off the heels of the field side end. We want the Mac linebacker to stay tight in his scrape. He runs through the alignment of the end's heels. He is a B gap defender, and he wants to square his shoulders and

get ready to take on a block. If he doesn't square his shoulders, he has no power.

The Will linebacker keys the near back though the offensive guard. We want him to tag step. That means we want him to slow down on flow away from him. He is playing the strongside A gap to the strongside C gap. He is going to bracket the ball if it breaks inside. He takes the number three receiver on all passes.

If the ball is in the middle of the field, the strength of the formation will determine which way we declare and to which direction we run our movement. On field Florida, we are coming with zone pressure from the Mac and Sam linebackers. We can give a nose call and drop the nose tackle into coverage. We can make other adjustments to this front. If we call field O-Florida, the field tackle aligns in a head-up position on the center. This is fire zone coverage. That means we are bringing a safety down to the side of the blitz. In this set, the strong safety will roll down to the blitz side, and the free safety will rotate to the middle of the field. The corners are playing three-deep coverage. The key to this pressure is we use the under front in our defensive package. If the only time you are in the under front is when you run this blitz, the stunt will not be effective.

The Sam linebacker is a blitz man. If the tight end blocks out on the Sam linebacker, he has to fight pressure. The worst thing the Sam linebacker can do is run upfield and get turned out. He is a contain blitz man. We want him to widen his alignment at the last second. We like to time up our blitzes on any motion the offense has. If they motion the flanker back inside, the quarterback is not going to stop the play and automatic out of it. It is important not to take false steps. We ask the Sam linebacker to curl his front toe. If he does that he will never step back up underneath himself. The worst thing the blitz man can do is drop-step before he comes. If the blitz man can't get to the quarterback, we are not going to send him. It makes no sense to send a player out of coverage who is not blitzing aggressively with an attitude.

The strong safety is coming down hot on the number two receiver to the side of the blitz. He is a C gap to D gap player in his run responsibility. He wants to stay high in his alignment and move down at the last second. We want to disguise the coverage until the last second. We time our movement on whatever the offense does to indicate that they are going to snap the ball. We get those tips and clues from a scouting report. On a running play, the strong safety comes down to a depth of five yards and sits in the C gap.

At some point, the path of the ballcarrier is going to get distorted. The ballcarrier is going to turn back inside or bounce outside. We are canceling gaps in the direction of our slants. People usually don't bring the ball back that way. If they do bring the ball back to the angles, good things usually happen for us. If the ball bounces outside, the safety becomes the D gap player.

We tell our middle of the field safety to always attack the line of scrimmage at the same angle the ball is attacking the line of scrimmage. If the ball is being run in an isolation-type play, the free safety attacks the line of scrimmage at the same angle of the running back. If the play is a toss sweep, the free safety carries his pads parallel with the line of scrimmage. The free safety starts to gain ground toward the line of scrimmage at the same time the running back starts to gain ground. He keeps his outside shoulder on the inside shoulder of the running back. That way he is not overrunning the play. The corners are coached to secure the number one receiver and keep the ball inside in front of them on running plays.

We have adjustments to every set we encounter. The more we learn about what we are supposed to do within the defense, the more complex it becomes. We start with the foundation and build upon that idea. We go into the defense with the idea that we are going to blackboard the defense. That means the way we draw the defense on the blackboard is the way we are going to play it. However every defense needs simple tweaking to make it effective. In every case the Leo end or

boundary end is going to be the flat coverage man into the boundary, except when we need a change up.

If the offense gives us a twin set into the boundary, we can game plan an adjustment called hank (see Diagram #3). This allows the Will linebacker to take the flat and the Leo to come inside to take the hot receiver coming out of the backfield. The Will linebacker is our best cover linebacker.

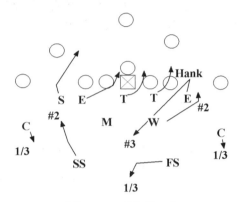

Diagram #3. Hank

The next blitz is called field Bama (see Diagram #4). The entire defense is played just like field Florida except for the movement of the Mike linebacker and the field end. On this pressure, the Mike linebacker goes first and attacks the B gap. The field end jab-steps upfield and follows the Mike linebacker by looping into the A gap. Everything else on the defense is like Florida.

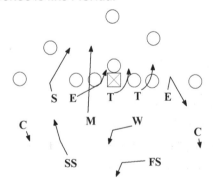

Diagram #4. Field Bama

Let's talk a about pass defense with these defenses. On every zone defense we play, we have a no-cover zone (see Figure #5). We ask our players to know the dimensions of the field. The first thing we teach our defensive backs is the distance the numbers are from the sidelines. The bottom of the numbers is seven yards from the sidelines, and the top of the numbers is nine yards from the sidelines. The outside third of the field in college football is 19 yards from the sidelines to the hash marks of the field. The middle third in college football is 13.33 yards. In any zone coverage, the no-cover zone is five yards from the line of scrimmage. If we are playing zone defense, we never want to have a player standing in the no-cover zone. We want our defenders to be ten yards deep with the ability to break back into the no-cover zone to make the tackle.

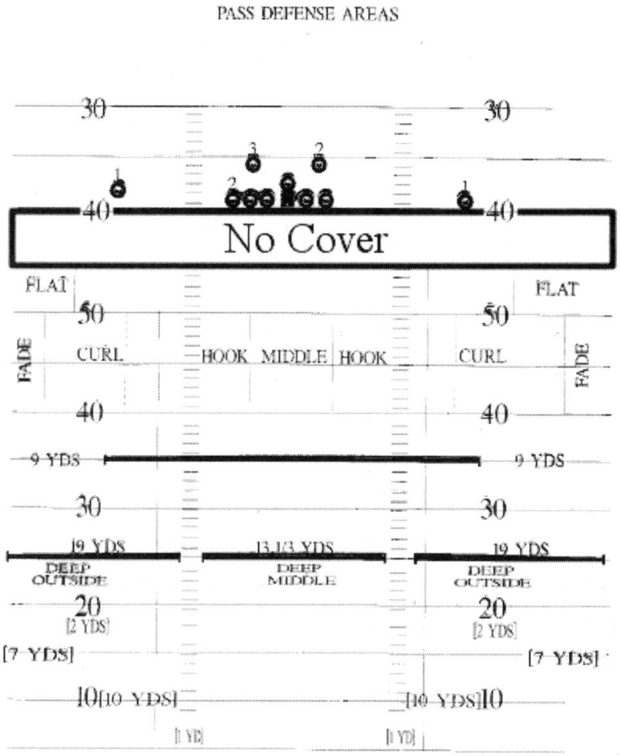

PASS DEFENSE AREAS

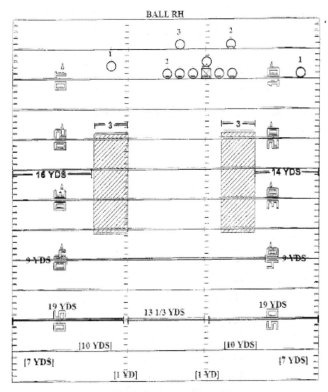

Diagram #5. No-cover zone

We ask our players in any zone coverage to be able to break to one-third the distance the ball is in the air. If the ball is in the air for 21 yards, we expect the defender to break seven yards on the ball. To be able do that, he has to have vision on the quarterback and break on the ball. We want eye control on the ball. When we watch film, if everyone in the coverage is not moving to the ball when the quarterback is releasing it, they are wrong. If we are using vision and break on the ball we can create a big hit on receivers. We may not be able to stop the ball from being completed, but we can make a sure and sound tackle after the catch. Every time the ball is thrown, we want to average five yards or less per attempt. When we score our performance, anything that is more than five yards for the offense is a loss for the defense.

There are seams on a football field within the zones of coverage. If you are an offensive coach, that is the area you want to attack. Seams stretch the defensive coverage. If the ball is on the hash mark in college football, the seam to the boundary side of the ball is three yards outside the hash mark and three yards wide. The seam to the open side of the ball would be on the college hash mark and three yards wide. These seams start at ten yards from the line of scrimmage and are three yards wide. The corner is always told, in three-deep coverage, if the number two receiver is down the seam, he has to have depth within his zone as to the point of his divider (see Diagram #6). The point of the corner's divider refers to the middle of the corner's one third. If the number two receiver breaks his pattern and doesn't come down the seam the corner's eyes go to the number one receiver and he squeezes him from the top down like man-to-man coverage.

Diagram #6. Three-deep seams

From the top down means the defender is going to play on top of the receiver squeezing back to him.

We ask our hot defenders to make sure they bump the number two receivers out of the seam areas.

The middle of the field safety is asked to go from seam to seam on his break (see Diagram #7). If the ball is thrown over 25 yards, he has to cover from seam to seam. If the ball is throw 18 yards or less, he has to cover from hash mark to hash mark. We are looking for a guy that has vision and can cover ground once the ball is in the air. We are giving the safeties guidelines so they know what is expected of them.

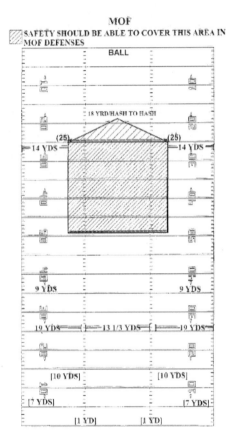

Diagram #7. Middle of the field safety

In fire-zone coverage, the strong safety and Leo end are what we call a hot to the number 2 players. The Will linebacker is what we call a hook to the number 3 player. The strong safety and Leo end should have a big hit on the number 2 receiver if the quarterback straightens up and throws the ball to one of those receivers. If the number 2 receiver goes to the flat, the safety and Leo match that move. They simply get width and match the move. They do not jump him in that area. If the ball is thrown into the flat, the safety breaks on the ball

and makes the hit. If the number 2 receiver goes inside or comes up the field, the defender bangs him out of the seam area and breaks on the ball.

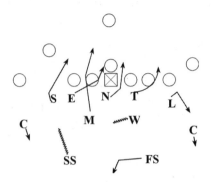

Diagram #8. Fire-zone coverage

If the number 2 receivers breaks inside the defender delivers the receiver to Will linebacker who is the hook man to the number 3 player. He jams him, calls over-over, and lets him go to the hook player. The Leo end plays the same technique on any receiver coming his way. He is a seam re-router and flat player.

The hook to the number 3 player could be the Will linebacker or the Leo end, if he is playing a hank technique. He is responsible for the number 3 receiver to either side. He drops to ten yards and vision breaks on the ball. He is simply leaning the way the number 3 receiver comes out. If the number 3 receiver breaks to the strongside, that is the way the defender plays him. If he breaks the other way, that is the side he favors.

We have a free safety going to the middle of the field. We tell him to lean toward the linebacker who is covering in space. In this case, it would be the Will linebacker. He has the middle one-third, but we are asking him to hang with the linebacker in space.

I want to talk quickly about our deep one-third players. We use the term divider to define the corner's play. A divider is a specific landmark for each corner that tells him where the midpoint of his outside one-third is located. The divider remains constant throughout the play, and the corners play off these in terms of horizontal alignment and actual play (see Diagram #9). If the ball is in the middle of the field, the corner's divider is ten yards from the sideline, or one yard from the top of the numbers. If the ball is on the opposite hash mark, the field corner's divider is five yards outside the hash mark and five yards from the top of the numbers. The boundary corner's divider is the bottom of the numbers. Those numbers will change slightly depending on where the ball is located.

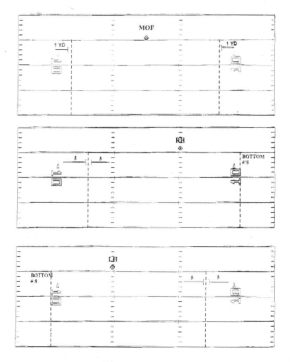

Diagram #9. Dividers

Our corner's stance is inside foot back, shoulders parallel, and eyes toward the football. His alignment is one yard by eight yards based upon his divider. That means if the receiver is outside the corner's divider, he would align inside the receiver. The divider remains constant up the field. If the receiver tries to stem the defender outside so he can run the skinny post, the defender has to stay on the receiver's inside so the receiver can't beat him to the post. The safety covers from seam to seam. If the ball is thrown outside the seam area, it is the corner's ball.

If the number 2 receiver breaks up the seam, the corner forgets about his relationship to the number 1 receiver, gets on his divider, and carries his depth according to the depth of the receivers. As he starts to run deep, he puts his butt to the boundary. If the ball is thrown deep to the outside receiver, he

wheels his head around, locates the ball, and goes for the ball. If the ball is thrown to the inside receiver, he plays the ball since he is facing that way. If the number 2 receiver is not up the seam, the corner's eye control comes to the outside hip of the number 1 receiver as he runs up the field. He starts to play strong man-to-man coverage on the number 1 receiver from the top down. If the receiver rolls up on his outside foot the corner knows he is running an inside dig and he attacks it from the receiver's inside, shoulder down.

As I said in the beginning, the defense has to be comprehensive in its approach. The nickel field Florida is another of these defenses (see Diagram #10). In this scheme, we have a fifth defensive back, represented by the star symbol and the money linebacker, who is our best cover linebacker. We rename the Will linebacker the money backer. He is represented in the diagram as a dollar sign. The nickel back is always to the field side of the defense. In this case, he is the blitz man. Everything else is simple field Florida. You can utilize the money backer with a hank call and get him in tight coverage on the number 2 receiver weak.

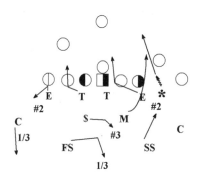

Diagram # 10. Nickel field Florida

Our 30-front is usually played with nickel personnel (see Diagram #11). If we wanted to play the 30 front with regular personnel in the game, we would simply call a 50 front. That means the defense looks like a 30 front, uses 30 rules, but has 50 personnel in the game. Offenses are using a lot of empty sets and four-wide receiver sets to spread the defense. With the 30 front, we align with our ends in heavy 6 techniques on the offensive tackles.

The nose tackle aligns in a 0 technique on the center. The Will linebacker becomes the money and moves out to play on the outside. The Leo end becomes the viper and plays a stand up linebacker position. When we play our nickel personnel, the Mac and Star are always on the same side, and the viper and money are always on the other side.

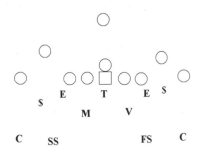

Diagram #11. 30 front

We can use the 30-front and run a Florida field defense (see Diagram #12). The stunt is the same. The star is coming off the edge. The field end is running the big stick with the Mac linebacker coming off his heels. The money is playing hot to the number 2 receiver to his side, and the viper is playing hot to the number 3 receiver. The secondary is playing the same fire zone coverage.

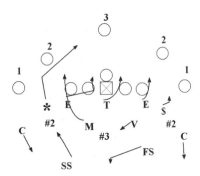

Diagram #12. 30 field Florida

In one day we can put in field Florida, nickel field Florida, 30 Florida, and 50 Florida. The stunt is the same, and the personnel change is not drastic. It is all the same defense, but it looks different to the offense.

With the 30 Vegas defense, we align in a 30-front (see Diagram #13). Instead of bringing the stunt from the field, we are going to bring the blitz man from the boundary. The boundary end and viper

run a Bama stunt on the boundary side. The money runs a blitz off the edge making sure to peel over the top of the running back's block for containment. The strong safety goes to the middle of the field to cover the middle third. The free safety moves out to take the money's coverage on the number 2 receiver hot. The star plays hot on the number 2 receiver to the other side, and the Mac linebacker plays the number 3 receiver hot. The corners play their fire zone coverage as they did on the other fronts. It is the same stunt, but we are bringing our money linebacker. When we blitz the money linebacker the stunt gets its name from places in Nevada.

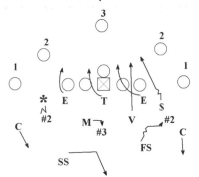

Diagram #13. 30 Vegas

Another example of zone pressure is called field Philly (see Diagram #14). In this defense, we align in our under front. The bubble is to the field side of the defense. The shade tackle loops to the field side B gap. The Mac linebacker goes first and blitzes the weakside A gap. The Will linebacker comes second and blitzes the strongside A gap. The 3 technique tackle loops outside like he did on the Florida stunt. The field side end does the same thing. The Leo end is playing as he did in the Florida stunt by playing the number two receiver hot to flat. The Sam linebacker is playing a 9 technique and is playing the number two receiver hot to flat. The strong safety is rotating into the middle of the field to cover the middle third. The corners are aligned in a press alignment but bail out to cover the deep outside thirds. The free safety rolls down into the middle linebacker's position and has the number three receiver hot and becomes a hitter.

If we want to change up the stunt we call Alaska. The alignment is the same for all the personnel. The only thing that changes is the pattern

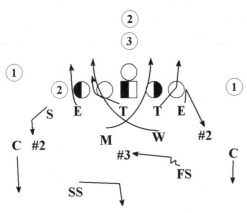

Diagram #14. Field Philly

of the blitz man. In the Alaska stunt the nose tackle loops across the center's face into the weakside A –gap (see Diagram #15). The Mac linebacker goes first into the strongside A –gap, and the Will linebacker blitzes the strong side B gap. Everything else in the defense is the same. We can always use a hank call to change up the secondary coverage. All you need to remember is the weakside number 2 and number 3 hot defenders exchange responsibilities.

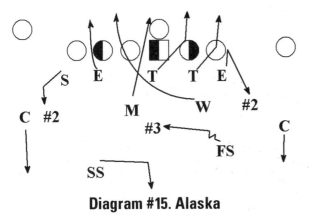

Diagram #15. Alaska

The problem you run into with the zone blitz scheme is in the event you don't get to the quarterback. Since we have only three men in underneath coverage, the quarterback is going to find holes in the defense. When that occurs, the only thing you can do is limit the amount of yardage after the catch. We did that against Miami in the championship game in 2002. They caught 26 passes against us, but they

only averaged 2.2 yards gained after the catch. That is extremely important to limiting the damage.

When I was a younger coach I tried to do as many things with schemes as I could do. But the more experience I got, the more I realized that schemes don't win games for you. Players win the games. Forget about the schemes, find ways to get you players to understand what you are doing, and let them play the game. Give them an opportunity to play fast and aggressively, and they will win games for you. Give them a chance to gain ownership in your system, and that will take care of the peer pressure that comes with playing.

The other thing you have to do is get their moral and spiritual values lined up with the importance of team play. When your players feel at home with your football family, you will find success will come in abundance. That has been proven over the course of time by Coach Tressel. It didn't matter whether he was at Youngstown State or Ohio State. Average players can become great players when they play fast, are aggressive, and play with confidence. As a football coach, you have to have a vision of what you want and talk small steps on the way to getting there.

There are more games won or lost by a small event that occurred within a game. Football is a game of inches. Some coaches can't figure out why they aren't successful. I think it is because of the intangibles in football. How you handle adversity on and off the field is one of the many intangibles you have to meet. Nick Saban always asked his players to do three things. He asked them to play with great effort, to play physical and to play with mental toughness, and know what to do. If you know what to do, you will play fast. The mental makeup of a person needs to be developed just as physical makeup needs to be developed.

I know I'm running over so I will close. Thank you for your time.

SECONDARY COVERAGE TECHNIQUES

Western Kentucky University

I appreciate the opportunity to speak at this outstanding clinic. I have enjoyed attending the clinics myself, and to be here representing Western Kentucky is a thrill for me.

I am going to talk about our single and double safety packages today. The first things I will cover are some coverage principles that concern our safeties and corners.

In our single safety package, we play three coverages. We play 3-deep coverage, man-free coverage, and what we call cover 7. In the double safety package, we have five coverages we play. From the double safety package, we play a 2-deep, 4-deep, ski coverage, invert coverage, and cloud coverage.

Our players have to be aware of the problems area in the 2- and 3- deep coverage. In those coverages are seams and holes (see Diagram #1). In the 3-deep zone, a seam runs down the hash mark on each side, three yards outside the hash mark. That is the area we do not want people running. We want to force receivers out of that area when we can. The middle zone on the college field is 14 yards wide. In the outside third, 14 yards from the sideline is three yards outside the hash mark. That is the seam our defensive backs have to be aware of.

The corners have to know where the midpoint of their zone is located. We call the midpoint of the zone the divider. If the ball is in the middle of the field, the divider is the middle of the numbers marked on the field. If the ball is on the hash mark, the corner uses a five-yard rule. His midpoint on the short side is five yards from the sideline, and his divider for the wide side is five yards outside the hash mark. There will be some exceptions on individual team and their wide receiver split, but this is a general rule.

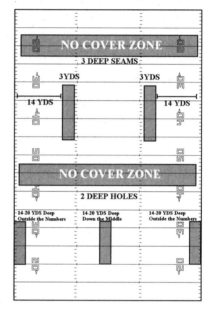

Diagram #1. Holes, seams, no cover

In the single safety coverage with a double width formation, the corner alignment is seven yards deep and one yard either inside or outside, depending on the split of the receiver (see Diagram #2). If the split of the receiver is outside the divider, the corner is inside on his alignment. If the receiver's split is inside the divider, the corner's aligns outside the receiver.

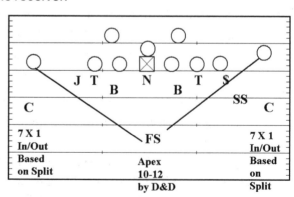

Diagram #2. Double width alignment

The free safety is aligned in the middle of the formation 10 to 12 yards deep. We call that an apex alignment on the distance between the two wide receivers. The strong safety aligns three yards deep and five yard wide of the tight end.

In the single width formation, the corner to the tight end side is in a five-yard by three-yard alignment (see Diagram #3). The corner to the wide receiver side is in a regular 7 by 1 yard alignment. The strong safety is aligned on the inside receiver five yards deep, and has a one- and two-back rule. If one back is in the backfield, the strong safety aligns one yard inside the receiver. If two backs are in the backfield, the strong safety is one outside the receiver. That alignment has to do with his run support on the set. The free safety takes his apex alignment on the formation 10 to 12 yards deep.

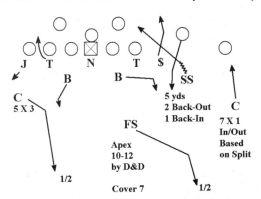

Diagram #3. Single width alignment

The one- and two-back rule on the alignment of the strong safety has to do with run support and zone coverage. If the offense comes out in a one back, double slot wide, the free safety is in a bind against four vertical routes. The strong safety aligns inside the slot and carries him to a depth of fifteen yards. That puts the slot receiver back into the coverage zone of the free safety. Under 15 yards, the free safety cannot cover the seam three yards outside the hash mark.

On cover three against a double width pro set, the free safety is in the middle of the field. The strong safety is three by five yards outside the tight end (see Diagram #4) On a drop back pass, he goes to a vision point 10 yards deep by 1 yard inside the alignment of the wide receiver. He is reading the number two receiver and reacting to the number one receiver.

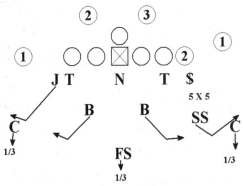

Diagram #4. Cover 3

The tight end is the number two receiver. If he goes to the flat he is in a no-cover zone. Then o-cover zone runs one to five yards deep. We do not have coverage in that area. The strong safety is not covering the tight end until he gets out of the no-cover zone. We tell the strong safety that if he can make the tackle for a two-yard gain when the tight end turns up, that is proper leverage on the tight end.

The inside linebacker is working number three-to-two in his coverage. He has the number three receiver, which is the back in the backfield. If number three does not release or stays in the no-cover zone, the linebacker is working under the new number two receiver. If the number three receiver comes up the field, the linebacker rides him out of the seam and works out under the curl and reacts back to the flat.

The coverage to the weakside is the same as the strongside. The Jam linebacker works to the 10-yard vision point. He works two to one in his coverage. If the number two receiver from the backfield releases flat, the Jam linebacker works two to one. The inside linebacker works two to one, moving out under the curl of one.

The corners are going to their divider and getting depth in their thirds. In a double slot formation where there is a possibility of four vertical routes, we want the underneath players to collision receivers out of the seam areas. That is particularly essential for the strong safety and inside linebackers to get their 45- degree angle drops inside on the number two receiver.

If the quarterback sprints out with the ball, the strong safety forgets about the reroute and gets into the vision point drop right away. If the receiver tries to break inside across the field, the defender maintains a two-yard cushion on the inside and makes the receiver pull up to get across the face of the linebacker. We want the receiver to cross over through the middle third. We do not want him in the middle short.

On the backside of a twins set, the corner aligns in a three-yard outside and five-yard deep alignment. If the tight end releases, the corner shuffles back to his third. We do not want him to bail out and run deep. If the tight end blocks, he turns his attention to cross-the-field patterns.

In the man-free we match up simple on the receivers (see Diagram #5). In the double width pro set, the corners have the outside receivers. The strong safety matches up with the tight end. To the backside, the linebackers have the number two receiver that way. If the offense gives us a twins set, we do not bring our second corner over. We play the strong safety on the number two receiver in the slot. If we bring the second corner over, that is a dead giveaway of the coverage.

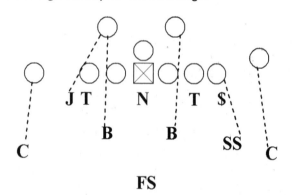

Diagram #5. Man-free

Our corners use the same divider in their alignments to determine their technique. We want the strong safety to take an outside technique as much as possible on the number two receiver. We do that for two reasons. If the play is a run, the strong safety has better leverage on the running play. The number one pattern the strong safety has to defend is the corner pattern. He can do it better from the out-side leverage. If the strong safety plays inside, he ends up trailing the receiver all the way to the sideline, and a good quarterback will wear him out. The strong safety takes away the outside and forces the receiver back into the free safety.

The cover 7 is a two-deep coverage coming from the cover-3 alignment (see Diagram #6). This coverage takes away the frontside hot patterns. In this coverage, the weakside corner goes to the weakside half, and the free safety goes to the strongside half. The Jam linebacker moves under the number one receiver weak. The inside linebacker takes the number two receiver weak. The strong corner plays under the number one receiver to the strongside. The strong safety plays under number two strong and the inside linebacker is responsible for number three strong.

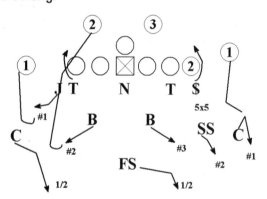

Diagram #6. Cover 7

This coverage is played as a change-up coverage. It is not meant to be a primary coverage. If we get a double wide slot or twins set, the defender covering the number two receivers have to make sure they reroute their receivers out of the middle (see Diagram #7). In the twins set, the strong safety does not have to expand under the number one receiver. He gets more aggressive with the number two receiver to make sure he does not get inside. From this coverage, we could bring the inside linebacker under the number two receiver and blitz the strong safety.

We align the strong safety inside the number two receiver because he is not the primary run support in this coverage. The corner is rolled up and becomes the run support with the strong safety filling inside of him.

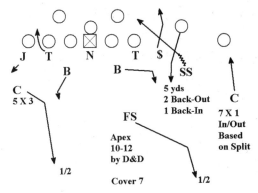

Diagram #7. Cover 7: twins

Those are the three coverages we play from the single safety alignment. From the double safety alignment, we play five calls (Diagram #8). Because we run a 50-defense we want to be balanced in everything we do. We still align our corners at seven by one on the wide receivers. The safeties are still 10 to 12 yards deep. We tell the free safety that if the ball is in the middle of the field, he aligns on the tight end box. If the ball is on the hash mark, he is aligned on the backside guard.

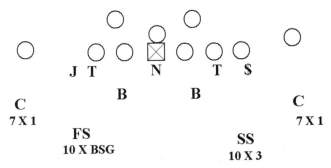

Diagram #8. Double safety alignment

The reason we align our corners at seven yards is to confuse the quarterback. Seven yards is a gray area for the quarterback in his read. He is not sure what the corner is doing. It does not help the quarterback in his presnap read on the secondary. As the corner starts to shuffle, the quarterback is not sure whether we are going to the third, rolling to the flat, or setting up to jam on the receiver. Because we are shuffling out of the stance, we can still drive on the slants and quick patterns.

On the tight end side of the twins set, we are playing three by three with the corner, and everyone else is the same in their alignment (see Diagram #9). The nickel backer is underneath the number

two receiver in the twin set. If the ball is on the hash mark, the free safety is aligned on the backside guard. The strong safety is aligned on the hash mark based on the split.

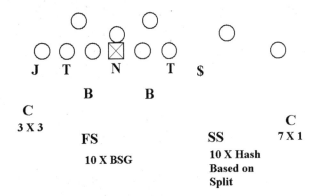

Diagram #9. Double safety: twins

If the corners play the squat coverage in the defense, they squat at five yards from the receiver, not the line of scrimmage. With the ball in the middle of the field, the safeties are dropping about two yards outside the hash marks. If the splits of the wide receivers are wider, we may go to four yards outside the hash. The corners want to reroute the receivers until they reach the depth of 14 yards. When they reach that depth, they sink to the corner. We want to protect the hole against the sideline in a two-deep scheme.

In the twins set, the nickel backer is aligned on the number two receiver. He has to wall him out of the middle. The corner in squat coverage reroutes the wide receiver and sinks into the corner with the strong safety playing over the top. The corner in the squat position is cocked inside so he can see what is happening with the quarterback and both receivers. The free safety is aligned on the backside guard and backs out into his coverage. The corner shuffles back, keying the tight end. He is watching for crossing patterns from the frontside.

Cover 4 is our quarter coverage from the double safety look (see Diagram #10). The alignment is the same as the cover 2 alignment. This coverage allows are safeties to get into the running game fits. The strong safety reads the tight end, and the free safety reads number one initially to the number two receiver in the backfield. The strong corner reads from the number one receiver to the number two receiver. The strong safety reads the number two receiver. If the tight end blocks and the wide receiver runs the post route, the corner has to take him. He cannot depend on help from the strong safety. The corner's primary thought is to protect the post.

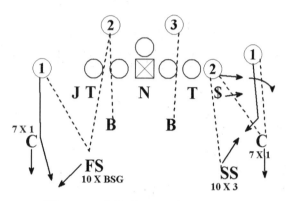

Diagram #10. Cover 4 quarters.

If the number two receiver runs vertical, the strong safety takes him and the corner stays with number one, playing outside in. If we get four vertical routes, the secondary is four deep. If the tight end runs to the flat, the strong safety looks for the number one receiver coming inside. He is playing the post and driving on the curl from the top down. The corner sees the outside move by the tight end and reads outside. He has to carry his depth to prevent the wide receiver from running the shallow corner, but is aware of the wheel route by the tight end and guards against it. The nickel linebacker is taking the tight end into the flat, but the corner can help him on the wheel route.

To the backside we play an inside-outside zone with the free safety and corner if there is no quick number two receiver (see Diagram #11). If the number two receiver is in the backfield, the safety is taking the inside moves of the split end, and the corner plays his outside moves. If number two comes out of the backfield to the flat, we are getting help from the linebacker, and the zone is played like the strongside coverage. The free safety is playing the post of the number one receiver and driving on the curl. The corner is helping the linebacker with the wheel route by the back. If the back runs a vertical

route, the free safety takes him. The drag routes coming from either side are played by the underneath coverage.

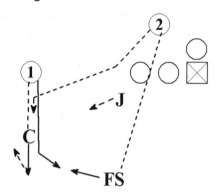

Diagram #11. Weakside cover 4

The pattern that hurts us in this coverage is the double deep route. That is the deep corner by the tight end and the shallow corner by the wide receiver. The nickel has to get under the patterns and make the quarterback throw over him. That gives the deep backs a chance to break on the ball. To the twins set, we can play quarter cover or check to the cover 2 call because the backside does not present a problem.

We play the sky coverage from the same shell. We roll to the cover 3 by bringing the strong safety down into the coverage (see Diagram #12). Everything is played from cover 3 rules, which I have gone over.

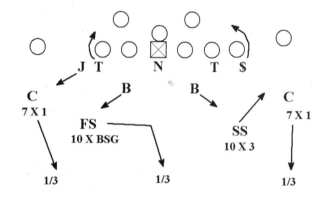

Diagram #12. Sky coverage

The invert coverage is weakside rotation from the two-deep shell (see Diagram #13). It is cover 3 with the strong safety taking the middle third coverage. We can check to this with motion from the offense. In this coverage, we can bring the Jam line-

48

backer since the free safety comes down into flat coverage. The nickel linebacker is playing the strong-side flat area. This coverage is exactly opposite the sky coverage as far as the safeties are concerned; it is played the same for everyone else in the defense.

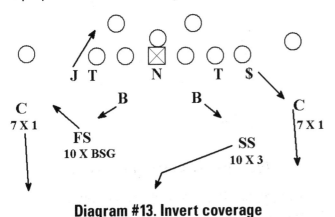

Diagram #13. Invert coverage

The sky and invert coverage does not change with the twins set; we run the same adjustment to the backside in both coverages. This allows us to come off the backside with pressure without going to two-deep coverage. If we want to involve the free or strong safeties in the blitz game, these are the scheme we can use.

The last coverage is the cloud coverage. This is rolling strong or weak with the corner (see Diagram #14). This allows the corner to do the same things the safeties do in the sky coverage calls. We can roll to the field or boundary depending on what we try

to stop. If we are rolling the field corner down, the strong safety takes his outside third. If we roll to the boundary, the strong safety goes into the middle third, and the free safety takes the outside third. It is cover 3 coverage after the movement for everyone in the defense. This movement allows us to include the corner in the blitzing game also.

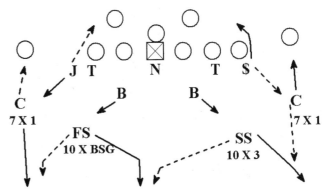

Diagram #14. Cloud coverage

In cloud coverage, we give up the reroute on the number two receiver. What we try to do is force the wide receiver wider toward the sideline. In a cocked position, the receiver has a difficult time deciding if the corner is inside or outside in his alignment. That makes it easier for us to sneak up and force him to the sideline.

I appreciate the opportunity to be here and thank you very much.

Darryl Drake

RECEIVER TECHNIQUES AND DRILLS

University of Texas

We have been extremely fortunate at Texas to have some excellent receivers. There is more to playing receiver at any level than catching the ball. That is the least of our worries at Texas. The receivers that we sign can all catch the ball. However, if you do not block, you will never leave the bench. When receivers come to college they think the only thing they have to do is catch passes. You have to set up the expectation and make them live up to those expectations.

There are only two fundamentals to catching the football. The first is to watch the ball coming into the hands. The second is to put the ball away in a secure fashion. You must coach your receivers to do this every time they make a catch. Even when the receiver is playing a simple game of pitch and catch, he must catch the ball and put it away.

Securing the ball has to become a habit and second nature to the receiver. Make sure the receivers can make different types of catches by using drills. When you do drills, make sure you are emphasizing watching the ball into the hands and tucking it away in the arms.

Teach the receiver to catch the ball naturally. In most cases, catching the ball in a natural fashion will be the proper way to catch the ball. Any style of catching is proper as long as the ball is caught. Do not beat up a receiver because he catches the ball against his body.

A receiver should catch between 50 and 70 balls during practice. During team drills, the receiver may catch one to five balls if he is the primary receiver. If he is not the primary receiver, he may catch none. During individual drills before and after practice is the time the receivers do most of their catching.

To have the receivers catch 50 to 70 passes a day, the coach must use two methods. The first method is to have the receivers catch what they can while they are working on their routes with the quarterback in passing drills. Records have been kept for a number of years on the number of passes a receiver had thrown to him in drills. During a standard drill with the quarterbacks and all the receivers, the individual receiver may catch five to ten balls.

You can do the same thing with your receivers. Have your manager track the receiver throughout practice and record the number of chances he has to catch the football.

The second method for catching multiple balls is in individual drills, in prepractice drills, and postpractice drills. The receiver coach cannot let his receivers leave the field without catching at least 50 balls.

The receiver must master a variety of catches. He has four main responsibilities in the passing game. The first thing the receiver must do in the passing game is to get open when he runs his route. The second thing he has to do is to catch the football. The third thing is to run with the ball after he catches it. The fourth point is maintaining possession of the ball when he is tackled. Catching the football and avoiding a fumble is the number-one responsibility of the receiver regardless of his talent.

From my own experience of trial and error, success and failure, and observing other receivers, it has become apparent to me there are about 20 different types of catches a receiver must master to realize his full potential.

To teach these catches, you put your receivers in bad ball drills to make them catch balls in an unorthodox position. They must catch balls in situations in which they are not normally involved. The receiver must be conditioned to make those catches because it is impossible to know when those types of bad balls will come up in a game. If a receiver works hard enough on catching that type of pass in practice, his chances of catching that type of pass in a game are greatly improved.

I believe fundamentals in the game of football are so important. It is a real timesaver when a receiver comes to us from a high school with sound fundamentals. The first fundamental to catching a football is to keep the eyes on the ball all the way into the hands. The last 15 inches of the flight of the ball are the most important in catching the ball. If the receiver does not see the ball go into his hands, he has little chance to catch it.

When we are on offense and the ball is thrown, it is not a free ball. The ball belongs to the receiver, and he must go get it. He can never allow the ball to be intercepted. If we have a player that has the ability to play at the next level, we tell him that every ball that is thrown to him has a million dollars on it. You have to convince them to be brave and go get the ball.

We want our receivers to catch the ball in their hands and not against their chests if possible. It is not always possible to catch the ball with their hands. In practice we ask them to catch the ball, tuck it away, secure the ball, and sprint at least 15 yards up the field. Do not let your receiver catch the ball and simply run back and give the ball to the manager.

We place cones 30 yards up the field and make the receivers run past the cones when he catches a ball. If he catches a five-yard ball, he runs the additional 25 yards up the field. If you do not make them do it, they will catch the ball, take three or four steps, and head back to the huddle. Make sure you coach extra effort with your receivers.

When the receiver runs his pattern, he runs it at full controlled speed. That means the receiver is running full speed, but he has control of his body and understands where he is on the field.

Pass receivers are made, not born. Receivers have to work on their moves and routes in practice until they become second nature to the receiver. Every opportunity the receiver has in practice, he needs to catch the ball. One of the simplest drills the receiver can do is playing pitch and catch with one of his friends. The football has to become the receiver's friend. The football can never be a stranger to the receiver. At night he can lie in his bed and toss the ball up in the air and catch it. The football must become part of a receiver's life.

The receiver must be alert to the ball, although he is not the primary receiver. You never know when the quarterback is going to throw you the ball. If the receiver thinks the ball is going to someone else, he still has to run his route and get open. He has to present himself as an open pass receiver to give the quarterback another option. If the receiver eases off the ball because he is not the primary receiver, he can't catch up if the quarterback looks his way.

The receiver needs to talk to the quarterback when he gets a chance, but never in the huddle. Too many times, coaches will not listen to players. The players are the ones who are playing, and the coaches should listen to them. The player may not be right, but the coach and quarterback should listen to what he has to say. The more the quarterbacks and coaches listen to the receivers, the more confidence the receivers have in the quarterback. When there is communication between the quarterbacks and receivers, a bond is formed of trust, confidence, and faith between them.

I always ask my receivers when they come off the field, what they think will work on the defender. They tell me the patterns they think they can run against the defense, and most of the time they are right. The more experience they have, the better they can read defenses and can tell what the corner is trying to do in their coverage.

The receivers need to learn the tendencies of the defensive backs. We need to know when the defensive back aligns inside or outside what he is likely to do. Each receiver should know certain things about a defensive back: his speed, how he reacts to fakes, and what his tendencies are in down-and-distance situations are some of those things. This type of information comes from film study and experience.

There are basic principles that a receiver has to know to play the game and be effective. He has to understand field position. If he is into the short side of the field, he may have to adjust his alignment to run the pattern that has been called. He has to be aware of the sideline and know how to work it to make the catch.

The receiver always needs to know the down-and-distance. That is especially true in a third-down situation where the depth of his pattern may mean picking up a first down or not picking it up. It happens time and again in games when the situation calls for a seven-yard pattern, and the receiver runs the pattern at five or six yards and doesn't pick up the first down. It is the receiver's responsibility to take the pattern the proper distance to meet the situation.

The receiver has to understand the time factor and the number of time outs remaining in a half or in the game. He has to know when to get out of bounds to stop the clock and when to stay in the field of play to try to pick up extra yards.

Natural conditions exist in every stadium. The receiver has to know the wind direction and what the wind is likely do to the ball. If it is a day game, he has to know when or if the sun will affect his vision. If the game is played at night he must know if the lights in the stadium are going to affect his ability to see the ball. He has to understand those conditions and adjust.

The receiver must understand the conditions of the playing field. He has to know if there is a crown on the field. He wants to know the condition of the turf. He has to know if the field is a slick field and if there are low or high spots on the field. All those things will affect his ability to make cuts and keep his footing.

The sidelines and end lines are enemies of the receiver. The sideline and end line represent the twelfth man for the defense. The receiver has to know his relative position to them and cannot let them bother him in catching the football. The receiver has to catch the ball first and get his feet down in bounds when he is working the sidelines. If he does not catch the ball, it makes no difference whether he was in or out of bounds.

There are some coaching points that should be emphasized in pass catching. The receiver has to look the ball all the way into his hands. He has to work on catching the bad passes so the spectacular catch looks routine to the average fan. He has to learn to run his routes at the proper depth to satisfy the timing of the pass and the down-and- distance situation.

He must learn to relax his fingers and hands in receiving the football. As he is receiving the ball, he has to cushion the ball with his hands and ride the ball to make the catch softer.

The receiver needs to run to the ball before extending his arms to catch it. If he runs with his arms extended, it slows him down. He wants to extend his arms on the last step before receiving the ball. If the receiver extends his arms coming out of the break, it is a signal for the defensive back to break on the ball. Good receivers use that technique to draw defensive backs up so they can go by them.

If the ball is not thrown to him, he becomes a blocker. He wants to help his teammates, and his team maximizes every caught football. The receiver needs to adopt an attitude that he can catch anything he touches.

Every defensive back is taught to catch the ball at its highest point. That coaching point is no different for a receiver. A receiver never wants to wait for the ball to come down. He must go and gets the ball at its highest point and takes it away from the defensive back if necessary.

The receiver must never be offsides in his alignment. He must use the official to align himself. The official will not tell him if he is onsides, but he will designate the line for the receiver. The receiver should never jump the snap count. He must key the football. In some cases, the crowd is making so much noise he cannot hear the snap count. He should never be offsides because his rule is to watch the football.

He has to know his quarterback and the types of passes he throws. He has to anticipate where the ball is going to be delivered and how fast it will get there. All quarterbacks are different when it comes to their delivery and timing. Balls thrown by left-handed quarterbacks have a different spin than balls coming from a right-handed quarterback.

The receiver needs to know the pass action so he can complete the pattern. He has to know the coverage and the adjustments that go with the coverage. We do not want the receiver to break his routes. When he does, the quarterback ends up throwing the ball to the defender in most cases. Even if the quarterback throws into coverage if the receiver is there he can keep the defensive back from catching it.

If the ball is thrown to another receiver, he must break toward that receiver. If the ball is tipped, the receiver has a chance to catch the tipped ball. If the teammate catches the ball, the second receiver can throw a block for him.

The next thing I want to go into is the techniques of route running. On each play, the receiver has to determine how wide his split should be and where he should align in the relationship to the formation. They must have what we call split judgment. When I first started coaching in college football, the route that was being run determined the split of the wide receiver. If we were going to run and out route, the receiver tighten up his split. The opposite was true if he were going to run an inside route. That principle is not true anymore because the defensive backs are starting to read the receiver's alignment.

We want to run every route we have from a normal split. The receiver tries to predetermine the coverage by the alignment of the defensive backs.

We listen to the calls of the defensive backs to pick up hints as to what they are going to do. We watch the eyes of the defensive back so we can see where he is looking. The defensive secondary are doing everything they can to disguise the coverage.

They may align on the outside during the presnap read and move to the inside as the ball is being snapped. We have to understand how the defensive back is being coached. In the past, if the defensive back was looking at the receiver, we could assume it was man coverage. Today, the defensive backs are looking at the quarterback in man coverage so they can read the three-step drop.

As the receiver starts to run his route, we do not want him to look to where he is going. I do not want him looking at the ground. Through repetition, the receiver should get the feel for depths of patterns.

I do not like to try to count steps in a pattern. It is hard for the receiver to count his steps when a defensive back is locked up on him beating the hell out of him.

If the defense is playing loose and off, the receivers there is nothing wrong with step counting to get depth on the pattern. However, when the defensive back is jamming and pushing the receiver, when does the count start in the route? You have to teach what you know as a coach. I have a hard time teaching steps with press coverage.

The defensive secondary either verbally communicates, or they use hand signals. The receiver, if he listens, will know the coverage being run. You can pick the hand signals up with film study. It is not that hard to watch and tell what the secondary is doing.

The normal release of the receiver is outside coming off straight. The time between the snap of the ball and the breaking point of the pattern is critical. The game of football has gotten so much faster. Defenders coming off the edge in today's game are running like wide receivers. The people playing the game of football have gotten so much bigger and faster that it is scary. The receiver has to get open in a hurry or the quarterback is killed.

Receivers have to approach the defenders and get in an advantageous position before they make their break. We used to tell the receiver to work to the defender's outside shoulder on outside cuts, and to the inside shoulder on inside cuts. That teaching is no longer accepted in today's game. The key to getting open is the release. The receiver has to get off the ball and do whatever is necessary to get open.

A great receiver is also a great actor. He has to make the defender think he is running one route when he is actually running another one. He has to have a feel and expression in his route running. You can't program the receiver and make him robotic. When the receiver is facing man-to-man coverage, he will have to use a move to turn the defender.

When the receiver is facing zone coverage, moves are not as important. The receiver is looking for seams and windows in the zones. When the receiver makes his final break, the first thing to turn is his eyes. He leads with his eyes and finds the ball. He has to see the ball in order to catch it. He has to get into a habit of coming back to meet the football. Coming back to the ball cuts the interception angle of the defensive back on the football. Coming back to the ball is especially true on all sideline patterns.

Once the receiver catches the ball he turns and gets upfield. We do not want them to run east and west after catching the football. A quick turn north and south will split defenders quicker than running across the field.

There are three different phases in execution of routes. The first phase is the release of the route. Everything in running a route starts with the release of the receiver. The release is getting off the line of scrimmage, in the right direction, with a minimum of delay.

The second phase is the approach of the receiver. The approach is the portion of the route between the release and the break. There are several different components of the approach. The first component in the approach is faking the defender. A fake is designed to create a difference of opinion between the receiver and the defender.

The second component is not to get in a hurry before making the final break. The receiver has to make sure he runs the prescribed distance of the route. If he doesn't, he destroys the timing of the pass and is covered when the ball is thrown. In a passing offense, timing and depth of the route are critical.

The receiver tries to get as close to the defender as possible. He should strive to step on the defender before he makes his break. The receiver looks directly at the defender as he runs his route. We don't want them looking at a spot on the ground unless it is part of the fake to move the defender.

When we teach a receiver to release, we have to give him some choices on the way he releases. If he takes an outside release every time he runs a flat route, the defender can figure out how to play him. If the receiver varies up his releases and goes outside one time and inside the next time, the defender will be guessing on the receiver's release.

The worst thing a receiver can face is a patient corner. If the corner is patient and does not get anxious, the receiver is going to have a tough time. Most corners want to get their hands on the receiver and manhandle him. The patient corner does not react to the fakes and moves the receiver is trying to put on him. If the battle comes down to a physical battle, the defender wins the battle because he spends a lot of time in the weight room.

Normally, for some reason, receivers that are trying to get deep get tense. They are more relaxed when they run a short route. The receiver should study his downfield blocking pattern and incorporate it into his pass routes. The receiver can make the defender's keys work against him.

If a receiver does not have confidence in a pass-catching move, it should not be used in a game. The thing he wants to guard against is overdoing fakes in his attempt to get open. The game situation will require less faking than practice does because the defensive back is afraid of getting beat deep in front of a crowd. In practice, the defender will not back up because he has no fear of the ball being thrown for a touchdown over his head.

The break is the point at which the receiver has completed all of his approach moves and is ready to receive the ball. The receiver should make the break as near to full speed as possible. The less the receiver has to gather himself, the more effective the break will be. The game has changed so much because of speed. If a receiver gathers and sinks before his break, the defensive back will be all over the throw. The reaction time for defensive backs at the college level has gotten so much better it is unbelievable. The receiver must make his break and get out of it as fast as possible. The less the receiver has to gather himself, the more effective the break will be.

If the receiver does not run full speed throughout the route, the ball will be overthrown. I have seen it too many times when the receiver tries to speed up in his route to catch the ball. If the pass is timed at full speed, that is the way it must be run in the game. The receiver can always slow down to catch the ball, but he cannot speed up to reach the ball that is just off his fingertips.

When the deep pass is thrown, any receiver can get open if he uses the proper technique. Getting open deep is not relative to speed. If the defensive back will let the receiver eat up his cushion, the receiver can get by him. The quarterback cannot wait to throw the ball because eventually the speed of the corner will catch up to a slower receiver.

There are two keys to getting deep on a pass. The receiver has to step on the defender's toes, and he has to have grass. Having grass means the receiver can never get closer than four yards from the boundary line.

If the quarterback throws the ball out of bounds, it is generally because the receiver got into the four-yard area of the sideline. The receiver must give the quarterback grass in which to throw the ball. If the defensive back stays in his backpedal too long, it allows the receiver to step on his toes, and he is beat.

The defensive back is coached to stay in his backpedal until the receiver gets within three yards of him. They all want to settle in the 10 to 12 yard area because that is the break point of most moves. Because of that sort of thinking, they allow the receiver to get closer than the three-yard cushion before they open to run with the receive. When the defensive back allows that situation, the receiver can go by him the defender and beat him deep.

If the receiver makes his break three yards from the defender, the defensive back will run with the receiver all over the field. The quarterback has to throw the ball over the outside shoulder of the defensive back into the grass area. If he throws the ball inside, it is an interception.

The next thing I'll discuss is pass-receiving drills. Drills are more effective if they are gamelike in relationship to speed and timing. We break our drills down into categories. We have different types of drills. The drill categories are warm-up drills, net drills, sideline drills, concentration drills, running drills, and conditioning drills.

The first drill is called pat-and-go (see Diagram #1). Divide the receivers into two groups with a coach on both sides of the field to throw the balls. The receivers start in their three-point stance and run across the field at half speed. The coach waits until the receiver runs ten yards before throwing the ball. The ball should be thrown with a good, high arch. The receiver catches the ball around mid-way, crosses the field, and strides across to the other sideline. After each player has gone one time in both lines, the drill is repeated using one-handed catches and over-the-head catches.

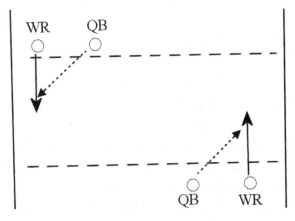

Diagram #1. Pat-and-go

The emphasis is placed on good running form, and not speed. These drills are run at half speed to let the receiver warm up his body.

The next drill teaches the receiver to develop both concentration and the technique of securing the ball quickly as he is being hit. This drill is the one-man concentration drill (see Diagram #2). One player with an air bag stands ten yards away, facing the receiver. The receiver comes off the line full speed, and the ball is thrown at the last moment. The receiver makes the reception and secures the ball before the collision. Just after the receiver makes the catch, the player holding the bag unloads on him.

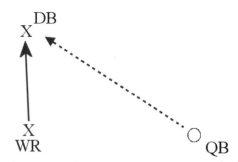

Diagram #2. One-man concentration drill

When the quarterback has to scramble, it is important for the receiver to come back to the quarterback. To enforce this, we use a drill simply called the running drill (see Diagram #3). The players line up about ten yards from a coach and run any pattern. The coach calls "Back," and the player runs the break off the pattern, he comes back to the coach, and catches the ball.

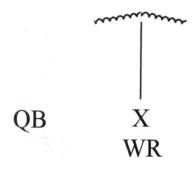

Diagram #3. Running drill

We use the play catch drill to improve the receiver's concentration when catching the ball (see Diagram #4). The receivers line up in parallel lines facing each other, about two yards apart. A receiver stands at each end of the gauntlet. The two receivers play catch while the others try to distract them by waving their arms at the ball. Each player catches four balls.

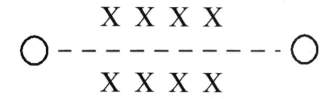

Diagram #4. Play catch drill

We run the wrong shoulder drill (see Diagram #5). This is like the pat-and-go drill except the ball is thrown over the outside shoulder. The receiver must take his eyes off the ball momentarily, get turned quickly, and catch the pass.

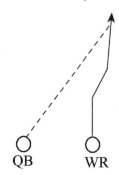

Diagram #5. Wrong shoulder drill

The next series of drills are what we refer to as net drills. The first one is called goalpost (see Diagram #6). The purpose of this drill is to make the receiver catch the ball with his hands. Have the receiver stand behind the goalpost with his chest against the post. The quarterback is 10 to 15 yards away and throws the pass chest high. The receiver catches the ball in his hands, or it bounces off the post.

Diagram #6. Goalpost drill

The next drill is done in front of a net strung under the goalpost. The net catches balls that are not caught by the players. The receivers line up about five yards from the net. The receivers run in front of the net at half speed, catching balls that are thrown low, high, or behind them (see Diagram #7). On low balls, the receiver concentrates on getting his hands under the ball and flexing his body to get low with the ball rather than trying to spear it. The thumbs are turned outward. On the high balls, the receiver concentrates on getting the arms into position to catch the ball in his hands. The thumbs should be turned inward behind the ball. The waist should be turned to get the upper body and hands in position to catch the ball that is thrown behind the receiver. It may require the receiver to make a complete pivot if the ball is way behind him.

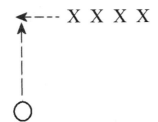

Diagram #7. Low/high/behind/drill

The quick ball drill emphasizes quickness, good body control, and body lean (see Diagram #8). One player lines up even with the goalpost in his stance. The coach stands ten yards away with four balls. The coach calls "Go," and the receiver starts running at three-quarters speed. When he reaches the midpoint, the coach throws the ball. The player catches the ball, runs to the other goalpost, tosses the ball out, and returns to the midpoint to catch another ball. He continues until he catches four balls.

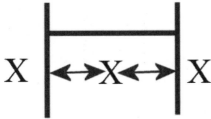

Diagram #8. Quick ball drill

The blind ball drill is designed to help the player develop his quickness in turning his body around for the ball (see Diagram #9). The receiver lines up ten yards from the coach with his back to the coach. The coach throws the ball toward the receiver. When the ball is halfway to the player, the coach calls, "Left" or "Right." The player turns as quickly as possible and tries to catch the ball in his hands. You can use a variation where the player turns his head and shoulders around as quickly as he can.

Diagram #9. Blind ball drill

The blur ball drill (see Diagram #10) is another concentration drill done in front of the net. One or two players are aligned eight yards in front of the net. The receiver runs at three-quarter speed behind them. The ball is thrown between the two distracters, and the receiver catches the ball in his hands. The two players wave their hands in front but do not touch the ball.

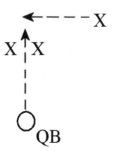

Diagram #10. Blur ball drill

You can do any number of drills in front of the net. We use a drill called crossing distraction. Two receivers face each other and run toward each other. The receiver going in front tries to distract the receiver going behind as he catches the ball. We also use a dummy interference drill. It is the same drill, except as the receiver is catching the ball, the coach hits him with a dummy.

The tap dance drill (see Diagram #11) is designed to help the receiver get his feet down in bounds. The receivers line up about 15 yards from the sideline. On the command "Go," the receiver starts to run at three-quarter speed toward the sideline. The coach throws the ball about five yards from the sideline. The receiver catches the ball, then plants one or two feet in bounds before going out of bounds. The coaching point is to catch the ball first and then position the feet. Make sure you do the drill going in both directions.

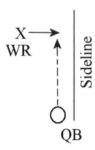

Diagram #11. Tap dance drill

The turn-and-up drill (see Diagram #12) is used to help improve the player's ability to catch the ball near a sideline and turn up the field instead of going out of bounds. This is almost the same drill as the tap dance drill. The exception is the ball is thrown eight yards from the sidelines. The emphasis is on catching the ball, then using good body control to stay in bounds and turn up the field.

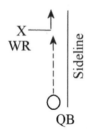

Diagram #12. Turn-and-up drill

It is important for the receiver to get north and south after he catches the ball. The feel the defender drill (see Diagram #13) teaches that skill. Align all the receivers to one side of the net. Have a coach or manager stand in front of the net 3 to 4 yards away. The receiver takes 3 to 4 steps toward the net, plants, and comes back toward the quarterback. The quarterback is 15 yards away from the receiver. The receiver catches the ball and the manager runs up behind the receiver on one side or the other. The

receiver feels the defensive back breaks the opposite direction and gets north and south up the field.

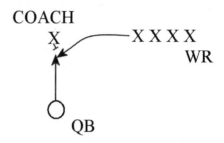

Diagram #13. Feel the defender drill

Another drill we do is called the high curl with a push drill. The receiver runs a curl in front of the coach or manager. The quarterback delivers a high throw to the receiver, which causes him to jump to catch the ball. When he jumps to catch the ball, the coach pushes him in the back.

In the strip drill we align our players with a receiver followed by a defensive back in a single line. The receiver runs back toward the quarterback with the defensive back trailing him. When the receiver catches the ball, the defensive back that is trailing the receiver tries to strip the ball loose.

The flat-and-up drill (see Diagram #14) helps the receiver work on catching the deep ball and keeping his four-distance from the sideline. It helps the receiver concentrate, lets him work on his jumping ability, and develops long ball skills. The drill starts with the defensive back and the receiver facing up field. On the command, the defensive back and receiver runs full speed up the field. The ball is thrown long and high with a high arch. The receiver tries to catch the ball, and the defensive back tries to intercept the ball.

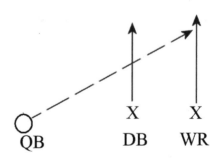

Diagram #14. Flat-and-up drill

The purpose of the curl drill is to acquaint the receiver with reading different linebacker drops (see Diagram #15). It also teaches the proper way to run the curl route. We start the drill with a large stand-up dummy in the place of a linebacker. The receiver runs his curl route around the dummy and comes back to the quarterback. After we learn the proper technique for running the curl, we replace the dummy with a linebacker and let him drop into several drop areas. The receiver runs his curl route off the linebacker's drop.

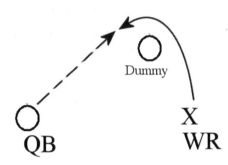

Diagram #15. Curl drill

We use what we call the watch ball L-R-over drill. This drill gets players in the habit of catching the ball over either shoulder, or also catching the long, arching ball that comes directly over the head. To run the drill, stand the receiver 40 yards or more downfield and have the quarterback arch the ball deep ball to the three positions.

We have several conditioning drills we use with our receiver and the ball. The first on is called the front and back drill. One player starts on the five-yard line, and the other starts on the goal line. They are facing one another. At the same time, the receiver on the five-yard line starts to run backward while the receiver on the goal line runs forward. As they continue down the field, they toss a ball back and forth between them. They reach the other goal line, take a short rest, switch positions, and come back.

We do the same thing in the side-to-side drill. Both players start on the goal line facing each other. They are about five yards apart. On the command of the coach, the receivers start running sideways down the field, tossing the ball back and forth. When they get to the other end of the field, they take a short break and come back up the field.

The quick ball drill is also a conditioning drill. The emphasis is placed on catching the ball and locking it in with the eyes. This drill starts with one to three receivers and quarterbacks. The receiver lines up on the goal line with the quarterback ten yards from him. The coach calls "Set," and the receiver runs out a pattern six to ten yards deep. He catches the ball and runs out of bounds or takes four steps up the field. The receiver moves to the next line, and the pattern is repeated. If the receiver drops the ball or the ball is a bad throw, everyone has to go back one line. A minimum of seven passes and a maximum of 12 passes are used to cover the field.

The take off and post drill is done for conditioning to develop the ability to catch the ball deep. Simply split the receivers out and let them run a takeoff or post at full speed. The coach should emphasize proper running form and not reaching out with the hands too early to catch the ball.

Obviously, we do not do all these drills every day. I have a drill chart to keep track of the drills we have done and the drills we need to work on. We pick and chose the drills we need for each practice based on what we need. I do not think you can ever do enough fundamental drills.

I really enjoyed being here. Thank you very much, and good luck to all of you.

BUILDING A WINNING PROGRAM

University of Iowa

I appreciate your being here. I want to share a few thoughts with you tonight. I just had a short talk with Gary Pinkel in the back of the room. We are all aware of the great job he has done at the University of Missouri. Gary told me he is looking forward to some enlightening things from my lecture. I am not sure I have any new ideas to share with you. As we go through coaching, we do develop some ideas and thoughts. I want to share those things with you.

One of the great stops in my career was back in 1980 at the University of Pittsburgh. I got an opportunity to go back to my hometown and work for my high school coach. His name is Joe Moore. He was the finest football coach I have ever been around. He certainly had a great impact on me and my life.

Last year was a rewarding and enjoyable year for our football team. We have climbed the mountain, so to speak, at Iowa. I went back to Iowa five years ago, and we hit our stride last season. We did improve a great deal in those five years. In our first season we were 0-8 in the Big Ten. In the 2002 season, we were 8-0 in the Big Ten and we finished up 11-2. We played in the Orange Bowl but did not do very well. That was disappointing, to say the least.

This past season, most people picked us to finish in the lower part of our conference. I think we were picked eighth in the preseason. We won our Bowl Game and ended up ranked eighth in the country. It is just a great feeling to know we did not take a step backward this past season. I am very grateful to be back at the University of Iowa. We have a great group of young people to work with. We have a great coaching staff that is easy to work with. The state supports us, and it is just a great place to be coaching.

I have had the chance to coach at all levels. I have coached at the high school level for a couple of years. I was an assistant at Iowa in the 1980s. I left Iowa to become a head coach at the University of Maine. Later I coached three years with the Cleveland Browns and three years with the Baltimore Ravens in the NFL. When I had a chance to go back to Iowa, it was a no-brainer. My point is this. I have coached at all levels, and I have been able to make a couple of observations.

First of all, I enjoyed coaching at all levels. Second, I have seen some of the best coaching at all three levels, and I have seen some of the worst coaching at all three levels. The last observation is that there is no perfect job out there. In our profession, we can spend a lot of time looking across the fence admiring other coaches and other programs. The important thing is what you do with the job that you have. If you spend your time thinking about doing a better job with what you have, I think you will find it to be very gratifying. Success in life is determined by the people involved and the attitude they choose to take. That is what my experiences taught me. With coaching, it starts with liking people. You must like the people you work with, the coaches you work with, and you better like young people. That is where it all starts.

As a coach you must know that players are not stupid. This is true at all ages, and as a result, you must treat them that way. You can not try to fool them or con them. The thing you must do is to be honest with the players. If you show interest in the people you work with, I believe they will come around.

It is important to shape the attitudes of the players you are involved with. To me, it is important in knowing your audience. Most coaches would agree that times are more challenging today than they have been over past years. We all must realize that young people today have a lot of choices. The commitment to our society and sports today is certainly not what it was back a few years ago. The youth of today are hearing a lot of different voices. I think it is important as a coach to know what those voices are.

I like to talk about the ESPN Generation. It started in the 1980s. I think ESPN has done a lot of good things for sports, but I also think it has done a lot of negative things. The ESPN world is very interesting. I like to pick on Dick Vitale because he was the person that did a great deal to promote college basketball. There is no doubt about that.

Our young athletes are exposed to a great deal today as a result of the media. For years, my dad would send me the sports sections from the Pittsburgh papers. He would send them to me wherever I was coaching. Some of you may have heard of Chuck Klausing. He is a wing-T guru and a successful football coach. He coached at West Virginia, and came back to Carnegie Mellon and did a great job there. He later took a coaching job at a private school. He officially retired from coaching in the 1980s but still is involved in clinics and football camps. He coached over 50 years. One of the sports writers from Pittsburgh interviewed Chuck. He asked him this question: "As a coach, how have the players changed over the years?" His answer was very simple. "The kids have not changed at all; their parents have changed." Those of you working with high school kids know exactly what I am talking about.

Chuck went on to tell the reporter that when he started coaching, parents respected authority. Teachers were respected, and coaches were respected. "Today, the kids are always right, and the coaches are wrong." I felt this was a good observation. I am sure most of you can relate to this.

I have been very fortunate. I have not had many player problems since I have been coaching at any level, young, old players. However, I have had some parent problems. That is the way it goes today.

In pro football you do not have to deal with the parents. But, you do have the agents to deal with. I advise you to take the parents over the agents. That is a better deal, believe me.

People in coaching can make a difference. I do not think there is any doubt about this. I used to think this was true more so at the high school and collegiate levels than the pros. But I think that may be changing a little today. Look at the Super Bowl this year. The impact the two head coaches have had on their players is excellent. With the salary cap in pro football, coaching is becoming more and more important. At the high school and college levels, without a doubt, coaching makes a big difference.

We can look at the University of Iowa to see firsthand exposure to this fact. Going into the 1981 season, Michigan and Ohio State had won or shared the Big Ten Championship for 13 straight years. They dominated the Big Ten for all of those years. In 1981, Iowa ended up getting to go to the Rose Bowl. We played against Washington and got beat. At least we broke the ice at that point and ended Ohio State and Michigan's streak of going to the Rose Bowl. Now, all but two schools in our conference have gone to the Rose Bowl. Things changed from that 1981 season, and other teams felt they had a chance to win the Big Ten. Obliviously, Coach Hayden Fry had a major impact on the program at the University of Iowa. He got the program up and running. He ended 19 straight years of losing at Iowa. One of our radio announcers said, "We only had two bad decades of losing. What the hell is everyone in Iowa worried about?" It is awesome the impact that Hayden Fry had on the program at Iowa.

Most of you know about Coach Paul "Bear" Bryant. He was one of the all-time great coaches. He had winning programs at four different schools.

In any endeavor you undertake, you must have objectives. You must have a plan. Our plan is not really involved. I am a line coach, so I do not know about all of the technical equipment we have. Our game plan is not real tricky. Most of the people come to see us practice and they go away disappointed. They think they are going to see something else. We are not real fancy, and we do not do a lot of trick plays. I believe what we do must be sound and we must think it out before we do it. It must fit what we believe. I do not think it is so much what you choose to do as it is how you implement the plan, how you can sell the plan, and how you sustain the program. That is what really counts. Putting the plan into action and getting them to follow it day by day is important.

One of the most influential coaches I have ever been involved with was Jim Young. Jim was an assistant coach at Michigan, and he was the head coach at Purdue in 1981. He coached for Bo Schembechler at Michigan, where they ran the heck out of the football. When he was at Purdue, they threw the football a lot. Purdue lost a tough game to Ohio State in 1981 and Jim resigned. He had a hard time dealing with that loss. But he did bounce back and ended up as the head coach at Army. I think that is the last time they won consistently in the last 30 years. But when Jim Young went to Army, they started running the wishbone offense. You talk about a contrast in style: that was it. That is a great example of two opposite programs, and he had success in both programs. He was very flexible in his thinking, and he adapted to the athletes he had at each school. Jim was a great football coach.

Another story that jumped out at me is Bill Muir of the Tampa Bay Bucs. I had an opportunity to visit with Bill last year. He had only been in the NFL one year. He told me it was a very interesting thing in watching their defense. I asked him what he meant by that. He said, "They do very, very little." It is obvious that Tampa Bay has good personnel on defense. Bill went on to tell me it was amazing to him to see how simple and how concise the defensive game plan was for them. He said they have players that know how to play the defense, and that the players understand the adjustments and all phases related to the defense. The players and the coaches understood the defense and how it worked. They knew how to coach the players. There are all kinds of ways to skin a cat, but I thought that was an interesting point.

On offense the Tampa Bay plan is much more complicated. They have 8 million plays and every formation ever known to man. Two schools of thought exist in football. This is a good example of the different styles that are successful.

You must have objectives to achieve the plan. I will tell you I would be cautious of how you coach your high school players.

We are all recruiting football players. Even in high school, you still have to recruit the athletes to your program. They have so many choices, they do not have to choose football. If I were a young high school coach, my first objective would be to get the young players to come back to play for the next week. Hopefully, they would have a smile on their faces and would want to come back the next season. That may sound crazy, but that is what I would do.

I hear coaches talk about their ninth grader team. I do not think you get any awards for winning in the ninth grade. If the players do not come back for their sophomore year or their junior year, you cannot win. I am not telling you to run a soft program. I am saying that you must teach the fundamentals and let the players have a good experience. The idea is to get them to return to the program the next year.

I think it is very important to teach the fundamentals of the game. I think you must accept the responsibility for that aspect of the game. A couple of stories jump out at me in this respect. I had a great experience when I coached in Cleveland. In the spring of 1993 or 1994, I can't remember the year, but I got invited to go to a clinic at Robert Morris College. A coach by the name of Joe Walton was the head coach there. The reason that was such a thrill for me was because I got a chance to hear Chuck Noll speak on Saturday morning. I grew up in the Pittsburgh area during the time when the Steelers were a great team. It was an honor for me to meet Chuck Noll and to shake his hand. I walked away from that experience, and I was amazed. Chuck Noll, whom a lot of people will tell you was the greatest coach ever in pro football, talked for 50 minutes about the art of hitting. He talked about the cornerbacks, the guards, the ends, and he was all over the place, but he talked for 50 minutes about the art of hitting in football. It you saw the Steelers in the 1970s you know they knew how to hit on defense. They understood leverage and technique. I listened to Chuck Noll, and with the passion he spoke about the subject, I knew why their teams were so good. This really made a great impression on me.

There is no way I could coach basketball. That is the worst job in the world. How could Shaquille O'Neil get so much attention when he misses so many free throws? He is a world-class athlete but he does not care enough about shooting free throws, or his coaches do not feel it is important enough to work on his technique so he can get better shooting free throws.

In football I am not saying that assignments are not important. In football, you must know what you are doing because that is important. But I will argue with you that anyone can learn assignments, and you can learn the simple schemes of the game. But I will tell you this; fundamentals are a lot more important than assignments.

In the position we are in in coaching college football, we cannot afford to waste time. Busy work and silly drills that coaches do just because they saw someone else do them is a waste of time. To me, we are all fighting the clock. We all know our opponents have the same clock. We have the clock and the same calendar to work with. This is what you must focus on and make the most of your time with your team and your staff.

Whatever you decide to do, you must figure out what is important, and that is what you must focus on. As a position coach, that is your job. You must decide what is paramount to your players. You must let the players know they must have success.

In addition to fighting the clock, we have to deal with the players. How much attention span do they have and how much can they take physically? I was fortunate to work with Ted Marchibroda for three years. We would be sitting in a meeting and he would say, "Let's make sure we are not getting too smart." This is a good point. You may think it is a simple plan, but when you get on the field on Monday, you have players looking at you wondering what is going on. You must keep this point in mind in designing your schemes.

Everyone knows about the Yogi Berra stories. He made the statement "You can observe a lot just by watching." This is simple but it is very true.

I think it is important to spend time with the players in situations where they are not involved in practice. You need to spend time with them when you can talk about things other than when they are in group meetings, or when they have their helmets on and you are discussing techniques related to football instruction. Spend time with them in the locker room, in the weight room, or the lunch room. This is very important.

We all have sources of information available to us. If you will take the time to listen, you can find out a lot about your program. Listen to the important people to your program. I go back to Joe Moore. The custodians at Upper Saint Clair High School loved Joe Moore. He saw everything. There are people in your building that can tell you a lot and there are people that can contribute to your program if you will seek information.

You must be able to evaluate what you are doing. Any time you are involved in a loss or in a disappointment, you need to go back and examine what went wrong. The other side of that story is when you have success. When you win a game, you need to know what was important in contributing to the win. You want to keep the same approach. The same thing is true after a very good season. I go back to Joe Moore. He would never let you feel comfortable. That was his nature. He always let you know there were some things you could have done better. He was always coaching and he was always looking for improvement.

Another factor I feel is important in a coach is that you must have a sense of humor. If you go through some tough times, humor is more important here than in other times. You must find time to laugh, and you must be able to relieve some tension. There will be tension when you are losing football games.

I remember back in the 1980s, we had things going well at Iowa. But in 1987 after seven games into the season, we were 4-3. We were struggling. We had to work hard just to be at 4-3. There was no confidence, and there was no continuity on the team. We knew that something was not right on our team.

We always started our meeting on Monday night at 7:15 P.M. We would start our meetings with the scouting reports and all of those related things. On this one night Coach Hayden Fry was late for the meeting. We had a walk-on receiver on the team that noticed that Coach Fry was late for the meeting.

At that time Coach Fry, was very popular in the state of Iowa. They had big life-sized cutouts of Coach Fry all over the state. The walk-on player got one of those cutouts and cut the face off of Coach Fry and came up to the front of the room. He held up the cutout facemask of Coach Fry and proceeded to go into what Coach Fry would be telling us in the team meeting. You can imagine what the reaction was with the rest of the team when the walk-on started imitating Coach Fry. They were in stitches. He went on for two or three minutes, and everyone was going along with the joke.

Soon Coach Hayden Fry walked into the back of the room and came up behind the walk-on. He did not see Coach Fry, so he just kept on going over the scouting report giving his best impersonation of Coach Fry. Now the players were rolling in the aisles with laughter. Finally, Coach Fry tapped the walk-on on the shoulder to get his attention. The place was just cracking up by this time. It was the first good laugh we had all season. All of this took place in about five minutes. It may be a coincidence but we went on to win six straight games that year. There is no doubt in my mind that what happened in that 1987 season was that five-minute session where the team got to laugh at the antics of the walk-on player imitating Coach Fry. Sometimes laughter can be the best medicine you can have.

If you are going to have a good football team, you must be able to identify and develop leaders. We have all been in meetings when the seniors are great leaders. Then other years when your team is struggling, you look for reasons you are not doing well. Then you realize the leadership is missing. What we do now at Iowa is to elect four captains at the end of spring practice.

I know other teams have selected committee members to represent the team by classes. They meet with the team members of their class and take their ideas to the committee. The committee reports to the coaching staff. This gives the coaches input, and it gives the players a chance to express their views.

Some teams select team captains for each individual game. Then, at the end of the season, they select permanent captains. This gives more players a chance to show their leadership ability.

The key to avoiding stress and to be successful is to be prepared. You must be prepared, and your players must buy into the program. I think this is an educational process. You must spend time in educating your players, and you must spend time with them to show them the value of the program. When players start seeing the rewards, they will begin to realize the extra time looking at film is worthwhile. I do not think that most things happen by accident for the most part in sports. You usually get what you deserve. It is based on your talent level, preparation, and how you compete. I think you get what you deserve and it all starts with preparation.

One of the great things our game teaches is perseverance. Players must understand you must persevere. Examples of that are countless. Football is a competitive game, so you have to be able to deal with unwanted results. My wife usually reminds me that only one-half of the teams win in football. That is the nature of the game.

Everyone knows about Abraham Lincoln. He was a failure as a businessman. He lost five major elections before he won the office of president. His comment after one of those losses was that he considered it to be a slip and not a fall. He had a very positive attitude. Henry Ford was a businessman that went bankrupt twice during his first three years in the automobile business.

I was reading about Dr. Seuss. His first book for kids was rejected by 23 different publishers. These are examples of people that kept the faith and kept on going in spite of early failures.

In our first 20 ballgames at Iowa, we had won two games and lost 18 games. People were friendly in Iowa, but the media was a little different. They started every article with the same lead: "The Hawkeyes, under Coach Kirk Ferentz, have a record of 2 and 18." Those writers love to point those things out. We had to endure that, and we learned to persevere.

The flip side of this is that you must be able to deal with having success. It may be more important than dealing with adversity. It may be tougher than dealing with the hard times. Since we were 2-18, we have turned it around and are 30-11. In the last two years, we have had a 21 and 5 record. The point I am making is that we have been through both processes. We would win a big game and then we would take three steps backwards. This is something you just have to learn.

We started out talking about our plan to guide our football program. Our formula is very simple. We are looking for a couple of things. We want to recruit players that truly love football. I know that sounds simple, but I really believe in this idea. I do not think there are a lot of magic ingredients in what we are looking for in a recruit, but we want players that love football. They are must easier to coach.

The other thing is you must have a great staff. A great staff is not just a staff with great resumes, or celebrities. I got criticized at Iowa because I took my time in hiring my staff. I did not want to hire someone and then have to replace them in less than a year because I made a mistake.

The second thing I got criticized for at Iowa was that the assistants I hired were not celebrities. The formula for hiring assistants is very simple for me. The first thing you must remember is that you must hire good people. Second, you must hire coaches that are good teachers. You must have coaches that can teach and communicate.

The third ingredient in selecting assistants is that you must have team players. If you want your team to be a team it starts with the coaching staff. You need coaches that are on the same page. That does not mean that we do not have discussions and differences of opinion. I think that is healthy. That is how you move forward. Your staff must realize that you must get something accomplished, and to do this you must have team players. We have a great staff at Iowa.

Another thing you must have is an environment that is conducive to success. Facilities are important. In college football, they are important because of recruiting. Some teams go to extremes on the locker rooms and do all kinds of things to draw attention to the team. At Iowa we do not have smoke when our team comes out on the field. That is just not our style. There are all kinds of ways to bring attention to your team. I think you need things that are functional. I think these things should be as first class as you can make them.

The other thing is we have great tradition at Iowa. We have had tradition for a long time at Iowa. If you do not have tradition, then obviously you are trying to build tradition.

Our plan is made up of two main components. We try to recruit good players and then we try to develop those players. I do not think this is any different in high school, college, or in the pros. In high school, you have to get the kids to come out for the football program. You must recruit coaches in high school. Going back to Joe Moore in high school, he had a knack of getting people into the school that were good teachers. Then all of a sudden, they became interested in football. He taught them what they needed to know about football, and they got the job done.

Another area you can recruit is support from your community. If you can get the right outside voices involved, it can be a great thing for your program. We have an Honorary Captains Program where we bring in a former player and he speaks to our team on Friday.

Development of players is big for us. We are not a glitter school. In the last 22 years, Iowa has sent 17 teams to Bowl Games. Four of those teams were Big Ten Conference Champions. To put it into perspective, I use an NFL term. At Iowa we do not get a lot of first-round draft picks." For us, we get the players that would go in the second round of the NFL draft. If we can get the right kind of players, we think we can develop those players.

I do not think you can give up on a player too soon in college football and in high school football. You learn this from your players. In the 1980s, when I was at Iowa, we had three players that played in the offensive line and only started one year for us. Only in their fifth year did they become starters. One of the three players came into the fall camp as a number-two player. He later won the starting job at guard. All three of those fifth-year players ended up in the NFL. One of them was a first-round pick and played 13 years in the NFL. The other player was selected in the fifth round and played for seven years in the NFL. The third player went in a later round and played in the NFL for four years. Those three players only started for one year in college. That taught me a great lesson.

Last year, we had three players drafted to the NFL. One of the three was a first-round draft selection. All three of those players drafted were former walk-ons. My point is this. Players develop at different times and at different ages. If the players are committed and they are putting the effort forward, you must keep working with them. Not many places can afford to give up on many players if they are trying.

In closing, I want to leave you with a couple of additional points. In development, it all starts with expectations. The players must understand what you are looking for. At our place we just ask for a championship level effort in three areas. The three areas are their personal lives, academics, and football. This is what we govern ourselves by.

In the first year at Iowa we talked about the core values we had. We talked about playing tough and playing physical, being sound and consistent, and trying to become a team. We tried to become closer as a team, and we tried to become more accountable. The turning point for us came last year. We had too many distractions. We challenged our teams to grow up, to become men, and to be accountable. I think it has helped us a great deal.

We talk about continuing to develop mental and physical toughness. To be more physical. It starts in the weight room. We have a great strength program.

The other thing we felt was important was that we wanted to learn how to win. Now we are at the point where we expect to win each game. We put an asterisk next to this point. The players must know what they have to do to achieve success in this area. They know they must be willing to work and pay the price for success. The other thing we talk to our players about is just not giving up.

In closing I will go back to Coach Joe Moore. He was a good philosopher. He came up to me one day and said, "When it comes down to it, there are two things that are important. First, you only get what you ask for and what you demand." I think as a coach you must continue to keep pushing the bar and you must be demanding. The second point Joe Moore made was this. He said, "Kids do not always need another friend." This goes back to the Chuck Klausing story. We must remember to take an active interest in our players. We are coaching players, and not just coaching people. You are there to support your players and you are there to help them. But coaching is no different than being a parent. Sometimes you have to tell the players "No." You must be honest with them. It is good sometimes for you to be their friend, but there comes a time when you must be able to say no to them.

I want to commend you for being here tonight. We are coaching a great game. You are taking you time to help others. I wish all of you the very best. Thank you.

LINEBACKER TECHNIQUES AND DRILLS

Marshall University

I have been extremely lucky, blessed, fortunate, or what ever you want to call it in my football career. My idols were my high school coaches. I always wanted to be a coach from the time I was about 11 or 12 years old. In 1981, I realized my dream when I graduated from Oklahoma State and was hired by my high school coach to coach high school football. I thought I had hit the lottery.

In 1984 I coached at the University of Oklahoma under Barry Switzer. I stayed there for six years before going to Marshall.

In 1966 Jim Mackenzie was the head football coach at the University of Oklahoma. After his first season at Oklahoma, he died of a heart attack. That also was Barry Switzer's first year at Oklahoma. Coach Mackenzie came up with something he called the "winning edge." This is something that has stuck with me through all my years of coaching. It applies to everything we do.

To get the winning edge:

- Play the percentages.
- Avoid losing first.
- Don't give up anything.
- Make them earn it.
- Play mistake free.
- Play field position football.
- Every coach knows more than he can coach/
  a) Confused players will not play well.
  b) Simplicity
  c) Security
  d) Consistency
- Don't coach caution to good players.

- Nothing is accomplished without enthusiasm.
- Look for and recognize your mistakes in coaching.
- The little things are done by the winners.
- Having a good team just gives you a chance to win.
- Physical conditioning precedes mental toughness, and discipline precedes morale.
- Players, not coaching, win games. Poor coaching loses games.
- Be yourself, not an actor; players can recognize phonies.
- Play like you practice. Make second effort part of your personality.
- Know the rules (players and coaches).
- Football is a game of critical situations.
- The kicking game is one-third of football. This is the phase of the game where big breaks occur.
- Prepare for psychological lifts and letdowns.
- Know what to expect of your personnel.
  a) Offense
  b) Defense
  c) Special team
- Always have a plan and believe in it.
  a) Don't compromise or lose your guts.
  b) Everything must be planned.
  c) Nothing good happens by accident
  d) Your plan will keep you from overlooking the little things.

• Form a team of winners, and surround yourself with players and other people for whom football means a lot.

We have a program at Marshall that enables some of our students to get additional assistance for their schoolwork. When I was hired in 1990, I met with the director of what we call our HELP program. That is an acronym which stands for Higher Education for Learning Problems. I wanted him to help me coach my players.

He told me there were different ways of learning. The first method is auditory. That means a student can learn by simply listening to an explanation of the topic. They can also learn through visual means. When you diagram a play on the board, show them a video, or give them a hand-out, you are using examples of visual learning. We find our players learn quicker if they walk through what we are trying to teach first. We take them out early for practice and walk through the new learning situations.

We go one step further and introduce the teaching into individual drills. From the individual drill, we integrate it into a group drill and finally into the team concept of learning.

The next method of teaching is the whole/part/whole method. The first step is to introduce and explain what we want to accomplish for team success. We want them to know what they must do at their position for our defense to be successful.

The second phase is to break down the defense into specific techniques, alignments, and drills that are used for individual success. When a player has individual success, it gives you a much better chance for the defense to be successful.

The third phase is a progression of the whole concept. We start out in a meeting room, explaining on the board what we want. From there, we go to the field and participate in a walk-through. In progression, we have prepractice work, individual drills, group periods, and team sessions to accomplish our objective.

At Marshall, we are an eight-man front with four down linemen, and we run an Okie package. We run this defense because it allows us to get more speed on the field. It is a great defense to stop the run because it allows us to play with leverage and outnumber the offense. It also allows us to get more men in the box to give us pressure looks and many possibilities to blitz.

The eight-man front is an easy defense to teach. The defense is designed to adjust to everything. That takes the personnel substitution packages out of the game. The only situation that requires substitution to adjust is the dime package. With our regular defense, the nickel package is already on the field.

If we go to the dime package, it looks like a 3-4 defense with three down linemen. It is a different front structure for the offense to work on. It gives you leverage, is balanced, and gives you endless possibilities, from running a simple defense to a maximum blitz defense.

On defense, you must have solid fundamentals. You have to tackle, get off the line, pursue the ball, and communicate. We tell our players they have to have six seconds of concentration to play each play. Each time the ball is snapped until the whistle blows is about six seconds. In college we get about 70 snaps a game. That is 420 seconds, which amounts to seven minutes a football game. We have eleven football games next year that we are guaranteed to play. We are going to work our tails off from March until December for one hour and seventeen minutes of playing time.

As part of our objectives, we want to stop the run. That limits the play selection the offense has. We want to use great disguise by stemming the fronts, making bluffs, and by having identical man-zone looks in the secondary. We don't want the offense to dictate how we play.

We want to attack the offense and make them defend themselves. We study how the offense reacts to pressure. We study and predict their protection schemes. Bringing pressure on the quarterback causes offenses to put fewer receivers into the patterns. We try to take away the hot routes and make the quarterback hold the ball. We want to take the game out of the press box and make the quarterback beat us.

There are things the offense tries to do in an attempt to be successful. They try to motion to get defenses out of their blitz patterns. They trade the tight end from one side to the other. The quarterback is always looking for one or two high safeties to determine the coverage and run support. They are trying to find the 3 technique player so they can trap or run the zone play at him. To combat all those items, we must stem and disguise our defense to look the same on each snap.

I have a pledge in my meeting room I require all my players to sign. There are 20 items on this list, which relates to our work effort. The chart is entitled "Insider Linebackers' Attitudes." It states: "We are the leaders of our defensive unit and we will base our work ethic and competitive spirit on that belief. Effort and physical toughness will be our trademarks and will provide us with a better opportunity to win. We will lead by example." I have the linebackers sign the chart each fall and spring.

If I find the player in any violation of the rules, I cross his name off the list. If they put their names on the pledge, they want to live up to it. It puts pressure on them because they see their names on that pledge each and every day. If their name is crossed off, everyone knows which linebacker is not living up to what he said he would.

We have 30 words that describe what it takes to be a great linebacker at Marshall. Some of the words on the list are discipline, dedication, unity, consistency, commitment, and effort. There are 24 other traits relating to those types of behavior.

We have individual linebacker goals and team defensive goals that we post in our locker room. Our linebacker goals are:

- Improve as a player
- Improve as a unit
- Be consistent
- Practice great preparation
- Win all home games
- Win all conference games
- Have a winning season
- Win MAC East
- Win MAC championship
- Go to and win a bowl game

When we break down after practice, we bring our players together in a core. When you think of core, you think of the core of the earth or the core of a baseball. They are rock-solid expressions. That is what I want our linebacker to understand. We are the core of the defense and are rock-solid. We are going to bring our lunch pail and hard hat to work each day.

Our base stance is aligned with the toes of the linebacker at 4.5 yards from the line of scrimmage. Our linebackers are downhill football players. We want them to press the line of scrimmage. We want each linebacker's feet slightly wider than shoulder width. We think that helps to eliminate a jab step or crossover step as they move forward. Any time you have to make a movement to get out of your stance, you are in a poor stance.

We want to get the weight on our knees and roll up on the balls of our feet. We are playing downhill, and I don't want the linebackers sitting back on their heels. The heels in the linebacker's stance should be light on the ground. I should be able to slide a sheet of paper under their heels in the stance. We want the head up, back flat, and the arms hanging relaxed, approximately at knee height, but not outside the knees. The linebacker has to remember that the closer he plays to the line of scrimmage, the less room there is for error.

When we attack a blocker, the thumbs are pointed at 12 o'clock. That keeps the elbows tucked into the sides of the body. If a linebacker plays with his hands wide, the elbows go outside, and we loose leverage on the blocker. We want our hands inside the blocker's hands with our elbows tucked inside.

There are times our linebackers play in an up stance. When we play this technique, we want a staggered stance, with our outside foot back. The stagger is in a heel-to-toe relationship. We want the depth of the linebacker no deeper than the heel line of the defensive front. We call this up, macho, or bluff.

The impression the quarterback should get is pressure coming from the linebacker. If we call up, we simply play base defense. If we tag a blitz to the call, we are coming. If the offense is watching film of our defense, they shouldn't be able to tell if we are playing base or blitzing in our up position.

If we are playing base, when the ball is snapped, we step to square our stance and play football. We want to make sure we are within that two- and one-yard limit of the line of scrimmage so the offense will include the linebacker in their blocking count.

When you teach tackling in today's world, you have to be extremely careful when you talk about the use of the head. You have to get your message over to the players without instructing them to use their head as a primary part of the tackle. What I use to describe the technique is called biting the biceps. I tell the tackler to bite the bicep of the arm that holds the ball. That places the shoulder as the primary focus. However, when we can place the hat on the ball with force, we can produce a turnover. The primary job of the defense is to get the ball back for the offense.

Turnovers don't normally happen; they are created by the defense. In our tackling progression, we start by teaching a fit position from the right and left shoulder position. We fit the tackler to the ballcarrier in a perfect tackling position. We follow that up with a fit-follow through drill. From the fitted position, the linebacker, on the coach's command, punches his arms through the ballcarrier's armpits. We want his head up, a sinking and rolling of the hips, accelerating of the feet, and grabbing high cloth. When he accelerates his feet, we want him to step on the ballcarrier's toes. To get the point across, I tell the linebackers they have to tackle with their feet.

The next step is form tackling, which is fit tackling from a distance of two yards apart. We coach the same techniques and emphasize keeping the

feet moving on contact. Missed tackles usually occur when the tackler's feet stop on contact.

The next thing we do is called a turn tackling. The linebacker turns his back on the ballcarrier. On the command, he turns to the ballcarrier and hits him with the proper shoulder. The proper shoulder is the one opposite the position of the ball in the ballcarrier's arm. When we tackle, we want to bite the bicep. We allow the ballcarrier to try to squirm out of the tackle.

We use angle tackling when we pin a ballcarrier into the sidelines. We teach the same technique of biting the bicep. That forces the linebacker's head across the ballcarrier's body. Upon contact, the linebacker must square his hips and drive the ballcarrier upfield. In this drill, we have the ballcarriers and linebackers 10 yards apart. If the ballcarrier is aligned on the 10-yard line and the linebacker is on the goal line, the five-yard line represents the line of scrimmage. I tell our linebackers that in this drill I don't want the ballcarrier to get to the line of scrimmage.

When you teach open field tackling, the first thing to impress on your linebackers is that toughness is not important. It is not important to have a big hit. It is important for the linebacker to get the ballcarrier on the ground. I don't want an ESPN highlight tape; I want them on the ground. We want to use the sideline if possible. Before we tackle, we gather our feet and gather momentum slightly before contact. We want to go from speed to power in this stage of the tackle. Keeping the proper pursuit angle eliminates the cutback run of the running back. We want to tackle higher than normal and keep our feet moving. We have to keep the body square throughout the approach and tackle.

When we do our goal line tackling it becomes a competitive drill. I do this at least twice a week. We want the best of the best in this drill. To set up the drills, use the sideline between two yard lines. A dummy is placed parallel to the sideline, two yards from the sideline. The running back is allowed to go only one direction. The linebacker puts his heels on the sideline, which represents the goal line. The running back faces the sideline and must cross the goal line to score. We want the linebacker to execute a high tackle using a combination of angle and open field tacking techniques. If the running back touches the yard lines, he is out of bounds and the defense wins. If the ball crosses the sideline, it is a touchdown. This is extremely competitive. The winner gets out of the drill, whether it is the running back or the linebacker.

Block protection is part of understanding gap responsibility. On every call, we make sure someone is assigned to a specific gap. The linebacker has to understand his gap responsibility and leverage dictated by the front, coverage, and play that is being run. He has to understand the relationship of the blockers in his area of responsibility. He has to have some idea of who is going to block him in the offensive scheme. When flowing to his gap, he has to maintain proper body position.

He has to keep his shoulders square to the line of scrimmage. If the ball is moving with speed, the linebacker has to move with speed. When arriving at the block, he has to deliver an aggressive blow to neutralize the blocker without over extending his body. After finding the ball, he has to get off the block as quickly as he possibly can.

If the ball stays between the inside shoulders of the offensive tackles, we refer to that as the ball staying within the cylinder. If that happens, we use what we call a frontal technique. In this technique, we key the movement of the blocker. The linebacker targets the landmark on the offensive blocker and puts his nose on the V of the neck to maintain gap control leverage. He punches with the heels of the hands, with the thumbs up and elbows in, as quickly as possible to shock the blocker. We try to snap the wrists inward to force the elbows in. His facemask will make contact, which helps to slow the momentum of the blocker. At contact, we dip squat and come out of our shoes while accelerating the feet for balance to stop the blocker.

When the linebacker attempts to shed the block, he has to know his gap responsibility. As he sheds the block, he physically throws the blocker opposite his gap responsibility.

If the linebacker has to play a low block, he has to get vision on the blocker. We call it burn and defeat the blocker with his eyes. If the linebacker is scrapping on a sprint-out pass with a blocker coming at him, he has to see the blocker. If he looks at the quarterback, he is going to get cut down right now. We want his eyes down on the helmet of the blocker. His wrists are below his knees, with his gap foot back, away from the blocker. We want his shoulders square. The linebacker gets his hands on the near shoulder and head of the blocker. He wants to steer the blocker east and west, and extend his arms on contact. He runs out of the block by extending his arms and accelerating his feet while he gives ground. Once he is clear of the blocker, he snaps his head up to find the quarterback.

We have a number of block protection drills. We start on the five-man sled, especially the first two days of practice, because the NCAA mandates no pads on those days. We start off with the perfect stance. We want the linebackers to attack the pad of the sled with the heels of the hands. The thumbs should be at 12 o'clock. We stress coming out of the shoes and rolling the hips. We are not taking any steps during this phase of the drill.

We want the linebacker to lock out his arms to simulate getting separation from the blocker. After the lockout, he releases the pad and shuffles to the next pad. He repeats the drill until he hits all five pads. Once the first man gets to the third pad, the second man starts on the first pad. At this rate, you should have three players on the sled when the first player reaches pad five. We repeat the drill coming back the other way. We start off at one-half to three-quarters speed and pick up speed until we reach full speed.

The second time we go through the drill, the linebackers are skipping pads number two and four. The coach is watching the pad level of the players as they shuffle down the pads. We want the pad level the same all the way down the shed. We want a shuffle with no crossover steps. After everyone has completed the drill going one way, we repeat the drill coming the other way.

When we go to the one-man sled, the drill is exactly like the five-man sled drill until the players reach the lock out part of the drill. Once the players lock out on the pad, they take short, choppy steps and drive the sled for five to seven yards. After they reach seven yards, they release the sled on the command of the coach. The second time, they repeat everything except when they release the sled, they throw it to the left. They repeat the drill a third time and throw it right.

The next drill we do is the shiver ball drill, which works on playing the low block. The drill uses four agility bags laid on the ground. We use three large rubber balls to simulate low blockers. The shiver balls are rolled between the bags to simulate the low block. The linebacker gets in a perfect stance and waits for the ball to be rolled through the first hole. As the ball comes forward, the linebacker shuffles, maintaining good pad level, steps up, and attacks the ball with the heel of his hands.

He steps back, shuffles over, and gets ready for the next blocker to appear again. After hitting all three holes, he accelerates downhill as he gets past the last bag. We turn and repeat the drill going the other direction.

The next drill is a block protection and tackling drill. You need to set up four agility bags about two yards apart to run this drill. Place a cone or dot about five yards behind, and at a 45-degree angle from, the bags. The linebacker starts in a perfect stance. He goes over each bag with a right leg lead step. He skims the top of the bags with his fingertips as a reminder of great pad level. After the linebacker gets over the last bag, he immediately turns, plants his foot, and hits the end of each bag, shuffling and simulating low block protection. When he hits the last bag, he turns and sprints downhill toward the dot, where a ballcarrier is waiting. As the tackler approaches, the ballcarrier simulates a rush. The linebacker executes a tackle on the ballcarrier. We repeat the drill going the opposite direction.

If you face a sprint out passing team or an option team, you had better work on low block protection.

If you don't, your linebacker will get cut all day long.

I want to get into some pass coverage techniques. We identify personnel grouping as they come on the field. We use a two-digit number to describe what personnel group is on the field. The two-digit number identifies the number of running backs and tight ends in the game. The first number equals the number of running backs, and the second number equals the number of tight ends in the game. The defensive personnel are relayed to the defense by the defensive end nearest the opponent's sideline.

If the personnel grouping in the game is "00," there are no running backs and no tight ends on the field. That means there are five wide receivers in the game. A "12" grouping would mean one running back, two tight ends, and two wide receivers. It will be extremely important to know the personnel grouping and the offensive tendencies from those groupings.

I have some general passing game thoughts the linebackers need to know. The first thing we want the linebacker to see is the level on which the ball is moving (see Diagram #1). With the ball moving on level one down the line of scrimmage, the linebacker should run with the possibility of a play action pass. The linebacker matches his speed to the speed of the ball. If the ball is going fast, it could be a speed option.

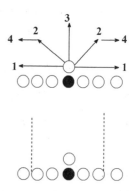

Diagram #1. Ball levels

If the ball is on level two, the linebacker is thinking, run first and pass second. It could be a sprint, half sprint, or play action pass. If the ball stays inside the cylinder, the linebacker treats it as a dropback pass.

If the ball is on the third path, the linebacker should think, pass first, and possibly draw. The linebacker on all pass actions must be aware of the possibility of a draw play. He should be thinking about the possibility of the draw until the ball passes the deepest back in the backfield. He has to remember to take on the blockers as close to the line of scrimmage as possible, but he can't break back to the ball too soon. Certain opponents force us to slow our pass drops considerably to defense the draw.

There are some clues to help tip the linebacker to a draw play. When a back runs a draw play, he has an atypical action, or a lateral hop, when he gets ready to receive the ball. When the offensive linemen start to look at the linebacker, it is probably going to be a draw. Linemen don't look at linebackers unless they think you are going to blitz. Linebackers have to react at the same tempo as the backs. The linebacker wants to mirror the running back's action until he sees the pass. When he reads the pass, he drives to get depth into his zone responsibility.

In zone coverage, it is a priority of the linebacker to see the set of the quarterback's shoulders. After the linebacker reads the set of the shoulders, he peeks at the receivers. The linebackers want to match up on receivers that attack his zone.

These next thoughts are some general comments on zone coverage for the linebacker:

- Know point of aim (zone).

- Work from deep to shallow (no cover zone).

- Keep head on a short swivel (girl friend analogy).

- Keep inside-out leverage on receivers in your zone.

- Know depth of QB on drop back pass; set when he sets.

- Learn zones by QB roll, by flood action

- On play-action pass, reaction is to sprint to responsibility

- Carry vertical threats in your zone responsibility to appropriate depth.

- Know when your QB's shoulder is set to you or away from you to determine how you set up (directional key).

- See QB's front hand on ball (delivery key)

- You must break for the ball as it is thrown and cover ground while the ball is in the air.

- Intercept the ball at its highest point.

When we are reading pass keys I tell my linebackers that offensive linemen don't lie. We are going to read offensive linemen and running backs. We are not going to read the quarterback. There are two keys we get from the quarterback. The first one is a directional key. That comes from his shoulders. The shoulders will tell you which direction he is going to throw the ball. The second key is the front hand on the football. When the front hand comes off the football, we say that is the delivery key.

When you put the two together, it gives you a break on the ball. The quarterback's shoulder points the direction, and the front hand tell you when he is going to deliver it. When the front hand comes off the ball, we break in the direction of where his shoulders are pointed.

Sometimes players make man coverage more difficult than it is. It is simple: "Look at your man and cover him." In man coverage, you have to look at the receiver and not the quarterback. The linebackers have to know the receiving skills of the man they are covering. The linebacker wants to look at the receiver's middle and pick up his stride in his vision. He has to know where his help is coming from so he can establish proper leverage.

If there is no help in the coverage, he has to protect against the deep throw first. He wants to deny the inside cut and make the quarterback throw the ball outside because that is the most difficult throw. He always has to be smart about seeking collision with a receiver.

If he is in a chase position, the linebacker looks at the receiver's middle and sees his hands. If the pattern is a deep route, he always wants to catch up and get stride for stride before he looks for the ball. If the defender doesn't have a chance for the interception, he should tear away the upfield arm and strip the football.

If the defense can make the quarterback change the trajectory of the ball, that is a successful pass rush. We know the delivery of the ball is coming when he takes the front hand off the ball. When the defenders see that happening, they get their hands up. If the quarterback puts more air under the ball than he intended to, that is a good pass rush. And if we knock the ball down, that is a great pass rush. I tell linebackers those things because I don't want them to get frustrated when they don't get to the quarterback and sack him.

Here are our basic fundamentals in rushing the passer. You have to take pride in sacking the quarterback. Pass rushing is 90 percent effort and 10 percent skill. To rush the quarterback, you have to anticipate when the quarterback is going to throw the ball. We know the down-and-distance, get a presnap reads of the offensive linemen's stance, see the offensive formation, and know the defense called to determine if it is a passing situation.

It is extremely important to get a great jump on the snap of the ball. The rusher must key the football. The pass rusher in his stance puts his weight on his back foot so his first step is a progressive step toward the quarterback. He has to explode and accelerate out of his stance. To be a successful pass rusher, he has to close the distance between himself and the blocker as quickly as possible.

When you rush the quarterback, the pass rusher has to have a plan to attack and defeat the blocker. When the defender has a contain responsibility, he attacks the upfield shoulder of the quarterback.

When tackling the quarterback, the defender must tackle him high and pin his arms to his sides. When sacking a quarterback, the defender should force a fumble 50 percent of the time. When recognizing a pass, don't leave your feet until the ball leaves the quarterback's hand.

The linebacker has to learn how to read the draw. There are many clues to see it. If the quarterback turns his back to the line of scrimmage on his pass drop, that is probably a draw. If the quarterback moves the ball from the shoulder area to the hip area on his drop, that is a draw clue. If the offensive linemen are staring a hole in the linebacker, that is a draw read.

We use most of the standard pass rush techniques that everyone else does. In the bull rush, the defender explodes into the blocker with the top of his helmet into the chin of the blocker. At the same time, he shoots his hands into the chest area of the blocker and grabs cloth. He has to keep his feet driving all the time. The defender wants to drive and lift the blocker into the quarterback's lap.

We use the butt pull with the bull rush. We butt the blocker with our helmet like we did in the bull rush. When we feel the blocker shift his weight to resist the move, the defender grabs cloth and pulls the blocker forward and off balance.

In the swat swim, the defender starts the move like the bull rush. As he gets into position to step on the blocker's toes, he gives the blocker a move opposite the direction he is headed. He swats his inside or outside hand to the elbow area of the blocker, pinning his arm down. As he pins the blocker's arm, he brings his other arm over the top of his body while shooting his hips through to the backside. When he brings his arm down, he should drive his elbow into the middle of the blocker's back and accelerate toward the quarterback.

When the defender uses the arm under move, he approaches the blocker, dips, and rips his shoulder and arm through the rib cage area and arm of the blocker. He explodes into him, turning his body, while at the same time shooting his hips and accelerating toward the quarterback.

The last pass rush technique is simple finesse. As the defender reaches the blocker, he uses foot, shoulder, and head fakes on the blocker. He is trying to slip by the blocker without making contact with the blocker. The defender must be able to step on the blockers toes before making a move.

I want to show you some of our man-free coverage. Against 21 personnel, the free safety is in the middle of the field. The corners are man to man on the wide receivers. The rover has the tight end man to man. Our two linebackers and the whip are working a three-way coverage in the middle (see Diagram #2). That means they are responsible for the two backs.

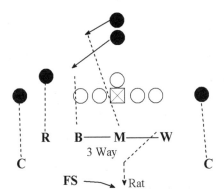

Diagram #2. 3-way RAT

If both backs flow to the strong side, the Backer and Mike linebackers take them in man coverage, and the whip is free in the short middle of the field. He can spy the quarterback or double a receiver.

If the backs split their routes, the whip takes the back that comes out to his side and the Backer linebacker takes the back to his side (see Diagram #3). The Mike linebacker is the RAT defender in the middle.

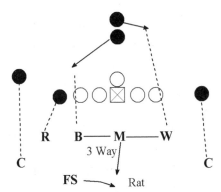

Diagram #3. 3-way split

If both backs release to the weak side of the formation, the Whip takes the first back out of the backfield (see Diagram #4). The Mike linebacker has the second back out to the weak side and the Backer linebacker is the RAT player.

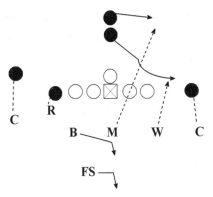

Diagram #4. 3-way weak

In the one back set with four wide receivers, we have a two-way RAT coverage. The personnel is called 10 personnel. That means one back, no tight ends, and four wide receivers (see Diagram #5). We match up with the corners on the number one receivers. The Rover and Whip have the number two receivers. The free safety is in the deep middle playing free. The Mike and Backer linebackers have a two-way coverage on the remaining back. One of the linebackers covers the back, and the other is the hole player in the middle of the field short.

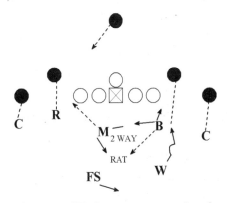

Diagram #5. 2-way vs. one back

If the back does not release in the pattern, the linebacker responsible for him should cover him in tight coverage. That takes the screen pass out as an option for the offense. The linebacker is a potential receiver if the quarterback is flushed and looking for somewhere to throw the ball.

We can play the same cover from the cover 2 look (see Diagram #6). The corners have the wide receivers. The Rover has the tight end man-to-man.

The free safety is going to the deep middle. The Backer and Mike linebacker have 2-way cover on the two backs in the backfield. The Whip is rolling down into the short hole in the middle of the field as the RAT player.

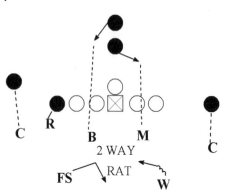

Diagram #6. Man free, cover 2

This is the same cover 2 look with the one back set (see Diagram #7). The corners have the number one receivers. The Rover takes the number two receiver to the weak side. The Backer linebacker, has the tight end with the Mike linebacker taking the one back in the backfield. The free safety has the deep middle and the Whip rolls down into the middle short hole.

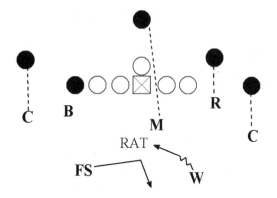

Diagram #7. Man free/cover 2 with one back

When we play man free, we don't like to get in chase positions with our defenders. To prevent that, we make cross calls and cut calls (see Diagram #8). In the two by two set we just showed, the Backer linebacker has the tight end man to man. The whip is keying the tight end from his alignment. If the tight end runs a crossing pattern, the Backer calls cross, and the whip calls cut. Instead of the Backer chasing the end across the field, the whip picks him up and the Backer becomes the short hole player.

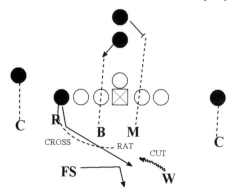

Diagram #8. Cut call

This sounds complicated, but it is easier to play than it sounds. From the same set, the Backer is playing the tight end. If the tight runs the crossing pattern he calls "cross" and passes him on to the Whip when he makes his cut call. The Rover has the number two receiver weak. If he runs a crossing pattern to the other side, the Rover calls "cross" (see Diagram #9). The Backer linebacker picks up the Rover's man running the cross, and the Rover becomes the short hole player. We maintaining leverage and are never in a chase position. We can play this coverage and are able to disguise it very well. It looks like cover 2, but we are playing a man free concept out of it.

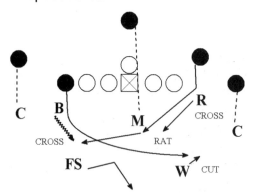

Diagram #9. Double cross

My time is up. Thank you.

THE 3-3-5 STACK DEFENSE

West Virginia University

I am going to give you an overview of some of the things we do on defense. However, the main thing I am going to do is to talk about our 3-3-5 off stack defense. I am not going to talk a lot about philosophy. That is one of the reasons coaches do not like to come to clinics today. You get so much philosophy and very little that you can use in your program. I will talk about our base alignment and our coverage rules, our techniques, and the fundamentals of our defense. I will go over our defensive philosophy, our defensive goals, and our grade sheets.

Our defensive system is an odd stack package of multiple fronts and coverage that is simple, flexible, and capable of attacking any offensive system that we may encounter. We use a multiple system that is based upon the learning and perfecting of a limited number of fundamentals and techniques through repetitions. Our approach presents problems for opponents by forcing them to prepare for the multitude of looks that they may see from our defense.

Our defense is not just a stack package. Two years ago, when we started at WVU, we were 103 out of 117 on defense in the nation against the run. After the season was over, Coach Rodriquez came in our defensive meeting and said "I want to run the type of defense Joe Lee Dunn uses." Our staff were all 4-3 guys, so we had a lot to learn. In the first year we used the defense, we went 9-3. Over the last few years, we have finished in the top 30 in rush defense in a predominately run conference. We do play some good teams in our conference.

Our defense is built around players who possess four primary attributes:

- Mental toughness
- Outstanding work ethic
- Physical conditioning
- Coachability

We believe these are characteristics that every player can develop and improve upon, regardless of the individual's talent level. These attributes are the foundation for our style of play. Our team will be recognized and known for the following characteristics:

- Disciplined alignment
- Excellent technique and fundamentals
- Relentless attacking and pursuit of the football
- Physical and punishing tackling
- Outstanding physical conditioning

Our practice and preparation each day reflects and reinforces the commitment to our approach on defense. It will take a great effort each and every day from everyone involved in our program to distinguish us as the best defense in the country.

I want to go over our defensive priorities. I will put them up so you can see what we are trying to accomplish:

- Stop the run. No one will run the ball successfully against our defense. We will commit as many people to the line of scrimmage as necessary to stop the run. No one will run the football against us.

- Control the pass. We are primarily a zone coverage team. We will take away the long ball and force our opponents to throw into our underneath coverage. By becoming proficient in disguising our intentions and being sound in our drop keys and responsibilities, we will break on the ball and create collisions, turnovers, and incomplete passes.

- Tackling. We will be the best tackling team in America. By doing reps on the fundamentals every day in practice, we will punish ballcarriers and develop the attitude necessary of a physical defensive football team.

- Pursuit. We will get 11 people to the football on every play. It does not take a great athlete to run with the red line effort to the football. It takes a football player with a great attitude. We want as many of our helmets on the ballcarrier as possible, and we want to wear down the opponent in the fourth quarter.

- Turnovers. We will create a minimum of three turnovers per game with our attacking and aggressive style of play. We will work fundamentals every day that force turnovers and create a short field for our defense.

- Eliminate the big play. We will force the offense to travel the length of the field by not allowing a run over 10 yards or a completion over 18 yards.

- Eliminate mental mistakes. Most defensive breakdowns that allow big plays are the result of a mental mistake. By practicing with total concentration and learning our assignments, we will eliminate mental errors.

- Sudden change. We must accept the challenge of stopping our opponent after we have turned the ball over. We will go into a sudden change series with the attitude of getting the ball back and regaining the psychological advantage.

- Discipline. We will be recognized as a disciplined defense. We will do what we are coached to do on each and every play. Discipline in practice will enable us to develop good habits.

- Have fun. We are fortunate to be involved in the greatest game in the world. Enjoy the game and everything that goes into winning a championship.

Our defensive goals are no different than most of your defensive goals:

- Win!

- Team hustle: +90 percent team grade

- 3.5 yards or less per carry

- 17 points or less per game

- Force 3 or more takeaways.

- Score or set up two scoring opportunities for our offense.

- No big plays. No runs over 15 yards. No pass plays over 25 yards.

- No TDs after sudden change.

- 4 or more 3 and outs per game.

- Win third down 70 percent of the time.

- 100 percent efficiency on fourth down.

- Less than 290 yards total offense.

Of course, the number-one goal is to win the game. If we win by a score of 62 to 61, we have met our number-one defensive goal. It does not matter what the score is as long as we win.

We want to force three or more takeaways. We do not want to call them turnovers because that is like the offense is giving us something. We want to be creative and take the ball away from the offense.

We have all of our defensive goals on a board in every defensive meeting room. The players get to see them every day. When the players come into our team room, the first thing they look at is the defensive goal board. If we meet our goal during a game, we put a star or a WVU Mountaineer logo for each of the goals we meet for that week. We may gain the first goal and not do very well on the other eleven goals, but we tell our players that it is all right because our number-one goal is to win the game.

I want to show you our team grade sheet. We put up a productive board with the kids' names on the board. We upgrade the board every week. After we grade our players, we put the results on the board to show how productive we were for that last game. We keep the board running and total the points for the year. I want you to understand this is not the grade that we are showing. We are showing how productive we are in games. This tells us who is making the plays.

We put the play grade in separately. Then we calculate the total points scored for each player. The last point is contact with the ball. That included the number of times you are involved in a play. If you played 60 plays and were involved in 10 plays, that would mean you were involved in one out of every six plays. We want our players involved in one out of every four or five plays if they are a lineman or a linebacker. If they are a defensive back, we want them to be involved in one out of every seven plays. All of our defensive coaches use this form. This is what we take into our meetings with the head coach on Sunday morning. After we talk about the scores in the meeting, we post everything up in the team room. Our kids have a lot of fun with the grading system. They look forward to seeing the grades each week.

The next thing I am going to cover is our player alignment in our stack defense. We play a 3-3-5 stack defense. We have three down linemen, three linebackers, and five defensive backs. I will go over each position and tell you how we align.

Coach Bill Kirelawich coaches the three down linemen. Coach Jeff Casteel coaches the three linebackers. Coach Bruce Tall works with our spur and our bandit. I have the three deep men, which include the two corners and the free safety.

We play with a head-up nose man. He is our 0 technique. Our two ends play 5 techniques. Our linebackers are our Lou, Mike, and Rob. We are in a true stack with the Mike stacked on the nose (see Diagram #1). Our Lou linebacker is in a 50 alignment. If the man lines up in a 5 technique and is off the line of scrimmage, we add a zero to the number, so we say he is in a 50 alignment. The Rob linebacker is also in a 50 alignment. They line up four yards off the heels of the down linemen so they are about 5 yards off the ball. We do not flip our linebackers. They play on the same side all of the time.

PLAYER PRODUCTION BOARD

	Total Plays	Assists	Tackles	Tackle for Loss	QB Harass	Sack	Big Hit	Exceptional Play	X Mile	Caused Fumble	Recovered Fumble	Pass Break Up	Caused INT	INT	Score on Defense	Missed Tackle	Loaf	Missed Assignment	Penalty	Play Grade	Total Points	Contact with Ball
POINT VALUE		1	2	3	3	5	3	3	2	5	5	4	5	7	8	-2	-1	-1	-2			
NAME																						

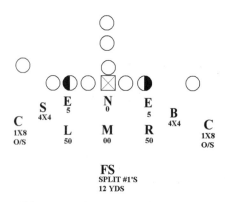

Diagram #1. Player alignment

Our outside spur and bandit have to think a little more. The spur is on the strongside of the formation. He is in a 4 X 4 split off the heels of our defensive end. We do not line up off the offensive end. We line up off our defensive end. Our bandit goes to the weakside and he is a 4 X 4 player off our defensive end.

We have a field corner. If the ball is on the hash mark, he goes to the wide side of the field. He is 1 X 8 outside. His alignment changes when the wideout lines up outside the numbers. Then he automatically goes inside with the wideout. The bandit is our boundary corner. This is the man we usually give the inside alignment. We tell our free safety to split number one. If the ball is on the hash mark, we move him over the tackle. He is 12 yards deep.

I will go over what we look for in a player for each position. Our bandit is the next best defensive man besides the two corners and free safety. He would be a safety in the 4-3 alignment. He is an athletic type that can cover and can play man coverage. The spur could be an outside linebacker. Our spur defender is larger than the bandit. He must be able to play on the tight end side and take on the blocker. He must be a physical athlete. We never pull the spur off the line of scrimmage. He is always in the 4 X 4 alignment. Our corners must be able to cover in man coverage. The boundary corner must be more physical than the field corner. Our free safety is the corner type player that we have moved back to that position. We recruit quarterbacks and tailbacks to play this defensive position.

Let me cover the gap responsibilities out of the stack alignment (see Diagram #2). We start with the nose man. The nose is an A gap player. He is the frontside A gap man. The Mike is the backside A gap player. The ends are C gap players. The spur and bandit are D gap players. The Lou and Rob linebackers are B gap players.

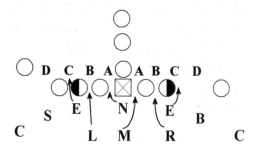

Diagram #2. Gap responsibilities

Our free safety is an alley player. The bandit and spur force the play, and the free safety fills on the play. The corners secure any play action pass or deep pass.

We always have a force man, a secure man, an alley man, and a cutoff man (see Diagram #3). What we call the cutoff man is the corner away from the action. If the play is a toss sweep to the tight end side, the corner on the backside is the cutoff man. He wants to get 10 yards depth and check for the reverse or throwback. He pursues the play gaining depth. He is the deep man on the pursuit. He can save the touchdown if he pursues the play properly. We make the backside corner tell us his responsibility when we are running the film and the play goes away from them. "What do you have on the backside corner?" We expect them to reply, "Cutoff man."

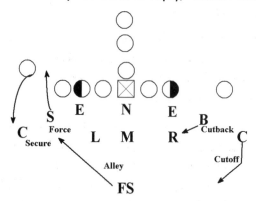

Diagram #3. Force, secure, alley and cutoff

Let me go over the toss sweep using this concept. As the spur sees the quarterback toss the ball to the tailback, he becomes the force player. He wants to get up the field to restrict the back from getting outside. We want him on the outside path of their fullback. He wants to make the tailback cut back inside. He does not want the play to get outside. This should be the easiest play in football to read. As he sees the quarterback turn and pitch. he wants to get downhill and get in the face of the fullback (see Diagram 4).

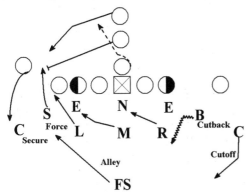

Diagram #4. As he sees the quarterback turn, the force player wants to get in the face of the fullback.

Once the spur sets the corner for us and there is nowhere for the ballcarrier to go but inside, he is going to get hit by the Lou, Mike, or Rob linebackers. We bring out linebackers over the top of everything.

Our free safety is flat foot reading, and his eyes are on the triangle. As soon as he reads the quarterback make the toss, he is up in the alley. That is the reason the corners are our secure players. The onside corner secures the play, and the backside corner is the cutback player.

The Lou linebacker is over the top of the tight end, the Mike linebacker is over the top of the guard, and the Rob linebacker is over the center. We use the bandit as the cutback player.

If the offense sends the outside man in motion to the other side, we kick the free safety over to the motion side and the corner comes back to replace the free safety (see Diagram #5). We move the shell. We do not move the spur on the tight end side.

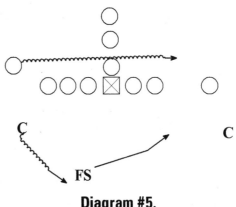

Diagram #5.

This is basically our stack against the 2 X 1 Set (see Diagram #6). Nothing changes for the linemen. It is the same as we have covered in the alignments.

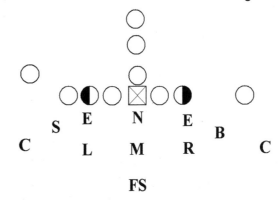

Diagram #6. Stack vs. 2 X 1 set

Next I want to talk about the stack vs. 2 X 2 set. This is the reason we started running the stack defense: because teams were using the spread offense. When you get into this alignment, the match-ups are good (see Diagram #7).

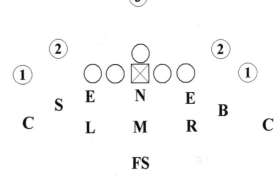

Diagram # 7. Stack vs. 2 X 2 set

The bandit and spur have inside leverage on the number two receiver. We count from the outside to the inside. So the bandit and spur have the two receivers in the slot. The corners still are outside.

Nothing has changed for them. The free safety still splits the number one receivers.

We play mostly cover 3 with this defense. The reason we like it is because it allows those linebackers to play. We think that is the key. Line them up, teach them how to play technique out of stack cover 3, go against different combinations in practice, and see what you are going to get. Then after you see the problems, you can work on adjusting the defense. This is a lot better than trying to teach cover 2, cover 3, and cover 4. If you teach a lot of different coverages it leads to mistakes. I like to stick with the coverage and adjust the players. If the offense sees the stack alignment, there is only one way they can block it. You will not see a lot of different blocking schemes up front.

We tilt our corners inside so they can read the quarterback. He is eight years off the line. He wants to be able to see the number one receiver, but he is reading the quarterback. The quarterback is going to tell the corner what is happening. The wideout will not tell the corner what is going on when the ball is snapped. We turn them inside and use a shuffle step and slide as the ball is snapped.

Next in our progression is the 3 X 1 set. That is a trey set for us. We adjust no different but we pull the defense. We pull the three linebackers one full man over to the trips side (see Diagram #8).

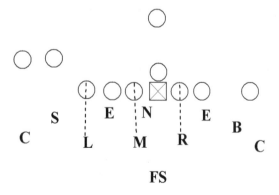

Diagram #8. Stack vs. 3 X 1 set

If one of the two wide receivers motion back to the split end side, we move the linebackers back to their original positions in the box. This is one of the things we like about this defense. We can move the cover players without making a lot of adjustments.

The responsibilities of the cover players do not change against the 1 by 1, 2 by 2, or 3 by 1 set. When we spot drop it in a zone, it does not change anything. As I said, we play cover 3 a lot.

The corner is a deep one-third player. He has outside leverage. He will play up tight against the quick passing game. The free safety is a middle one-third player. His alignment is splitting the number one receivers. He is a middle one-third player. The other corner is a one-third player.

The bandit and spur are flat players. Their landmark is to the numbers on the field. They want to get to a depth of 10 to 12 yards deep. They play everything from the top downhill. They must get depth and width on his drop. That is the hard thing for them to do. They want to stay skinny and not get deep enough and not wide enough. We tell them to get to the numbers, and we will coach them from there. If the quarterback pulls up on his drop, they must back up and get depth.

Out of the spread sets, we see the bubble screen play with our soft corner. That is why we have to move our corners up and down on the receivers. We have the corners come up like they are going to press to play man coverage, and then we retreat into one-third coverage. We mix it up by playing man cover as well. We do different things with the corners. We do not sit them in a 1 by 8 alignment all of the time.

The spur and bandit align with their inside foot up. They look inside to the quarterback. As soon as they get the read and they know it is a pass play, they come outside, keeping their eyes on the quarterback. They want to get depth and width.

The Lou and Rob linebackers are hook-curl players. They work 10 to 12 yards deep. The Mike linebacker is a hole player, and he is 10 to 12 yards deep.

What we are talking about here is basically a five under with three deep. We play against some great quarterbacks. In cover 3, if we hit the right landmarks, we should have the players covering the flat, hook-curl, hole, hook-curl, flat, one-third, one-third, and one-third (see Diagram #9).

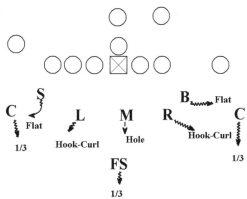

Diagram #9. In cover 3, if we hit the right landmarks, we should have the players covering the flat, hook-curl, hole, hook-curl, flat, one-third, one-third, and one-third.

If we want to blitz one of the linebackers, we end up with a four- under-three-deep coverage. We move the linebackers in and out of the gaps to mess with them. We can show the blitz and drop off, and we can walk them up and blitz. The same is true with the corners. We move them up and fake man coverage. We move them up and play man coverage. We mix it up with the coverage.

The key is that we want our linebackers aggressive. Against play action, we want them to play aggressive. Our linebacker coach tells them, "Stick your face in the fan." Remember, our number one priority is what? Stop the run! Right! If the offense runs play-action plays, we are telling our linebackers to stop the run. We tell the other backs they must play man-to-man when they read play action pass.

I want to talk about cover 1 for a few minutes. Everything is from a loose alignment. With our corners, we have inside leverage, and we line up at seven yards deep. We stagger the stance. We do not care which foot is back. We used to coach it one way, but it really does not matter. We want to get all the weight off the back foot. If the weight is on the front foot, the corner can go in any direction. If he is going back, he must push off the front foot. If

he needs to get downhill, he can push off the front foot and get moving forward. He wants all his weight on the front foot.

Against the trip set we roll our free safety and bandit if they line up on one side and motion back to the other side. We do not move across the formation (see Diagram #10).

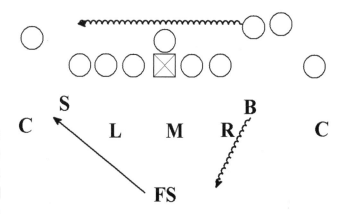

Diagram #10. Invert coverage vs. motion

In talking about our drills for the secondary, we do stance, start, and back peddle every day. The key is to relax the arms. We tell players to play the piano with their fingers. When we back peddle we want them on their toes. We stress keeping the elbows in tight.

I do want to show the film on our drills for our defensive backs. We have a net that we use in our defensive drills. In all of our drills, we have the defensive backs slap the ground before they start the drill. That is a just a reminder for them to stay low. We make the players get in their stance, slap the ground, and then go. If you want to get more on our drills, drop me a note. We use a lot of different techniques. I like man-to-man techniques the best.

That is a little about our defense. If you want to visit us you are welcome. If we can do anything for you, let us know. Thank you.

Al Groh

AIM FOR THE BULLSEYE

University of Virginia

It is a treat for me to be with you. There are 19 Coach of the Year clinics around the country. If there was one clinic that I would choose to attend, it would this one. Here is why. It is a nostalgic for me to come back to this area. I grew up on the other side of Long Island. I spent eleven years between the New York Giants, New England Patriots, and the New York Jets. I had some of my best experiences and memories in those three places. I made the association with Bill Parcells and Bill Bilichick during that time frame. This has served as a foundation for my career. So I am happy to come back to this area to give something back for my great experiences here.

I really love football. I like football coaches, and I like to talk about football. Obviously, you feel the same way, by being here. When I was asked to speak, I was asked to speak on some technical phase of football. When you are the speaker at a clinic such as this, I think you should chose a topic as if you are going to be the only speaker at that clinic. Speak as if no one else can redeem your presentation. As a speaker the objective is to make everyone in the room feel, by virtue of what you present to the audience, that it made their attendance worthwhile. My job is to make each of you feel the trip to this clinic is worth your time and effort. If every speaker can do that, you will have a great clinic in terms of your enrichment of football. My job is to make everyone here feel the best 90 minutes they spent listing to this lecture was the best time spent at this clinic.

If I take one specific area such as cover 2, all of a sudden a lot of the people in the audience are disappointed because they coach the offensive line. If I tell you I am going to talk about our off tackle play, then the defensive coaches get up and leave. Some

of them may physically leave the room, and some of them may mentally leave the room. So I have tried to find something that everyone can relate to, and something where everyone can get something out of the lecture.

For the subject I am going to talk about with you I do not need any notes. The only reason I use notes is because I have tried to put together a sequence that will help you understand what I am trying to convey in my message. I am going to talk about things we believe in and things we practice daily. The content of the subject is easy, but it is the organization of the material that took a little time.

Everyone is here, myself included, to stimulate our mind about football and to get some information that will help us win. Obviously if this clinic were billed as providing information on how to lose, no one would be in attendance. Everyone is here because they want to get ideas, techniques, plays, and inspiration to help us win. That is why we are here. That is our objective. That is why my topic is "Aim for the Bull's-eye." The picture I have of the bull's-eye is one similar to the archery targets. They have all of these rings around the target. We all have heard the phrase "Keep your eye on the target." The target is not good enough in our analyses. That is why I say "Aim for the Bull's-eye." The bull's-eye in the target for me is winning. Winning is the bull's-eye of what we are trying to do.

I am not an expert on winning, but I have some ideas about it. We feel very confident in our approach to putting a team together because of our basic mentality toward teams has proven to be very successful in two places. Other ways to do things exist other than the way we do things. Our system has stood the test of time in very competitive situations.

I want to talk about some issues that are critical to winning. These are things I think a head coach would be very interested in. From my perspective everyone in this room is a head coach. You are either the current head coach, or you would like to be the head coach. I think all coaches in their positions are head coaches of the positions they coach. You are the head coach of your position. That is the way I approach it with my staff. You need to think and act as the head coach for your position. By doing that, you are preparing yourself for the circumstances, and second, you come across a little strong with your players than you would if you see yourself just as a simple assistant coach. Everyone here is a head coach of some sort. You may be the head coach of the offensive line or the head coach of the linebackers. Everything has pertinence to you if you see your position from that particular perspective.

Winning is the most important thing you can aim for. Sometimes winning is diminished a little. "It is not important who wins or loses, but how you play the game." I attended a clinic last year and the speaker did a great job of presenting his message, and at the end he made a statement that I disagreed with. He said, "As coaches we have to have a perspective that we are about something other than winning. Winning is not the most important thing we do." I know what he was trying to say. He was trying to say developing values and standards in a direction of life with the players is very important. He stressed the fact we must give emphasis to the academic side, which is as important as winning.

I understood his perspective, but I did not agree with the statement. I think winning is the focus of everything we do. Winning is the bull's-eye of the target. It makes you pay attention to all the details and all of the nuts-and-bolts issues that bring about success. That is what we are driven by: winning as much as you can. You want to make your program as successful as it can be. You do everything within the legal limits to make your program the best. When you do this, everything becomes important.

People say take care of the little things and the big things will take care of themselves. What are the little things? If they are all important and can affect the outcome of the program, then they are important details. Everything counts. This is why team discipline is more important than ever. That is why study hall is more important than ever. That is why player development is more important than ever. All of those things are important to what you are trying to accomplish.

I think this enhances everything you do. It enhances team discipline, academic performance, and how your players present themselves to the community. If winning is the bull's-eye of everything, you must pay attention to all details that bring about success.

Here is what we are all about. We do not have a long list of objectives. We have some things that we work on to try to get to these objectives. It is important for the players to see the bull's-eye as well as the coaches. This is what we want to accomplish:

- Win the conference championship.

- Win the postseason game.

- Graduate all players that are involved in the program.

If you win the conference championship, you are in the postseason. We want to get into the postseason, and we are trying to win. We have won our last two postseason games. We want to establish the mentality if you can win your way into the postseason, you have a responsibility to win that postseason game. It is a pleasant time for the players to go to these games. There are some nice social events for them to attend.

If you ask any of the players that had the opportunity to play in a postseason game if they ever show off the watch they received from the postseason game if they lost the game, they do not show off the souvenirs they receive from those games if they lost that game. The object is to win that game.

In our conference, we do not have to set our goals any higher. The ACC gives us the opportunity to get a lot of attention from the media. All you have to do is win the ACC, and you are in the tournament. You do not have to talk about winning the national championship. That is a little beyond what our focus has to be. We want to win the conference championship. If we can get into the postseason game and win that game, we will be right there at the end. It is a very simple formula. Those are easy things to try to get your players to focus on. We want to win the conference championship, get into the postseason game, win the postseason game, and we want to maximize the academic performances. Those are our goals and all the little things get our attention.

Let me talk about some of the things that bring about winning. I want to cover some issues and elements that have been proven very successful. First of all, I think football is the greatest of all team sports. There is no other game in the world like football. There is no other game that is more challenging to coach. No one coaches as many players as football coaches. We have different age groups on the team. Because of the number of players involved, it is more difficult to coach the team. It is more challenging than any other circumstance.

We do not have a lot of signs in our team meeting room. We do have one sign on each side of the walls in the team meeting room. We talk about this frequently in these exact terms: The best players do not always make the best team, but the best team always wins!

That is our challenge every week. That is a big statement. That is not just a ninety-minute lecture; that is an entire weekend lecture. If the best players do not make the best team, but the best team always wins, how do you create the best team? What does this mean? That means execution, awareness of game situations, and creating a sense of teamwork. I am going to stay away from the football specific issues, but I will give you a little hint as to what some of those are.

Let me give you an example of what I mean. I am sure you have read the sports page where Team A has gained 450 yards of total offense. They had 12 penalties, three turnovers, and had a punt blocked.

Team B has 250 yards of total offense. In the jousting match of offense against defense, Team A has 450 total yards and only allowed 250 total yards. Team B has 250 total yards and gave up 450 total yards.

After the game you will hear someone on Team A say, "The best team did not win tonight! They did not have a better team than we did. They were just lucky." The team A player just does not get it. They will lose again. You can't be the best team regardless of your production if you get penalized 12 times. You are not a good team if you turn over the ball three times. You are not a good team if you get a punt blocked. What you are is a team that may be able to gain a lot of yards on offense. You may be fair at stopping the other team. You are just not good at winning games.

You can have more talented players on your team, and bigger and faster players, more experienced players. But we said the best players do not always make the best team, though the best team always wins. That is execution, understanding the game of football, and all other phases of the game. These are all things that make this the most complex game to coach and play.

The challenges to us as a head coach or intermediate head coach are significant. One, you have to put the team back together every year. We are all in that stage in the off-season. After the national signing date, a curtain gets pulled down on that cycle of football. It was official over three days after the Wednesday signing date. The bowl game was in December, and the signing date was on February second. On February fifth, a new cycle started. We did have a few weeks in the indoor program, but a new cycle started on February fifth. Now is the time to put the team back together again.

We finished strong at the end of the season in 2003. We won our last three games, and we beat Pittsburgh in the bowl game. This is second year in a row that we have finished strong. People said to me, "Coach, the team had a great finish. If you could just pick up right where you left off, you would have a great season next year." That is exactly what cannot happen. You cannot pick up where you left off last season. You "pick up" where you started. The cycle starts all over again. You have to put the team back together again. Some players are leaving the team, and some players are coming on the team. Even if everyone was coming back, you still have to put the team back together again. Each player is different and his circumstances are changing somewhat. That includes playing time, proficiency, and academic situations. Individuals change. They do not stay the same. You still must put the team back together again. That is one of the most challenging things in coaching.

You must put your team back together each year. You must think a lot about how that occurs. It is a big project. You must evaluate your talent. You must decide what you can do differently the next year. You need to study the strong points and the weak points on the team. You must decide who the leaders are for the upcoming year. We must decide how we are going to integrate the young players into the program. If you do not have a plan to make the young players a fabric of the team, then they will remain outside the team.

The seniors are always a part of the football family, but they are no longer a part of the team once they walk out of the locker room after that last game. They were no longer on the team. We had a new team after that game was over. The new team will operate without the seniors until August. They will get used to working together from the bowl game until August. Then in August, we have about twenty new players come into the program. Coaches and players must understand the importance of integrating the new players into the team. You must have a plan for that process. The older players have all experienced this and they know if the plan worked or not.

Once you have put the team together and we have established the makeup of the team, you must determine what the identity of the team is going to be. What are we going to be good at? What are we going to feature? Players must understand the iden-

tity of the team. If the team does not establish an identity, then it becomes a collection of players.

We want the players to establish an identity. They must understand who they are in the program, what they stand for, and what they are in terms of the system for that year. Everyone must be comfortable with that identity. That issue may take some time going into the season. It may take two, three, or even four games to develop, and for the team to understand its identity.

Once the identity is established with the goal of being the best team, you must be ready to reshape your identity every week. You must decide you are going to be the best team each week. You get that part established, and your team has an identity.

From game to game, things change. They change based on the results of the previous game. If you win the game, the team's mentality is different than it is if you lose. When they come back to practice on Monday, they are a different team than the one that played the game on Saturday. They are a different team based on the psychology of results. If the team loses, they are a different team in another way. They are not coming back to you as the same players. The results of the game have changed them.

The match-up for the next week has changed them as far as trying to be the best team. You must consider the next team you are going to play. It is too easy to say, "Look, guys, if we just do what we do, we do not care what the other team does. All we have to do is to do our thing."

Your thing is defined by the profile of your team and the identity you have established. But that is too easy. It may be the psychological circumstances that you are in. It may not fit the match-up that you are involved in that week. This means you must reshape your team every week. As we see it, this is the biggest challenge to the coaches. It is the most invigorating challenge. Regardless of what we have and what the other teams have, the challenge is, how can we make our team the best team on Saturday? If you approach each game in this manner, you can beat a lot of teams that you could not beat in practice. You do not lose to a team that does not have the athletic talent you have. Again, we are looking at it from the standpoint that the best players do not always win, but the best team always wins.

The great satisfaction comes when you can figure out how you can make your players the best team each week. When that happens, you must feel that if anyone else were coaching the team, they would not win. We must figure out a way to play better football against the opponents that may have better players and more talented athletes.

I am leading up to the fact that winning is the big deal. If we are trying to be the best team, then leadership is where winning starts. The team is a direct reflection in terms of how it is coached. Leadership is the catalyst to winning.

When I was the head coach at Wake Forest back in 1981 my offensive line coach was John "Jack" Henry. He is now with the New Orleans Saints. He is a dear friend of mine and he wanted to give me some advice. He had been on a staff at a small college in Pennsylvania, and the coach gave him this statement, which he passed on to me. I bought into the statement, and it has helped me over the years. There are some very serious words in this statement.

If we are talking about leadership, and leadership is where winning starts, then "the supreme function of the leader is to set the standard and demand compliance to that standard." We can all relate to that statement if we are the head coach, the principal, the head of the English department, or just a dad. The supreme function of the leader is to set the standard and demand compliance to it. That is more important than deciding if you are going to run the one back or two back offense, or play two deep or three deep. If you want any backbone to your program, and an identity to your program, here is where it starts. The leader sets the standard. Give some thought to what those standards are.

This is where it gets to be a challenge. "Demand compliance to the standard." It is one thing to set the standards, and another thing to demand compliance to the standards.

Do not set standards that sound appealing to you. Don't articulate the things you want the players to say and do that sound appealing to you unless you are willing and know you can demand compliance to them. You must choose things that you are personally willing to step up to the plate with and demand compliance to. It may be the environment in your school building, in your community, and in your booster club. There may be some issues that you find it difficult to demand compliance to.

A leader must be willing to step up and demand compliance to issues such as class attendance, players' behavior, or game performance. You must make sure you are willing to step up to those things and make sure you have the backing of the people around you so you can continue to support those issues.

Let me give you a few examples of what we are talking about here. One of the big factors that we feel help to make the best team is not getting penalties. We say, "No one wants penalties because penalties will cause you to lose."

When I want to the New England Patriots in 1993 with Bill Parcells, we looked at the number of penalties the team had the year before we took over. The Patriots had gotten 112 penalties, and their opponents had a lot fewer penalties. It was a significant differential in the number of penalties. The record before we took over was 1-15. There was a significant difference in the number of yards gained by the opponents. We were interested in the number of yards gained. Ball movement is the issue. Penalties create ball movement.

In the next four years, the Patriots were plus 93 in penalties against their opponents. That included two playoff games and a Super Bowl Game. We went to the New York Jets, and it was the same situation. In the first year we were 2-14 and we had a minus 11 in penalties. The next year we were 9-7 and went to plus 13 in penalties. Other things were involved, but those things were a big factor.

The year I was the head coach of the Jets, we were first in the league for the least number of penalties. In the years I have been at Virginia, we have been the least penalized team in the ACC. Players do what you make them do. Players don't do what you don't make them do. We will come back to this point later.

I was the head coach of the Jets and we went through the preseason practice getting ready to play the regular-season games. At the start of the season, we put up this sign in the locker room to help us become a better team. The sign was very simple: "No one is worth penalties because penalties make you lose."

We go to Green Bay for the first game of the season. In the first half, our left tackle had four penalties that really killed us. One penalty resulted in a touchdown called back, and two of the other penalties took us out of the red zone and prevented us from scoring. We only took seven offensive linemen to the game with us, and the players we took as subs were not as good as the other players.

As the game went on, I started thinking about that sign we had in the locker room. I had to make a decision. Should I replace the left tackle that was making all of the penalties and risk putting in a player that was not as good as the left tackle, or should I wait until I got back home and sprint to the dressing room and take that sign down before the players had a chance to see it again?

I made the decision to stick to my plan and sent in the sub for the left tackle. We had no penalties in the fourth quarter and won the game 20 to 16. As I said before, before you set these standards, be ready to enforce them when the time comes to act. That was a hard decision to enforce because it was going to weaken our lineup. Not only did it help us with the game, but it helped that player. I think he only got two penalties the rest of the year.

The next point that goes along with the best team and leadership is the phrase collective mentality. The establishment of a collective mentality of your team is absolutely essential in taking a group of individuals and turning them into a unified team. That collective mentality is based on what you have set up as the profile of your team. It may be toughness, pursuit, or eliminating penalties. Your team must have a collective mentality to the identity of the team you are establishing. They must have a collective mentality to game situations in order to be the best team.

If you are in the two-minute situation of the game and nine of the players know exactly what is going on, and two players are out in left field, then you do not have a collective mentality. It may be that those two players will cause you to lose the game. You must establish the collective mentality every week: "This is what we must do to beat our opponent this week."

A team has an agenda every week for a game. Someone is going to set that agenda, and it may be the parents, the booster club, the students, and in some cases, the press. Other people can set the agenda for your team. It is very important for you to set the agenda before anyone else sets it for you. That is the only way you have a chance to have a collective mentality. Often I have read the newspaper and I found our players quoted in a story. Very often the player is saying something that we told him in our team meetings about the upcoming game or why the game turned out the way it did the week before. When I see that I know our players have the collective mentality. The player is on our agenda. This is important in going into the season and it is part of being the best team.

We want a collective mentality of those principles that we think are important overall to the identity of the team. They include the things we consider essential for winning a particular game. It is not good enough to just say our defense has to play hard. We must be more specific in what we must do to be successful. We must have a collective mentality of what must be done in the game. It is more than just playing hard. If you can do that, you will have a unified effort instead of just a group of individuals. Now you are on your way to being the best team even if you do not have the best players.

I am going to move to another idea. I hope you can see how this all ties into the things I have covered. I strongly encourage you to think about what you team needs. It is hard for me to do, and it is hard for anyone to do. I recall hearing someone at a clinic say, "The hardest thing man has to do is to think." People would rather do physical activity than think. I can think of many examples in my life where that was the case. There comes a time when you need to turn off the projector, stop looking at plays, stop working on practice plans, and just start thinking about the team. "What does the team need this week? What does this player need to hear? Does he need to hear encouragement? Does he need a challenge? What does the team need?" Spend time thinking about your team. This will help you be in touch with your team. If not, then you are just coaching plays.

I have three points that come into play in thinking about your team. These things do not come into play all at the same time. First, be creative in your thinking. I do not mean you are to be bizarre and re-create the wheel, but be creative in your thinking. Be willing to get outside the box.

Second, take some risks, whether it is in your planning or in the play calling. I do not mean gamble. That is easy to do. Take some risk that will help you win.

If things are not going well, be willing to make changes. You can get a better idea of this after you establish the identity of the team. List those things you do well, and list the things you are having problems with. How are you going to fix those problems? Will the problems continue if you just change the scheme? Do you need to change personnel? If changes do not work, do not second-guess yourself.

Players do what you make them do. Players do not do what you do not make them do. By and large, your team will look the way you want it to look. They will wear their uniforms the way you want them to wear them. They will dress for road games the way you want them to dress. They will pursue the ball the way you want them to pursue the ball. They will avoid penalties the way you want them to avoid penalties. They will be responsible for their academics if you make them do it. Figure out what the identity of your team is. Have a picture in your mind what you want your team to look like and how you want them to perform and act. Players do what you make them do. Players do not do what you do not make them do. That is why you are the coach.

The best players do not always win. The best team always wins. That is a simple saying that I think summarizes a lot of things in football.

Players know what is expected of them, and you establish accountability with this. Players must be held accountable for what you want them to do. There are consequences if they do not do what you want them to do. That does not mean you're heavy-handed. You are running the team. Some people will say some coaches are "control freaks." What is the opposite of control? Out-of-control is the opposite. So that is a compliment to be called a control freak.

Players do what you make them do. Players must be accountable to the standards you set for them. Players must know the consequences for that accountability is. We have found over the years that you can demand a lot out of a player, and the bottom line is the player will know you are on his side. If a player knows you are on his side, he will respond. You can be an easy coach, but if the players does not think you are on his side, he will not respond the way you want him to. You can be a hard coach, but if the player believes you are on his side, he will respond.

Every sports team must decide what their kind of guy is. It does not have to be the NFL or colleges. You must know the profile of the players. Know what your kind of player is. What do you want to make the players do? Every organization should know this information.

In closing I want to thank you for your time. Good luck next year.

KEY ELEMENTS IN THE WEST COAST OFFENSE

Tampa Bay Bucs

This is my first clinic lecture in fifteen years. I am excited about doing this lecture. Coach Johnny Majors was my first boss at the University of Tennessee. He asked me last spring if I would be interested in doing a clinic. I told him I would be very interested in doing a clinic. Whatever Coach Majors tells me to do, that is what I will do.

I was a grad assistant in 1985 at Tennessee. I did not really know anything about football, but I was the scout team coordinator for the defense. Coach Majors was sitting up in the stands of Neyland Stadium watching practice one day. It had the wrong script for the practice period. They were in the perimeter period and were running screens and waggles. I was in our blitz period for the session. I was blitzing the hell out of the offense. I heard Coach Majors yelling at me from the stands. "Hey, GA, you are in the wrong period." I had to work hard to overcome that mistake, but he did allow me to come back to practice the next day.

I know many of you coach high school football. My dad was a former high school coach. I have a real appreciation for what you guys do for young people. I am talking not only about players, but also people in general.

Having moved to Florida from Indiana late in my high school career, I know football is good down here. It is as good as it gets in Florida. It is amazing the speed of the athletes in Florida. The way you guys coach the players is fantastic. It is a real privilege to be here, it really is. I am looking forward to some fellowship with you guys.

You and I have a lot in common in terms of football. We love the game of football. We have to develop players, and we have to develop our team. To do that, we must study and we must be together. We must find new ways to do things.

When I was asked to give this talk, I had no idea of what they wanted me to talk about. Most of my experience has been on the offensive side of the ball. When I got the brochure on the clinic and I saw my topic was "The West Coast Offense," I kind of laughed. Today I met 15 to 20 coaches in the lobby that run our offense. They told me, "Hey, Coach, we run your offense." My reply was, "I guess that means I am running your offense." What I have learned over the last seven or eight years in this style of football is the perception out there is this: If you run a slant pattern, you run the West Coast offense. If you run a wide flare pass, you run the West Coast offense. If the quarterback has to reset and pull the ball down, you run the West Coast offense. If you run the split backfield set, you run the West Coast offense. It is almost to the point where it is ridiculous.

The way I see it, the West Coast offense is Bill Walsh. Bill Walsh was trained by Paul Brown in the late 1960s. Bill put together an attack with the San Francisco 49ers that was very exclusive to them. The West Coast offense was a tag that was created by the media. There is not a playbook that Andy Reid has in Philadelphia, that Mike Holmgren has in Seattle, or that we have in Tampa that is exactly the same. We all interpret the game differently. I think we all appreciate that fact.

I have seen some of you here today working on the field. Several of you coach the triple option. But none of you coach it the same way. That is how football is in general.

I want to try to give you some feedback on how we coach our offense in Tampa. It does not matter if you call it the West Coast offense or the Gulf Shore offense. In Philadelphia, we called it the Jersey

Shore offense. In Oakland, we called it the silver and black attack. I really liked that title. It does not matter what we call it, we all have a philosophy of the game.

In college, I learned football under Walt Harris. It was the run and shoot offense. I was a freeze option quarterback at the University of Dayton. So I have been around a lot of different people in football. Whatever your philosophy is, I think it is important to have a mindset. So before I get into the offense, I just want to talk about the mind-set. A lot of defensive coaches are in here today. So I am going to talk offensive football for the next hour or so. I want to come clean with you, and I want to tell you how we convey our offense to our players.

We are going to coach our offense with a defensive mind-set. When we get in our meeting with our offensive team, we are going to coach them very much like Monte Kiffin coaches the defensive team. We are going to be physical. At times, we are going to be very violent, legally, in how we play the game. Legally, we are going to punish the defense with a physical style and a relentless attack.

Our tempo is going to be fast, and our style is going to be unique. We are going to punish the defense, and they must know that every day they step on the field. We are going to finish plays. Every play in our offense is designed to score touchdowns. That is not always the case. When the defensive corner or safety or linebacker makes a tackle to stop us from scoring a touchdown, we like to see him getting up with his helmet turned sideways. We know he's probably thinking, "Gee, I feel like a train just hit me!" We try to establish a mind-set that we are gong to be physical on offense.

We are study our opponent's defense. We find out what base front you are using. We are going to find out what your primary coverage is. We are going to try to find a weak link in the front and the coverage. We try to find match-ups where we can get our best players against the worst defensive player. We try to exploit that match-up as much as we can. That is a big part of our offensive mind-set.

I looked up the word offensive in Webster's Dictionary. I found two meanings. The first definition is this: "An attempt to score in a game or contest." The other meaning is "a painful or unpleasant sensation." For example, we can talk about an offensive odor. In some of the games when I have called the play, we have stunk it up. We were very offensive. We have had some offensive games where we were brilliant. So your team needs to understand you are going to be very good if you execute at a premium level and that you are physical. There is a chance if you are not going to do this you can really stink the game up. Your team must understand this concept. So that is what offensive means.

I am going to get into a video tape and give you a presentation of the film. Instead of showing you plays on the overhead and showing you the techniques we use at Tampa Bay, I want to use the film to illustrate my points.

When I was a high school quarterback I was not very good. When I was a Division III quarterback at the University of Dayton, I was not very good. As a result, I never had access to a film to see myself on tape. When I went to Tennessee as a GA, I got to see all kinds of film. They took film from the end zone, from behind the huddle, from the sideline, and with handheld cameras. I learned a long time ago that "what you see on film is what you coach." We can go to all the clinics we want, and I can tell you about the things we do, but those things by themselves are not necessarily what we are coaching. So I want to take this time to show you some things that I think are important.

This is a tape we will show to our football team and to our young quarterbacks. I made this tape especially for today.

I want our players to know the players are going to practice their butts off in Philadelphia. I know that because I once coached there. They are going to practice hard in Green Bay. They are going to work their tails off, and they are going to be in the playoffs. I know this. They are going to be ready for us in San Francisco. Practicing hard is not what the game is all about. That is because all teams are going to practice hard. They do it from coast to coast. But in Tampa Bay we say we are going to practice hard and we are going to practice smart. Regardless of the style of offense or defense you run, you better have a great program in terms of practice.

I want to talk to you about a few things I think will help you win a championship. It does not matter if we are talking about winning the Super Bowl, National Championship, State Championship, or League Championship. To win a championship, you must practice.

The first thing we want to do is this. Do not underestimate the importance of the center-quarterback exchange. The worst thing about the center-quarterback exchange is that we waste a lot of time. You can get this problem ironed out before practice. Get the centers and quarterbacks together before practice, or in a gym class, or after practice. We do not waste our time with the center-quarterback exchange. There is nothing more defeating than not being able to get the snap on the football field. We make a big deal about this.

We really want to coach the huddle. When you get into the huddle, you must call out the play clearly and distinctly. "Flip right – double X jet - 36 counter – naked waggle – at 7 X quarter – heads-up at 358 – bull's-eye on one." You really have to spit it out loud and clear. We want to get everyone's attention.

When we break the huddle, we want to line up briskly. We want to get our butts in and out of the huddle, get up to the line, and get set so we can attack the defense. We may assign a coach to coach the huddle. If that coach does not like the way we broke the huddle and if we are not crisp and sharp, we will redo the huddle and break it again. I think it is important to film your huddle. Film the huddle in training camp. The huddle is habitual. If you take pride in the way you break the huddle, the players will break it the way you want it to be broken. This is something worth talking about. A lot of information must be conveyed in the huddle. When we come out of the huddle, we must take the proper splits. Then we must come off the ball and go hard.

This is the progression we believe in. It all starts in the huddle. It all starts with the center exchange. We have used this system from coast to coast, and it has worked for us. If you want a copy of this tape, I will send it to you.

I do not want to waste a lot of time on the practice field yelling at players to hit someone. Instead, I want to coach our system. I want the players to know we are not going to grab jerseys. We do not want our defensive players to grab jerseys. That is why we have so many poor tacklers in football. They are all grabbers now. I want to show them what we want to do and why we do not want to grab jerseys.

We let our players know we do not want to hit a defensive teammate. We do not want to hit him on the practice field. We show it to them on film so they know what we want. We do not want our defensive backs or our linebackers splattering our receivers all over the practice field. There will be plenty of time for that in the games. The receivers have to take an unbelievable amount of punishment in games.

This is a big point. I want to have a certain amount of etiquette on the practice field. Before we get into any type of scheme, we want to make sure we are not going to hurt our own people. Defensive players and coaches tend to get upset because they are the ones that want to kill the offensive players. At the same time, we let the defensive linebackers know we are not going to peel back and crack block on them and try to put them out of the game. We want to make sure we practice with a certain amount of etiquette, and we want to show the players what we are talking about.

I want to make a couple of other key points. We want to make sure everyone stays away from the quarterback in practice in terms of contact. This may be a point that fits with pro football, but bear with me for a minute. If you beat a back on a block, or you get past the tackles pass block and you have a chance to make a play on the quarterback, stay away from him. Again, we tell the players not to grab jerseys.

We have a lot of players that like to fight. I have a meeting before we go out on the field to let the players know there will be no fighting. If they fight, someone may get hurt and they may get hurt real bad. We spend time with our players going over these things because we think they are very important. I think these things are worth spending 20 minutes on with them.

Our players better understand the snap count. There is nothing worse than spending 15 minutes of practice because of a fumbled snap, or when players cannot stay onsides. I watched our football team self-destruct this year. It was because we could not stay onsides in key situations. We are paying a quarterback six million dollars, we are paying our two tackles thirty million dollars, and we can't stay onsides. It is because of a lack of concentration. That can not be tolerated. We make a big deal with that part of the game.

We tell our defensive players not to bat footballs down. We are paying our secondary coach, our receiver coach, our wide receivers, and our secondary players a lot of money. In fact, we were paying one of our receivers too much money. I don't want them to bat balls down. I ask the defensive line coach to work with the players on this. I want to be able to see the film and I want to be able to see the route the receivers are running. I want to see our players catch the football.

If you are going to play for Tampa Bay, or for any team, we are going to finish plays. It is hard in a game to catch a pass and go the distance. If you do not practice making long runs, you will not make them in the game. Is the left tackle going to get the cutoff block? Is he going to finish the play? It is hard to catch the short pass and go the distance for the score. You must practice with that mind-set of being a great finisher. As coaches we enforce this point all of the time.

It is very difficult to make a long run in the NFL. I know a player in the NFL that carried the ball 500 times, and his longest run was 48 yards. You have to work to get your yardage. You have to work to finish plays. To become great, you must practice with that

state of mind. It just takes a great effort. You must practice finishing plays. That is how you are going to play. When we practice an inside period or a team period, we want to see our players finish the play.

You must practice with gamelike speed. The defense must go full speed, and they must pursue the football. To make the great play, you must make them in practice. It is the same as you do when you make a routine play. We try to sell this point to the players.

The great players have a knack of finishing the plays. I show these clips to our football team so they will know what is really going on in terms of great effort.

A player that could finish was a friend of mine. Keith Byars, the 257-pound fullback of the Miami Dolphins, ran 77 yards on Thanksgiving Day of 1993 on a simple fullback belly play. It is the still one of the longest running plays in the history of the Miami Dolphins. He was a finisher.

Another thing we stress is to never hit a defenseless teammate. In 1996, Green Bay had four players on injury reserve because our players were hit by our own players in practice. We must be smart in terms of our work ethic. Again, there is going to be plenty of time to get your team to make the plays in the game.

We tell our team they must know how to start practice, and they must know how to finish practice. You have some players that come out to practice and have a couple of nice periods, and then they just can't finish. We have some slow starters that finish strong. You must have a state of mind when you hit the practice field. You must be able to get it done. We want them to get ready to play fast. We do not want them to wait until period four to start to play. You must have an instinct for the jugular vein. You must be able to finish things off.

You must be like Michael Jordan against Cleveland; end it for them. That is the state of mind we are looking for with our football team. You must be the closer in the ninth inning of the World Series. You have to finish the game. Sell this point to the team. Some of our great closers in our lifetime are also good starters. It carries over to your play. At some point and time, you are going to play 58 minutes and 51 seconds and you will have to close the game out. You are going to have to finish the game off the right way to win, or the wrong way to lose.

I try to make it a big point to our football team on these issues. You must have a strong state of mind. Start fast, finish strong! The key in practice is that you must have a championship mind-set. When you step on the practice field, you better think like a champion. You must have a great state of mind because, before you get the first snap, a lot of things are going to happen. Those are the keys we go over with our football team in terms of how we practice.

Now I will go over some key components of the West Coast offense. Since 1992 the Green Bay Packers have had one quarterback start every single game. We all know that quarterback is Brett Favre. Think about that for a second. How many players have you coached at one position since 1992? You say Green Bay should be good since they have had the same quarterback since 1992, right, guys?

In the offense we are talking about today, you must have an offense that suits your quarterback. The system must be adaptable to your quarterback. You may have plans for the first- and second-string quarterback, but what plans do you have for your third-string quarterback? The reality of it is you do not know who your quarterback is going to be at the end of the game. The point I am trying to sell you on today is to have an offense that suits your quarterback.

If you have three quarterbacks it is like having three sons if you are the offensive coordinator. They do not all like the same kind of ice cream. They do not all like the same movie. They do not all like the same things. Let's have a system in football that truly allows them to do their best. If we do not do that, then we are not very good coaches. That is my opinion.

The passing offense we are looking for is a high percentage, low risk offense. We would love to see the quarterback complete 70 percent of his passes with a lot of touchdowns and with very few interceptions. When we won the Super Bowl, Brad Johnson threw for 64 percent on completions, with 22 touchdowns and only six interceptions. That was outstanding. That is a high percentage, low risk offense.

We talk to our team a lot about team route distribution. I cannot stand to see wide receivers and backs stacked on top of each other. We want to get five receivers dispersed very quickly all over the field. We want great route distribution. We want disciplined routes. We want to see decision making by the quarterback that is very sound.

A good example is a play like 22 hank. That is a play all of the West Coast offensive teams run. You let the five eligible receivers go out. You are running two hooks and two flat routes, and are putting the tight end over the ball in the middle. We read it from the inside to the outside. By the end of the day 22 hank is like a five on a dice in Las Vegas. Do any of you roll the dice? Hank means hook. We have two outside receivers running the hooks, we have two intermediate receivers in the medium flare control, and we have the tight, who is the primary receiver, coming over the middle to the ball. However you set hank up, it's a play with great route distribution and a play the quarterback has to read.

No matter how you set the play up and no matter how you coach the quarterback, you want to try to get quick, disciplined route distribution and let the quarterback make a high percentage decision. That is what we are talking about. It is a low risk play. We will throw the short pass and let the receiver run after the catch. It is high percentage, low risk football. We will get into the routes another day.

I think you must have a conservative protection plan. When we have meetings with our staff, the line coach has a lot of clout on how we are going to handle pass protection. We must have a conservative mind-set to protect our quarterback. We do not want to tell the quarterback how important he is and then send him out in a game and allow the defense to knock his butt off. We must have some type of conservative protection plan. That means we must be able to audible, and we must have hot receivers. If there is a defensive end that we are having trouble blocking, we may have to send a back or a tight end that way to help against that man. We want a conservative but well-understood protection play.

We must rehearse the protection plan. There comes a time when you know the defense is going to blitz that bubble on the weakside. We ask our quarterback to recognize that situation. There are things you can do to help the situation. You can change to a three-step drop and throw the ball quickly. If you recognize the blitz and you see trouble, you go to a conservative protection plan. The defense may not be successful. But you must take that into account.

You may be playing a team that runs a two-deep five-under zone concept. This is a hard defense to throw against. Your protection play should allow you to be able to get five eligible receivers out to attack a two-deep five-under zone defense. You must have an audible for the quarterback to get you out of trouble. You must have a hot receiver that the quarterback understands. The more you release tight ends and backs into the patterns, the more vulnerable you are to the blitz. That is something to consider.

If you empty the backfield, you need to have a play called for the blitz. To attack that two-deep five-under defense, you must be able to get the receivers out on their routes. So you must take into account that the more people you release into the pattern, the more you open yourself up to the blitz situation.

We stress to our backs that they have a responsibility to pass block. If the man they are responsible for does not come on a blitz, they are to check to see if someone on our line is having trouble with their man before they release into the pattern. If their man does not come, they are to check and then release. That is their checklist for the game. A block by the back can take the sting off the quarterback,

and that is what we are trying to do. We tell them to check, to chip block if we need help, and then to release.

You must have a conservative protection play. As you well know, a great pass rusher can ruin a good day for a passing team. It does not matter how good your schemes are; without a great protection plan, you are not going to be able to block some of the premier rushers. If you can't block those guys, you can be in for a long day. It may be too late in the game before you pick up what the defense is doing if you are not prepared to have a conservative protection plan. It is something for you to think about.

I am trying to show you that what you see on the film is what you coach. We are not all perfect, and that is for darn sure. But we are going to practice the protection plan restlessly. It is important for your backs and quarterbacks to be able to go to sleep the night before the game looking forward to the blitz. They should look forward to the process. You may have to walk through the blitz package you expect to see for a game. You may want to go out a few minutes before, or stay a few minutes after practice, and walk through some of the blitzes you expect to see so the quarterback feels comfortable about the situation. You want to make sure your offensive backs and line are ready to go against anything the defense can throw at them.

The protection play must be executed, and it must be well rehearsed. The quarterback has to get the play from the sideline, go into the huddle, and convey the play to his teammates, and you want his state of mind to be confident. You do not want him to be worried about getting knocked on his rear end.

You must have drills to find out which of your backs like football. You must find out which one of your backs loves to catch one of the safeties on a blitz and knock him on his butt. We practice picking up the blitz. It may just be a walk-through, with the defense showing the quarterback where they are coming from. You do not need a lot of players involved to show the quarterback where the blitz is coming from. We want to make him comfortable with the protection system. We can let the guards make the calls on the protection. You would be shocked how many reps you can get done in 30 to 40 minutes.

Another factor in the West Coast offense is that we are going to use all five eligible receivers. That may get some of the players upset. Some receivers want to be the primary receiver on every pattern. The way I have learned this system is that we are going to use all eligible receivers whenever we can.

Here is another play: red right 22 Z in. I am sure some of you may have read about it in Bill Walsh's book. The 22 Z in is a strong side triangle with strong hot protection (see Diagram #1). It is a simple play. It is a strongside play where the quarterback is taking a five-step one hitch drop and throwing a 12-yard turn pass to the flanker. If the flanker is not open, he dips his front shoulder and kicks it to the Y square. If he does not have the Y square, he resets and throws the ball to the tight end that is running the short drop route. The X receiver runs an alert post on the weakside for the full blitz read. We have a two-by-two check down by the protecting back. The play is designed to throw the ball to the flanker on time.

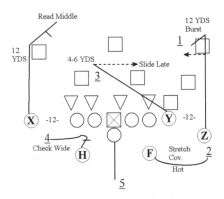

Diagram #1. Red right 22 Z in

There may be times when we you run the West Coast offense where the quarterback does not like the throw on the play. He may not want to throw the ball to the flanker. You may have to get the ball to the ball on the play. There may be times when the defense covers the flanker on the play. We are running the patterns in the triangle. All three receivers are active. There is a progression in which the quarterback is going to work.

The offense is about high percentage throws and route distributions. It is about keeping the chains moving. If you are going to run the West Coast offense, all five receivers must run their routes hard. You have to sell the receivers that they must run hard on all routes. If you are going to have a strong hot protection and you see a team that runs the strong zone dog blitz, you must have a hot receiver.

You must work on the contingency plan. We practice the contingency plan over and over. If the defense brings one more man than you have, the bubble must go somewhere. At some point you may have to take your quarterback and let him practice with the receiver on the route. You may have to practice the route over and over again with them. It all starts with rhythm.

You want to see if the quarterback can recognize the blitz and if he knows the contingency play for that play. He must be able to get us out of the bad play and into a good play. So we work on a contingency plan of changing plays.

Another key element of the West Coast offense is that we want to present to the defense an illusion of complexity and sophistication. I even try to learn three- and four-syllable words so people think I am a lot smarter than I really am. I was a 2.2 GPA student when I was in high school. I know very little about anything. When you start using words like illusion and complexity and sophistication, it sounds like you are a smart guy.

I want the defense to say this about our offense: "Man, they have a lot of stuff on offense." But in our minds we are real simple, and we are real basic. Think about that as we look at some other plays.

Here is a simple play you all have seen. You can call it smoke or whatever you want to call it. This is our 200 jet smoke route. (see Diagram #2). You have two slant routes and two flat routes. I have even run this play out of a two back set. It was a good play against the Raiders when they had 12 men on the field.

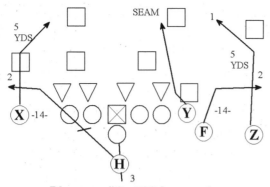

Diagram #2. 200 jet smoke

You can come back the next week and line up in a double tight end set. You can move the one end from left to right. You can use motion to get the quarterback to work away from rotation. It is an illusion of complexity and sophistication. Each week, we are going to have the 200 or 300 jet smoke play in our package. It does not have to be the whole game plan. It could be an audible play. We do not care who we throw the ball to on the play. There is nothing better than a slant pattern because you have a chance to score if you have the right receiver.

You can run the play from trips. You can send one back in motion across the formation and still run the play. It still is 200 jet smoke to us. Every week, we are going to have the play in our game plan, and each week it will be run a little different. It may be from two tight ends with the flanker in motion, or it may be from backfield motion. There are several ways to run the 200 jet smoke play. The next week, we change it to 200 jet drag.

Then we take the tight end out of the game and run it with four wide receivers. It is still 200 jet smoke. You can run it on first down or on third down. It is a good play. And as I said you can use it as an audible.

The key is we are using the same play out of different formations. It is the illusion of complexity and sophistication in the play that makes it a good play. We are just looking for completions. We want to fast break and get the ball out of the hands of the quarterback. We want to distribute the ball to all five eligible receivers. We try to find different ways to run the same play that our quarterback likes to run, and run them over and over.

We like to use an array of personnel groupings in formation. We want to have different combinations of players so we can use them when the situation calls for it. If we need a strong running back, we want to have that grouping available. We want to use this technique with the understanding that if the defense has not seen it they cannot prepare for it. When our defense works all week, they practice against plays they have seen before. The hard thing for them is to prepare for something they have not seen before. We take that into account every week.

We look at film and we may see a team that has problems with any kind of adjustment. They may have a lot of different fronts, and they are trying to play man-to-man coverage. We may start the game with a regular formation with two backs, a tight end, and two wide receivers (see Diagram #3). After a play or two, you may want to start shifting. You can bring the tight end into the backfield and send the two backs outside. You may want to throw a quick pass to keep the defense off-balance. Then you can come back with two tight ends and two backs. You can shift into a different set, and you can go into motion. You want to force the defense to always adjust to you. We are going to run plays that are very simple and plays that are understood.

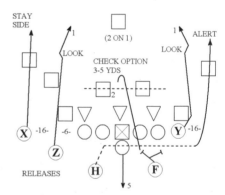

Diagram #3

We are going to game plan to force the defense to adjust to what we are doing. You can try to figure out what adjustments the defense is going to make. We want to have the tempo so fast the defense will have a hard time making the adjustments.

We want to give them a wide variety of formations and a lot of different personnel groupings. We must be ready for the blitz once we get inside the red zone. Give the defense an attack that they have not seen before and something they have not prepared for.

Another key point in designing the game plan is this. We like to start out the game by running several plays that look exactly the same. They look exactly the same, but they are different.

We want to find new ways to get the ball on the perimeter. We want to find new ways to get the perimeter offense going. Sometimes the most routine plays are the hardest plays to make.

If we start out the game with our 22 Z in route in one game, the next week we can run the same play but throw a screen pass to the backside. The defense is looking to stop the 22 Z in slant route, and we run the screen pass. So that is another key component of the West Coast offense.

Where are you in situational football in terms of the passing game? We try to break our staff down into specialized areas. We say one coach is the goal line expert, one is the short yardage expert, and another coach is in charge of two-minute situations. Each is the expert in one area. When we come together as a staff, we want someone that can identify what the other team is doing. They look at that aspect of the game all week. It is situational football. We only see a few short yardage situations. We want to be sure our football team knows what to expect on those situations.

Next I want to talk about goal line situations. It is hard to practice goal line live during the season. But you must practice on the goal line so you will be ready for it in the game.

In the two-minute drill we were very good this year. Last year we were seven for seven in fourth-and-one plays.

It does not matter if you are an option team or a passing team. At some point in time you may have to throw the football to win the game. We also use a four-minute drill similar to the two-minute drill.

(Editor's note: The last five minutes of the lecture were not recorded due to tape malfunction.)

SUCCESS — A STANDARD OF EXCELLENCE

Boise State University

It is awesome to be here because I am with a group of people I respect a great deal. Recently I was at a clinic and saw one of my former players from UC Davis. I asked him what he was doing now. He replied, "I am just a high school coach now." I looked at him and said, "Don't ever say that. Don't ever say you are just a high school coach." High school coaches have a great opportunity to mold young people's lives. I could go back to being a JV coach at any high school any time. Coaching is coaching. The opportunity to make an impact on the player's life is awesome. Don't ever underestimate that fact.

One thing I have learned at different levels of coaching is this: there are good coaches and there bad coaches at every level. I tell our staff to go see the high school coaches to learn football. I do not encourage them to go to the NFL to learn football. If you want to learn, go see some JV program where the coaches take some 170-pound kid and try to teach him how to block a 200-pound man in front of him. You can learn from that coach.

I think X's and O's are important. That is the heart of football. The sad thing is I used to go to clinics and the speakers would get up and talk about something we could not use or were not able to implement in our program. That was disappointing. I want to give you something that will help you in your program regardless of the offense or defense you use.

I have had an opportunity to be successful at a lot of different levels. When I send out my bio, it always has my record for each year I have coached. But when people ask me what I want them to say when they introduce me, this is what I tell them. I tell them just to say I have been married for 21 years to an awesome lady, and I have four great kids. This means a lot more to me that any of those stinking records that I have accumulated over the years.

I want you to know I do not have all the answers. But what I have done over the years is to try to get a handle on the things that contribute to a winning program. Some people think it is money that leads to a good football program. Some people think it's wins that lead to a quality program. It is not wins! When I became a head coach, I tried to put all of the information together that I had learned as a player and as a coach. I got my master's degree in administration and tried to put all of this information together. Going to Boise State was a big question. Could I go to a new situation and re-create what I had done before, and would it work again? When I became the head coach at Boise State, the question was, could I raise the bar once more as a head coach?

The things I am going to cover are things I believe in, and I believe they are the most important things in a winning program. We have won a lot of championships. We have used a lot of different defenses and different offenses. We have used a lot of different styles on offense. A lot of common things are extremely important.

I want you to know I am not a very smart person. I did not make most of the things I am going to talk about up. I have taken the good points from other coaches and put them into our program.

We talk to our team about this all of the time: "You cannot assure success, but you can deserve success." We ask our kids all the time, "Do you deserve to have success? Have you earned it, and have you paid the price?" If you don't deserve a chance to win, then you are leaving it up to chance.

Coaching takes a lot of time. I speak to businesses and organizations often. I use the analogy of a chair with four legs. If they took one of the four legs off, they could still sit in the chair. If they took two of the legs off the chair they would have a hard time sitting in the chair. If they took three of the legs off, it would be almost impossible to sit in the chair. Being able to balance out your life is important. You need to take time with your family. You must maintain your health, which is very important. You need to have a balanced quality of life.

We talk with our players all of the time about having a balanced quality of life. It is important for them to get their education. It is important for them to have a degree so they can coach at any level. Becoming an expert and having a lot of knowledge is important in any field.

Being able to network is important. We may not have all of the answers, so we have to be able to call on others in our field to help us at times. We must be able to talk to other people to find out how to solve problems.

If you want to have a successful organization, you must have a standard of excellence. I try to keep my administration aware of what is going on in our program. I believe things have to happen from the top.

I think it is important to have the right chemistry for any program to be successful. I continue to stress the leadership at the top and I want the administration to know what has to happen for us to have a chance to be successful.

As far as the football part of it, I really believe you must be good on defense. That is number one. We have led the nation in scoring three of the last four years at Boise State. We have had some great offensive teams the last few years. But the thing people do not realize is the fact that we have had some awesome defensive teams.

The next point relates to eliminating negative plays. The only goal we have on offense, defense, and special teams is turnovers. That is it. It is not first downs, time of possession, or completions. It is turnovers. We emphasize this in all phases of the game in practice. This is very critical in football.

The other thing we stress is this: We want to be able to create big plays. I totally believe in a solid running attack. It does not have to be fancy. If we play 7-on-7 out in the parking lot and no one was rushing me, I could be a good quarterback. Again, we want to eliminate negative plays. We want great quarterback play in our offense. I think the quarterback has to be the toughest player on the team at all levels. Not everyone will agree with this, but it is probably right.

If there is one thing I have changed as far as my philosophy is concerned over the years, it would be this. It is the "big play potential." I am all about launching the ball. I kid with my coaches a lot, but when I get the head set on for a game the thing that goes through my mind is this: "Houston, you are ready to launch." I am all about the vertical ball. It is nearly impossible to put twelve perfect plays together. It takes just as much work to protect for a 12-yard curl pass route as it does for a 40 yard takeoff route.

I do not believe you have to be very fast to run pass routes. I do not believe the quarterback has to have a rifle arm to be effective. But, I am all about getting those big chunks of yardage. I think it helps in our mentality. We are going to attack the defense. We do not play just to win. We attack our opponents. This is true on offense, defense, and special teams. We try to block kicks. We have never downed a ball on a kickoff return. Why? You cannot score a touchdown if you take a knee. On offense, we are going to launch the football.

To have a good team, you must have good talent. You must have ability on the team. You must have experience and depth on the team. Your team must have a good attitude about winning. I totally believe in preparation. We say talent plus attitude plus motivation plus motivation equals performance.. All of this leads to confidence and success. I believe it all falls together in this sequence. You gain confidence through preparation.

It's said, "Fundamentally, the Zen master seeks not the target, but rather to become the bow."

What does all of this mean? It means the more you try to win the less you are going to win. The first time I told our players this they looked at me like I was a German shepherd. What does this mean? It means we are going to try to do things right. We are going to try to become that instrument of excellence. To say you are going out to win is important. But I can tell you that Martin Luther King, Thomas Edison, or Gandhi did not take a knee, so I am not going to take a knee. The whole deal is your philosophy and your style. It is who you become. You must try to exude that. It is really your personality. So we are not just trying to win a game. We are trying to become an instrument of excellence.

Here is another way of looking at success. Mihaly Csikszentmihalyi used something like this to describe success. You can find more on the subject by reading material by an Austrian psychiatrist, Viktor Frankl, who put that same thought into these words: "Don't aim at success. The more you aim at it and make it a target, the more you are going to miss it. For success, like happiness, cannot be pursued, it must ensue as the unintended side-effect of one's personal dedication to a course greater than oneself."

In other words, it is the journey, and the way we perceive that journey, that brings happiness. It is not reaching a long-sought goal that makes us happy.

That is what football coaches do. We are trying to create magic. We go to the movies and we laugh, cry, and have great emotional experiences. Football should be a great experience. You must be willing to throw yourself into the situation and become a part of the total situation.

I want to talk about some key things that people in successful organizations do. The first point is goal-setting. I am really big on this. I have four kids, and I used to read to them at night. I used to read Alice In Wonderland to them. There is a scene where Alice is going through the Enchanted Forest.

She comes up on a Cheshire cat and asks the cat if she could help her get out of the forest. The cat asks her where she wanted to go. Alice said, "I am not real sure." The cat replied, "It really does not matter which path you take."

Now how does all of this fit into this lecture? There is one fundamental question we ask our team several times during the season. "Are the things you are doing getting you close to your goals or are they getting you father away from your goals?" That is very simply put. That takes some courage to look into a mirror and answer that question.

I ask this question of myself as a husband, a father, a coach, and as a person every day. Am I getting closer to my goals, or am I getting farther away from my goals? This question is all I have to ask the players. It is very simple to ask, but difficult to answer at times.

"A sailing ship which knows no port finds no winds favorable." This saying has great significance for me. If you are a sailboat and the wind blows, you have no idea which way to attack it if you do not know which way you are going. There are all kinds of offenses and all kind of plays you can run in football. In the grand scheme of things, that does not matter to me. All that matters is that you know where you are going and you know what you are trying to accomplish and you work toward that goal. That is the most important thing.

When I was a high school coach, I used to run around in the off-season looking for better plays. I would go to clinics and look up coaches to show me new plays. Now we spend more time on our own deal. We watch our own film and evaluate how we do things. We are not so worried about what the plays other teams are running. It is about us. We focus on our team and what we do.

We have goals, just as most of you have goals. We have achieved most of our goals. We sit down with our team and come up with our goals. Then I have them back that up with what it will take for us to achieve those goals.

It is easy to shoot low in setting goals. You become a target if you shoot too high. In our players' minds, they think they have a shot at winning the National Championship. That is one of their goals.

We talk about dealing with adversity. Anyone can play when you are ahead. Anyone can coach when you are way ahead. When you are behind, you find out who you really are. We try to turn setbacks into comebacks. We know we must be willing to take risk. We have to get out of our comfort zone when bad things happen. When things go bad, we can go into a tank, or we can use the incident to get better.

Here is a very powerful book. I mentioned a quote from it earlier. It is Man's Search for Meaning by Viktor Frankl. He was a Jewish doctor that had his mother, his father, his wife, and his job taken from him by the Nazis in World War II.

In the book, Frankl says, "The ultimate freedom in life is determined by the attitude in a certain set of circumstances. He who has a desire to live can bear almost any out."

If you study the concentration camps, you know why he said that. One reason he made it out of the camps was because he found joy in living in the most undesirable circumstance.

How many of you have seen the movie Life Is Beautiful? Get the Italian version with the English subtitles. The movie has a great message. I do not want to spoil it for you. The star in the movie is carrying this big anvil. He starts telling his buddy with him it too heavy and he cannot lift it. As the anvil is getting close to the ground, he repeats the fact that it is too heavy and he cannot carry it outside. His buddy tells him, "If it hits the ground, I will shoot you!" Immediately he replies, "It is not that bad, I can do it!"

I think the whole idea of learning to appreciate something when it is tough takes some mental work. We all know it is easy when things are going good.

I watch a lot of pro games during the year. I see them line up to punt the football and see them fake the punt very few times. I know fake punt plays are wide open, but few teams take advantage of the situation. I went to a friend of mine in pro football and asked him why they did not fake the punt more in pro football. He said, "No one ever got fired in pro football for not faking the punt."

It is not easy sometimes to play it safe. We are afraid of failing. We are not willing to get out of our comfort zone. That is a hard thing to do. I use the story of Roger Bannister to illustrate the point. Doctors told him he could not run a mile under four minutes. They told him his heart would blow up if he went that fast.

Roger Bannister ran the first sub-four-minute on May 6, 1954. It was the first sub-four-minute mile in recorded history. The 25-year-old native of Harrow on the Hill, England, completed the distance in 3:59.4 at Oxford. The next year, the sub-four-minute mile was run ten or twelve times. Others believe they could do it because Roger Bannister did it. We have to develop that appreciation.

Here is another way at looking at adversity and taking risk. It is a quote by Anais Nin: "Then the time came when the risk it took to remain tight in a bud was more painful than the risk it took to blossom."

The fact we have led the nation in scoring three of the last four years had much more to do with our attitude than it did with our X's and O's. It is not about us failing or making mistakes. I talk to our players all of the time: "Get the bat on your shoulder and swing it." We are going to do that.

We can rationalize a lot of things. We are a no-excuses outfit. We believe everything is possible. We are going to shoot that way.

Marianne Williamson says, "Our deepest fear is not that we are inadequate. Our deepest fear is that we are powerful beyond measure. It is our light, not our darkness, that most frightens us. We ask ourselves, 'Who am I to be brilliant, gorgeous, talented, and fabulous?' Actually, who are you not to be? You are a child of God. Your playing small does not serve the world. There is nothing enlightened about shrinking so that other people won't feel insecure around you. We were born to make manifest the glory of God within us. It is not just in some of us: it is in everyone. As we let our own light shine, we are liberated from our fear."

When your anxiety level starts to go up, your performance goes up. There are two things to consider. In practice, you want the anxiety level up. We want the energy level up. We are going to go hard, and we are going to go fast. We are going to coach them hard, and we are going to work fast in practice. We want a good tempo in practice.

When we get in a game, we want to be able to relax. We want to have fun in the game. It must be in that ideal area here. This is how I explain this idea to our players.

If we relate football practice to practice driving a car, we can see the point Lets say all week you drove a small Volkswagen bus and on Saturday someone gave you an eighteen wheeler to drive, you would have some concerns. You would say, "That is not what I practiced on during the week." This is what happens with your emotional level in this case.

People ask me about my pregame talk. They want to know what I tell our players before a game. We have three goals for each game. We want to play hard, play smart, and have fun. I tell our players all the time. "This is a great game. Go out and have fun playing this great game." Typically I can tell what our team or the other team is going to do for a game based on their anxiety before the game.

Chuang Tzu wrote, "When archers shoot for a prize of gold they begin to see two targets; when they shoot for the brass buckle, they get nervous; when they shoot for enjoyment, they have all of their skills."

It is a fine line on this point. We are not trying to teach our players to win. I am really not teaching them to win. We do not talk about winning. We go back to talking about doing it our way and correcting ourselves. We talk about playing hard, solid football. We want to live our philosophy. When we come back in after the game, we want to be happy.

An unknown person said, "Only those that risk going too far will ever know how far they can go."

We talk with our team about this all of the time. I am asking them to do the unnatural. Have you seen the movie Secondhand Lions? There is a very interesting scene where Robert Duvall is telling his kids what it takes to be a man. One of the kids asks him, "Is it true?" Duvall replies, "It has to be true because we have to believe in something." A lot of times that is what happens in sports. We have to believe in the altruistic values the game of football will give us. This is what we are trying to get our players to do. We want them to live the unnatural. I am asking them to be abnormal and I know it. I understand it. I want them to be a success.

I want my guys to get on the horse and cut it loose. That is all I want them to do. I do not want them to be afraid to fail.

Hoka hey! Does anyone know what this means? It means, "It is a great day to die." I like to study Eastern philosophy. The people of the East spend more time developing the mental life than we do. Hoka hey means to us that we are not afraid to cut it loose. We are ready to get on our horse, ride into battle, and cut it loose. That is what I want our players to do. I want them to get on in life and cut it loose and not be afraid to fail.

After we lost the game to Oregon, there were some people that were upset with the officials. When we got into the locker room, this is what I told the players. "I do not want anyone to blame the officials for our loss today. If you blame someone else, basically you are taking your hands off the steering wheel. We had a bad snap on a punt, we missed getting the first down on a fake punt, and we had them on a third down and 18 yards to go, and could not stop them. We have no one to blame but ourselves for the loss."

I love it when someone is late and they give me some silly excuse. "It wasn't my fault, coach; the alarm clock did not go off. What should we do to this player? Should we take his scholarship away? Should we get him another alarm clock, or kick the alarm clock off the team? What should we do? We must tell them they must take responsibility for what they do. We all have a slice of responsibility in everything we do.

Our players expect to win, and they expect to play well. Some teams expect to lose the game before it starts. I use this analogy with the players to get this point across. If you walk up to the foul line with no time showing on the clock and you have to shoot two free throws to win the game, what is the first thing that enters your mind? "I hope I do not miss the free throws!" Isn't that right? That is usually the first thing that enters the mind. It should be something like this when a person gets that opportunity. "Hey, man, I have a chance to win the game. This is awesome, baby. This is where I want to be.."

Another analogy I use to illustrate this point is with my son Cody. When we moved to Boise, they moved him up a level in the baseball league. It was tough on him to move up to the next level. In his first dozen or so times, he struck out. I went to see him play one day and could not find him. I asked where he was, and someone told me he was in the dugout. I went down to the dugout and asked him what the problem was. He told me he had an upset stomach. I told him that was not the problem; the problem was because he was afraid he was going to strike out again. What happened was he would get up to bat and take a pitch to see if the pitcher could get the ball over the plate for a strike. After the first strike, he would stand there and wait for a second strike. By that time, he was certain the pitcher could not throw a third strike, so he took the next pitch. And three strikes and you are out in baseball.

I told Cody he had to think about what he was doing. I said, "If I give you a dollar for each time you swing the bat, will you get the bat off the shoulder and make an effort to hit the ball?" He told me he would take three swings of the bat instead of taking the three strikes. He started doing much better hitting the ball after that. I told him to go out and play and to have fun and things worked out a lot better for him. I told him to think about hitting home runs instead of striking out.

I asked Jerry Pettibone, who was the head coach at Oregon State at the time, what he noticed about programs that were outstanding. He said the one thing he noticed was that their locker rooms were immaculate. Every good team had an immaculate locker room. It was cleaned up, and it looked nice. I think this all goes back to what your standards and expectations are. Once you make the decision to go first-class it filters across the board to all phases of your life. It has nothing to do with football. It has to do with your philosophy and what your standard is.

Mihaly Csikszentmihalyi said, "The best moments occur when a person's body is stretched to its limit in a voluntary effort to accomplish something difficult and worthwhile. Optimal experience is thus something that we make happen."

I recall a coach saying this a long time ago. "You must have a mental picture in your mind of how a play was supposed to look and how it was supposed to work." I still believe that is true today. Most great businessmen, religious leaders, politicians, and coaches have a real strong vision of what their programs should be like.

I talk to our captains about this all of the time, and I believe it as a head coach. "If you are not making things happen it is time for the manager to say it is impossible." That is a fine line. I really think this is the difference between a manager and a leader. A leader is going to find that magic dust or that magic potion that makes things happen.

I told my wife this last year because of the success we have had in the past couple of years. Sometimes coaching is a little like being on a mountain top. At times it is not a comfortable place to be.

We talk about having a positive atmosphere at our practices. Pro scouts come by to see us and they tell us they do not hear us screaming and yelling at our players. They do not hear us using profanity, and they do not hear us screaming at players. That is just not our style. I believe the practice field must be a positive environment. We do not allow our players to make fun of other players. If they do, they have to do pushups right there.

"Don't sweat the small stuff." Do the small things and the big things will take care of themselves? This is what it is all about. You better sweat the small stuff. I read an article after the winter Olympics in Utah. The difference between the medal winners and the nonmedal winners was two percent. In 2001, we were 8-4. We lost a close game to Louisiana Tech, and we ended up second in the conference. I asked the team after the season where we could find two percent more for the next season. That is really not a lot. But that is what football is all about. In football and life, the difference between good and average is very small. The difference between good and excellent is very small.

I believe in continuity, consistency, attitude, and how you do things bears itself out over time. I am not saying that there has to be change in this process. You may get to a point where you may want to change your philosophy and your offense and the way you do things in the middle of the season. You may want to dramatically change things. But I think it is best to be consistent and make changes gradually.

We talk to our players about winning on the field and losing off the field. What does that mean? Nine times out of ten the things that pop up for us have nothing to do with football. We tell our players to take care of the problems off field so when they do get to the field we can cut it loose. If we can do that, we have a chance to win. Otherwise we have a bunch of holes, and we will have to plug up those holes to keep the boat afloat. We end up just trying to patch things up, and it is hard to win like that. Again, we are not perfect. Our team understands if there are a bunch of issues off the field, it is going to make it difficult for us to be successful.

Is the whole idea of success winning? We say it is the process of winning that is the most important aspect of the game. We have to invest in the process. The sad thing about Division I football is this. If you do not win enough games, you get fired, and it does not matter about the process. They fire you if you do not win. But still you must be clued in as to what the process is. You have to live that process.

You can go out and play a good game and still lose. You can go out and play a crummy game and still win. You can win some games, and it still feels like a loss because of the way you played. The players get this feeling depending on how the head coach talks to them. I am not concerned about the score. I am concerned about how we do things.

We talk about Big Team and little me. It is all about having a role on the team. You win with material, and you lose with potential. We do not talk about "should be"; instead we talk about "being here now." We do not want excuses. We just want to get it done. No excuses; get it done.

I tell our coaches this all of the time: "When a kid makes a mistake on the team that is the coaches' fault." If you are going to take the responsibility to coach the players, it is your fault if they make mistakes. Don't be like the math teacher that tells his friend he cannot teach his students because they are knuckleheads. That is the job for the teacher. That is what the teacher is there for. If the kid makes a mental mistake, don't blame the kid; blame the teacher.

I recall an incident that sticks with me that indicates my views on this subject. When I was an assistant at UC Davis, we were walking out to the practice field. The head coach asked me to work with one of the players on his techniques that day. I told the head coach I was having trouble with that one players. I said, "I have gone over the techniques with that player a thousand times, and he still does not get it. He must be the dumbest player in the country, and he still does not get it." The head coach got up in my face and said, "You must be the dumbest coach in the country because if you told him a thousand times and he still doesn't get it, you better change your teaching techniques." I got the message very quickly that day. I really believe this is true more than ever now in football. If a player continues to make mistakes, it is as much the coach's fault as it is the player's fault.

I want to talk about the positive side of success. One of the worst things you can do with the growth of your team is to embarrass them, humiliate them, and cuss them, or beat them down. If you do that, they will not play to win; they will play not to lose. It is the first major hurdle to get you over to being what they should be. If you want a better marriage, better kids, or a better football team, do these things.

Everyone wants a sense of belonging. They want to feel like they have people on their side. I have our staff fill out a card for each player on how they are going to get each player to develop this sense of belonging. Everyone wants a sense of power. Everyone wants to have an impact, and they want to have a say in things. If we do not get those things, we do not feel like we are important. I always give our staff and players a chance to voice their opinions on how we do things so they feel they have an impact on what we do.

Everyone wants to feel they are good at something. The only I can not figure out is golf. We are all bad at golf, and we still play the game. You know how that works. But generally we all want to be good at something. I tell our coaches to find out what their players are good and work with him to become better. It they are not good at something, I tell them to make them good as something. I want them to make the players believe they are good at something. If you want to make your players feel good, walk around and tell them, "Hey man, you are unbelievable in picking up the blitz. I know I can count on you most of the time." That player has a good feeling about himself. He thinks, "Hey, I am doing something good."

Everyone is needed. Everyone has a role to play. I try to play as many of our players as possible. We play a lot of players. If they can do something consistently we are going to get them in the game.

One of my favorite books is by Phil Jackson, and the name of the book is Sacred Hoops. Here is a quote from the book. This is a good point: "The most effective way to forge a winning team is to call on the player's need to connect with something larger than themselves. A successful team is essentially a spiritual act. The trick is to experience each moment with a clear mind and open heart. When you do that the game, and life, will take care of its self. Our journey is a sacred quest. This is when the spirit of the team forms.

"In basketball as in life, true joy comes from being fully present in each moment. Stop worrying about whether you are going to win or lose and focus your full attention on what is happening right this moment."

If your program is all about football, you are missing the point.

Here is what Bill Walton said about Coach John Wooden in talking about success: "Coach Wooden created an environment where you expected to be your best and outscore the opponent: where capturing a championship and going undefeated was part of the normal course of events. Coach made the extraordinary seem normal. I can't describe how exciting it was to be a part of that, the joy he created in preparing us for competition."

I focus on the line where he said, "Coach made the extraordinary seem normal." That is what it is all about.

I speak to a lot of high school groups. I bring out this point to them, and by no means am I bragging. Unfortunately, in our society, it does mean something. Basically, I have had the opportunity in the last couple of years where I could have taken jobs where I would have made over a million dollars a year to coach football. That is a lot of money. For a coach that was not making a thousand dollars at UC Davis that is a lot of money. But the only thing I have ever tried to do was to get better. All I have ever tried to do was to improve. I have always tried to be the best I can be. I have never been about all of the other stuff.

People ask me if my goal is to coach in the NFL, or if it is to coach in the Rose Bowl. My goal is to coach football. The following quote sums it all up for me. Bret Butler said, "When I get to the pearly gates I doubt that St. Peter will care that I hit a lifetime .290. What matters most is that I made a difference."

I want to make a difference. I want to have a positive impact on the lives of the players. I want to make a kid's life better, and I want to make his life and his marriage better.

Some people ask me if my goal is to lead the nation in blocked punts, or scoring, or touchdown passes. It is not the point. I coach because it is fun and I want to have an impact on the players I work with.

Do not underestimate your power as a coach. You have a chance to be a mechanic. You can change a player's engine; in other words, his body. You can make him a whole different "car" by the time he leaves your program. When they come to us, all we can do is run them through like a car wash. We can shine them up and brush them off, but we can't take the engine out. We may be able to give them a tune-up, perhaps. But the high school coaches are in a great position.

I hope I have given you some information that will help you in your program.

I continue to read and search for new ideas that will help our program. I saw an article in the paper today that reminded me of an incident that happened to us on our home field. We had a team come into our stadium and dance on our Bronco logo. We went on to defeat that team 77 to 14. This reminded me of one of my favorite sayings: "Speak softly, but carry a big stick!"

I appreciate your time very much. Thanks.

RUN AND PASS IN THE SPREAD OFFENSE

University of South Carolina

I am going to talk about the spread offense. I will cover how we have progressed to this offense. Most of the time, we are in the multiple spread offense, and about thirty percent of the time, we are in a two backs set. When I coached at Connecticut I was in two back sets almost seventy percent of the time. I believe in running the football. I believe that is the way you win football games. There are a lot of ways to run the football. Some people throw the ball, some run the option, and some people run the power game. Regardless of whether are mentally tough, I believe they should be able to run the football.

In our first year at South Carolina, we were 0-11. We played the SEC teams, and we did not have the same talent they had. Hopefully we have closed the gap in talent somewhat. We were 0-11, and we were an awful two back offense. It used to be when teams got into a two back set teams went to an eight man front. Today, if you get into the two back set, you will see the nine man front. The two safeties are going to find a way to run downhill.

After the season, we saw the problems. We could run an isolation play and have everyone blocked, and the safetyman would come up and make the tackle for a gain of three yards. The next play, we would run the power play, and a defensive lineman would make the tackle for a loss of one yard. We would run another play, and again the safety would make the tackle for a gain of three yards. Now it was fourth-and-five, and we had to punt the football.

We sat down as a staff and tried to figure out a way to get the safeties out of the box. Teams are playing quarter coverages and match-ups that get everyone involved in the running game. That is why we went to the spread offense.

For us, the offense must complement the defense. Even though we are in the spread offense, we are not going to throw the ball 55 to 60 times per game. We are running the spread for a number of reasons, but we are in it first to complement our defense. We want to make first downs and control the football. Coach Holtz is an old-school thinker. He learned under Woody Hayes and Earle Bruce. They ran the ball for three yards and a cloud of dust, and then punted the football. They wanted to force the offense to drive the ball 80 yards to beat them. They were determined to win the game by a score of 10 to 7, or 14 to 10.

In the last four years, we have been in the top four teams in the SEC in rushing. We have converted over 40 percent on third-down plays. We are in the top three teams in the SEC in turnovers lost. This year, we led the SEC in the fewest turnovers, with only 15. When people think of the spread offense, they think of a high-risk offense where they throw the ball on every down. Last year we threw the ball 380 times and only got sacked 11 times. The spread offense helped us in this regard.

Productivity in the red zone has been our strength the last few years. The last two years we have gone 5-7 and 5-7. I am not standing up here beating my chest over those two years. But if you will look at our games, you will see the difference in winning and losing is only one or two plays. We were only three or four plays away from being a 9-3 team instead of 5-7. What we have done with the spread offense is to give us a chance to win in the fourth quarter.

First, I want to talk about our running game. We picked up a play last year that we call the mid zone. We had always been an inside and outside zone team. The reason we used the zone plays was because so many defensive teams were running stunts against us. Teams stunt to stop the run as well as the pass. We ran the mid zone last year 180 times. We averaged 6.0 yards per carry. But the way we evaluated the play was to see how many times we were able to gain 4.0 yards for us.

That is how we evaluate our run plays. We want to know the percentage of times we gained four yards on the play. Some plays may go for ten yards and then go for zero yards, and that comes out to an average of five yards. But that is a hit-or-miss play. In our mid zone play we had a 71 percent of plus four yards. On our inside zone play we averaged 6.2 yards, but we only converted the four yards on 80 tries.

The other running play for us is the counter, which is a misdirection play. Also, we run the outside zone play. It is not a big play for us because we are running the mid zone play. Then we have an option zone play. So you can see the zone plays are four of our five running plays. They are very similar, but the steps are just a little different.

When you get in the spread offense, you have two options. You can run play action and throw the ball down the field, or you can fake and throw the screen passes. You can fake the run and throw the ball, or you become a great screen pass team. It does not take talent to run the screen play. It does take execution.

We have a 15-minute session each day that we run our SDD period. We run nothing but screens, draws, and delays in this period. I will cover the bubble screen, the slow screen, the iso draw play, the reverse, and our middle screen.

I mentioned recruiting a few minutes ago. I want to tell you a story that I think will illustrate some of the issues we face in college recruiting today. The story is about a coach that dies and goes to the Pearly Gates and asks to see St. Peter. St. Peter comes to see the coach and says, "You have run a clean life, but when I look at the total picture, you are on the bubble. You could go to heaven or you could go to hell. You could do either one. I will give you a chance to decide if you want to go to heaven or hell. You can spend one day in each place and then decide where you want to go." The coach said that would be fine.

The first day he went down to hell. He got off the elevator and immediately saw a few of his old buddies. The people in hell were playing golf, playing cards, sitting around the pool, chasing women, and having a good time. His first thoughts were "It is not all bad down here in hell."

The next day he goes to heaven. The people were walking in the park, and going about their business. It was peaceful and quiet and everyone was content.

The next day he went back to see St. Peter. He said, "St. Peter, I never thought I would say this, but it was not all that bad in hell. I really think I would rather go to hell after visiting both places." St Peter told him that was fine and that he could have his wish.

St. Peter put the old coach on the elevator going back to hell. The elevator doors open and the fire and brimstone were shooting out at him as he got off the elevator. The people in the background were screaming and yelling something awful. He got off the elevator and saw Satan. He went over to Satan and said, "Satan, I was down here yesterday and everyone was having a good time. Everyone seemed so happy. What happened?" Satan replied, "That was your recruiting visit!" That always puts things in perspective when recruiting.

Why the zone play? We were a young team last year. We lost nine starters from our offense the year before. We lost four offensive linemen and our receivers. We wanted something on offense that was simple. You will see a lot of carryover with the rules on our plays. We want to make sure our players know what we are doing. This offense is good against all defenses. If the defense wants to move around or if they want to twist and run games, the offense is designed to handle those things.

We can run the offense of our multiple backfield sets. We can run the offense out of split backs, the I formation, one back set, motions, and multiple formations. We can get in the "I" formation. We can run 3 wide with 2 backs, we can run 2 tight ends and 1 back, we can run 1 tight end and 3 wide receivers, and we can go with 4 wideouts.

What we decided to do was to run the play about 200 times. That breaks down to almost 20 times per game. But we were going to run that same play from about ten different formations a couple of times. You cannot get in the same set and run the same plays over and over. We wanted to make it simple for the linemen, but at the same time, we wanted to dress the play up a lot of different ways.

As we go through these zone, plays, you must be able to answer a few questions to run the plays. You must be able to block frontside support. When you get into four wide receivers you must be able turn and block the frontside support to be able to account for all of the blitzes.

There are a number of ways to do that. You can keep the tight end in to block the support. If you do not have a tight end in the game, you can block with the motion receiver. You can use the back to block if you are in a two back set. Also you can use formations to block the support. You can put trips to the field and allow the inside receiver to block inside on the safety if he were an issue.

The other thing you must be able to do is to block on the backside. How do we block the backside? You can leave the 5 technique unblocked because you do not think he can run the play down from the backside. You can put a tight end to the backside. You can motion the wide receiver. You can put the quarterback in the shotgun set and have him read the backside end. These are the things you must consider when you are running the inside, middle, and outside zone plays.

Let me talk about the mid zone play. We call the play Ranger. We have set up our offense where we can call everything in a "no huddle" situation. We found that we were getting too wordy with everything, so we tried to make it simple. We are a rule offense. We give the players rules that will cover all defensive situations. Let me go over the rules for Ranger.

The frontside tight end has the D gap. It could be a 9 technique, or a strong safety outside. He has the D gap. He must listen for the tackle to make a call. If the tackle makes a help call, the tight end helps the tackle on a combo block. The end is going to block the D gap first with a midreach, or he is going to combo block if the tackle makes a call to the end.

The frontside tackle has on. He has the midreach. He has no help on the man over him. He can make an overcall to the guard if he does need help on the man over him.

The frontside guard has on. He works with the center. The center is on zero. He works with the frontside guard. Everyone on the backside, including the guard, tackle, and tight end, block the A, B, and C gaps.

The key to the mid zone play is the block. We have three zone blocks. We have a tight reach, a midreach, and a full reach block. That is where we spend most of our time with our offensive linemen.

You have seen the plastic donuts with the holes cut out in the center that Gilman Gear has for offensive linemen steps. We take those donuts and put the hole over the right foot. We want the lineman to take a lead step with the right foot, and take a step with the left foot gaining ground, and we try to put the left foot in the crotch of the defensive man we are blocking. If we are the tackle and we are trying to reach the 5 technique on the outside, we get the first lead step with the right foot, and then step with the left foot upfield. We want to step into the crotch of the defender. Then I want to get the shoulders square from there.

If it is a tight reach, we put the right foot just inside the defender's left foot, or inside of the defender's outside foot. Now the left step has to come almost straight upfield. We never want to cross our feet, and we want to keep the shoulders square.

On the full reach, we put the foot all the way on the outside of the defender's outside foot. We take a lead step, cross over, plant, and then shuffle up to the inside to turn everything back. When we talk about our zone blocks, I will call it a midreach, a tight reach, or a full reach block. We do a lot of drills on these three blocks. We work on the steps of each block over and over. That is the key with what we are trying to do with our offensive line.

For the receivers, if they motion to the play, they block the support. If they motion away from the play, they block the end.

The quarterback steps at 4 o'clock if he is under the center. The aiming point for the tailback is two yards outside the tight end. He is reading the hat of the tackle. His steps are a lead step, crossover step, and then he plants and takes it two yards outside the tight end landmark. You must hammer home for the tailback to read the hat of the tackle.

This is the way we would block the different defense on the tight end side.

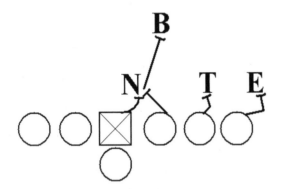

Diagram #1

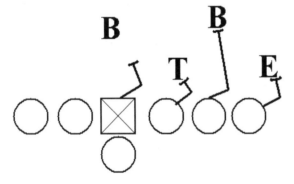

Diagram #2

When we first put this play in, I was not totally sold on the play. I was not taught never to chase a linebacker. I was taught to let the linebacker go, and to turn back and get the inside seal block. This is one play where we teach the linemen to chase the line-

backer. We want to chase the linebacker and push him by the hole. We want to push him past the point of attack because about ninety percent of the time, the play looks like a cutback play. It is really a cut up the field and not a cutback.

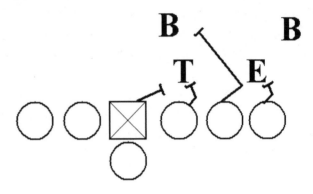

Diagram #3

As the guard takes his three steps, he looks inside to help the center. He takes a lead step, a step with the back foot upfield, and then pushes off the inside step to get upfield to get to the linebacker. He does not run to scoop block the linebacker. He wants to kick him past the point of attack.

If our quarterback is under the center, we must find a way to block the backside end. We could turn him free or we can use the man in motion. The way we are going to block on the frontside is with the tight end. Our tailback is seven yards deep on the play. They take the lead step, cross over, and on the third step, they plant and cut upfield (see Diagram #4). We are trying to give the defense the image that we are running the outside zone. On the third step, they are planting and going down hill.

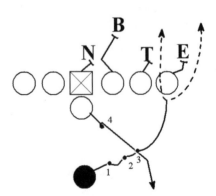

Diagram #4

On the inside zone, the blocking is the same for the frontside. This play was a little more productive for us. For the front five men, the rules are exactly the same. The only difference is now it is a tight reach. We do not cross the feet on the tight reach. We are trying to get movement on the down lineman and move them out of the hole. We have tightened up the running back. He takes a lateral step, a crossover step, and plants on the third step. He is not going outside, so his aiming point is the outside leg of the guard. He is reading the first down lineman (see Diagram #5).

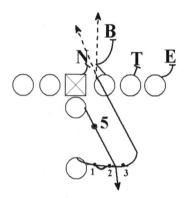

Diagram #5

We can run the play toward the 3 technique or we can run the play toward the shade technique. It does not matter; he is still reading the first down lineman. The center and guard are working together on the shade or the 3 technique man. If we can not reach the 3 technique man because he is too wide, the back is going to cut back inside. If the 3 technique man goes inside, we take him down the line and the back cuts behind the block.

The quarterback is in the shotgun and he is reading the backside end. If he quarterback is under center, we ask him to step at 5 o'clock and then to go straight back to 6 o'clock. We do that because we do not want him to go back at six o'clock and then have to redirect, and come back to five o'clock. If he comes back at 5 o'clock, he does not push the running back too wide because we want the quarterback to give the ball to the tailback as deep as possible. This gives the tailback a better cutback lane. That is why we do not stay on the straight tract at 5 o'clock on the drop to hand the ball to the tailback.

The tailback takes a lateral step, then a crossover step, then plants and cuts upfield reading the first-down lineman.

With this offense it is a great offense if you have a quarterback that can run. In high school, you want to put your best athlete at quarterback or running back because you want the ball in his hands. In this offense, the quarterback gets a chance to make a lot of plays.

Here is another concept that has been effective for us. We are running the zone play to the tight end side. We do not need a lead blocker because we have the tight end to block the alley. We run the zone to the tight end.

If we call "Orbit" we are going to run the option to the backside. The onside back fakes toward the tight end side. The quarterback goes toward the defensive end on the line. If the defense squeezes the play, the quarterback is going to option the support man on the outside. He does not option on the defensive end. He goes outside and options off the support man outside (see Diagram #6).

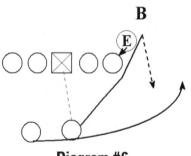

Diagram #6

Let me get to the counter play. Although this play has not been our best play, since it ties in so much with what you do with the zone plays, it has been our most productive play for the last couple of years. We average over eight yards per carry. We run the play about 60 times per year. We probably should run it a whole lot more than that. It ties in so well with what we do on our zone play. If your run the one back this is one of the best plays you can run. It is nothing more than an isolation play out of the one back set with the backside tackle as the blocking back. That is what it boils down to.

The rules are simple. The tight end has the D gap. The frontside tackle and frontside guard have the number one and number two men on the line of scrimmage. The guard has one on the line, and the tackle has number two on the line of scrimmage. The center has the nose man or the zero man. The backside guard has the number one man on the line. The backside tackle pulls and kicks out on the line-backer.

The tackle pulls and turns up in the first hole past the center. He is looking to kick the linebacker. We are not going to log the linebacker. We want to kick him outside. (see Diagram #7).

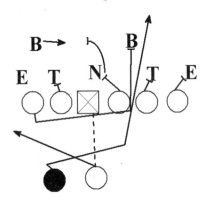

Diagram #7. Counter vs. 50

In a 4-3 defense, the middle linebacker has a hard time seeing the tackle pull. We have run the play with the guard pulling. Our tackles run decently. The problem you have with pulling the guard is two-fold. First, you have to block the center to the backside on the 3 technique man, and you do not get the point of attack blocked as well on the shade technique. The second point is the fact the linebackers do not read the tackles pulling like they do the guards (see Diagram #8).

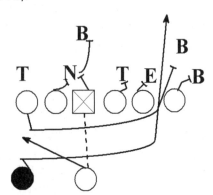

Diagram #8. Counter vs. a 3 technique

In the backfield, we are trying to do is to take the movement on our zone and ranger plays and step away from the call to give our tackle time to get into the hole.

If we see a double eagle defense, we call "Bear." That is an exception the blocking rules. We are going to double the center back or the 3 technique on the playside, and that tells the tackle to kick the defender outside instead of leading through the hole on the linebacker.

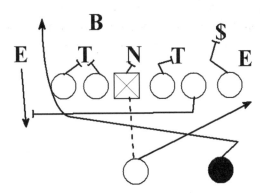

Diagram #9. Counter vs. bear defense

We found this was a better play to the shade than it was to the 3 technique man because of the double team block. We have run the play both ways, so we do not give the play away when we are running it to the shade technique.

We tell the ballcarrier he has to take a hop step away from the play. If that tackle does not move very well, he may have to slow the run down to give the tackle time to get to the block.

We can run the plays with the running back or with the quarterback in the shotgun. We can let the quarterback keep the ball on the bootleg if the backside end does not stay at home and honor the bootleg.

When we line up in the shotgun, we can have the running back on either side of the quarterback. We can run the quarterback on the zone one way, and the running back on the counter play the other way. We can run the zone either way, and you can run the counter play either way.

Running the football is tough and it is a mindset. The thing I worried about getting into the spread offense and becoming a zone team was that everything would come down to a finesse game. A lot of teams run the zone offense and that have the linemen drop stepping and all of the other finesse moves. We do not drop step. We want to move forward and come off the ball. For us, it is toughness and a mindset of coming off the football to run the ball. We get in a mindset that we are going to run the football when we get in the spread offense.

Once we were able to establish the run, the thing we wanted to do was to eliminate our turnovers. After, we were able to do that we wanted to make sure we had a high completion percentage. That is where the next package comes into play. I am talking about our screens, draws, and delays.

We break the offense down into these areas. We have our run game, which I covered. Then we have our screen game, our quick passing game, and our dropback passing game. I will not have time to cover all of this here, but I will talk about our screen game.

Everyone that has ever been in the spread offense runs the bubble screen. We run the bubble a number of different ways. We will run the bubble out of a 2 X 2 set and a 3 X 1 set (see Diagram 10, Diagram 11, Diagram 12, and Diagram 13).

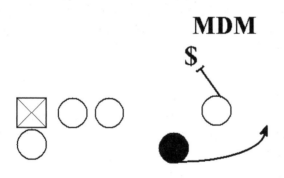

Diagram #10

Predominately we will bubble to our inside receiver. We will also bubble to our middle receiver and our outside man. We are going to make you cover our receivers down low.

Some teams associate this play with the running game. Teams will move a linebacker outside and

split the difference between the receivers. They set the man outside and have him key the quarterback. If he sees the quarterback come up to throw the ball, the linebacker comes outside to play the pass.

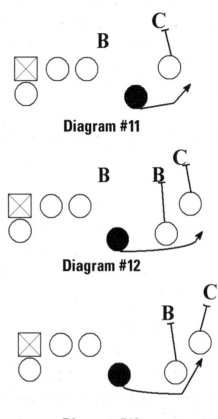

Diagram #11

Diagram #12

Diagram #13

In the 2 X 2 set, we bubble the inside guy. The rule for the man on the outside is the most dangerous man. In the three deep, that is the strong safety. In a two deep, that is going to be the cornerback. The quarterback's read is on the down defenders outside. We never throw the bubble if both receivers are covered down low. If they put the linebacker on the inside man and the strong safety on the outside man, then we can't run the bubble screen. I will talk later about our options when that happens.

In our trips set, the only rule we have is if everyone is covered down low. The rules are the same for the receivers on the blocks. We block the most dangerous man. We block the strong safety and the corner. We let the alley defender go.

What teams started to do to take away our bubble was to play us in three deep. They took the strong safety and put him on the inside shoulder of our middle receiver. As the play develops, the blocker stalks the strong safety. As the ball is released, he comes up the field and does not allow us to get any width on the play. That forces the receiver to turn back inside, and that is where the pursuit comes from.

So what we started doing was to run the crack block on the inside man (see Diagram #14). The outside receiver came down inside and stopped the penetration of the strong safety. The middle receiver prevents penetration until the block is made, and then he releases and goes upfield to block the corner.

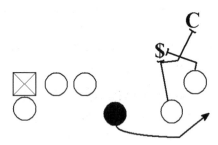

Diagram #14

That is what we did when we started getting heavy outside leverage on our number two receiver to run the bubble. We run the play from trips and get the ball to the third receiver. We can run the play to the split end side. The play has been good to us in all three sets.

The play that is dynamite is our bubble deep. It is a great play to get the ball down the field. I talked about our talent level. We do not have the talent to say we are going to play four wide outs and throw the ball down the field until we score. I wish we had that kind of talent, but we don't. Our talent is not quite as good as our opponents in most cases. So we must find ways to get the ball down the field. This is a good way to do that

We have the inside receiver stalk block on the under defender. He will stop to set his block, and then he will take off down the hash mark. The outside man will stock block and stop and go down the sideline. The receivers stalk the man head-on and then they go vertical down the field. The quarterback pumps the bubble and then lays the ball up for the receiver to run under.

One of the problems we have is our receivers all run the bubble differently. One receiver will run it hard down the field, and the next man will run a soft pattern down the field. So we have tried to give the receivers some guidelines to make everything uniform. We tell the bubble man to put his inside foot up. As the ball is snapped, we are going to turn our back to the quarterback and sprint three steps sideways. This gives the quarterback a target, which is the middle of the receiver's back. He takes the three steps straight across the field toward the sideline. The quarterback is throwing the ball right at the receiver's back. When the receiver gets to the third step, he shuffles gets turned around, and faces the football, where he can catch the ball and run with it. We should be able to complete that pass. I do not have very much patience with an incompletion on this play.

I tell you what makes the play special. The offensive line and the running backs run the inside zone play. If the defense moves outside and covers down on all of our receivers, we are going to run the inside zone play. We make a zone-bubble combo call. The quarterback can make that read from the shotgun. We do not run the play from under the center. We only run the play in the shotgun. We have a combination check to give the quarterback some guidance on checking to the run. We can run the zone play toward the bubble, or we can run the zone away from the bubble. It is a great play, with the tight end to the backside, and trips to the wide side of the field.

We ran the bubble play close to 80 times this year. We are going to make the defense go outside and cover everyone down. When we went to this offense, we wanted to be able to run the ball. We wanted the defense to cover our outside receivers down so we could run the football. With our quarterback in the shotgun, we can run the ball against the six man front even though we only have five blockers.

The bubble pass is really a sweep play for us. It is getting the ball out on the perimeter where we can make yardage. It is not a big play for long yardage for us. We want to get eight or nine yards on the play. If you have a sweep play that gives you eight or nine yards per carry, how many times do you call it?

We can run the play from the empty set. We run the double bubble and let the quarterback run the zone play. If the defense covers the bubble, we are going to have the quarterback run the ball on the zone. If they do not cover down on our wide receivers, we run the bubble screen. It is a good play to run on first down and it is a great third-and-short call, and it is a good second-and-medium call. You cannot go wrong calling the play. If you are going to run the spread offense, you must be able to get the ball outside in a hurry.

If you asked us to tell you the thing we have done the best job with in the last three years, it would be our slow screen pass. Our linemen are not great athletes, and they are not speed guys. But this has been a good play for us. There are a couple of coaching points on it that I want to cover. Here are the rules for the slow screen play.

The receiver that is closest to the play crack blocks. If we are in a tight end and flanker set, then the tight end would be the closest receiver, and he would crack block on the first linebacker in the box. If we run the play to the split end side, then the inside receiver is the man that crack blocks back inside on the linebacker. If we run the play to a single receiver side, then that single receiver crack blocks inside. The closest receiver to the ball, inside out, is the man that is going to crack the inside linebacker. If we run trips to the right and call the screen to the right, the inside receiver is going to crack block inside on the linebacker. All of the other receivers are DMMS, Deep Man My Side. They get downfield.

The tackle sets the depth. He sets up and cuts the defender at six yards (see Diagram #15). The guard jams, locks, and releases. That is our timing on the play. JLR is what we call it. If the defensive line comes, we want to jam them, lock the arms out, and then release them. We do not give a count of 1001, 1002, and 1003. We have found that does not work well for us. We call it JLR. The guard is going to go flat and kick outside.

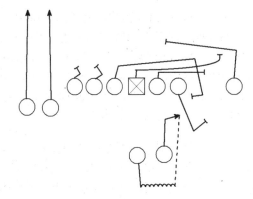

Diagram #15. Slow screen

The center is going to go JLR and then go flat and turn up. The backside guard does the JLR and then he peels and seals. He comes down the line and peels back, looking for any defensive lineman that is chasing the play from inside out.

Here is a big coaching point. We want our guard, center, guard alignment to be no more than two yards apart. We want those three men running straight down the line. The running back sets up like he is blocking on a pass play. He sets up behind the guard. He does not leave until the guard goes. When the guard goes, then the tailback leaves. The running back wants to be behind the wall of the blockers, so he never takes a shot. He turns his back to the line of scrimmage, and we are going to protect him as he catches the ball.

When the quarterback puts the ball in the air, the tailback makes a "Go" call. He steps up and fakes the block. As he sees the ball in the air, he calls out, "Go-Go-Go." Now we want everyone to turn and go upfield. If he has not called "Go," then the linemen are not allowed to turn upfield.

The quarterback is in the shotgun. He takes a three-step drop. He takes three steps and holds he ball as long as possible. We want the defenders coming to the quarterback. We want the quarterback shifting to the side of the call. He wants the defenders coming toward him before the throws the ball to the back setting up behind the guard.

We run the iso draw. We run the play out of the two backs set, or we can run it out of our one back set with the quarterback. We use the same rules as we use on our counter play. The quarterback flashes the quick pass to the side away from the play side. The running back isolates on the frontside linebacker. The quarterback takes the snap, drop steps, and shows pass to the side of the back that is getting the ball. We do not run an isolation play, but we do run the isolation draw. If you run the isolation, the linebackers come up and try to fill the hole, and there is no separation. By showing pass, we are trying to get a little hesitation to hold the linebackers.

The reverse play may be one of the best things we do because we run it out of so many different formations and different backfield actions. We have a lot of fun with the plays because we only run the reverse one way in each game. The players want to know who is going to get to carry the ball on the reverse each week. We can run the reverse off the speed option and the zone plays.

When you do not have the talent of your opponents, you have to find ways to move the football. We have tried to be simple with our zone concepts so we all know what we are doing. We let the defense dictate where we are going to run the ball instead of trying to push teams around that have us outmanned. We have done that with our screen and delay game. I do not know if I have helped you with this session, but if you could just take one thing back, it would be this.

This is what we do. Get something you can live with. Get married to it, teach your players what you are doing, and stay with it. Don't change so much. We all are guilty of adding things we see during the year that we think worked well for someone else. Do what you do best and take that philosophy and be simple. Thank you for your time. I really appreciate your attention.

PUNT RETURN AND KICKOFF RETURN

Vanderbilt University

It is an honor for me to be here, and it humbles me to be talking about Vanderbilt football. I obviously don't have all the answers. If I did, we would have beaten some of the teams we lost to this year. We are working on our program, trying to get better. We are excited about Vanderbilt and the opportunity we have. We realize Vanderbilt is a top-20 academic institution and plays football in the SEC. There are not many schools that have that combination.

The attendance here at this clinic makes a great statement for the game of football. In the middle of February, we have a room full of people trying to get better at what we do. I just want to ask you one question. Do you all know it is Valentines Day? My wife asked me what we were doing for Valentines' Day. I told her I was going to Louisville to do a football clinic. That didn't go over too well.

My topic today is about our kicking game. Before we get started on that, I would like to talk to you about our overall philosophy. I have been where you are, and know what you are thinking when the head coach starts out talking about philosophy. I didn't want to hear it. But this fits in with my talk today.

We have a very simple philosophy at Vanderbilt; don't beat yourself. We play in a league with teams that have great athletes and great coaches. If we tried to do what everyone else in this league was doing with their athletes, we would be in trouble. We are trying to make sure we don't help the other team. The kicking game fits into that train of thought.

There are things that you can do to keep from beating yourself. The first thing is to control the football. If you give Florida the football a bunch of times, they are going to put points on the scoreboard. We think the best way to control the ball is to run it. We want to do well on first down so we can have some manageable third downs. If we end up in third-and-six or more, we are going to be in big trouble.

I have seen teams control the football by using the controlled passing game, but we don't try that. However, if you control the football, you have a chance to be in the game in the fourth quarter.

The second thing we try to do is minimize turnovers. Turnovers are a part of the game, but there are some turnovers that are worse than others. When people are playing hard and running backs are trying to get that extra yards, the ball is going to get knocked out. But when you have blocked kicks and interceptions, I believe that is one of the biggest momentum builders in a football game.

The third thing is to minimize penalties. When I was head coach at Furman in the Southern Conference, we were the least penalized team in the conference just about every year. Basically, we were able to do that by avoiding postscrimmage penalties. Those are penalties that are selfish acts by your players. They hit someone out of bounds or after the whistle blows, which is a useless act. If you can eliminate those types of penalties, there is a good chance you will win the penalty battle every week. The past two years we have been at Vanderbilt, we have been the least penalized team in the conference. I don't know if it is the job we do coaching, or the referees just feel sorry for us.

The fourth thing is to be sound on defense. We say being sound on defense means not giving up the big play. At Furman, before becoming head coach, I was the defensive coordinator. We won seven conference championships, and in most of those years we led the league in defense. In 1988, when we won the national championship, we led the nation in defense. Every year, fans and alumni wanted to know why we didn't blitz more. The answer is simple. When you put yourself in a position to give up the big play, it is going to happen. That is true when you are playing teams with athletes better than yours. That was the case at Furman, and right now we are facing the same problem at Vanderbilt.

The fifth thing is to be sound in the kicking game. That is my topic today. The schemes I am going to cover today are our punt and kick-off return schemes. They are different than what you normally see. I think they will work for you to have a sound kicking game.

To be sound in the kicking game, you must avoid the big plays against you. When we are in a kicking situation, the other team has the opportunity to score. I am going to place a lot of emphasis on that part of the game. When you punt the ball, the defense can block the kick or return the kick and get the ball in the end zone. On the kickoff return, the offense can return the ball for a touchdown. I am going to spend most of my time and focus on those two aspects of the kicking game.

When we are taking possession of the ball, I spend less time and focus on those teams. Our punt return and kick-off return teams do not receive the same focus as the other special teams. We want to make sure we don't have the ball returned against us for a big gain.

A blocked kick really excites the fans and turns the momentum of a game. How many times have you seen a team line up to kick a field goal, have it blocked, and then that leads to points for the opponent? It is a total negative experience for your team. Usually blocked kicks lead to big plays for the opponents.

One other situation that I think is extremely important is committing penalties that deny you possession of the ball. If it is fourth-and-three and you jump offsides trying to block the punt, that act denies you possession of the ball. Roughing the kicker or running into the kicker are penalties that can deny you possession of the football.

When we get a chance to gain possession of the football through a punt, our major focus is on catching the ball. The second goal is to enhance our field position with a return. If we can get ten yards on the return, that is one less first down our offense has to get.

We want to make plays in the kicking game when the opportunities present themselves. We want to have returns and blocks in our package to take advantage of the opportunities when they are there. The pooch kick has an important use in the kicking game. We were fortunate to have a punter who could pooch the ball. He knew the importance of getting the ball over the line but keeping it short of the end zone. Giving the opponent the ball at the 15-yard line is better than kicking it into the end zone.

Field goals are tremendously important in today's football planning. There are so many games won with field goals today than ever before. Last year, we had a tremendous field goal kicker. We were number one in the SEC with red zone efficiency because of this kicker. He transferred after the recruiting season, and we were left without a kicker. We went from first to next-to-last in red zone efficiency in one year's time. All those types of things make a big difference in what you do.

You have to believe in your kicking game as a staff, because you have to commit the personnel you need for those teams. The punt is the first play of defense for us. If that is the case, we need to have the best players on that team. The kick-off return is the first play of offense for your team. You need to commit good offensive players to that team.

When I first became a head coach, I gave lip service to the idea about committing the proper personnel to those teams. I didn't do it, and it cost me some games. The second thing you have to do is commit the practice time to work on the special teams. We have two different sessions in our practice schedule each day to practice some aspect of our kicking game. When we are practicing those special teams, those teams have the focus of our entire staff. When we are working on the punting game, we have six coaches working with that team.

We divide up the front line among the coaches. We have a coach working with the snappers. We have a kicking coach working with the punter. We have someone watching the protection. We have to commit to the kicking game. If we don't commit to the kicking game, the players will know it. We record and document our success or failure and show it to our players. Our punter last year was not nearly as good as the one we had the year before, but our averages were about the same because we improved our coverage.

I am going to go over our punt protection. We have been using this protection and formation for six years, and we have yet to have a punt blocked. It was pretty consistent, and we ended up having a good net punting average. Our number-one goal when we punt is to get the ball off.

In our formation we lined up unbalance to the side on the punter dominant foot (see Diagram #1). We had a left-footed punter and our unbalanced was on the left side. If you have a right-footed punter, the four man side is to the right of the center. Toward the two man side we put two wing backs to that side. The personal protector is to the punter's dominant side. We feel like we can do a good enough job with our zone blocking scheme to take care of anything the rushers give us.

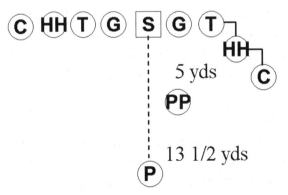

Diagram #1. Punt formation

Some ideal situations do occur within a game, where we can get one-on-one blocking. That lets us release quicker, be more aggressive, and cover better. It also gives a built-in wall for our punter and gives him more confidence. We are going to give two calls every time we go out to punt the ball. We make one call for the kicking side and one call away from the kicking side.

The center is extremely important on your punt team. We have an outstanding coach working with our centers at Vanderbilt. He is one of the best technique teachers there is coaching that position. Robbie Caldwell is our line coach, and he does outstanding work with the center. Whatever stance the center needs to get the ball back there is fine with us.

The punter aligns at 13.5 yards deep instead of 15 yards. The ball arrives in .72 to .75 seconds. The key men in the protection are the two guards. Their stance is extremely important. What we are going to try to do is make sure we don't get anyone up the middle. They are going to be bunched in on the center. The guards are foot to foot with the center, with their inside toe aligned on the heel of the center. They are staggered back from the center so they can interlock with him after the snap. We want the stance of the guards very narrow. On the snap of the ball, the guards are going to hop back and interlock their legs with the center and the tackle. They can't interlock before the ball is snapped.

The personnel we put in those guard positions are big defensive end types who can run. We don't ask the center to do a lot. We may ask him to lean one way or the other, but mostly he is going to snap the ball and try to get big. The tackles are foot to foot with the guard. The tackles are in a normal stance as far as their width. Their heads are up and their tails are down in a good football position.

When the ball is snapped, the tackle steps down the line of scrimmage and punches with both hands outside. He can't go backward. If there are two men in the gap, he has to punch hard enough to go through the first man in the gap to get to the second man. It is extremely important that they do not move their inside leg. The guard is interlocking with his inside leg. If he moves it, a big hole is opened up to the inside. The personnel we use for the tackles are fairly big guys in the linebacker type category.

The head hunter is the outside tackle in the unbalanced side to the punter's leg side. He does the same thing the tackle does. He steps down the line of scrimmage and punches outside with his hands. The head hunter could be a safety type. The contain man to the unbalanced side is in the end position. He hinges back and makes sure no one from the outside comes inside of him. He punches everyone outside and makes them run the hump. In the contain position, we could use corner backs.

To the side away from the punter's kicking leg, the head hunter is off the line of scrimmage. He is one foot outside the tackle's outside leg. He is slightly turned to the outside and cannot give ground. On the snap of the ball, he takes a step up and takes on everything inside out. He can't allow anyone inside of him. The contain man to the away side has his inside foot on the outside foot of the head hunter. His relationship is exactly like the head hunter relationship to the tackle. He does the same thing the head hunter is doing. We make everything to that side run the hump outside the head hunter and the contain man.

The personal protector is at a five-yard depth. He is responsible for up the middle first, to the leg side next, and the back side last. He has to keep his head on a swivel looking for seepage in the line. The punter is at 13.5 yards and punts the ball in two steps. Since we have gone to this protection we have never had a punt blocked.

If the rushers overload to the left side by putting six rushers left of the center and three to the right, we ask the center to lean left. The guards will tell the center which way to lean. Everything else in the zone protection scheme is the same, with the center helping the left guard because he has a man inside and outside of him (see Diagram #2). If the overload were right, the center would lean to his right.

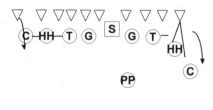

Diagram #2. Zone/zone

It is important for the punter to know the strongest side of the protection. He wants to punt the ball behind the strongest side of the protection.

If the situation fits itself to the scheme, we want to build a stronger side for the punter.

If we have five men to each side of the center, we give an overload zone call (see Diagram #3). That means we are going to identify the outside rusher to the left side and let him go free. The contain man, head hunter, tackle, and guard can get a hat-on-hat to their side. The left guard tells the center he has only one man inside him, and the center can lean right. The right side blocks zone like the normal punt blocking scheme. The personal protector takes the outside man to the leg side.

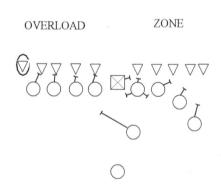

Diagram #3. Overload zone

There is one thing that is important about this formation. The reason we have the two wing players to the right side is to give us two eligible receivers to that side plus the personal protector. That makes three receivers who could run patterns to that side. For that reason, we very seldom get pressure coming from the side with the wing set. If people are going to try to block the punt, they will come from the other side.

Since we don't retreat on our protection, we can be more aggressive on our coverage. We can jam and punch the rushers, stop their charge, and get down the field.

Let me show you what some people try to do against us with their overload schemes (see Diagram #4). They put six rushers to the left and four to the right. We still can overload the left side with our call. That means we identify the outside rusher and let him go free. The left guard knows he has two rushers in his gap. He tells the center to lean left and hit the man in the gap. The left guard is interlocked and gets big to jam up the inside gap. The tackle punches his man outside. The head hunter blocks the man to his outside and the contain man blocks his inside gap. They can control their men and get downfield in a hurry. The outside rusher is released, to be picked up by the personal protector.

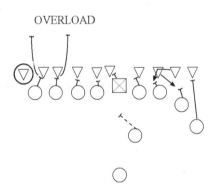

Diagram #4. Overload man

To the backside, they are blocking a man scheme with zone principles. The reason they do that is to pick up any twist stunt that may be run to their side. The tackle is punching out but not moving out or dropping back. He can pick up an X stunt coming from the outside. The head hunter and contain man are stepping up and protecting inside.

If the rush overloads to the wing side, we can do the same thing we did the other way (see Diagram #5). To the left they are blocking man-on-man. The center leans to the right side. The right guard interlocks and gets big. The right side tackle punches out

through two men if he has to. The head hunter and contain man protect inside and make the rushers run the hump. The personal protector steps right, looking for seepage over the guard gap and working outside. We are blocking zone right and man blocking left. On the left side, we are blocking a man scheme with zone principles. That way we can pick up any stunts.

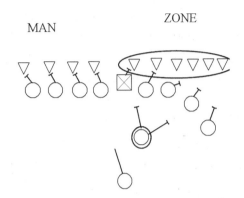

Diagram #5. Overload right

If we have a great return man to defend, we split our head hunters in our formation (see Diagram #6). We split him into the wide side of the field. Our protection doesn't change because the defense has to cover the head hunter, and that means one less man inside.

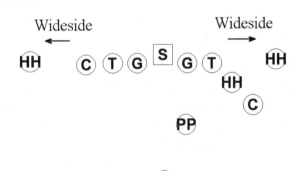

Diagram #6. Split head hunter formation

When we are going into the opponent's territory and have to punt the ball we often use the pooch kick (see Diagram #7). In this formation, we split both head hunters. We drop the contain man to the leg side into the wing set, where he becomes eligible as a pass receiver. We usually man the protection and try to get down and down the ball inside the ten-yard line. On the pooch kick, the head hunter will release past the return man. If he is giving a fair catch signal, we run by him and get between him and the end zone.

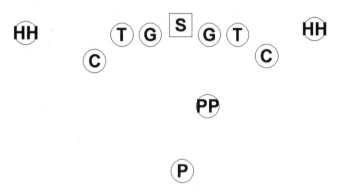

Diagram #7. Pooch formation

After you protect the punt, you have to cover the kick. The punt coverage lanes will be determined by where the ball is caught, not where it is kicked from! We will use field landmarks to set the coverage lanes for each defender (see Diagram #8).

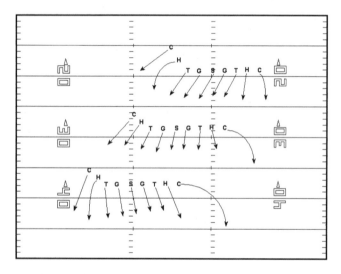

Diagram #8. Coverage lanes

As each punt team member releases from the line of scrimmage, he must do four things. He has to fan out and cover the field for the first 10 to 15 yards. He has to realize where the ball is being caught. We key the return man to find out where the ball is being kicked. You may peek for the ball, but don't look for the ball unless you want to get lit up. When he sees where the ball is going, he adjusts his lane in relationship to where the ball is being caught. He squeezes to the ball and breaks down to make the tackle.

The head hunters are going directly to the ball, and the contain men are fanning out to keep the ball inside of them. We practice punting the ball off of each hash mark and from the middle of the field to get the coverage lanes exact.

If the ball is caught in the middle of the field, the snapper is going down the middle of the field (see Diagram #9). The tackles are covering two yards outside the hash marks. The guards are half the distance between the center and tackles. The distance between the snapper, guards and tackles is about five yards. The contain men are covering down the top of the numbers. They are keeping everything inside of them.

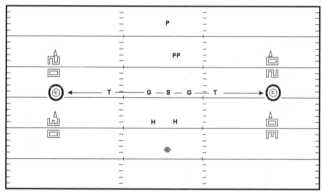

Diagram #9. Coverage lanes middle

The head hunters are going straight to the return man if they are not held up. If they anticipate being held up, they give a switch call to the contain man. The contain man changes responsibility with the head hunter. The head hunter covers on an outside-in angle. The halo rule doesn't apply anymore, so the head hunter has to time up his hit on the return man so as not to arrive before he touches the ball.

The personal protector covers five to seven yards behind the first wave of coverage. He mirrors the ball. If the snapper, guard, or tackle gets pushed out of his lane, he fills in for him. If he sees a wall forming as he leaves the line of scrimmage, he gets behind the wall and covers at full speed.

The punter covers 15 yards behind the coverage wall. He mirrors the ball as he comes downfield. He tries to force the ball out of bounds.

If the ball is caught on the hash mark, the snapper is splitting the distance between the hash mark and the middle of the field. The boundary side guard is two yards outside the hash mark and the field side guard is up the middle of the field. The boundary side tackle is down the top of the numbers and the field side tackle is five yards outside the field side guard. The boundary contain man is between the sideline and numbers. The field contain man is two yards outside the hash marks. The head hunters, personal protector, and punter have the same rules of coverage as they did on the middle coverage (see Diagram #10).

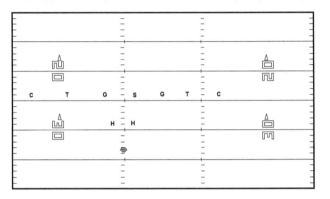

Diagram #10. Coverage lanes hash

The quickest way to give up a punt return is for the coverage team to turn in to the ballcarrier. They have to keep their pads square as they cover. They want to squeeze the ball, but not turn their pads to chase the ballcarrier. If the return man starts inside and breaks outside, the coverage has to stay square on his movement.

The snapper covers down the hash mark. The boundary guard is between the numbers and the hash mark. The field guard is halfway between the middle of the field and the hash mark. The boundary tackle is on the bottom of the numbers. The field tackle is cover down the middle of the field. The boundary contain should be three yards from the sidelines. The field contain-man covers down the field hash mark. Rules for the head hunters, personal protector, and punter are the same (see Diagram #11).

As much as we practice the protection of the punter, we practice our coverage lanes. One man out of position can result in a touchdown. Most times we are using defensive players on our punt

team. That means they are getting tackling practice every day. They have to apply their tackling-in-space rules in their coverage.

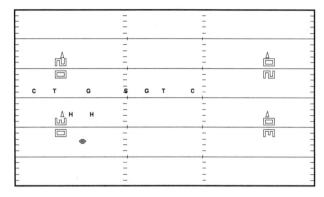

Diagram #11. Coverage lanes outside the hash

I want to show you our kickoff return before I run out of time (see Diagram #12). It is extremely easy and you do the same thing over and over. We align our front line across the field at the 47-yard line. That is two yards over the free kick line. We distribute them across the field to guard against any onside kick situation. You can go back to 15 yards from the ball, but that leave you vulnerable to the onside kick.

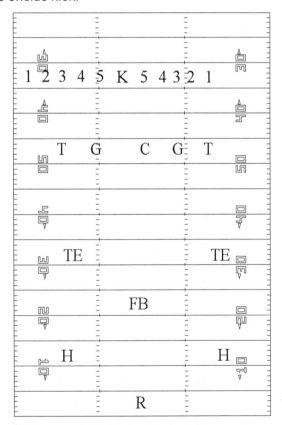

Diagram #12. Kickoff return formation

The ends are aligned on the 30-yard line just inside the numbers. The fullback is in the middle of the field at the 20-yard line. We have two halfbacks who align inside the numbers between the 10- and 15-yard lines. The return man is aligned on the ball around the goal line ready to go.

The front line is playing the onside kick. The tight ends are going to play the bloop kick. They never back up to catch a ball. If the ball is over their heads, the halfbacks make the play on the ball. The halfback never backs up to catch a ball unless the return man tells them to take the ball. The fullback never backs up to catch a ball. If the ball goes over the fullback's head, the return man has to get the ball. If the ball is moved to the hash mark to kickoff, we adjust accordingly.

No matter what the coverage teams do, our return rules will stay the same. We are going to run a double wedge (see Diagram #13). When I was at Furman, we ran this one return all year. We led the nation in kickoff returns, and our return man leads the nation in kickoff return average. We ran the same return for the eight years I was there.

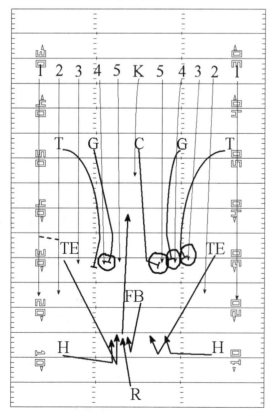

Diagram #13. Middle double wedge

Our tackles are going to ensure the kick and run toward the football to around the 30-yard line. They are going to turn and block the first thing coming outside of them. Most of the times in coverage, the two men on the outside of the coverage team are contain men or some kind of safety backs. We don't block them at all. The good thing about the tackle's block is they don't have to be vicious blocks. All they want to do is move the defender outside. It is like pushing a rusher past the quarterback in a pocket.

The guard does the same thing by dropping inside and blocking outside. They block the first man inside the tackle. The center drops to the wedge and blocks one of the two defenders coming down the middle of the field. If the front five can stop the charge of the coverage, we have a chance to return the ball all the way.

The fullback sets the second wedge 12 yards in front of the ball, wherever it is kicked. He never takes the wedge outside of the midpoint between the hash and the numbers. The fullback has to set the wedge exactly at 12 yards. If he doesn't, the outside defenders will get behind the wedge and blow up the return man. The tight ends have to hustle their butts to the fullback and get shoulder-to-shoulder with the fullback. The two halfbacks come inside and get shoulder-to-shoulder with the tight ends.

The return man gets the ball and starts up field. As soon as he has momentum and feels no one can get behind the wedge, he calls "Go." The wedge has to move. They can't stay there and catch people. When we were at Furman with 12,000 people in the stands, you could hear the "Go" call. At Tennessee, with 109,000 people in the stands, the fullback has to anticipate the call because he can't hear it. At home we might be able to hear the call, but on the road we have to anticipate it.

As the wedge moves forward, the halfbacks are going to block the first thing that comes outside of our offensive tackles. They have to block the crazy guys who are trying to knife through the wedge. The fullback and the tight ends are going to lead the return man to the promised land. If we are lucky, we will have 10 men blocking on seven. Kickoff teams are coached to stay in their lanes. We let them stay in their lanes and run by them.

The return man has to be fearless. He has to take the ball and run as hard as he can and trust the back wedge. He is depending on them to protect him from any screamer that is coming down that field. With any luck at all, the return man is going to run right off the fullback's block, and everyone else will be past him and down too deep. That is what we do every time on our kick-off return.

If the ball is kicked outside the hash mark, the fullback never takes the wedge outside the mid-point between the hash marks and the numbers (see Diagram #14). The return man has to bring the ball back to the wedge. It is his job to get the ball back to the wedge. If the screamer is coming down the sideline into the corner where the ball is kicked, it is the halfback's job to make sure the return man gets back to the wedge. He may have to leave the wedge to do that.

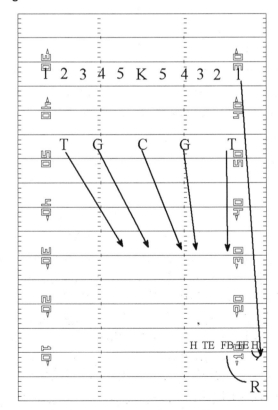

Diagram #14. Double wedge outside the hash

The Southern Conference and the Southeastern Conference are a little different when it comes to the athletes in the league. When we went to Auburn they sent a 6-7, 300-pound athlete who could run like a deer down as a wedge buster. He almost killed our fullback. We felt like we had to have an answer for that kind of play. We decided to put in a side return to help us out (see Diagram #15). When coverage teams stays in their lanes this return will not work. However, since we have been at Vanderbilt, people send everyone to attack our wedge.

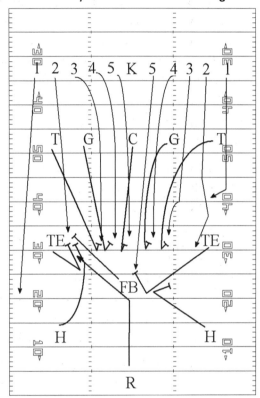

Diagram #15. Right or left return

We tried to make everything look the same as the double wedge return. Everyone in the front wedge is going to block away from the side of the return. The halfback to the side of the return kicks out the contain man to that side. The fullback and tight end to that side are going to double-team the second man to the outside. We are not going to run this return if the number 3 man in the coverage is staying in his lane. If he is cheating and going for the wedge, we are in Fat City. The offside tight end takes the missile coming down the middle. The offside halfback makes sure the return man gets into the sideline by cutting off the outside.

I am out of time. I appreciate you being here. Thank you.

DEFENDING THE SPREAD OFFENSE

University of Dayton

Coaches have more influence on the young men today than anyone else in their lives. I think the football field is the best classroom a kid has. Coaches have to set good examples and be good role models for our players. Kids do not care how much the coach knows; they only care how much he care about them.

Twenty-seven years ago, the only defense was the Oklahoma 5-4 defense. That was where we began and what we have run all of these years. Over the years, we have kicked the front, reduced sides, and made adjustments as the offenses changed. We developed different schemes in the secondary, but our defense is based on the Oklahoma package.

Everyone who plays with the spread offense today is generally in a double slot or trips formation with the one-back set. The problems we started to have with our 50 package were purely athletic ones. When people began to spread the offense, we ended up with people in coverage that could not cover. In our package, we had to get more speed on the field.

We play two packages against the spread offense. We run a 50 package and a 40 package. In the 50 package, we have three defensive linemen, two linebackers, two corners, and four safeties. We take our outside linebackers out of the game and replace them with secondary players.

In our 50 package we play six coverages. We play a 50-base defense, which is a three-deep, three-under, and five-man rush. The 50-X coverage is three-deep, four=under, and four-man rush. We play a coverage called 35, which is a three-deep and five-under zone coverage. We play a man coverage called 35 man, which is a three-deep and five-under

man coverage. We play 50-man free and 50-load/cover-4 banjo, which are man coverages. That is what we play in our 50 package against the spread offense. I will take each of the coverages and explain them to you.

The 50-base is the regular 50 defense (see Diagram #1). We rush five defenders, play three men in underneath short zones, and three men in deep zones in the secondary. The strong safety goes to the two receiver side if the offense has a two-back set in the backfield. In this coverage we give up the weakside flat zone.

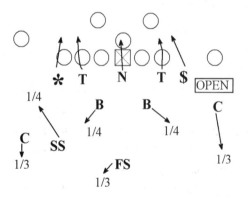

Diagram #1. 50-base

If the set is a double slot with one back in the backfield, we call "Check-X" (see Diagram #2). The X call refers to one of our nickel backs in the game at the defensive end position. The nickel and dime backs are represented in the diagrams as the dollar signs ($) for the nickel and asterisks (*) for the dime back. In a two-by-two set or double slot, the free safety will determine the side of declaration. A double slot set is a balanced set, so it does not matter where the free safety declares. However, he generally declares into the wide side of the field or to defense's left. The nickel back aligns opposite the strong safety. We play a four-under and three-deep zone coverage in the secondary. We rush with four defensive linemen.

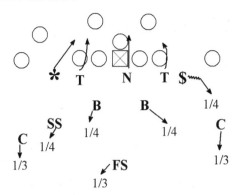

Diagram #2. 50-base check X

The nickel on the X call stays on the line of scrimmage until the ball is snapped and drops into his underneath zone. If he gets an "X-now" call, he adjusts his alignment to the inside shoulder of the number-two receivers to his side and goes as wide as that receiver may go. His reads and responsibilities are the same from that position as they are from the tight position.

If the offense comes out in a trips formation, we check the coverage to a "Rip/liz" call (see Diagram #3). The strong safety declares to the three-man side. We angle the front toward the trips set. The nickel and dime backs are both dropping into coverage. The nickel is opposite the strong safety to the one receiver side. We play three-deep and five-under in this coverage. If the offense motions from the trips set to a double slot, we check the coverage to X. If they motion from a double slot set into a trips set, we check the coverage to rip or liz.

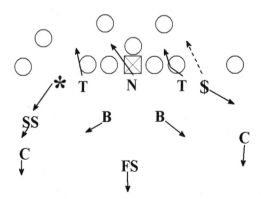

Diagram #3. Rip/liz

One adjustment we make is blitzing the nickel back off the one receiver side. That is a scouting report type of play depending on the tendencies of the offense.

We can call the 50-X at any time we choose. If the offense comes out in a two-back set, we can call the X coverage and drop the nickel back opposite the strong safety into coverage. I have shown you the 50-X coverage. If the offense motions off the strong side and changes the strength of the formation, we bump our safeties over (see Diagram #4). The strong safety goes to the middle, and the free safety bumps down to the motion side. Since the strength of the formation has changed, the X coverage is always run opposite the strong safety.

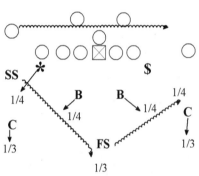

Diagram #4. Bump/motion

With a trips set in the 50X defense, we check to a rip/liz call (see Diagram #5). We slant to the trips side with our down linemen and play a five under scheme with three deep behind them. This situation gives us an opportunity to bring the nickel defender off the backside on a blitz. The nickel can run an X-stunt with the backside tackle and come inside with the tackle going outside.

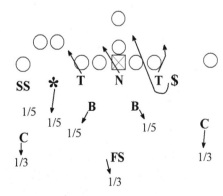

Diagram #5. Rip/liz X-stunt

The next coverage we can play is called 35 (see Diagram #6). That coverage is a three-deep, five-under coverage with a three-man rush. Against a three wide receivers and a two-back set, the strong safety aligns inside of the split end. The dime back moves out to cover the slot back in the twins set. The nickel back aligns opposite the strong safety and walks out on the split end to his side. The linebackers are in the underneath coverage with a three-deep scheme behind the under zones. This type of defense is a maximum coverage defense. You should not expect to get pressure on the quarterback with a three-man rush. What you want to do is make him hold the ball and not let him scramble.

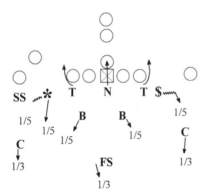

Diagram #6. 35

If we get four vertical patterns from a double slot formation, the free safety has to alert the defense. If the ball is on the hash mark, the first thing the safety says is "Watch the seams!" The throws the quarterbacks take are the two middle seams and the short sideline vertical pattern. He seldom tries to throw the ball deep to the wide side vertical against the sideline. The underneath defenders carry the receivers through the short zones to a distance that allows our free safety to break and get to the ball on either side of his zone. We squeeze the wide side zone toward the middle with the wide side corner.

The thing we learned in the 35 coverage when we face trips is to stay in the coverage with all motions (see Diagram #7). We do not bump and adjust back through the middle with our safeties. We make the adjustments with our linebackers. If the motion comes from the trips set into a double

slot, the dime back comes back inside, and the nickel widens with the motion. If the offense runs motion from a double slot and moves to trips, this is how we cover it. The inside linebacker moves outside and covers under number three receiver to the trips side.

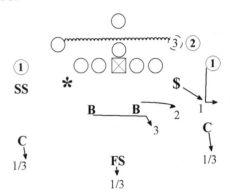

Diagram #7. Motion with 35

The companion defense for the 35 defense is 35-man (see Diagram #8). In this defense, we run a three-deep secondary with five men playing man coverage underneath. In a two-back set, the strong safety, nickel, and dime backs are in coverage on the three wide receivers. The inside linebackers are locked on the two remaining backs. If we get four wide receivers in a double slot, the inside linebacker to the side of the extra receiver comes out in man-to-man coverage. If any kind of motion occurs, everyone runs with their man. We do not switch men. Each defender takes his man wherever he goes.

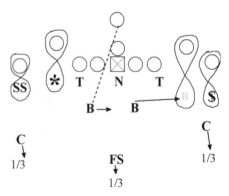

Diagram #8. 35-man

If we get the trips set with a 35-man coverage, we use an inside linebacker to take the third receiver to the trips side. If there is motion on the play, the defender assigned to the receiver runs with the motion. Against the bunch look by the trips set, we have a number of ways we play. We play man and disregard the bunch, check to zone coverage, or use an inside-outside man scheme versus the two receivers off the line of scrimmage. The defender covering the receiver on the line of scrimmage would take him man-to-man. The outside defender takes the receiver breaking outside and the inside defender takes the receiver breaking inside.

When we go to the 50-man free coverage we rush five defenders (see Diagram #9). The corners play man-to-man on the number-one receivers to their side. The strong safety takes the number-two receiver, and the linebackers take the backs in the two-back set. The free safety is free in the middle of the field. I think the most important thing for the defender playing man coverage is to be aware of where his help is aligned. He generally has sideline help or free safety help. That allows the defender to adjust his alignment to force the receiver into his help and allows him to overplay away from his help.

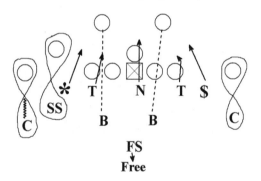

Diagram #9. 50-man free

With a free safety in the middle of the field, the man-to-man defender does not need to run on top of the receiver. He trails him with help over the top from the safety.

In the double slot formation, in theory, the second receiver to the weakside belongs to the inside linebacker (see Diagram #10). We make a switch call between the inside linebacker and the nickel back. The nickel takes the slot receiver to his side, and the inside linebacker rushes the quarterback. He runs a stunt with the down lineman or blows the gap in front of him. The defense disguises what they are doing.

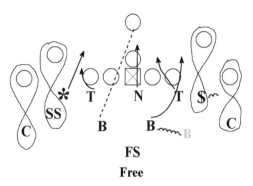

Diagram #10. Man free switch

If the offense gives the defense a trips set, we use a switch call to the three man side (see Diagram #11). The corner takes the outside receiver, the strong safety takes the outside slot, and the dime back takes the inside slot. The linebacker stays inside and blitzes as he did in the double slot adjustment. If there is any motion, the defender assigned to the motion back runs with the motion.

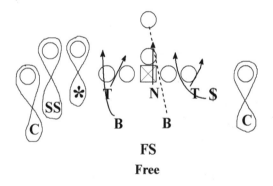

Diagram #11. Man free trips switch

The coverage we like to blitz from is called 50-load/cover-4 banjo. (see Diagram #12). That means we involve our free safety into our man coverage. The corners take the wide receivers, and the strong safety matches up on the slot receiver in the two-back set. The nickel and dime backs have containment and match up on the backs coming their way. The load call means the inside linebackers come on a blitz of some kind. We like to run a middle stunt with the noseguard slanting to the weakside A gap and the inside linebackers blitzing the strong side A gap and B gap.

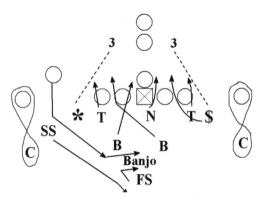

Diagram #12. 50-load/cover-4 banjo

In this particular diagram we banjo the slot receiver with the strong safety and free safety. If the slot receiver likes to run an inside crossing pattern, the free safety jumps that pattern, and the strong safety takes the middle of the field and plays free.

If the offense runs a double slot set. our coverage changes slightly (see Diagram #13). Instead of taking the nickel back into coverage on the slot to the weakside, we make a Sally call. That means the free safety covers the weakside slot and the nickel back is rushing. The nickel and dime backs have the third receiver if he release toward them.

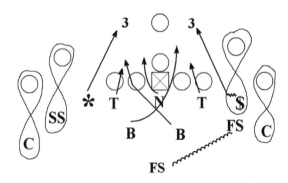

Diagram #13. 50-load Sally

In the trips set, the free safety makes the Sally call and has the third receiver in the trips set. Everything else in the defense is the same reaction for the linebackers, nickel backs, and dime backs. That is the same 50 package we always run, except we have taken our outside linebacker out and replaced them with safeties.

Our 40 package is a four-man rush scheme. We use the term "box" to describe the coverage. From this package we play five coverages. We play a two-deep zone, quarters, cover-3, box man, and box load coverage.

In this package, we play the nickel back but we have another defensive lineman in the game instead of the dime back. If you are an even front team, this may be the package you want to play. In this package we have four down linemen, two linebacker, two corners, and three safeties.

When we play the two-back set, we use a cover 2 box zone (see Diagram #14). This defensive alignment is a half coverage look. If the offense has a tight end, the nickel back is aligned to the tight end side. If there is no tight end, the nickel back aligns according to the wide side. The inside linebacker opposite the nickel back steps out on the weakside slot receiver, if there is one. Everything we do in this coverage is based on the number-two receivers.

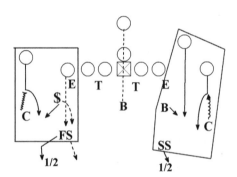

Diagram #14. Cover 2 box zone

The free safety, nickel back, and wide corner take the number one and two receivers to their side. The strong safety, linebacker, and weakside corner take the number one and two receivers to their side. If the number two receiver runs to the flat, the safety gets over the top of the corner's coverage. The corner reroutes the number one receiver inside and sets up on the number two receiver coming to the flat. If the number two receiver releases vertical or across the field, the corner locks the number one receiver in man-to-man coverage. The nickel is keying number two to number one. If the number two receiver goes outside, he looks for the number one receiver to run some kind of curl or in pattern. If the number two receiver comes up the field, the nickel back carries him down the seam and tries to wall him outside.

In the trips set we have a problem (see Diagram #15). We have an inside linebacker responsible for a wide receiver on a vertical route. The way we solve the problem is have the backside safety keying the number three receiver to the trips side. He is going to play the number three receiver in the trips set on the vertical route. The free safety, nickel back, and the corner are playing the 2 outside receiver in zone coverage as they did in the double slot set. The corner to the backside is playing the 1 receiver in a man principle with help from the inside safety.

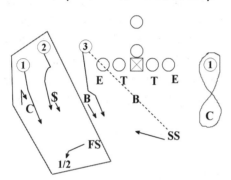

Diagram #15. Box, zone 2 vs. trips

In our box quarter coverage from a two-back set, the corner generally aligns in a press position (see Diagram #16). Before the snap of the ball, he bales out and has the number one receiver in man-to-man coverage. The nickel back plays under and keys the number two receiver. If the number two receiver goes vertical, he looks for number three crossing his face or bubbling to the outside. If number two goes to the flat, the nickel back has him. If the number two receiver goes under to the other side, he sinks under the number one receiver.

The safety keys number two also. If he goes vertical, the safety has him. If he goes diagonal, the safety takes him unless he knows he is going underneath a linebacker. If he goes under a linebacker, the linebackers will pass him along between them. If the number two receiver goes to the flat, the safety looks for the post cut from the number one receiver. If the number two receiver goes to the flat and the number one receiver disappears, he looks to the backside.

To the backside, the corner bales and locks on the number one receiver. The number two receiver is aligned in the backfield. If he does not come out, the safety has no number two receiver. He looks to the number one receiver on the post cut and plays the technique of the front side safety.

If we play a box quarter coverage against a double slot set, the front and backside are played exactly alike. The free safety, corner, and nickel back have one box, and the strong safety, corner, and linebacker have the other box. If you are worried about the linebacker getting beat by the wheel pattern run by the number two receiver, you can check the coverage and go to zone.

To play the box quarter coverage against the trips set, the secondary has to make a decision (see Diagram #17). We play the quarter coverage with the free safety, corner, and nickel back playing against the two outside receivers. When we do that, the backside safety plays a three away coverage and takes the number three receiver if he goes vertical. Otherwise, we play the rules for the quarter coverage to the strong side.

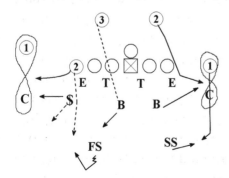

Diagram #16. Box quarter coverage

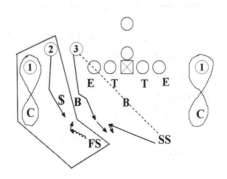

Diagram #17. Box quarter three away

The problem is the backside corner is on an island. To help us with this situation, we have an adjustment called nickel zone (see Diagram #18). That allows the strong safety and corner to play a two-on-one zone to the 1 receiver side. To the 3 receiver side, the corner has the wide receiver man-to-man and the free safety, linebacker, and nickel back play quarter coverage on the two slot receivers.

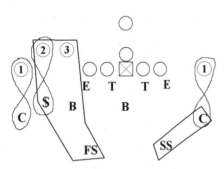

Diagram #18. Nickel zone

We only play the nickel zone against a trips set. We play a box 3 zone from this alignment. We play cover 3 rules and rotate down opposite the nickel back. That means the corners go into deep outside zones and the free safety rolls to the middle third. The strong safety rolls into the weakside flat, and we play three deep and four underneath. We show the four-man front and two-deep secondary and roll into the three-deep scheme.

We can run the box 3 against the trips set. It is not ideal, but we can keep the coverage (see Diagram #19). The inside linebackers drop their coverage toward the trips side. The nickel back drops under the number one receiver, the frontside linebacker drops under the number two receiver, and the backside linebacker drops under the number three receiver. The strong safety drops down under the number one receiver on the backside.

The box man is a two-deep, five-man-under concept. We play press coverage with the corner and nickel back on their receivers. The inside linebackers have the backs in the backfield. If they do not come out in a pattern, the linebackers are free. Where we might get in trouble is in a double slot or trips set with a linebacker in man coverage on the second

man weak or third man strong. In the trips set, the strong safety gives a "Three away" call to the linebacker covering the third receiver. That gives the linebacker help on any vertical run by that receiver.

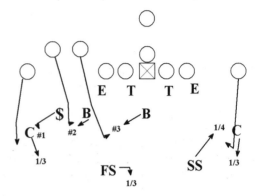

Diagram #19. Box 3 vs. trips

We play a load scheme with the 40 package also. We give the "Box load Sally" call, which means the safeties are coming down into coverage (see Diagram #20). The corners match up on the wide receiver in either a press or off technique. They do not have help because the safeties are responsible for the back coming out of the backfield. This is a six-man pressure package. Both inside linebackers come on a blitz from any number of angles. We run those blitz on scouting report data. The safeties need to be aware of the screen to the backs. If the backs block, the safeties make sure they know what is happening before they try to help someone. If the offense lines up in trips, we do not check the coverage. We match up with them and go get them. You have more rushers than they have blockers.

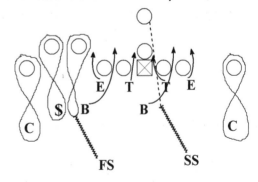

Diagram #20. Box load Sally

Those are the two packages we play against spread offenses. I hope you got something that you can use in your program. Thank you.

MOTIVATING THE DEFENSE

UCLA

It is a great pleasure to be here representing the UCLA staff. This was our first year at UCLA, and it was a big challenge for us coming into this program. We incorporate a new philosophy of what we do on and off the field. We put in a new offense, defense, and kicking game. We got used to playing new opponents in the PAC-10 and across the country.

I spent ten great years at Colorado State. I loved the atmosphere of working with Coach Lubick and had a great experience there. This is a new challenge for me and something that I look forward to.

We are going to build a program we think will be very successful. As we went through the PAC-10 Conference this year, we learned a lot about the conference. We found out everyone in this conference is equal except for Southern California. USC had an outstanding football team. The way we look at the situation is they have a three-year head start on our program. Our goal is to challenge them, and I think we will have a chance to do that down the road.

In order to achieve that goal, your players have to understand where you are coming from and what you do. You must bring a philosophy in which your players will believe. The philosophy has to be something that they buy into and can understand.

We believe you must build a relationship with your players. You build a bond with them so you can count on them, and they can count on you.

When we got to UCLA, we wanted a chance to get to know our players. The foundation we laid was the reason we were successful this year. We asked our players to do something on defense that was totally different. We told our seniors we could be successful if they bought into the philosophy and led the rest of the team. Our senior bought into our philosophy and gave us a chance to win this year.

We talked to our team about being faithful. Faithful means having a belief in the team. If you can get your players to believe in each other and believe that everyone is working together, you have a chance to win. They have to be accountable to each other. Everyone has to understand there are consequences for their actions. Everyone in our community and at UCLA knows who the athletes are. What they do and how they do it relates to everything your team does.

We do not have a lot of rules. However, the rules dictate that the players must understand what they do affects their teammates. We want our players to do the right thing. We want them to go to class, be on time, and treat others like they want to be treated.

We want our players to be teachable. Coaching is teaching. We take the information, pass it along to someone else, and see what results we get. To be a successful teacher, the students have to be teachable. They have to be willing to listen and learn. They have to accept positive and negative criticism because everything that comes from the coach is not positive.

Sometimes the coach has to admonish his players for options they chose that are not what the he wants. When you discipline a player, they have to understand that you attack their performance and not them. I think it is important to lay that foundation before you do it. As long as the player understands, he will listen to the coach. If the only thing that comes out of the coach's mouth is negative, the players turn him off.

When we have practice, we have a philosophy that goes with the way we do things on the practice field. The attitude of your football players determines so much. The player's attitude reflects how he contributes to making the team better.

There are a number of intangibles that a team must have. There has to be discipline in all areas of the football team. The discipline exercised off the football field carries over to the football field. Discipline on the field has to do with penalties, errors, and assignments. Discipline is so important in how a player takes care of business and what he does.

When the discipline becomes a peer pressure discipline, that is when you have things rolling. When the players demand each other to do things right, you have your program going in the right direction.

When we talk about a system, we refer to eleven players working together. Any system that is going to be effective over the long haul has to have execution. Execution depends on players working together. If players will trust one another, you can build something special on your team. You have to create situations on your team so players can have fun playing the game. Football has become a full-time job for the players that play the game.

It is difficult to keep the morale up on the team with all the things the players have to deal with. Winning is one way to keep morale up, but it is not the only way. One of the things I have done over the last ten years is to have a defensive Olympics. It is amazing how our players get involved this activity. We try to put it in the middle of the season during the bye week. That is when players are getting tired, and football is beginning to be drudgery.

We have the defensive Olympics among our defensive line, linebackers, and defensive backs. Each group gets together and picks the players that compete each day for their group. The first day, we have a field goal kicking contest. We score the results ten points for first, five points for second, and zero for third. The second day is the singing contest. The third day is the passing contest. We have three players for each team throw and add up their total throws. The last event is a question-and-answer quiz from the scouting report. We have the competition in the defensive room on the Friday before the game. We have the competition before we watch tape on the opponent we play the next day.

I give each team an easy question worth five points, a medium question worth ten points, and a hard question worth twenty points. The whole purpose was to get the players thinking about whom we were playing and what the key issues were going to be in the game. Everyone had a good time and we got what we wanted from the exercise.

We recognize our players for their efforts. We recognize our players with the Player of the Week Award. We make tapes of our players who make big plays in a game. It is important to praise your players and let them know you appreciate what they do within your program. Find reasons and ways to recognize what they do and make a big deal out of the award.

A big part of your in-season and off-season program is conditioning. Our players get up at six o'clock and participate in our running program. The off-season conditioning program is where you build a football team. Our team is growing in terms of understanding after the first year. Our players know where we are lacking and what we have to do to get better. It starts with getting stronger, quicker, and physically and mentally tougher. They are doing these things when it is tough to do them. No fans in the stands are watching them participate in this kind of conditioning. This is the critical period of time in the development of the team.

The ability to run is critical to our defense. The different between good players and great players is great players can perform great for longer periods of time. The great player has endurance and can play great in the fourth quarter. That is what we want from our players. When it gets tough in the fourth quarter is when you build your team. The ability for a team to dominate in the fourth quarter is critical.

I want to give our players a chance to be successful. Our defense is not vanilla, but it does not change from week to week. We build our defense with repetition to the point where it is simple. The offense sets the tone for the game. The defense is a reactionary unit. It reacts to what the offense does. The less the players think and the more they know, the quicker they react.

The players need to understand the defensive package as well as the coaches. At halftime of a game, the first thing the coaches do is meet quickly to discuss what is going well and badly, and what adjustments we need to make. The coordinators meet with their groups afterward and do the same thing. We want our players to tell us what they think is going on within the game and what we can do to get better. We get good feedback that way.

Because our plan is simple, if something goes wrong we know exactly what it was. We can go to the point of the problem and not have to worry about changing an entire plan. When we know the defense and where the play broke, we know who made the mistake. We can go to the player and ask what happened. He will tell you what he did wrong. That is what your execution is all about. When your players know as much as we do, that opens up the lines of communication.

By keeping your defense simple, you eliminate big plays. We are not a team that plays a lot of pressure packages and press coverage. If the offense scores, they have come up the long field and earned the score. We do not like the phrase "bend but not break" when it applies to our defense. But we like that better than trying to sack the quarterback ten times and then giving up three long touchdown passes. Our philosophy is to make teams earn the score. We led the conference this year in pass defense because we did not give up the big play.

Being simple allows me to gamble as a coach. We are in a position where we can pick and chose when we do our special blitzes and trick defenses.

We believe in playing percentages and not beating ourselves. We study our opponents and know their strengths and weaknesses. You have to know the strengths and weaknesses of your team also. After you generate all the data, you can play the percentages to keep the game in control. You have to examine and prepare yourself before the game so you can be flexible when things occur in a game that you do not plan.

Do not panic in relationship to the game plan. You have practiced all week and have prepared to handle things in practice. Do not panic when something goes wrong in a game. Stick with the plan and tweak it during the course of the game, but do not scrape it. We can tweak and correct mistakes at halftime. The good news this year was we shut out six teams in the second half. The bad news was some of those teams got a bigger lead in the first half than we could overcome.

One of the biggest indicators in success and failure in football is the turnover margin. We want to know how our defense reacts when our offense turns the ball over. Your players have to be conditioned to handle the sudden change. You have to talk about it before the game and have a mindset of how to handle that situation. We practice the sudden change in practice to build confidence.

I try to build a mentality within our player. The mentality is called play one play at a time. There are five phases to every play in a football game.

The first phase for the defense is to get into the huddle and gets the call (phase 1). That sounds simple, but too many times players come out of a huddle and do not know the coverage. That is unacceptable because we cannot be successful if players do not know the huddle call. That call tells the defense exactly what to do.

To play effective defense, the players have to recognize the formation of the offense (phase 2). From that information, the defense sets their strength according to what the offense does. After the formation has been recognized, the defense has to communicate all adjustments.

After the communication the defense has to line up. They get into an alignment on defense. It is essential for the defense to align correctly (phase 3). Too many times, the defense gives up a big play because they align incorrectly. Alignment is critical and you have to demand your players get lined up correctly.

The next phase is probably the most important that teams work on religiously. That phase is keying (phase 4). The key is the tool that gets the defense to the football. It tells you what kind of play the offense is going to run.

The final phase of the play is to execute the defense at full speed (phase 5). There are four or five plays in every competitive game that determine the outcome of the game, and many of them occur in the fourth quarter.

To be successful on Saturday is determined by what you do during the week at practice. A successful practice starts with tempo. Teach your player what you want from each drill and the speed you want the drill done. At our practice, this year for the first time we got to wrap up receivers in the 7-on-7 drill. We actually got to tackle receivers in a drill but not take them to the ground. That lets the defensive secondary make the play instead of simply saying, "I could have tackled him." This was a foreign practice at UCLA for the receivers. When you do things like that, you have to be smart about it. We do not want to hurt anyone by taking an exposed shot on a receiver. We simply want to experience tackling in the secondary on pass receivers. If you have bad habits in practice, they carry over to games.

There are fundamentals that have to be executed every day. Every day you have to tackle, do agility, create turnovers, and practice pursuit with proper angles. What I am going to get into now is something I show the players every week. I am going to go through these fast and show you the tape of I have on them.

Our philosophy on defense is run and hit. We talk about two things we want our defense to do. We want our defense to play fast, and to be physical. Those are things we try to stress. After every game

I talk to the team about the following seven areas:

- Tackling
- Pursuit
- Turnovers
- Sudden change
- Eliminating penalties
- Goal line defense
- Enthusiasm

We take the items after every game and look at them on what we call a challenge sheet. We are stressing those things in practice. For example, we tackle every day in practice. Our staff has individual tackling in their group period daily. It does not have to be full speed. Some of our best tackling drills are done without pads. We have one team tackling drill. During that period, the entire staff is together, and the players as well, as the coaches get to watch team tackling. The number-one fundamental in football is tackling. If your defense does not tackle, it does not matter how good the players are, where they line up, or how they play. If they do not tackle, the defense is no good.

I want our defense to run hard to the football. I want the offense to know we have tremendous pursuit and are going to have people around the ball. We practice pursuit every day. Our pursuit drill is a staple of what we do and what we believe in. It shows in a football game. If you do not practice it, it shows in the games also.

Everyone talks about creating turnovers. You have to practice forcing turnovers if you want to have a shot at getting any. If the ball is on the ground, you have to know how to get on it or when to pick it up. You have to have drills that teach going to get the ball out of the air. When we got to UCLA, we did not have defenders going after the ball at the highest point. Getting turnovers during the course of a game are the number one indicator in wins and loses.

We have talked about sudden change already. It is the mindset of the defense to go out and stop the opponent.

Eliminating penalties was the bugaboo for the year in our program. I came from a school where we led the conference for five straight in least amount of penalties. A lot of things are involved in eliminating penalties. You have to be disciplined. You have to demand it from your players. Your players have to believe it is important. We were penalized more this year than any team I have been involved with. Defensively, we were a part of the heavy penalties total at the beginning of the year. By the end of the season, we were playing well with regard to penalties. We did not have a penalty on defense in the last six games.

When you do not have penalties it helps you play better. You are not giving the opponent extra opportunities to beat you. You can have a third down and 22 yards for the first down, make the stop, and give up the first down on an interference penalty. Elimination of penalties on both sides of the ball is critical to your success.

Goal line defense is the place you have to stop the offense. The defense can't retreat anywhere. They have to make a stand. That is why I like to practice goal line defense live in practice. It is amazing how many plays you have in a game from the one- to six-yard line. In the old days, we practiced goal line defenses 15 minutes a day. The philosophy has changed in the goal line situation. With so many spread offenses, you do not have a definite goal line package.

The last point is enthusiasm. To teach your players to have fun and make plays is a big part of the game.

I am going to show the challenge sheet we give our players. This is our challenge sheet from our Washington game. We have the seven points of emphasis on the sheet, and I will talk about them one at a time. The first thing on the sheet is tackling. If you can keep the number of missed tackles under ten, you are doing a heck of a job. In the Washington game we had four missed tackles.

In addition to charting the missed tackles, I want to know how many additional yards were gained as a result of the missed tackles. In this game, the four missed tackles cost us 25 yards of field position. I want our players to see how great tackling leads to success. We have a point chart, and our players get points for their tackles. However, they also get negative points for the missed tackle in a game.

The next area is pursuit. We want to have great pursuit in the game, but that is a hard goal to accomplish. Against Washington we had one great pursuit and zero poor pursuits. I tell my assistant coaches they do not give a great pursuit unless they see something that is absolutely phenomenal and that makes a difference. What I do not like to see in these areas are loafs. In the Washington we had three loafs. We really grade hard on loafs in a game. Also included in this area are the hidden yard totals.

We put these numbers on the challenge sheet and keep a cumulative total for the year. The next section is the turnover numbers. If our defense can get the ball back for our offense or score on defense, that is a big statistic. We had several big plays off of turnovers, which will be shown in the tape.

In the game we had one situation of sudden change. The defense went into the game and stopped the offense. That is what we are looking for from our defense. As you can see, in the first five games, we had eight turnovers, and we only stopped the offense three times. The offense scored two touchdowns and kicked three field goals. One of the field goals is counted as a win for the defense. The offense got the ball on the 10-yard line, and we held them to a field goal. That is good and we let our players know that.

The next column is the penalty area. As you can see we were not good at the first part of the season. I do not like to give the offense an additional chance with the ball. That Saturday we had five penalties. We had two pass interference calls. We had one face mask penalty. That is a result of poor tackling and lazy play. Grabbing the face mask comes from a player being out of position and reaching instead of moving the feet. I harp on those penalties big time.

We had one holding penalty and one late hit. We teach our defense to play snap to whistle. By teaching that way, we may get a late hit on occasion. If the player is playing hard and the hit is clean, we do not complain too much. The hit out of bounds or the flagrant hit well after the whistle is never accepted. I do not want the stupid play that is going to cost the football team dearly.

I felt in this game we could have lost because of the penalties. That is a lack of focus and discipline. We really got after the players about the penalties in this game. If you look at our cumulative total for the remainder of the year, you can see the zeros in the game totals.

On the goal line I count from the one- to the six-yard line as a goal line situation. In the Washington game we never had a goal line situation, but previously we were 0 for 3 chances. We have not stopped the offense yet in that situation.

The enthusiasm part of the sheet is the entire situations taken together. We are looking for reactions on turnovers, sacks, tackles for loss, and big stops. Big stops could be a big hit on a third down play or a goal line hit. The big stop or hit is generally a momentum changer. On the enthusiasm I talk in general terms to the team.

Enthusiasm is the excitement factor. When we make a big play, I want our players coming off the field excited. I want them jumping up and down. I do not want any individual celebrations but I want that team celebration. That is what defense is all about. It is fun. It is going out on the field and getting after people and having a great time doing it. When a defender makes a play, he celebrates with his teammates because it took ten other guys doing their job for him to make that big play. This film is a picture of what I have been talking about.

At the beginning of our practice every day we have pursuit drill (see Diagram #1). It is a simple drill. We place the ball on the 25-yard line. One coach stands on the line of scrimmage to represent the tight end, and one stands on the goal line. We call a defense, snap the ball, and I point a direction for our

running back. The players get in their pursuit angles and sprint 25 yards to the coach on the goal line. He either gives a thumbs-up or thumbs-down. If he gives a thumbs-down, they come back and do it again.

In the drill I do not want to see defensive linemen run past linebackers.

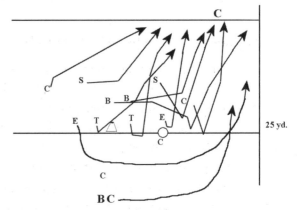
Diagram #1. Pursuit drill

We do a second drill on reaction to a screen. On this drill, I stand behind the line of scrimmage. (see Diagram #2). The linemen rush and the linebackers and backs drop into their coverage. The ball is thrown to the coach behind the line. Everyone breaks on the ball using proper angles.

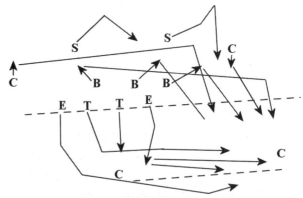
Diagram #2. Screen drill

The final drill we do is the intercept and score drill (see Diagram #3). The linemen rush, and the linebackers and backs drop into coverage. When the ball is thrown, everyone breaks back to the ball. When it is intercepted, everyone gets in front of the ball and we score with the ball. We emphasize blocking above the waist and making sure we have someone block the quarterback every time.

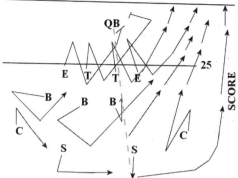

Diagram #3. Intercept and score drill

The next point you see on the film are some of the tackling drills we use in practice. This first drill is called the string out drill (see Diagram #4). In the drill, we have two blockers and a ballcarrier. We do not expect much from the blocker. They try to cut the tackler. He plays them off with his hands and makes a cross-the-bow tackle on the ballcarrier. I want the coach in a position to see the tackler's eyes. The emphasis is on running the feet at contact and running through the tackle.

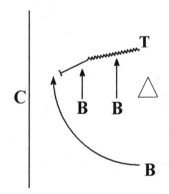

Diagram #4. String out drill

We use all kinds of tackling drills that require the defender to use the skills he has to apply in a game situation. We use goal line tackling drills and open field tackling drills. We do this daily.

The next drill is a 2-on-1 drill teaching the support man how to keep leverage and the fill man to get his fit right (see Diagram #5). The corner comes up in support, keeps proper leverage, and makes the tackle. The second defender could be a linebacker or safety back. He fits into the pursuit angle and finishes up the tackle.

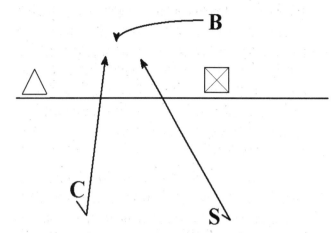

Diagram #5. Support and fit

With the film, you are giving your guys a picture of what you want to accomplish. The rest of the film is game footage of the skills we have been teaching. The first things are examples of pursuit. I want our players to see how important it is, and I make a big deal of it. On the tape, put all kinds of individual pursuit that shows extra effort.

The next thing on the film is turnovers. We were losing at halftime in this game. The first series after halftime we got a fumble, took it in for a score, and turned the momentum of the game. The tape shows interceptions and how they change the momentum of games. We have a defensive tackle intercept a shovel pass and run 65 yards for the touchdown. We won that game by three points.

You can talk to your players all you want, but these films give them pictures of the things you are talking about. It is a great motivation tool. We show them plays that relate to each of our points of emphasis.

You are going to be good at what you emphasize. If you are a defensive coach, I think the one thing you should emphasize over everything else is tackling. You have to find ways to do it without pads. Do it daily and create drills that let the defender practice the situations he has to face in the game. Make him tackle in space, against the sideline, and on the goal line. Find a way to critique your player in games. Thank you for your time.

MESHING THE ODD AND EVEN FRONTS

University of South Florida

I am very happy to be here today speaking for the Nike Coach of the Year Clinic. It has been a very satisfying season for us at South Florida.

It is a pleasure to be here. I think truth is funnier than fiction. I was out of a job, looking to find a position, when I got an inquiry from Dubuque University in Dubuque, Iowa. I was in Birmingham at the time, but I grew up in Florida. I had never been to Iowa, let alone a place called Dubuque. They had not had a winning season in forty years. I got the job. I remember I was paid $12,420 for teaching psychology at night, and was the new strength coach and counselor. The best part about this whole story is that I did not know I was also the new defensive coordinator. I went to the first meeting, and everyone was looking at me. I asked why they were looking at me. That is when they told me I was the new coordinator. I did not know what they had run the year before, but I had always been an odd-front guy. I found out they had run a 4-4 defense and that is what the head coach wanted to run.

I left there but couldn't find a job, so I went to Iowa to finish my PhD. I was 34 years old and was a graduate assistant, making $5,600 and happy as a lark. I was there at the same time as Kirk Ferentz, who is the head coach at Iowa now. I lived in the football office and loved every minute I was there. I went to every clinic I could and just spent time soaking up everything about the game I could.

I finally caught a break and went with Bill Snyder to Kansas State. What happened there was really important in my coaching career. Bob Stoops, who is now the head coach at Oklahoma, was the secondary coach. At the time there were 107 schools in Division I football. Kansas State ranked 106 in defense.

Coach Snyder called Bob Stoops and myself into his office and told us he wanted us to be co-coordinators of the defense. He told us to go out that night, discuss the possibility, and come back to see him in the morning. We went out that night and argued about the situation, but could find very little common ground. We went back the next morning and asked Coach Snyder to make a decision on one of us. He told us he had made a decision and we were co-coordinators, and he would see us in staff meeting tomorrow.

Bob Stoops and I shared the co-defensive coordinator job for six years at Kansas State. That was a life-changing experience for me. I learned a lot from Bob, and I would hope he would say the same thing. But what helped me the most was to get rid of the ego I had. I learned how to listen and not try to force my ideas on someone else. We worked together for those six years and went from 106 in the nation in defense to the number-one defense in the country.

The year I took the head job at South Florida, I flew all over the country because we had the number-one defense in the nation and people thought I knew something. We were doing the same thing when we were 106, but people did not want to talk to us then. That was eight years ago.

When I went to South Florida, that was a great opportunity for me. It has been a great situation. We started in a trailer with no desks, no filing cabinets, no bookshelves, no anything. I had never been a head coach and took a cut in salary to go to South Florida. It was never about the money; it was the opportunity. I had four coaches on the staff that worked for a dorm room and meals. The other four coaches worked for $12,000. The first year our program we went 5-6 and we have won ever since. We have won because we have had good people. We do not outrecruit people. We won three double overtime games this year. I just hope we do not loose three double overtime games next year.

The past three years we have gone 8-3, 9-2, and 7-4. We have had some talent. We have three guys who played at South Florida who have Super Bowl rings. We went 7-4 this year and finished third in Conference U.S.A. We beat Memphis the last game of the season and had eight first downs. We did not have a strong offense, but the guys did a good job of coaching.

The things I am going to tell you have not changed much since I was at Kansas State. I am going to give you some philosophical statements and then get into the X's and O's. I put this together real quick so I could fly with it. I have never wanted to run any kind of defense without a free safety. The only time we bring a full blitz is when we have a free safety, like the back of the end zone.

If the offense is on our 10-yard line, we feel like we have to make something happen. However, the offense cannot get too deep on us because of the back of the end zone. That serves as the free safety for us. We want to put a free safety in the middle of the field to stop the big play from happening to us. We work extremely hard to make sure we stop the big play in the run and pass.

We feel that to play good defense, you have to stop the run. We are going to do everything we can to stop the run. We load the box with the defenders to accomplish that goal. I was on the sideline this year at one of the bowl games and watched a coach let the other team run on him all day long, and he never loaded the box.

If we get beaten in the passing game because we are loading up the box, they are going to beat us. We try to make the offense one-dimensional.

We have to create turnovers. We work extremely hard at getting people to turn the ball over. We work on fumbles, interceptions, and scoring on defense. Against Memphis, we got seven turnovers. We had a free safety play in the North-South game. He was a walk-on for us, and now he may get a shot at the NFL. That shows you how smart we are. We hear these stories all the time. We have the great character kids that want to come, and we are so stupid we do not take them.

The kicking game is a huge part of any program. Most of your good defensive players are going to be on the kicking team. They can generally run fast and know how to tackle. We have a bunch of defensive backs on scholarship. When we travel, we take 11 or 12 defensive backs. Our kickoff team is almost all defensive backs.

The front line on our kickoff return team is made up of linebackers and strong safeties. We lead the nation this year in kickoff returns. College football has changed in its thinking about the kickoff teams. They are all going for speed on the kickoffs, not size. At South Florida, I am the coach who coaches the special teams.

The great equalizer in college football today is emotion. Your team has to play with emotion if you expect to win games. I am an emotion kind of guy. I go nuts and do silly things. South Florida was on TV a number of times this year and I am sure you hear all kinds of stories, but most of them are true.

You need to know the down-and-distance when you call defenses. You have to focus on third-and-short. You have to practice that situation so you and the players will know what we are going to do. On the third-and-three or less, your players should know what defense you are going to call. On third-and-seven or more, we will have your nickel package in the game. That adjustment gives you a good match-up in the third-and-long situation.

In our spring practice and in two-a-day practices, I put the ball on the six-yard line and work on goal line defense. I tell the offense to run the ball right up the defense's rear. We do that in the first practice. I want to see what kind of attitude we have on defense. I tell the defense the offense has four downs to score from the six-yard line, and every time they do, the defense is going to run four gassers.

If the offense does not score from the six, I move the ball to the three. If I am in a really bad mood, I will move it to the one-yard line. When we first started our program, the offense took the ball and scored eight times. Our defense could not stop anybody. After practice we ran 32 gassers. I ran with them because I want them to know I am suffering, too.

The next day I put the ball at the three-yard line, and the offense never got off the line. They could not run the ball anywhere. It was all different because all night long those defensive players thought about that drill. They came out in a frenzy, and the offense could not do a thing. The difference was not the scheme, because we used the same one from the day before. It was the mind-set, attitude, and emotions. That happens so much in football it is amazing.

We do our pursuit drill the first day we have practice. If we have one guy who does not go full speed, we do it again. When we first started the program here, we spent an hour the first day teaching pursuit drill. Do not compromise your teaching. If you have a guy on that team who will not put out, get him off the team or do the drill until he does it. Do not stop the drill until it is done the way you want it. If you are soft on the team, you are hurting them. Do not be soft with your team because you want them to like you. After practice is the time you spend with your team. That is the time you talk to them, hug them, and sit and listen to their problems.

On Tuesday and Wednesday night I sit on a bench outside of our locker room for two hours after practice. I sit right there until I have seen every player on our team. I spend time with them, talking and finding out what they have on their minds. I let them know how much I think of them. You have to let them know how you feel about them. If you are going to drive your team, they have to know that you are doing it for them. Do not play games with your team because they will see right through that. If you do not care about and love your players, you need to get out of coaching.

There are some fundamental ideas I sincerely believe in. I believe to play good defense, you have to play aggressive. When we practice, I go first offense personnel against first defensive personnel to bring out the competitive fires. Good defensive teams always tackle well. We had a good defense last year and finished second in our conference, but we still miss too many tackles. One of the chief fundamentals on defense is the pad level at which players perform. The man playing with the lowest pad level wins the battle. To stop the run, the defense has to play gap sound techniques.

Those fundamentals are the same ones we emphasized at Kansas State when we had the number-one defense in the nation. We were number one in conference U.S.A. until the last game, and Memphis nosed us out in that game. We won the game and they won the statistical battle on defense. We do okay, but we are not good enough yet. We have got to be a great defense.

I am going to show you a few things that you have seen before, and maybe a few new wrinkles. The first thing we want on defense is as much speed and attitude as we can on the field. If a player has speed but I cannot coach him, I do not want him. He has to be willing to do what I want him to do and be tough about it. If I have a guy with quick feet and he is tough, even though he may not be fast, I can work through that. I have to have the proper mind-set of everyone playing on the defensive side of the ball. Those players have to tough, ornery, mean, and want to hit.

We run the 4-3 defense, but we are going to load the box almost every time (Diagram #1). I want our down four as close to the line of scrimmage as they can get. I go completely out of my mind if any one of them gets reached. We always play with the inside hand on the ground. We are going to play gap responsibility football and are going to be gap sound at all times. The noseguard has to be able to draw a double-team. If he cannot, he is not very good, and you are going to have problems there. We are going to jump the ball and come off the ball with a mission.

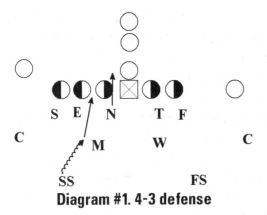

Diagram #1. 4-3 defense

The linebacker's keys are going to be the fullback and the guard pulling. We play them with their heels at five yards deep. They have to see the fullback and the guard pull at the same time. If the fullback goes one way and the guard pulls the other, we come back on the guard.

Our strong safety is aligned two yards outside the tight end and eight yards deep, but he is going to work that depth down before the ball is snapped.

We play the corners in man coverage and drop the free safety into the middle of the field. That is a transition from the way we did it at Kansas State. The way we play the secondary today makes it clearer how to play the deep ball because the safety is in the middle of the field. That allows everyone to play more aggressively.

We align the Sam linebacker on the tight end. He plays at a slight angle and cannot get reached.

The problem we have with the extra man in the box is the play action pass. The offense knows we are three deep, and it makes it hard on the defense. If you sit in that reduced defense, someone is going to make you pay.

We have made some adjustments that are really fun for our players to run. We have recruited a strong safety who is a big horse. We have a Sam linebacker who can really run. We bring our Sam linebacker off the edge and he creates havoc for the offense (see Diagram #2). The defensive line is looping one gap away from the Sam linebacker. To do this we move the nose guard off the 1-technique shade of the guard into a tight end shade on the center. That gives an odd look instead of the 4-3 look. The

3-technique tackle is looping outside the offensive tackle and the rush end is dropping to the flat area.

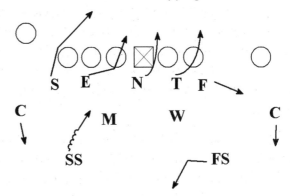

Diagram #2. Sam off the edge

I cannot tell you how many times the Sam linebacker has gotten to the quarterback or made big hit on the run for losses. The guy we had playing that position was a freshman out of Jacksonville. They have to be good athletes and be able to run. You can play this against one or two backs in the backfield.

If you are facing a one back set with the extra receiver in the weakside slot, you can walk off the rush end to align on the number two receiver weak (see Diagram #3). Another way to handle the adjustment is to put the Mike linebacker man-to-man on the tight end, roll the strong safety to the middle, and bring the free safety down on the number two receiver. You do not do that as a primary coverage because it is not as sound as other coverages.

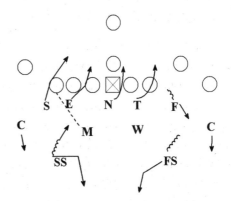

Diagram #3. One back adjustment

Our primary alignment for our disguise is a 2-deep look. We very seldom play a 2 coverage, but we will play it on occasion. If the corner is in a 1 or 3 coverage all the time, he has to play soft on the wide receivers. If he is in man coverage he is soft, and if he is in 3-deep coverage he is soft. We want to get the corner a chance to unload on the wide receiver to keep him off balance. We can do that from a cover 2. We may only run this coverage two or three times a game. But it allows the corner to play aggressively and keeps the wide receiver off guard as to the technique of the corner.

I want the down linemen moving and stemming on the line of scrimmage. When they leave the line of scrimmage and loop inside, they are reading hips as they go. If the hip is moving away from them, they get in the hip pocket and go with it. Our players are not as big as other defensive lines, but they can all run.

You can blitz from this defensive adjustment playing either man or zone blitz coverage (see Diagram #4). You can bring the Mike linebacker behind the loop of the defensive end into the B gap. If you play zone blitz coverage, all the defensive backs are looking at the quarterback, and they can make more plays on the ball. If you play man coverage, you only have the safety looking at the quarterback.

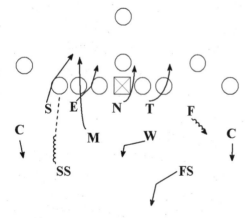

Diagram #4. Zone blitz Mike

At South Florida we are starting to get some corners that can match up in man coverage. When I was a Kansas State, we played man most of the time, and I am sure we are heading in that direction at South Florida. We want to move or front to get penetration (see Diagram #5). The offense is running so much zone-play offense, we have to get penetration. Penetration destroys the zone-running

offense. We get the nose guard and the 3 technique moving into the tight end side. We loop the nose guard through the strongside B gap and the 3 technique tackle through the weakside A gap.

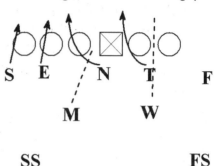

Diagram #5. Strong loop

I think you are going to see teams go back to the old double eagle defense. We ran a bunch of double eagle defense when I was at Kansas State, and the old Chicago Bears ran that with their Super Bowl team. If we get into the double eagle, it holds up against all runs except the option. It is hard to stop the option game out of the double eagle. We run the double eagle against one back or two back sets (see Diagram #6). We move the defensive end outside in a wide 9 technique or an 8 technique and angle him down. The Sam linebacker moves into a 6 technique head up on the tight end and locked on to him. We bring the rush end down into a 3 technique position to the weakside, and the Will linebacker moves out to a 5 technique off the line of scrimmage. The noseguard is head up on the center, and the 3 technique tackle is in a 3 technique strong.

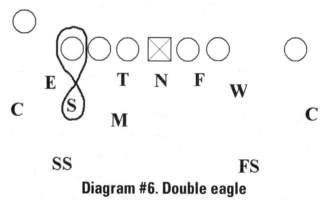

Diagram #6. Double eagle

We want to move into this front at the last second. You have to practice the move a lot to keep from jumping offsides because the Mike linebacker is going to call "Move." The Mike linebacker backs up to a depth of six yards. A huge coaching point for the Mike linebacker against a one-back team is to make sure the zone play commits to the frontside. He cannot let the zone play cut back on him. If the zone plays cuts back on the Mike linebacker, the only thing between him and a touchdown is the free safety. The Mike linebacker has to keep the zone play going frontside.

If you are going to use the double eagle, you have to practice it and know what the weaknesses of the defense are. People will use the double eagle only against one-back sets and with nickel defensive personnel on the field. We use it against a 2-back set with some adjustments (see Diagram #7). All the movements I have shown you are done at the last second from a disguise alignment. We do not line up in these defenses and let the quarterback automatic out of the play. We shift to the double eagle and move the Mike linebacker to the strong-side into a 40 technique on the offensive tackle. We bring the strong safety down to play the second linebacker into a 30 technique on the weakside. The free safety moves into the middle of the field.

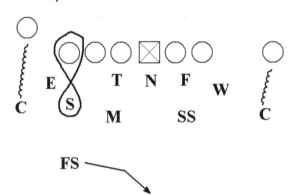

Diagram #7. Double eagle vs. 2 backs

The adjustment you are going to use against any team is something you are going to do during the week before you play. You do not need to adjust if you are stopping the run game from the 4-3. If they start to move the ball on you, load up the box or increase your movement with stemming. If the biggest problem you have is doing a million things, do not do a million things. Do a few things, but do them perfectly. You do that with unlimited reps in practice.

I want to show you one other movement that comes from the other side. This has been big for us (see Diagram #8). Our noseguard is in a weakside shade on the center. The rush end aligns in the 5 technique to the weakside. On the strongside, the tackle is in a 3 – technique, and the end is aligned in a 6 technique and comes off in coverage if it is a pass play. We are getting a strongside slant by the rush end, nose, and tackle. The Will linebacker is coming outside off the edge and is blitzing. The coaching point is to make sure the Will linebacker knows he has to cover the bootleg. When he blitzes. he has to come on the upfield shoulder of the quarterback.

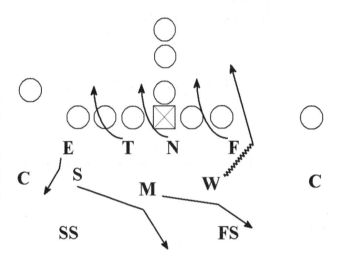

Diagram #8. 4-3 weakside blitz

We can run our reduced front and the 4-3 defense, which we can move to or away from the tight end. We can run the zone blitz package and the double eagle. The secondary coverage we play behind all those fronts and adjustments are man-free coverage or cover 3. That coverage depends on the ability of the corners to play man coverage. Even when we did not have those types of corners at Kansas State, and to a certain extent at South Florida, we had to get to the quarterback. The way we play defense is to move the front and load up the box.

The sets that give us the most problems are the two-tight end set and the four-wide receiver set. We are going to play our regular defense against those sets and do the best we can.

Gentlemen, thank you for your attention.

LINE BLOCKING TECHNIQUES AND DRILLS

Purdue University

It is a pleasure to be here. I have a bunch of old friends attending the clinic today, so I have to mention that I am originally from Poca, West Virginia. For people who are not from West Virginia and are not familiar with Poca High School, we are proudly known throughout the state as the Poca Dots. My name is Bill Legg, and I am the offensive line coach at Purdue University.

I have taken all these ideas from guys I thought were good football coaches. I tried to piece their ideas together into something that fit what I believe. I can take these ideas to the players and teach them with full conviction.

I firmly believe it is not what I know that is important. It is what my players can learn, understand, and execute that matters.

You have to teach your players in a manner they can learn, understand, and execute. The game of football comes down to the players on the field, not the coaches in the press box. I believe strongly that fundamentals win football games. We can talk about great schemes, but the guys that block and tackle best usually win the game.

The system in football allows your team to be successful, but it is the players within the system that win games. For the players to win games, they have to be allowed to play. Do not turn your players into robots by overcoaching them. The major concern of the coach should be that the player is getting the job done within the framework of the system.

My topic today is run blocking techniques. At Purdue, the first objective in running the football is for our offensive linemen to cover up the defenders. That means leaving no one unblocked on the defensive line. The second objective in the offensive line is to create movement.

Movement in our philosophy could be laterally down the line of scrimmage instead of off the line. It does not have to be vertical movement for the linemen to be successful.

To accomplish these objectives and goals, we start with the offensive linemen's stance. At Purdue, we are going to run and throw the ball an equal amount of the time. I want our linemen in a stance that does not indicate what they are going to do prior to the snap of the ball.

For us to have a balanced stance, the first thing we have to teach is the base. We have some tall offensive linemen whose stances have to be modified. However, for the average player, his feet are going to be shoulder-width apart. I have two players that are 6 foot −7, and they have to take a wider stance to get their hips down.

The toes in the stance are pointed straight ahead. By pointing the toes straight ahead, it gets the rest of the body pointed in the same direction. Our right side players get into a right-handed stance, and the left side players get into a left-handed stance. We get in those stances to accommodate the passing game rather than the running game.

We stagger our feet in our stance. The guards align in a toe-to-instep stagger. The tackles are in a toe-to-heel type of stagger. That allows the tackle to kick out of his stance quicker in pass protection against the wide outside rusher. That allows him to get his feet in position prior to having to move.

For us to have a balanced stance, the weight must be on the linemen's feet. We use the expression full-footed to teach our weight distribution.

The full-footed philosophy of the stance is going to depend on the flexibility in the players' ankles. The guard can get his inside foot flat on the ground because his stance is a toes-to-instep stagger. The outside foot of the offensive lineman has the weight on the ball of the foot. I want as little air as possible under the outside heel of the guard. With the tackles, I am more forgiving with the air under his heel because his stagger and the width of his stance are wider and longer.

After we get both feet as flat on the ground as we can, we talk about loading the spring. I talk to my players about being coiled up like a spring. From that position, they can explode. The linemen set their feet and squat to get down in their stance. We want to create good power angles in their ankles, knees, and hips.

The body posture in the lineman's stance creates a squatter's arch in his lower back. The forearms are relaxed and resting on the thighs. The lineman's chest is up in his stance. The description of a squatter's arch refers to a weightlifting technique that is done in a leg squat exercise.

If we are going to use a two-point stance, we stop in that position and get ready to play football. This is basically our two-point stance we use in our passing scheme. We can run the ball out of the two-point stance because this is a sound stance with all the fundamentals of a three-point stance.

To go to the three-point stance, we let the appropriate hand drop down and hang in front of the lineman. I tell the lineman to take six, which means to take six inches in front of the dangling hand and put the hand down. The rule is that the lineman is not allowed to use his thumb when he puts his hand down on the ground. If he does not use the thumb in the stance, the offensive lineman cannot put enough weight on his hand to get out of balance. The weight is centered over their hips, legs, knees, and feet.

When the hand is dropped to the ground, the weight will shift slightly forward. However, the hand can be pulled off the ground without the lineman falling forward on his nose.

The only time the thumb is allowed to go to the ground is in a short yardage or goal line situations. In those situations, the offensive line will be crowding the ball.

The first thing I teach when we go to run blocking is footwork. The reason I work on the offensive lineman's footwork is to increase the odds of him making a successful block.

The first movement in the lineman's footwork is called the set step. The purpose of the set step is to set the angle of the body at the target.

The length of the step depends on the position of the blocking target. If the defender is in front of the offensive lineman, the set step is picked up and put down in almost the same position. If the defender has to be reached, the first step is longer. The first step is not moving the lineman forward; it is putting his body into position to attack the target.

After the set step, the next step is an attack step. If the blocker is going to the right, he pushes off his inside foot and points his toe at the target to set the angle. The next step is an attack step. The offensive linemen attack the target with the second step. If the blocker attacks on the first step, he is going to have problems because of the slanting and twisting defenses. Offensive line schemes are more zone-blocking schemes than man-blocking schemes. If the linemen get too much weight forward, they cannot adjust on the second step to hit the target. The second step is a six-inch power step that regenerates the weight going forward to the aiming point.

You have to work the two-steps routine into your practices daily. I use T-boards to teach the two-step technique (see Diagram #1). You can set the T-board at different angles so the linemen can set their first step at different angles. The objective behind the T-board is to get the first step pointing in the same direction as the T and to get the second step down before the feet cross the T. We get power and explosion, and the base is still underneath the lineman as he moves out into his block. We use the T-boards in conjunction with the chutes as our first drill period of the day.

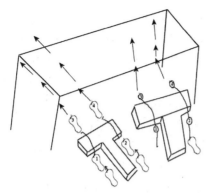

Diagram #1. Chute and T-board drill

My chute does not have any divider under it. It is 25 feet long and 48 inches high, and allows me to create any angles that I want to use. You can also pull and trap in the chute. I set the T-boards in the chute and go through a variety of angles very rapidly. For an offensive lineman to hit the target consistently, he has to understand the take-off. The take-off has to be ingrained.

The next thing in the blocking progression is target practice (see Diagram #2). When we take target practice, we use what we call a two-step punch mentality. The type of running play will determine what the target is going to be. If the play is an inside run, the target is the outside number of the defender tight to the sternum. On an outside run, the target is the armpit or the outside shoulder of the defender. On a gap blocking scheme, the target is the near hip of an inside defender.

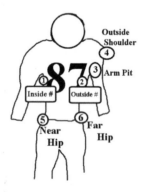

Diagram #2. Target practice

I always start with the target in close proximity to the blocker. Those techniques put the target at arm's length from the blocker. The blocker takes two quick steps. His nose and eyes should be on the aiming point of the defender.

In offensive blocking, I believe the blocker has to lead with his face. I do not think you should teach hitting with the head, but wherever the head goes, the body will follow. You cannot expect the offensive linemen to put his head on the outside numbers of the defender if he does not lead with his face.

The reason we do so much work in the chute is to stay low. We do not want our body angles to change drastically. We want the butt and head to stay down as we come off the ball. The blocker wants to surround the target with his hands, provided the target is big enough. We are leading with the face, but we want the hands to get to the target before the face.

The blocker, as he takes the set step, pulls his hands off the ground. On the second step, he shoots his hands to the target. We call that pull and shoot. We teach shooting the hands on the second step to get inside the defender's hands. The blocker rips the wrist, drives the elbow, and locks out on the defender. The punch, which comes from shooting the hands, has nothing to do with strength. The punch to lock out is nothing but speed and timing. You can drill the punch in the winter, spring, and fall programs to perfect the lockout.

Sometimes the target is too small to hit with the hands. When a lineman has to gap block on a defender, it is difficult to shoot the hands because the target is too small. To solve that problem we train two points of contact. On the big targets, we teach "hat and hands to the target." On the small targets, we teach that the shoulder and forearm are the points of contact. As the blocker comes down on the hip of the defender, he puts the ear hole of his helmet on the aiming point and brings up the forearm. The blocker is using the front part of the shoulder pad and his chest muscle to get into the defender.

After we work the offensive linemen with the defender in close proximity, we vary the distance. When we start to vary the distance, the target is removed from the area around the lineman. His block could be on a linebacker, a trap, or a log type.

We use what we call an arm's length rule. The rule states no matter how far the blocker has to run, when he gets within an arm's length of the target, he goes back to his two-step scheme. The blocker repeats the same skill as he did when the target was close to him.

After we teach the skill, we time it with target practice. We have the blocker fire up on a linebacker at linebacker's depth and watch his technique. We practice the technique of pulling and logging on a defensive end to perfect the angles of the offensive blocker. We pull a guard on a power play and let him turn up on the linebacker. We give him all the situations he has to handle in his blocking scheme. We rep it and practice it until the blocker has confidence.

In practice, the footwork drills are the first period after stretching. They are part of my warm-up drill every day. On Sunday afternoon, once we get our footwork drills and warm-up completed, we go to target practice drills. We start them on reach blocks and go to linebacker blocks. After that, we cover all the situation blocks that may occur in our scheme.

In the target practice drill we are checking their hats, eyes, hands, and shoulders. We want to make sure they are where they belong. We move the defenders around so the linemen have to work covered principles and uncovered principles in the drill. We call the play and work the two-step movement. We continue on with the drill, working aiming points for covered and uncovered defenders. From there, we work the angles and fits of the hands on the defenders. The key to finding success in these skills is repetition.

After we work on our footwork and fits into the block, we work on uncoiling and exploding on contact. The reason we do this drill is to maximize the leverage of the blocker. Defensive coaches are telling their defensive linemen the same thing I am telling my offensive linemen.

At some point in blocking low, you reach a point of no return. That means if the blockers get too low,

all they do is hit the defender and fall on the ground. Most contact between the blocker and defender is going to be like two rams butting each other in the head. When this takes place, the hand placement, forearm extension, and explosion are important to maximize leverage. We have to literally think we are running through the defender. When we do this drill, the contact has to happen fast.

We want to think in terms of diving off a diving board into a swimming pool. The offensive blocker wants to dive through and snap the wrist in the explosion of the block into the defender.

To run through a defender, the blocker has to keep his feet moving during contact. The reason blockers lose their feet at contact is because they try to jump off both feet. To finish the block, the lineman has to explode and take the next step. The step before the lineman hits the defender is important because that is the plant step for the explosion. When that foot hits the ground, the blocker drives his knee up to take the next step and explodes from the toes up through his body. The hips have to unlock because that is where the power is coming from in the block.

We do not teach our players to roll their hips. We do squats, cleans, dead lifts, and vertical jumps, and none of those exercises are hip roll exercises. Those exercises snap the hips and explode out, but they do not invert the hips. We want to use the same kind of movement that is required to perform a standing vertical jump. We want the hips to go through the shoulders.

When you do that type of exercise you maximize the power, and you maintain power angles. We want our butt behind the contact at all times. We want the butt to go through the shoulders.

The blocker wants to feel his arms lock out on the defender. If you were doing this blocking technique on air, it would look like the lineman is diving into a swimming pool and doing a belly flop.

The first thing I am going to do with the linemen to teach this technique is to get them in a six-point stance (see Diagram #3). They are going to get down on their hands and knees and rock back on their haunches. If we are not wearing pads, we may want to put a hand shield in front of them to break their falls. On the command, they explode from that position, with their knees going through their hip area, the hips going through the shoulder area, and the hands coming up in the punch. The movement is one motion, and they dive out and catch themselves on their chest.

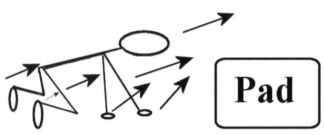

Diagram #3. Six-point explosion

The next part of the drill is to put a player in front of them with a hand dummy about arm's length from the blocker. The linemen do the same thing from the six-point stance, and the blocker can feel it as he explodes through the dummy.

We go to a fit up drill where the block and defender are placed into a fit position just before contact is made (see Diagram #4). This is the position a blocker would be in after the two-step punch. His nose is on the target, with his hands surrounding the target. He takes the next step, which is to explode the hips as fast as he can through the defender. The emphasis is on taking the next step so he can finish the block and locking out with his hands.

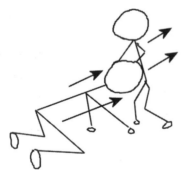

Diagram #4. Fit drill

In that whole process, the blocker is creating explosion, quickness, snap, and lock out. The third phase of the drill is to back them up and take them through the technique of the covered lineman. That allows the linemen to go from the stance through the block.

The defender is going to move at the offensive blocker. Even though we are exploding out and punching our hands, we are not going to get to the perfect lockout position. The blocker will never get completely uncoiled unless the defender is terrible. However, if the blocker can explode violently enough to get to the lockout position, he is in control.

On the second day of practice, we warm up with our footwork drills. We do a few target practice drills, but the primary work is done on explosion drills. The second day of the practice week is a big contact day for the offensive linemen. On Sunday, we did target practice, and on Tuesday, we are going to do the same drills, except we are doing the next step, which is explosion. If you do not do these drills full speed and live, the players will never improve their technique.

The finish to the block is the next part of the progression. Finishing off a block begins with attitude and effort. We want to use a sprinter mentality on the finish because we want to maximize the pressure on the defender. No matter how good the offensive lineman is, chances are the defender is a better athlete than he is. When they hit each other at the same time, there is not going to be much movement.

The fact there is no movement is fine with the offensive lineman. We are looking for a stalemate with the defense because eventually the defender has to get off the block. If the defender is going to make the tackle, he has to separate from the offensive blocker. If the offensive lineman wants to stay with the block, he has to maximize the pressure on the defender. The sprinter's mentality starts with the movement of the feet, the lower body, and the legs.

As the blocker starts to run through the defender, his toes will slowly move outside. We want to get as many cleats in the ground as possible. This allows the blocker to push an immovable object with maximum pressure. It allows him to change direction when the defender changes direction. The blocker's arms are going to be somewhere near lock out, and his eyes are totally focused on the target. That lets the blocker feel and see what is happening in front of him.

We do a drill to help the blocker finish the block (see Diagram #5). When we start the drill, we begin at the point where the blocker has exploded and nearly locked out the defender. On the whistle, the offensive blocker starts to crank his knees up and let the toes go out to get as many cleats in the ground as possible.

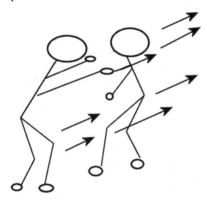

Diagram #5. Finish drill

The defenders start out the drill by not exerting much resistance on the offensive lineman. I will tell the defender to exert half pressure on the blocker. As the drill continues, I tell the defenders to load up and not let the offensive blocker move them. The defender makes the blocker run as hard and fast as he can in place. The defender has to eventually separate to make the tackle.

When the defender tries to separate, the blocker feels the movement. The blocker moves his feet rapidly and will not lose contact on the block. The defender has started the movement the offensive blocker needs to bury him. As the pressure from the defender lessens, the blocker's steps get larger as he maintains contact with the defender and continues to push.

We use a fit drill to practice the finish of the block. We fit the blocker and defender together with the blocker in his coiled position (see Diagram #6). The offensive blocker goes from an explosion to a speed finish. We do not narrow the base of our feet when we get into the sprinter's mentality; we simply increase our foot and knee movement. The key to keeping the wide base is the position of the toes. If the feet are pointed straight ahead, the feet will come together. If the toes go outside, the feet stay wider apart.

Diagram #6. Fit and finish

As we did in the other fit drill, the blocker backs up and executes the entire block from two-step to explode and to finish.

On the third day of practice, we are three days from the last game and three days until the next game. This is our second contact day of the week. We warm up with footwork drills and take a few shots of target practice, and a couple shots of explosion drill. For the next fifteen minutes of our practice the offensive line will work on finishing blocks. The pancake block comes from the finish of the block.

When we do separation drills, we work a one-on-one drill (see Diagram #7). I stand behind the offensive linemen and tell the defenders which way to try to get off the blocks. The offensive and defensive lineman locks up in a stalemated situation. When I blow the whistle, the defenders separate and the blockers work on their finish.

If a blocker is running as hard and as fast as he can, trying to run through a brick wall, his steps are short. However, if a defender is trying to get off a block, to run to the football, the blocker strides lengthen and automatically adjust.

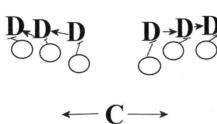

← C →

Diagram #7. Separation drill

We are going to do additional drills to improve our technique. We take the target drill and make it a moving target drill (see Diagram #8). Defensive linemen are not going to stand in one place and let the offensive linemen come out and hit them. The defenders are going to be moving or stunting to the ball. The key to the moving target is the second step. The first step is our set step. That step gives us direction in our charge. If the defender moves, the second step can adjust to that movement without destroying the base.

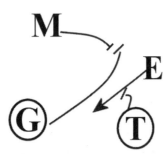

Diagram #8. Moving target drill

The next drill we do is called the replacement drill (see Diagram #9). If both players are trying to get their hands inside the other, in reality they end up with one hand inside and one outside. Each player has one hand on the chest and one on the shoulder pad. It is hard to get both hands inside at contact, but if the blocker works hard enough, he can get his second hand inside on the finish of the block. That is what we work on in the replacement drill.

To do the drill, we fit the linemen with one hand on the chest and one hand on the shoulder. I designate one of the players as the blocker and the other the defender. When I blow the whistle, the offensive blocker starts his finish drill and wheels his outside hand up underneath the defender's arm and replaces it inside on his chest.

Diagram #9. Replacement drill

Sometimes the blocker misses with both hands. When the whistle blows, the blocker wheels both hands inside during the finish working one hand inside at a time.

Throughout our drill work I am trying to create carryover for our players. If the blocker has a man over him and he is trying to create vertical push, I call that a drive-block. If the blocker is trying to get outside leverage on a defender, that is a reach-block. If a backside tackle has a man over him and he is running away from him, it is a cutoff-block. The drive, reach, and cutoff-blocks are similar blocks in relationship to the aiming point.

When a tackle has to down block on the man inside of him, it is a gap-block. If a tackle has to block out on a defender outside of him, that is a fan-block. The last block is a pulling block where the offensive lineman traps or logs a defender. Those three blocks are similar in the aiming point and punch.

To create carryover with all these blocks, the offensive lineman has to realize that the targets change. The second thing the blocker has to learn is that as the target change, so do the angles. The first step is the set step, and that sets the angle for the blocker. As the target and angle change, the adjustment occurs in the first step only.

The next thing we have to discuss is how that works into our two-man schemes. We have built carry over into every individual block. The individual blocks carry over into the two-man scheme. The offensive linemen have to get used to working with their blocking partner. If we run an inside tight scoop scheme as with the inside zone play, we block that play with a tandem block (see Diagram #10). In this scheme there is generally a covered lineman and an uncovered lineman. We have a blocker who base blocks the man aligned on him and a blocker inside of him feeling his way through the playside gap. We tell the covered blocker that the defender covering him is his assignment until he is pushed off by the blocker to his inside. We tell the uncovered blocker to track through the near hip of the down lineman, up to the linebacker, unless the linebacker fires through the gap.

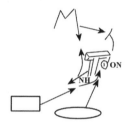

Diagram #10. Tight scoop

If the covered defender slants inside, the blocker adjusts his second step and goes from a two-handed punch to an inside forearm shiver on the slant defender. As the defender slants, he covers the uncovered blocker. Both blockers wedge the slanting defender up to the linebacker. One of the blockers will come off the wedge to block the linebacker. The linebacker will determine which blocker comes off. If the linebacker comes outside, the outside blocker comes off the wedge to block the linebacker. The inside blocker will take over the slanting defender and seal him.

There are several coaching points to this type of block. When the covered defender slants inside, we use the forearm instead of the hands. If the blocker tries to use his outside hand on the defender, his shoulders will turn, and he and the inside blocker will be pushing against one another. If the linebacker comes inside, the inside man comes off on the linebacker, and the outside blocker uses his outside hand to push the defender down the line of scrimmage.

We want to control the line of scrimmage first before we even think about the linebacker. We want to be patient with the tandem block and not be in a hurry to get off for the linebacker. If we are getting good movement on the down lineman, the blockers will not come off their double-team until they get to the same level as the linebacker. If we have a great defensive tackle and we are not getting movement, we stay on the double-team until the linebacker gets all the way up in the hole.

The full scoop goes with our outside zone play or the sweep (see Diagram #11). The covered offensive lineman is reach blocking. His aiming point is the outside arm pit of the defender. He is going to open, attack, and track the outside arm pit of the defender. The uncovered lineman is going to cover up the defensive lineman. His aiming point is the playside number of the defender. He is reading on the run, and has three steps to decide what to do.

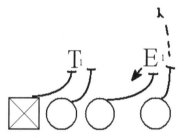

Diagram #11. Full scoop

The covered blocker stays on the defender until he is pushed off by the inside blocker. If the defender slants inside the covered blocker, he stays on top of the block, knowing that the inside blocker is watching the defender and coming to over take him. On the full scoop, we have two reach blocks working together.

When we combo block, we are aiming at the inside half of the defender, with the inside blocker and the outside half of him for the outside blocker. Both blockers are using forearms and not hands to secure the down defender. The inside blocker has his inside hand free and the outside blocker has his outside hand free. When one of them come off for the linebacker both offensive blocker engage the defender with their hands.

I appreciate the opportunity to come to talk to you.

DEVELOPING SPEED AND QUICKNESS

University of Notre Dame

Today is a special moment for me. I go all over the country speaking, but today in get to speak in my home area. I was born and raised in this part of the country. I attended Ambridge High School, where I played football, and graduated in 1983. I went on to West Liberty State University. It is fun to get to talk to some of my home folks. I am excited to be here.

My topic today is "Incorporating a Speed Program into High School." Basically, I am going to talk about the things you can do to help your athletes become faster.

The successful high school coaches start very early developing their athletes. You cannot do much about the athletes you get in high school, so you have to develop them. Everyone wants their players to become faster. I am going to share with you today some of the things we do that will help you with the pre-training you are involved in.

First I want to start with our program philosophy. Why are you doing what you are doing? What kind of results are you getting? This is what we stress.

You get what you emphasize. If you emphasize squats and bench presses, with no agilities and no running exercises, then that is what you get. You get players with big thighs, big barrel chests, and big rear ends. They cannot get out of their stance. If you do athletic drills and speed drills, change of direction drills, and reaction drills, the players will be able to move out of their stance. You get what you emphasize.

As a coach, you emphasize how you want your players to act on and off the field. It is the same thing in the weight room. If I just open the weight room and allow the players to come in and do the things they want to do, then that is the type of program I will get. We emphasize technique just as you do on the football field. We stress two things in our program. We stress technique and effort. If you have great technique in whatever you are doing, you are halfway there. Now we want them to give us the effort.

The second point is this: You get what is tolerated. If you tolerate giggling, horseplay, and unsupervised behavior when they are in the weight room, then you are not going to have a successful program. You get what you tolerate. Football coaches and strength coaches need to understand it all starts in the weight room. The season is over in December. The first thing for the next season is to step into the weight room. That first day or week in the weight room better be what you want in your program all year. It better be what you are asking them to do off the field. If you tolerate horseplay and silly behavior, that is what you get.

If you emphasize all lifting and no running, you get a big, strong team that cannot move. You must take this into consideration when you are developing your program. This goes with speed training, agility training, power training, strength training, flexibility training, and math training. It does not matter. You get what you tolerate.

The other thing you must have is a great attitude. Attitude and effort are everything. The first question I am asked by pro scouts is this: "Are they coachable?" We make our players coachable because we emphasize hard work and discipline. If someone would ask me to tell them about our strength program, you would hear the word accountability over and over. We stress accountability for being on time, and for players' actions. We set penalties if players are late for practice. In football, if the players make a mistake and goes the wrong way, the quarterback is carried off the field with an injury. It is like jumping offsides. It is not the player that jumped offsides that has to go back five yards; it is the entire team that has to go back five yards. What happens in the off-season with one player, the entire team has to suffer the consequences of or give up something to help the team achieve our goals. Attitude is everything.

You can tell when a player is having a good semester at Notre Dame. The schoolwork is going well, his bench press has improved, and his speed has improved. He comes into the weight room, and he is happy as can be. On the other hand, if he comes into the weight room and he does not have a smile on his face and he is not full of energy, you can tell he is having problems. It may be in the classroom, a problem at home, or a problem with football. If they have a great attitude, we know the players are on their way to success.

The last thing I try to do every day, and I think everyone in coaching should do, is to educate, motivate, and cultivate our athletes. My job is to motivate them. Sometimes players do not want to work hard. You have to motivate them to work hard.

We have to cultivate them as young men. We need to help them to mature and teach them to take care of their body. They must understand how important the strength and conditioning program is in football.

As in any sport, we must have a systematic plan. You must work on weaknesses. We work with each individual to see where we can help them. We ask them what their weaknesses are. If an athlete tells you they do not have a weakness, then they are lying to you. You have to work with the individual players on this matter.

We have to hold everyone accountable. This means everyone in our program. This includes the coaches in the indoor program. If a coach is not serious in the indoor program, then get them out of

there. I have had to do things by myself in the indoor program. Make sure the person that is working with you in physical training has a passion for what you are doing. They must have a passion for the kids. They must be willing to put in the time with the kids.

We want to reward great attitude and work ethic. We want to reward great accomplishments. But I still like to find ways to reward the players that are not the great athletes. The record boards are great. I try to take every aspect of training to judge the players on so that everyone has a chance to be on the record board. We include speed, strength, agility, change of direction, and conditioning on our record board.

We encourage coaches to use their coaching abilities and their God-given gifts in working with the players in the weight room. This is a very critical factor now in college and high school athletics. A coach must decide what he can do that will help make a difference in the lives of the players he works with. The question at times is simply, can the coach make a difference? If you cannot make a difference in a player's life in society today, then you need to take your name tag and give it back to the principal and move on. I know that is not the case with those of you here tonight because you are trying to pick up one or two ideas that will help you and your program.

Let me talk about motivation. These are the things we do at Notre Dame to motivate our athletes:

- Testing
- Timing
- Goal Boards
- Atmosphere
- Goals
- Aesthetics
- Competition
- End Results

Day in and day out, the players are not going to come into your program cheery-eyed and full of pep and ginger. That is not reality. So first, for us, is testing. This is the one way to make sure they are accountable for what you are doing. We use the NFL combine items and test in our program. That is our test. It includes the 225 bench press, pro agility test, three cones, and all the other things they do in their test. That in itself is a motivation for our athletes.

The second point is timing. I am talking about handheld electronic timing. The topic is speed training. How do you know if they are getting faster if you are not timing them? Timing is big in terms of speed training. We take the human aspects out of the timing device. In high school, you may not be able to do that.

We have goal boards all over our weight room. I meet with every player twice a year, and we talk about individual objective and subjective goals. I send a sheet home to the parents to let them know how they are doing. Then they have to answer to their parents.

We try to put our athletes in the best training atmosphere to achieve the best possible results. We do not have Beethoven's music playing. Back in the 1960s, they did a study at West Point where the maximum lift of a bench press was done with the aid of a gunshot or a starting pistol, as used in track. They reported a twenty to twenty five percent increase by using the starting pistol. Now, we can not take a gun into school, obviously. You must have something to excite their central nervous systems. The atmosphere is a key to any program.

We know everyone has a budget to follow. We paint the walls and put up nice boards for our goals. It does not take much to put up some nice logos. You can get the art department to help you with logos.

We use the aesthetics as much as we feel is necessary. We have weight room signs and other motivational techniques. I like the Rocky II stuff to motivate the players.

In most of the drills we do, we try to make them competitive. We have them work against each other. We push them to the limits. That is how you get the best results.

Let me get to the strength/speed plan. Here is the ultimate plan for high schools.

- Ultimate (Five days per week)
- Lift three times per week.
- Football speed two times per week.

From here we progress to the next level. Now we go four days per week.

- Lift two times per week
- Football speed times per week.
- Some of the small schools may not be able to work five days per week. That is why we say it is the ultimate schedule.

If the players come to you and tell you they are doing the weights hard enough, you can switch to the two-days-per-week lifting schedule. If they are not lifting hard enough, then you should continue to lift three days per week.

All of our speed training is done in the off-season. Research tells us it is almost like riding a bicycle. Once you learn it, you have the skill, and it will stay with you for awhile as long as you use it.

If you do not give the players the proper amount of time between runs, it becomes a speed endurance program. Football coaches do not want to give them a minute and twenty seconds between sprints. Some coaches only want to give twenty to thirty seconds' rest. That is when it becomes speed endurance and conditioning and it is not speed training. One day in the summer would be sufficient if you did it in the off-season. I am only talking about speed training, and not conditioning.

If you are on a four-day program, I suggest you go two days of lifts and two days or runs. If you have the time, some coaches want to go four days of lift and two days of running. We do two lifts and two runs. You should always avoid football speed work immediately after heavy leg training. There are two reasons for this. One, you are setting the players up for possible injury. The second point is this. To get true speed training the athlete must be fresh. The best thing is to do the running before the leg training. You must set your program up to your situation.

Football speed is the ability to accelerate to and from different angles, positions, and techniques. True speed will never be reached before you complete 40 yards. Maximum speed occurs at 50 yards to 60 yards. In football, how many times does an athlete go from zero to sixty yards? You can count them on your hand, and that is just for one player. That is the player that runs back kickoffs and punts. So the question is this: Are we really into true speed? We are not really into true speed. A lot of people will say football is a game of speed. I do not agree with that statement. The reason is because we are never into speed. Football is a game of acceleration from different angles. It is movement at different angles from different positions. Change of direction and agility is football speed.

We talk about speed of limb movement. We discuss linear movement, which is straight-ahead running. Lateral movement is change of direction and reactions and quickness drills. Change of direction and acceleration drills are the things you need to work on.

Next I want to talk about factors that affect football speed:

- Strength (power)
- Technique
- Overall conditioning
- Flexibility/mobility
- Explosiveness (quick twitch)
- Ability to play faster
  a) Aggression
  b) Mental knowledge
- Strong convictions
- Competitiveness

The baseline of your speed program should be the baseline of your strength program. A stronger muscle produces more force. There is no question on this fact. Speed or acceleration is the amount of force you apply to the ground when you run. That is what you are looking for. The stronger you are in the weight program, the better they are going to be in their speed program. It is true of plyometrics as well.

For the high school situation, techniques must be one of the factors that affect football speed. So many athletes waste so much energy they lose their running form. This should be a key in your program.

The better-conditioned the athlete, the easier speed training is for them to adhere to. Just being a better athlete is going to help them with conditioning. Look at the Olympic athletes. How many of them do you see that are not well conditioned and trimmed down? They are usually athletes with only three, four, or five percent body fat. Body fat corresponds with speed.

Flexibility is a key issue in injury prevention. It all depends on the range of motion you have around your joints. That is very critical in speed training. Mobility is moving flexibility.

We call explosive work the quick twitch. It relates to plyometrics and side drills and hurdle drills. They are real quick explosive moves. They also affect speed.

The result of improved speed is the ability to play faster. If a player does not know where to go, he cannot play faster. If a player is soft, he is not going to jump into the heat of battle and tear someone's head off. We want players playing faster, and we want them playing with aggression. Mental knowledge of the game is another factor that allows players to play faster.

I talk to our athletes all of the time about strong convictions. The players must be convinced they can become faster. They must be convinced this program is the right one for them to become faster. It is the job of the coaches to convince the players that this is the best program. Sometimes you may have to use outside influences to help with this. That is because we have so many different sport institutes and speed gurus. They are all over the place, and that is fine. They have clinics, just as we do. Go to one of their clinics and see if you can find something you can use from their program.

If you want your athletes to be faster, then something has to be competitive for them to improve. Also, they need to have rewards, and punishments if they do not improve. It may be as simple as doing push-ups, but you need to have something to motivate them in the drills.

First you must have a comprehensive strength program. It needs to be a year-round deal. The second point is to have a football speed development program. Third, flexibility and mobility must be included in the program. Some football coaches hate flexibility programs. The more flexible the athletes, the move productive they can become. Whatever you are doing in a program, you must have accountability. Athletes must be held accountable, just as coaches are held accountable for wins and loses. Nutrition and recovery must be a part of the football speed program. If you are going to train hard, you must eat right. You need a rest period because it goes into the equation, just as much training does. At times our athletes get confused. They say, "I though you said we were supposed to rest." We tell them train a muscle, feed a muscle, and rest a muscle. It is not the other way around.

Here is our football speed format:

- Dynamic Warm-up
- Mobility/flexibility
  a) Hurdles
  b) Wall drills
- Plyometrics
  a) Low level (dot drill, jump rope, etc.)
  b) Moderate (vertical jumps)
  c) Movement (power skips, bounding)
- Technique
- Linear
- Lateral speed and agility

- Football position technique
- Movement runs
  a) Speed improvement drills (high knees, skips, shuffle)
- Acceleration (Starts)
  a) Speed stance/starts
  b) Ground starts
  c) Ball drop starts
  d) Resistive starts
  e) Competitive
- Power speed conditioning
  a) Harness
  b) Sled push/pull
  c) Hill running

Speed endurance
  a) Sprints/limited rest

High-end sprints
  a) Sprints/maximum rest

The first thing we do is the dynamic warm-up. We do whatever it takes to get the body structure loose. Our second thing we do is the mobility/flexibility drills, which include the hurdles and our wall drills. We have three levels for our plyometrics that we do. We have a low level, a moderate level, and a high-intensity program.

The first thing we talk about in plyometrics is lower-body strength. You can not take a sophomore and have him do the high-end workout. You have to start the young players off slow. We do not want them to get shin splints and knee problems. The power skips and bounding are the high-level movements.

We always try to throw the component of football into our speed training. The last ten yards of a sprint may be from a linebacker's position. We have them take two shuffle steps and then turn and go. We may have a lineman take his pulling steps and then turn and sprint.

To us it is not just about the 40-yard dash. Who cares about that? He is either fast on the field, or he is not fast on the field. Although the 40-yard dash is important in accountability and testing, we know we have to work on it. I am more concerned how they move on the football field.

Next we go into our movement runs. These include the high knees, the skips, and the shuffling drills.

Most of our work is done in accelerations or starts. We go 5 yards, then 10 yards, and then 15 yards. You do not run much further than that distance unless it is a big play.

We work on speed stance and starts. I see some of our linemen get down to run the 40-yard sprint, and they have their hand two yards behind the starting line. They have to run 42 yards. We work on ground starts where the players have to start from a ground position. It may be on their stomachs or on their backs. In football, if you get knocked on your tail, you must be able to get up and go. We have a ball drop start, where we drop a ball and the players react on the drop of the ball. That is a reaction drill, which is a part of acceleration. The other thing we like to include in the acceleration program is the competitive aspects.

The power speed conditioning is the harness work. We push and pull sleds. Also, we run hills to develop speed and conditioning.

Speed endurance is sprints with limited rest. That is what we talk about in the summer. You may have lines of eight players run together. That is more like speed endurance. It is speed work, but it is more endurance. This is close to what everyone does. True speed work is with maximum rest. In football, you do not have that much time. High-end sprinting is more what the track teams do with their sprinters. It is high-end sprinting with a lot of rest.

I will show you our dynamic warm-up and flexibility program on film. It takes us about ten minutes to go through. Basically, it is the drills to fire all the muscles in the body. We call this our linear day workout:

- Walking knees to chest
- Walking lunges
- Cradle/butt kick wall
- Straight legs walk
- Straight legs skip
- Walking hip rotation
- A skips
- High knees
- Butt kicks
- Backward run
- Back pedal
- Fast feet
- Quick pace
- 75 percent runs

We tell our players the key to running is to get the elbows locked at ninety degrees. You can't just tell them to get the elbows in tight. They are not going to get that move. We tell them to get the elbows at ninety degrees, and that the rotation must come from the shoulder joints. When they are speed training, their hands are loose. In about eight weeks, you will find players that could not run very well at the beginning are running more fluidly. A lot of our speed work is to shuffle 5 yards and then turn and sprint 15 yards. We may say backpedal 5 yards and then turn and sprint 10 yards. We make it a transition-type run. It is not just straight-line running.

We teach the players how to run a 40-yard dash from a three-point stance. We like the ground starts because that is more like football. If you get knocked down, you have to get back up in football. Also, I like the resistance running. Again, this is more related to football.

Here are the mobility drills we do:

- Hurdle mobility
  a) Over-under
  b) Lateral straight leg
  c) Lateral over under
  d) Over-over

- Wall drills
    a) Leg swings front to back
    b) Leg swings side to side
    c) Hip rotation with internal rotation
    d) Hip rotation with external rotation

Here are the plyometrics we do:

- Quickness (5 to 10 seconds)
    a) Dot drill
    b) Line hops
- Vertical jumps (8 to16 reps)
    a) Power jumps
    b) Truck jumps
    c) Cone hops
- Horizontal (10-20 reps)
    a) DBL Leg hops
    b) Power Skips
    c) Broad jumps
    d) Bounding

Next we talk about the techniques used in linear/lateral/change of directions:

- Walking
- Marching
- Skipping
- Fast movement

Our movement runs are:

- High knees (fast)
- Back pedal (fast)
- Fast feet (fast)
- Position start and transition

Our transition runs are:

- Shuffle/run
- Carioca/run
- Back pedal/break
- Cut n touch
- Decelerators
- Tapioca/run

We do the following starts/acceleration:

- Speed stance
- Ground stance
- Resistive starts
- Ball Drop starts
- Competitive

We do the following power speed/conditioning:

- Sled pull/push
- Resistive runs
- Hill running

For speed endurance, we run short sprints from 10 to 40 yards. We have a limited rest period. For high-end sprinting, we use a maximum velocity of 40-plus yards with a maximum rest.

Next is our lateral speed/agility format. We start with our dynamic warm-up:

- Knees to chest
- Walking lunges
- Cradle/butt kick wall
- Straight leg walk
- Straight leg skip
- Walking hip rotation
- High knees
- Butt kicks
- High knee carioca
- Carioca
- Shuffle
- Cut 20s (Zigzag)

For the mobility we do the following drills:

- Hurdle mobility
    a) Over-under

b) Lateral straight leg

c) Lateral over-under

d) Over-over

- Wall drills

a) Leg swings front to back

b) Leg swing side to side

c) Hip rotation with internal rotation

d) Hip rotation with External rotation

Next we have our agility drills. We use these six drills:

- 4 corner cone drill
- Pro agility drill
- Open hip drill
- Shuttles 20/30/40/60
- Bag drills
- Mirror dodge

We do the following for conditioning. We do these in the off- season and in the summer:

- 60-yard shuttles
- Mini gassers
- Stations
- Basketball conditioning
- Relay teams

We play basketball as a conditioning drill. We break up the teams and they have a draft and have a lot of fun with it. When I was a coach in high school, we did relays for our training. This creates a lot of spirit. We tend to make things so hard for the athletes. It should not be that hard. We say things like, "Lift more than you did the last time. Run faster than you did the last time. Block better than you did last week." We do not need to make it that hard for the athletes.

We do what we call finishers with competition. It may be the tough man contest or strong-man contest. Again we have competition in the drills:

- Relays
- Walk of doom
- Tire flips
- Wall sits
- Tug-o-war
- Grip hangs
- Navy Seal workouts
- Team runs (stadium, hills, dunes)
- Speed groups

This is how we set up our program. You can get a better idea with the tape.

Question: What is your view on stretching?

Static stretching must be done when the body is warmed up. We do not do a lot of time before practice stretching. For us it is all moving drills. As we progress in our warm-up we progress with our speed.

Let me get the film going. I appreciate your attention. Good luck next year. If you need anything, just give me a call. Thank you.

DEFENSIVE LINE TECHNIQUES AND STUNTS

University of Notre Dame

My topic is coaching the defensive line. The defensive line is critical in playing defense. If you have a good defensive team, it is because you have a good defensive line. If you have great linebackers and great defensive backs, but only an average defensive line, your defense is average.

The defensive line coach has to be a great teacher. I take pride in my defensive linemen being intelligent. Do not pigeonhole your linemen by saying they only need to know a few things to do the job. If you do not teach your players the entire aspect of every stunt and defense, you will have problems with their performance.

I know we have a lot more time than high school coaches, but I give my linemen a mini-playbook every day. They have a tip sheet for everything we do in practice that day. I think you have to do a great job in the little things in teaching.

The defensive line coach has to be a great motivator. The best way to motivate your players is to make them accountable to you. The only way I know to make them accountable is to give them a grading system. I grade players with a plus and minus on techniques. If the only grades you have are plus and minus, you run the risk of having a robot who is a good technician but never makes a play. We grade all of our players on a production chart. In addition to positive points within the grade system, there are negative points.

The first thing our players want to see after a game is the production chart. I think a combination of plus and minus grades and a production chart is a good way to motivate your players.

I think defensive linemen are special people. To coach those people, you have to have a great passion and enthusiasm for the game. Your players will feed off the defensive line coach. If the coach is having a bad day on the practice field, the players in his group will have a bad day.

When you coach the defensive line, you have to be demanding, but also consistent. From the beginning of practices, the players must know only one way exists to do things. They have to do things your way, or it is not acceptable. When someone does something wrong, he hears about it. There is no one in the program who is protected form correction.

For a defense to be successful, they have to stop the run. My teaching motto is SATKR. That is an acronym for stance, alignment, technique, key, and responsibility. All those traits have to be present for a player to be a great defensive lineman. If one of the traits is missing, he will not be as good as he can be.

When our players come to camp at the beginning of the year, I treat them as if they know nothing. The stance we put them in is not the only stance in America, but it is the one in which we believe.

When we teach our stance, we talk in terms of a three and a half- point stance. The best stance to be in is a four-point stance, but it is impractical. You cannot pass rush and stem as easily from the four-point stance. I want to make one point, which I will make again and again tonight. What you see on film is what you are coaching. We want our defensive line at Notre Dame to be the best technique line in the country.

The first element in the stance is the width of the stance. We want the stance to be shoulder-width apart. That equates to how the player walks.

That is how wide the feet should be apart. If the stance is too wide, the defensive lineman has lost time in getting to the man he is facing.

A defensive lineman wants his toes and heels in a straight line. That is critical to a good stance. The most important thing about coming out of a stance is how fast the defender can get to player he is against.

I want the defensive lineman to have the weight on the inside of his feet. In linemen's stance, they should be knock-kneed. If you make them grab grass with their big toe, that will put pressure on the inside of the foot.

We want a toe-to-instep relationship in the stagger of the feet. When the defender comes off the ball, he is always gaining distance toward the man he is against.

The inside foot of the player's alignment is back. To get in the three and a half-point stance, we start in the four-point stance. Once we get in the four-point stance, we lift the inside hand off the ground.

The player's hands are loose as he gets into his stance. We do not want him to form a fist with his hand. That keeps the player tense. When you get in a stance, the shoulders are square and straight. That is the stance from which we want to play the run.

I am not going to spend too much time talking about alignment. Everyone in America is playing gap control defenses. That is what we tell our players. They will align as to their ability to control their gaps.

If the defender has a B gap responsibility, he has to align on the offensive blocker in an alignment that allows him to get into and control the B gap. If that means his inside foot is down the crotch of the offensive blocker, that is his alignment. If he cannot control the B gap from that alignment, he has to get wider. The problem, obviously, is the further the defender gets away from his technique, the more susceptible he is to other blocks.

When we talk about technique, I never mention footwork to our players. We want to explode our face and hands toward the target, and the feet will follow. A key point about contact is to explode with the heels of the hands through the man, and not to the man. If you do not talk about punching through the man, you end up playing patty-cake.

We want to punch to grab. We do not want the hands to fly off the target after the defender hits the man. When we talk about hand placement, we want our hands above our eyes. That allows the defender to play with his chest over his knees, which puts the defensive lineman in a good hitting position.

We never talk about rolling our hips in our explosion drills. The only time we roll the hips is during the tackle. If the defensive lineman rolls his hips, he is belly to belly with an offensive lineman who outweighs him and is going to hold him. We want the natural separation that comes from playing with the hands out.

When we key a blocker, we look right at the face mask. I try to convince players there is no one on the practice field or the game field except the man on which he is aligned. If you can get that point over to your players, you will win more battles than you lose. The defenders who get in trouble are the ones that are looking all over the place for the ball.

The only thing I tell my players about responsibility is for them to get their hips in the heat. We are a shade team, and most of the blocks we play are reach blocks. I do not want to hit and steer the blocker. I want the hit and to get my hips to where the force is coming from. In most cases the force is coming from up the field.

If the offensive blocker knows where the defensive lineman is going, he will win more than he loses. He knows the snap count and is probably bigger than the defender. If the defender plays a perfect technique, we still will lose. The defender must have the ability to go three ways. The offensive lineman has to wonder where the defender is going. The offensive blocker has no greater fear than missing the defender completely. We angle, loop, and stem to give us movement from a shade technique against an offensive blocker.

When you teach your linemen to stem, make them take pride in the movement, and do not let them get sloppy. We want them to move quickly. If you are a stem team, make sure you work on angling. If the offense snaps the ball while we are stemming, that charge becomes an angle charge. We continue the movement off the stem into an angle charge to our responsibility.

You can cue your lineman to stem in three ways. You can let the linebacker make the call, or the noseguard make the call. If you know the opponents cadence, we can stem off their cadence.

The last thing I want to cover before we get into the angle movement is the criteria for loafers. We did not do a good job of this last year. That is my fault, not the players'. I put the product on the field. If I do not teach them well enough, that is my problem. You can never justify a player loafing on the field. To grade a loaf, you have to define what it is.

We base our loaf grades on the following criteria: changes speed running to the ball, teammates passing him in pursuit, caught lying on the ground, and not laying out on the pile before the whistle blows. The last criterion is critical to being a great defense. We were an average defense last year because of that. Two years ago we had a great defense because we kept coming until the whistle blew.

There are some techniques involved with the three-way-go scheme. When you play a shade defense, offensive line coaches tell me the most difficult thing they have to deal with is the defender angling across the blocker's face. There are some critical points to these kinds of movements. Never cheat the alignment to run an angle stunt. If we are angling inside, we only have to play two blocks. We have to play the drive and reach blocks. If the block is a cut-off block, by angling we have played the perfect squeeze technique.

The defender is aligned on the outside shade of the blocker. On a drive block, the offensive blocker is angling outside to get to his block. That makes it easier for the defender to angle across his face. The reach block is better because the aiming point on the defender is wider than the drive block.

When the defender angles from a shade alignment, he always reads the man he is over, not the man to his inside. As he angles, he wants to narrow his stance. The most important thing in the angle technique is to gain distance with the first step. The angle is not a forty-five degree angle. We never step forward on the first step. It is a flat step to the line of scrimmage. If you step forward from a shade technique, the defender runs into the blocker every time.

By taking the flat step down the line, the defender, on his first step, is over the blocker's head gear. If the blocker tries to reach the defender, his helmet goes outside on the defender. When the defender reads that, he does not try to come back across the face. He plants his inside foot, comes off the blocker's butt, and runs flat down the line of scrimmage to the outside.

If the blocker tries to drive block the defender, on the first step the defender's head is inside the drive blocker, and he wins the battle. If the blocker goes inside, the defender squeezes inside and comes off the offensive blocker's butt. This technique applies to every position we play in the defensive line.

The defensive end playing over the offensive tackle has a tough time if the offensive tackle knows he has containment responsibility. The tackle thinks he can come off hard every time, and the end will never come inside. When we give the tackle the inside angle, that slows him down immediately. If our end has containment, we tell him to come late on the containment, when he has an inside angle.

We frequently call two stunts in our run defense. The first stunt is called a spear stunt (see Diagram #1). The aiming point for the defensive end is the offensive tackle's hip. If the tackle did not move, our defensive end hits him right in the hip with his face mask. He is coming flat to the line of scrimmage. We tell the end he can never be wrong. The only way he is ever wrong is to get too high. If the tackle blocks out or pass blocks on the defensive end, the end should be under the block.

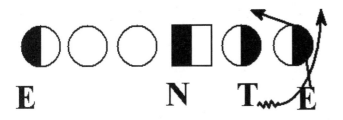

Diagram #1. Spear stunt

We do not tell him to get under the block. He is on a railroad track coming flat down the line of scrimmage. He is taking on anything he meets on that track. The 3technique defensive tackle cheats three inches back in his alignment. That allows the defensive end room. On the snap of the ball, the tackle takes two shuffle steps to the inside. The thing that destroys this stunt is the defensive tackle getting in too big a hurry to run the stunt.

The defensive tackle has to give the defensive end time to get down inside. If the offensive tackle is coming down on the defensive tackle, the end crushes his charge and knocks him down. The defensive tackle never has to worry about getting blocked. If the tackle gets too fast, he ends up forcing the defensive end wide, and that becomes an awful stunt. The tackle wants to come off the end's butt and become the defensive end. The defensive end becomes the 3 technique.

The defensive tackle cannot run up the field. This is a run stunt, not a pass stunt. If the tackle runs up the field, a huge gap is left on the line of scrimmage. He is able to tell whether it is a run or pass by the offensive tackle's block. If the blocker disappears down the line, the defensive tackle needs to stay on the line of scrimmage. If the blocker has set up in a pass blocking set, he rushes the passer.

The linebacker playing behind the stunt does nothing. He plays as if there were no stunt. His technique has not been affected. The linebacker is not involved with the stunt. If there is a tight end to that side, the stunt is off. We only run this stunt to the open side of the formation. This is a good stunt to run with the under front.

When we play the over defense, we use this stunt. This stunt is similar to the spear stunt, but different. We run a whip stunt. (see Diagram #2). Before the snap of the ball, the Will linebacker walks up on the line of scrimmage and does the same thing the defensive end did on the spear stunt. We want the defensive end to tighten down on his 5 technique, cheat inside, and back off the line of scrimmage. That gives the Will linebacker room to get inside. If the end is wide, the Will linebacker bows his charge. The defensive end has a rule that controls the way he plays. If the tackle blocks on him or inside, the end comes around late. If the tackle blocks out on the Will linebacker or uses a pass set, the defensive end goes inside.

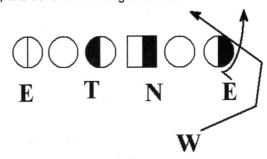

Diagram #2. Whip stunt

These are two good stunts we run to the open side of the formation, against the run.

The jet alignment is a technique we use for our defensive end (see Diagram #3). The end is in a cocked 5 technique stance on the offensive tackle. We want his inside hand exactly two feet from the outside foot of the offensive tackle. That is critical in this technique. The end has his inside foot back in his stance. On the snap of the ball, we go two steps as hard as we can, extending and thrusting our upper body and hands at the hip of the offensive tackle. Our aiming point is his hip, not his headgear.

This technique is where we talk a great deal about closing the air between the blocker and the defender. That is the catchphrase we use to describe the space between the defender and the blocker. Whenever the tackle's hip goes away, the end has to close the air with his feet. The end runs a straight track down inside at the hip.

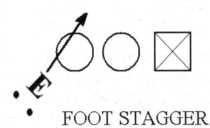

FOOT STAGGER

Diagram #3. Jet alignment

As the end attacks the hip of the tackle, everything happens. The first rule the defensive end follows is to have no air between the end and tackle. We know on nine out of ten blocks, the hip is going away from the end. If the hip goes away, the end continues to close until there is no space between him and the tackle. At that point, the end squares his shoulders and shuffles down looking for the cutback run or bootleg.

There are a number of blocks the defensive end has to play from the jet alignment. The first block is the base block. If the offensive tackle tries to base block the defensive end, he completely blows up the offensive tackle. He runs his track inside with such speed that the offensive tackle cannot turn him out. This allows you to play this position with an undersized end that has speed.

On the reach block, the tackle is closing the air with the block (see Diagram #4). When the defender sees the helmet come outside, he squares his shoulders, gets his hips to the heat, and rips upfield. "Getting the hips to the heat" means he turns his hips upfield against the blocker and upper cuts or rips upfield with the inside arm.

Diagram #4. Reach block

If the tackle goes inside and flattens out but does not cross the line of scrimmage, the defensive end knows it is probably the bootleg (see Diagram #5). If the tackle goes away inside and fans up across the line of scrimmage, the defensive end know it is a reverse. If the offensive guard is pulling to protect the bootleg, the end attacks the guard and gets his hips to the heat.

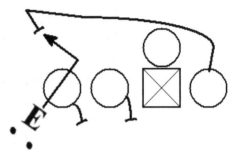

Diagram #5. Bootleg

We do not tell our defensive end to look for the blockers (see Diagram #6). If the defensive end closes all the air between him and the tackle, the offensive blockers will find the defender. The defensive end spills the blocks coming from the fullback on the kick-out or the pulling guard on the counter. However, I want him to take the block on with his head inside, but I want his hips working upfield. He spills the ball, but he tries to get out of the block to help with the tackle.

KICK OUT

COUNTER

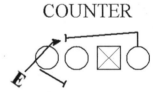

Diagram #6. Kick out and counter

If the defensive end did nothing but close the air on the down block and get as close to the tackle as he could, that is a great technique. He does not have to find the blockers because they have to find him. If the defensive end does not close, he is in trouble.

We have a saying at Notre Dame. The saying is, "If you cannot play a 6 technique, you cannot play at Notre Dame." That is a true statement. We take unbelievable pride in how we play the 6 technique. A 6 technique at Notre Dame is nose to nose and toes to toes on the tight end.

There are three types of blocks the 6 technique has to play. He has to play the power scoop, the cut-off, and the influence block. We play our 6 technique with the defender's outside foot back in his stance. We are firm believers that you cannot attack one man and key another man. The combo block of the tackle and tight end on the 6 technique gives me nightmares. No worse feeling exists than what you feel watching a tackle and tight end zone block the 6 technique with the linebacker trying to scrape to the ball.

The reason we play with the outside foot back is to be able to maul the tight end (see Diagram #7). If the tight end tries to power scoop the defensive end, the 6 technique puts him in the backfield. If you have an average defensive end, have him run off the football as hard as he can. Have him put his face through the tight end and drive him back. As soon as the 6 technique gets his feet to the line of scrimmage, it is time for him to get his eyes inside. Knocking the tight end back off the ball eliminates the power scoop.

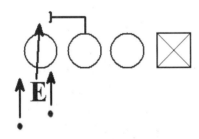

Diagram #7. Power scoop

There are some negatives to playing that type of technique. If the tight end releases outside on a pass, the 6 –technique's momentum runs him away from the quarterback. The second thing is the cut-

off block. We have never worried about the cutoff block because we are bigger and more physical than the tight end. We stuff the tight end back into the hole and make the tackle with his butt.

The 6 technique end is a C gap player. Any time a lineman pulls across the face of the 6 –technique, he can void his C gap as long as he stays inside the football. If the ball cuts inside the 6 technique, he is wrong. The linebacker is pursing outside the defensive end.

What teams try to do to our 6 techniques is influence them (see Diagram #8). They know the tight end cannot block him so they fake the outside reach block. They hope he widens and becomes an easy target for the fullback to kick out. Anytime we see the helmet go outside, the 6-technique closes as quickly as he can on the offensive tackle.

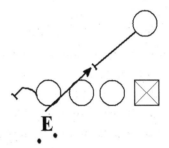

Diagram #8. Influence

We have one coaching point for playing a block. Too many times the defensive lineman becomes an offensive lineman when he plays the block. They do all the technical things correctly except they do not look for the ball. When they attack the blocker and get their hips to the heat, they have to get their eyes back inside. The ball is going to be on the inside most of the time.

To be a successful pass rusher the player must believe that no one can block him. When the offense wants to throw the ball, generally there are five blockers and four rushers. We challenge them on a pass play by telling them that three of the four pass rushers will be in a one-on-one situation with the pass protector. As hard as it is to pass block, if the rushers cannot get to the quarterback, they need to go to the offense.

Do not teach a lot of pass rush techniques. Pass rushing is like wrestling because we shoot the move and make the lineman cheat to stop it. After we shoot the move, we have a counter move that gets us clear. We have five moves we teach. I do not expect all the defenders to use all five of the moves. They find what they do well, and use it. We teach the bull rush, speed club, slap club, counter club, and spin.

In the bull rush, the defender explodes with his hands. He attacks half of the offensive lineman. We make three-point contact with the offensive lineman. We contact the chest with our hands, and the chin with the face mask. We want to accelerate the feet and push with the hands to get to the quarterback.

In the speed club, we club with the arm and leg together. If the arm and leg are not together, we are beat. We club the middle of the offensive linemen's back, grab jersey, and rip through the outside arm. The hands and feet have to keep moving to be a good pass rusher.

The slap club is a slapping movement on the offensive blocker's hand by the opposite hand of the defender. That allows the defender to get the speed club into the middle of the offensive lineman's back.

On the counter club, the defender has to sell the outside move with alignment and foot movement. On the first step, we sell the outside move. On the second step, we plant and come inside and club using the club leg together with the arm.

In the spin moves, we sell the speed club on the first step. We plant the shoulder into the numbers, swing with the arm all the way around, and slap the back of the offensive lineman. Make sure you accelerate the feet coming out of all moves to the quarterback.

Before I quit, I want to show you some games we use in our pass rush. The first game is between the 3 technique and the 1 technique. It does not matter who is in those positions. We call this a twist (see Diagram #9). The "t" in "twist" tells us the tackle goes first. The tackle comes first and gets

his helmet to the hip of the center. If the tackle gets his helmet into the crease, we win. If the guard comes off the tackle to block the nose, the tackle makes the sack. The center cannot block him with his helmet on his hip. The nose guard attacks the center on his shade side. He delays and comes off the tackle's tail into the gap of the offensive guard.

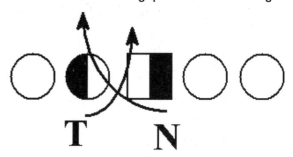

Diagram #9. Twist

We use the thumbs game on the outside (see Diagram #10). The tackle goes first, and the end comes second. This involves the 3 technique and a 5 technique or 6 technique end. The end is the key to the game. He has to get off the ball fast to make the offensive tackle open his hip to him. The 3 technique is speed clubbing on the guard and working for containment. The end plants and comes underneath the offensive tackle. Nine out of ten times, the center is waiting for the end. The end is running full speed and should beat the center's block.

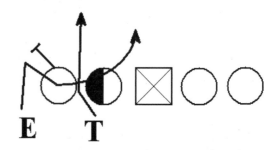

Diagram #10. Thumbs

If we want to bring the end first on a game we call "ears" (see Diagram #11). The "e" in "ears" means the end comes first in the stunt. On the end's first and second steps, it looks like the thumbs game. On the second step, he comes under the offensive tackle using a spin or counter club. The tackle takes two shuffle steps inside to freeze the offensive guard. He plants and goes outside for containment. If the end gets his headgear in the crease of the guard, the defensive tackle makes the sack.

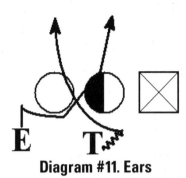

Diagram #11. Ears

When the defense runs a stunt, they cannot be selfish. If they cannot get the sack, they must make sure their buddy does. We run the Ed game with the 1 technique and 5 technique (see Diagram #12). That would occur on the bubble side of the under-defense or the weakside of the over-defense. The nose guard has to occupy the center and the offensive guard. He cannot smother the center and let the guard come off on the end coming underneath. The end sells the upfield move and comes under the tackle. The noseguard occupies the center and guard, and comes outside for containment.

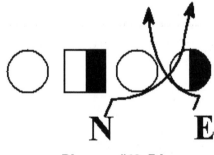

Diagram #12. Ed

Do not run games just for the sake of doing something on the defensive line. Have a purpose for running each game you run. If you think the offense is going to run the draw, the twist is a good move. It screws up the offensive scheme and protects your linebackers. Any time the offense is protecting by using turn back protection, the ears game is an excellent call. If a team runs a lot of sprint draws against us, we run the Ed game.

If we do not know what to run, we run a four-man game. That means no matter what the offense is doing, they will be in the wrong protection. This game is called Tex (see Diagram #13). Everything is planned, and we are not grab-bagging just to be running something. On this stunt we run a thumbs to the 3 technique and 5 technique players, and an Ed to the 1 technique and 5 technique players.

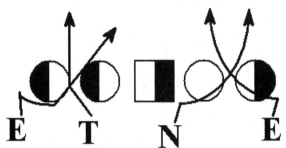

Diagram #13. Tex

We run games because we know what the protection is going to be. Against a shotgun set with a back sitting next to the quarterback, that tells you the center generally blocks away from the set back's position. We give a "green" call, which means we come off the center shade and run two 3 techniques (see Diagram #14). We know the center is turning away from the back. We run no stunt inside toward that direction. We void the center gap and run the stunts to the outside and the center's backside. We can run double thumbs and double ears and bring pressure without running into the center.

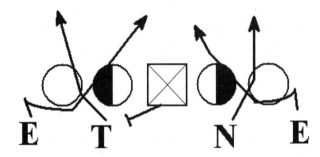

Diagram #14. Green double thumbs

Thank you for your time and attention, and thank you for having me.

Noel Mazzone

SCATS AND SCREENS IN THE PASSING GAME

North Carolina State University

Today I want to share with you some things I think we do well. I think we do a good job with the screen pass. It does not matter what kind of offense you run, wing-T, wishbone, spread, or any other offense, any time you can get the ball to the perimeter, it is good.

I am going to cover our two- and three-man scat routes, our screens passes, and our play action passing game. I will cover our screens off our bootleg. If I have time, I will cover how we game plan. Stats are stats. Stats do not win football games. They do give you a barometer of where you are on offense.

First I want to start with our scat passes. We had a good quarterback that really made our offense go. He made us good coaches. He threw for 4400 yards and 37 touchdowns, with only 7 interceptions. He is a great kid. Is he a great passer? No! But he is smart. Our attack has always been simple for him. If you look at the numbers in our two- and three-man scat game, we are throwing the ball with 83 percent completions, and we are averaging 8 to 9 yards per completion. We think this is good for our offense. It is something that Norm Chow started when he was the offensive coordinator.

Before I get to the scat routes, I want to talk about our goals on offense. If we can throw for 250 yards, we will win the game. Not true! If we can run for 100 yards, we will win the game. If we can throw the ball for 58 percent completions, we will win the game. These are good goals to have, but do they really have any bearing on if you win or lose the game? You may only complete 2 passes out of 10 attempts and win the game.

Two years ago, we took an idea from Ralph Friedgen of Maryland related to goals. All of the goals are secondary goals. These are the goals that really make a difference. We take the offensive penalties, sacks, turnovers on fumbles and interceptions, and dropped passes and look at those. We add all of those things up and divide them by the total number of plays you run in a game. If you can get that number under 12 percent, you have a 90 percent chance of winning the football game. In the games we won, we achieved that goal of 12 percent. In the games we lost, we were over the 12 percent except for one game. When you think about this, it makes sense.

OFFENSIVE OBJECTIVES FOR 2002

GAME	PENALTIES	SACKS	T-O FUMB. & INT.	DROP BALLS	NO. PLAYS	%	W OR L
NM	4	0	2	2	73	11	W
UNC	3	1	0	1	70	7	W
G-T	6	1	2	1	70	14	L
B-G	2	1	0	2	87	7	W

If we have two sacks, two offensive penalties, one turnover, and three dropped passes, it comes to a total of eight. We divide the total points by 73 plays and that comes out to 11 percent. Just think about this. Because you rushed for 150 yards does not mean you are going to win the football game. What our stats do is to keep us on track as a play caller. What throws you off-track? Penalties! We all can live with second-and-ten, but I hate second-and-fifteen. We all know the turnover is the great equalizer at any level in football. If you drop the football, it is hard to win the game. So this is something we sell to our players. We want them to get the total mistakes down below 12 percent, and we can win the game. We do not have to call any trick plays, or any other thing. For us, this theory was right 23 out of 24 times.

Now let me get into the two-man scat routes. Our X end is the man running the scat route. We want the formation spread from the hash marks to the hash marks. If the ball is on the right hash mark, we want our X on the left hash mark. You must get the spacing correct on the play. He splits about five yards out from his tackle. He wants to run the route between the two linebackers inside. He splits the difference five or six yards deep. He does not cross the center of our formation. He works in front of the guard and tackle box (see Diagram #1).

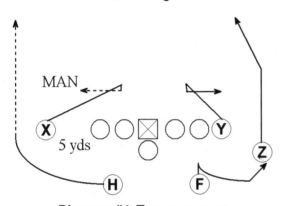

Diagram #1. Two-man scat

If the X receiver is open, he gives the quarterback his eyes. If he is not open, he does not give the quarterback his eyes. Against the man coverage, we tell him to run the pattern inside and use a punch-and-pivot move. He comes inside and punches, then pivots, and works away from the linebacker.

The H back wants to release and gain ground. He is running downhill. If the defensive man closes on him, he runs the wheel down the sideline.

On the three-man side, the tight end is running a scat route. He is the third look in the progression for the quarterback. He has from the center to the area outside the tight end area to run his pattern.

The F back checks and then releases. The Z receiver is running the deep post route. We call it a glance route.

Let me talk about the protection on the play. We want to get the back on a free release. We are in a seven-man protection scheme (see Diagram #2).

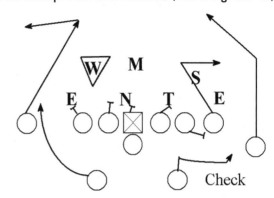

Diagram #2. Seven-man protection scheme

The protection to us is our 60 scheme. If we call "60 Will," it tells the H back he is the hot receiver. If the Will linebacker comes on a blitz, the H back has to look for the hot route. If we call "60 Sam," it tells the F back he is the hot receiver if the Sam linebacker comes on a blitz.

Out of the one-back set, we have a cluster on the right. The Y receiver runs the post (see Diagram #3). The Z receiver runs the scat route. The H back runs the swing route. Now we must be in our 50 protection. We must release the back on the outside on a hot route because we have only five protectors.

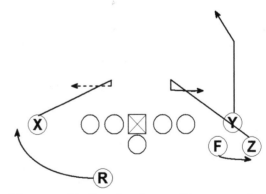

Diagram #3. One back set, 50 protection

The offense gives us two advantages. We can line up wherever we want, and we know the snap count. That is the only things the defense gives us. Other than that, we do not know what is going on.

We all have heard of the phrase, "Familiarity breeds great defenses." If you have a stagnant offense and you line up in the same set all of the time and run the same plays over and over, it makes it easy on the defense. We are not going to have a lot of plays. We are going to run the two-man scat, three-man scat, throw some screen passes, throw the curl - flat game, and throw a couple of verticals, and that is it. We are going to try to improve as much as we can. To do that, we are looking for plays that do not take a lot of thought process and a lot of adjustments by our offense. We want to keep it simple for our guys. We are a team that tries to out-leverage the defense. We want to make the defense make adjustments against our offense.

You can run the two-man scat with any two receivers. You can run it out of any formation.

Now we are going to add the third man into the route. Now it becomes a three-man scat route. We go into a game with three ways to run two-man scats, and six ways to run the three-man scats. We are going to do that by changing formations. First, we want to make them stop the two-man scat, and then we give them the three-man Scat. The plays complement each other.

We call the play red right zip – 60 Sam - Y corner - Z (see Diagram #4). The X receiver runs a glance route and looks for the ball on the seventh step. The Y receiver runs the corner route. The Z receiver runs the scat route. We can motion or line up with scat splits.

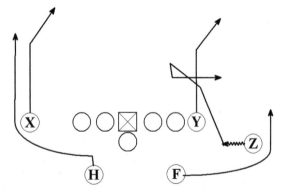

Diagram #4. Red right zip/60 Sam – Y corner -Z

We want the quarterback to look at the Y receiver on the corner route. Next, we want him to look for the back on the swing route. If they are not open, then he looks for the scat route.

We run a basic scat route, with the Y receiver running a square in route. The X receiver runs a corner route. It is what we call a collect corner. He wants to go inside and attract the Will linebacker's attention to come outside. The Y receiver runs the basic route, which is a square in route (see Diagram #5). The Z receiver runs the scat route. The rule is this. If we call "basic," he can never cross the face or the receiver. He is a punch-and-pivot receiver and is in what we call auto reverse. He is trying to pull the Sam linebacker outside. The backs check release or run the free release swing.

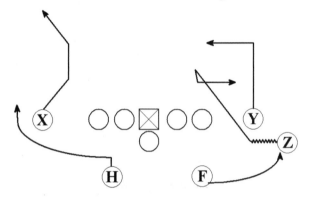

Diagram #5. Red right zip — Y basic - Z

When we get into the red zone, we call "Y PAC Z." When you get deep around the 20-yard line the safeties start setting their feet. They are not as deep, and they are ready to sit on the basic routes. We want the Y receiver to give the safety the corner move and then run the post route. PAC is a double move route (see Diagram #6). He could give him the post move and then run the corner, depending on what we have been doing in the game. PAC gives him the option of running the post or the corner. It should be POC for post or corner, but we call it PAC. We are trying to throw the ball in the end zone. When we call "PAC," that is the first receiver the quarterback looks for on the route. If he sees cover 3, he will look for another receiver. If he does not like what he sees, he goes to the scat receiver.

We run the mesh, which is help for a two-man scat route (see Diagram #7). We get the same scat spot move. We get the same reads: zone, sit, man, run. Everything else is the same. You have to teach your receivers to get a tight mesh. It is the same configuration the quarterback is used to looking at.

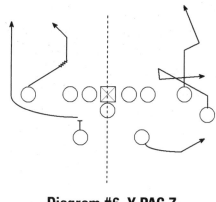

Diagram #6. Y PAC Z

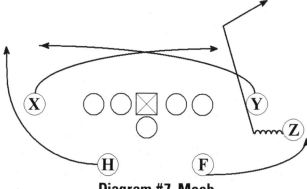

Diagram #7. Mesh

The coaching point on the mesh is this. You want the same splits, but we are going to take a little tighter split with the Y receiver. We have a five-yard split with our X receiver. The Y receiver is a little tighter now. The Y receiver is going to mesh. He is always going to set the mesh. It is the same as he does on the scat. It is five to six yards deep over the football.

The X receiver works off the mesh by the Y receiver. He comes under the mesh by the Y receiver. It is the same principle as the two-man scat. This is one play you have to work on. The hard thing on the play is to make sure the Y receiver makes the mesh before they look for the ball. The receivers want to start peeping at the quarterback before the mesh. We tell them not to even think about catching the football until the mesh.

If the defense is playing man- to-man, nothing changes on the route. The Y receiver still sets the mesh. The X receiver is working to rub off the mesh. If it is man coverage, all we tell them to do is to butterfly. We have to work on these plays.

We threw our screens close to 100 times. We were 88 percent on the screens, and averaged nine yards per throw on the play. When we start practice, we take ten minutes to set the tempo for that day. We put the ball on the 10-yard line going in. We take the popup dummies and set them where the linebackers would be lined up. Let's say we are playing a team that week that uses cover 4. It does not have to be exact because it is an assignment and hustle drill. We put the defensive line in the drill. The object of the drill is to get every popup dummy knocked to the ground (see Diagram #8). These are popup dummies, but we are throwing our body blocks on them. We never run by a bag that is standing up. We have players and dummies flying all over the place on the drill. We get a lot out of the drill because our linemen are looking to knock the crap out of the dummies. One man may knock down a dummy and as it pops back up, a second blocker may hit it. The last two bags represent the two safeties. Those two bags get worn out.

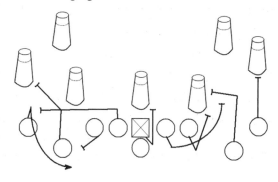

Diagram #8. Screen drill

After that drill, the offensive line leaves, and the backs and receivers work on our scat and mesh the same way. The offensive line coach takes his people and they go do what they do. I still have not figured that part out, but they do what they do. We have our receiver coach holding one of the bags. As the ball is snapped, we lean the bag toward the receiver. The receiver will come to the bag, smash into it, and then work off the bag to the ball.

The next time we run the play, the receiver coach throws the bag on the ground. What does that tell the receiver? It is man coverage. He has to punch and pivot and run outside. We rep the play over and over so we are comfortable running it. We give the receivers as many different looks as we think we will see that week.

Then we work on the mesh route. We have two quarterbacks throwing in the drill. Everyone must know how to set the mesh, and everyone must know how to work off the mesh. We are teaching them to play with their eyes. We just do rep after rep.

On the screen play, the key is to find a player on your team that is a good screen runner.

This is our rocket or laser screen. We call it ace – right – rocket lex (see Diagram #9). We ask the playside tackle to set up and then release to the force player. We do not want him to lose ground. We ask the playside guard to set up to the most dangerous defender. He releases to block in the alley. The center sets up to a gap defender. He releases to the first inside backer. The backside guard sets up to the B gap defender. He releases flat and kicks out the flat defender. The backside tackle drops in a deep set and shot puts to the hunt.

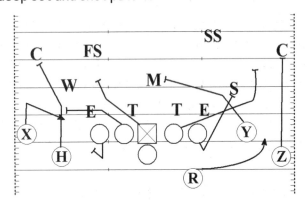

Diagram #9. Rocket lex

The offensive line coach explains the blocks to the players. He does not tell them they have the Mike, Will, or someone else. You know how the linemen are. If you tell them they have to block someone, they will go looking for them. If the defensive man goes all the way across the field, our lineman will chase his butt.

The way the coach explains it is like this. From the top of the numbers to the sideline is called the sidewalk. From the top of the numbers to the hash mark is called the alley. He gives them those terms. He teaches them to quick set and release right now. It is set and go (see Diagram #10).

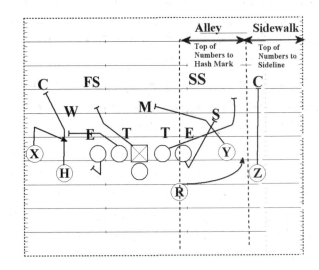

Diagram #10. Alley and sidewalk

This is the way the line blocks the play. A key is for the linemen not to get tied up with the defender on the line of scrimmage. We want them coming upfield on the rush.

The right tackle quick sets, then blocks the first man at the sidewalk. The right guard quick sets, then blocks the first man at the alley. The center punches away from the defensive man on the line and then goes and blocks the first man in the alley.

The left guard sets away from the defensive lineman, releases flat along the line of scrimmage, and blocks the first man at the sidewalk.

The right tackle sets vertical, which is straight back and not out, and then he is going to turn and hunt. In other words, he is going to hunt for the first opposite jersey he can find.

It does not matter who the defensive player is, we do not let him cross our face. The tight end is going to crack down on the first linebacker in the box. The back takes five hard steps and looks for the football. He must gain depth as he releases. The Z receiver has the first man on the sidewalk.

Over on the X receivers' side, the H back takes the first man on the sidewalk. The X receiver takes two steps downfield and comes back to the football. He goes one, two, three, plant, and comes back to the ball, running through the ball. The key is for the quarterback to put the ball up high so the receiver does not have to stop to make the catch. We want the quarterback to throw the ball right at his face. Once the receiver catches the ball, he cuts off the blocks of the linemen.

The H back must push off toward the Will linebacker. If Will drops back, he goes to block the corner. If Will comes, he must block him.

On the rocket, the back wants to have his outside foot splitting the stance of the offensive tackle. He leaves when the quarterback catches the ball. He must get a good inside-outside relationship with the tackle. We tell the tackle to set and then go. That is what you want. He does not want to lose any ground.

The quarterback looks at the defense. If the 5 technique comes off the line and plays the running back on the right side, he turns and throws the screen to the X receiver on the backside. It is a great play.

We were a good screen team. Some years you can run the screens, and some years you can't. I think the drill we do on the goal line really helps us on the screens. We do the drill every single day. Our line does a good job of getting out and finding someone to block on our screens.

One thing you really need to work on with the screens is the quarterback. We run a drill to get the quarterback to throw the ball up and over the defensive end. He has to be up on his toes to get the ball up over the defensive end.

We like to throw the screen passes off routes and off running plays. We throw screens where it looks like we are running a scat route and where it looks like we are running the ball. We like to give the defense different looks. We run the screen pass of our stretch play. We want our line and backs to sell the running play first. Then we release a sidewalk and an alley player, which will be the backside guard and tackle.

If there is a hot blitz, the quarterback is throwing the ball on the swing route. It is the same on the scat routes.

On our play action passes, we wanted to fake the zone run play one way and throw back the other way. The old adage of never run left and throw right did not fit our style. We threw that out the window. We wanted to create voids away from the playside. The defensive backs are going to run to the football. We will boot off the play and throw the voids away from the action. It is always the same route on the play. It is either an over and V or an over and stalk on the route (see Diagram #11).

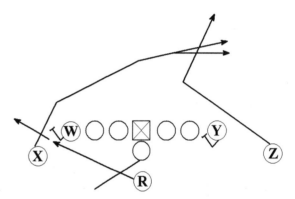

Diagram #11. Purple right air 29 X - over V

I think the best play action formation is the I formation. First, you run the sprint draw, and then you run the play action pass off the sprint draw. What makes it such a good play? It is because both plays look the same to the defense. Year in and year out, good sprint draw teams are also good play-action passing teams. With the one back formation, it is hard to do.

Our base plays are stretch and inside zone, and bootlegs and plays like that. We want to get the ball down the field. How are we going to do that? We are going to do it with play-action passes off our other plays. The play-action pass was our deep throw. It clicked for us this year. We threw the play-action pass 67 times and completed it 74 percent of the time, for 25 yards per completion. That is a good average.

The key is when you call the play. You have to call the play at first down, or after a turnover, and when you think the odds are that the defense will not blitz you. The second point is that you must sell the run for the pass to be effective. The offensive line must sell the run until the pass rusher gets in their faces, and then they have to pass block the rusher. If the defender is still playing runs, the lineman is still blocking runs. You must make the linebackers chase the back on the fake. We try to sell the run real hard.

After we have run the air 29 X-over V, we come back and run air 29 seal X over V. We pull the quarterback up, look for the bootleg, force the deep backs to come up, and then we are going to throw the X-over V route on the other side (see Diagram #12).

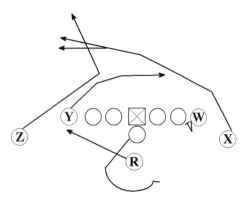

Diagram #12. Air 29 seal X – over V

The last way we run the play is off the bootleg series. Our X receiver runs the called route. The Z receiver runs a called route. The Y receiver slams and then releases to the flat. The back fakes the 24 or 25 play and protects to the outside. We set the pocket to one side and throw the ball back to the other side (see Diagram #13).

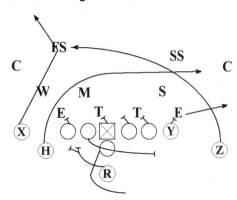

Diagram #13. 25 bootleg

We are going to pull the quarterback up and change the launch point for him. This will give us a

chance to make the deep throws on the defense.

The line is gap protecting except for the guard. The guard pulls and protects the quarterback. The back fills for the guard and picks up any run-through or anything coming from the outside. We are bootlegging the quarterback, but the pulling guard is thinking it is a pocket pass. He does not log the man on the outside.

For the drag receiver, he does not want to be deeper than 10 yards. The over receiver is at 12 yards in depth. The two receivers mesh as they come across on their routes.

Next, is the game planning for the offense? What you need to know is this. What formations do we gain an advantage in? Once you decide what the defense is going to use against those formations, you can select the plays that work best against that defense. If you gain an advantage with two tight ends, you must select the plays that work against the defense you anticipate the opponents will line up in against that formation.

The last thing that fits in the picture is the shallow routes. (see Diagram #14). We have run our two-man and three-man scat routes. We ran the mesh routes, and now we are going to look at the shallow routes. The shallow routes are all run from 50 protection. Now we are working on a high-low game on the Mike backer.

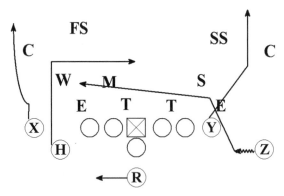

Diagram #14. Z shallow

The Z receiver is going to run the crossing route, and he is never going to stop. It is mandatory that he goes under the Mike linebacker. The Y receiver is running the stretch route. He runs an outside release, and against man coverage, he works for a rub with the Z receiver. Our X receiver runs the fade route. The backs run the free release swing. He is hot off the linebacker to his side. The H back runs the hunt route. The read is easy for the quarterback. All he has to do is to read the Mike linebacker. As the Mike linebacker looks to wall off the shallow route by the Z receiver, the H back hunts for the route. If the Mike linebacker drops, he fills the void and looks for the football. If he blitzes, he is filling the void and looking for the football.

If the H back is to the shallow side, he runs a curl. If he is the first receiver away from the shallow call, he runs the hunt. He must be alert. No matter what formation or who we call to run the shallow route, the rules stay the same. We can call any of the receivers to run the shallow route.

On a cover 2, the quarterback is looking to work on the Mike linebacker. We are going to try to high-low the Mike backer. If the Will backer blitzes, the H back fills the void and looks for the ball.

If we call the Z shallow from the bunch set, the H back runs the flat route, and the X end runs the void on the back side (see Diagram #14).

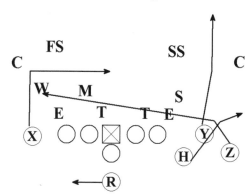

Diagram #15. Bunch right – Z shallow

I do want to make a few comments about our two minute offense. We have two mindsets in our tempo. We have Indy, and we have Nascar. On Indy, the ball is snapped with 18 to 20 seconds left on the clock. On Nascar, we go as fast as we can. We have listed the plays under Indy from 0 to 10. It is not very hard. It is a blast. This is our two-minute offense. In Nascar, we have plays from 1 to 3 listed. You do not have to use 10 plays in your Indy game. You could use

fewer if you want. We start using these plays in two-a-days. We use the plays during the conditioning period. There is no huddle in the drill.

Here are the plays we use with Indy.

0 = 3 man scat

1 = Rocket - Lex

2 = Mesh

3 = Cut (gun run)

4 = Drive

5 = Stone (hard count)

6 = Curl

7 = Trap draw

8 = Vertical

9 = Truck (toss)

10 = A special play

I know this seems like a lot of plays, but it really isn't. We drill the plays against air. We get in two formations. We get in a 2-by-2 or a 3-by-1 set. If we are on the left hash mark from the sideline, we start yelling, "Right – Right – Right." We get them lined up to the right. We call out, "80 – 0; – 80 – 0." The quarterback repeats the call. Everyone knows that is our three-man scat route. The players know they take the scat splits, and the receivers know they are going to run the 3 man scat route.

If we call, "Indy 5 – Indy 5," we all know that is the hard count. He gets under center and calls the cadence. If no one jumps offsides on defense, we run the pattern. If the defense jumps offsides, our offensive line field goal protects. The two outside players take off. We figure we are going to get the five yards, so we take a shot downfield. It is amazing how many times the corners will stop on the play. It is a free shot for the offense. Last year, we scored six touchdowns on this. If the quarterback calls, "Indy 7 – Indy 7" everyone knows that is the trap draw play.

You must have a directional call in your cadence. The quarterback calls out "Indy 7 – Indy 7 – Larry – Larry." Everyone knows that is the trap to the left.

We put the clock on during this drill. We want the ball snapped with 20 seconds left on the play clock. This is really a whole offense.

In Nascar, we use these three plays. This is hurry-up offense for us. However, you can use the offense any time. It is a sprint offense because we are going as fast as we can go. We only have these three plays.

1 = Toss

2 = Bubble screen

3 = Quick game (hitch routes)

We will be running the plays and the quarterback will call out "Nascar - Nascar - 91 - 91." As soon as the official marks the ball ready for play, the ball gets snapped. That is our Nascar, or hurry-up offense.

ESTABLISHING THE SPREAD OFFENSE

University of Utah

I am going to talk about the spread offense. We are in a shotgun set where we look to run the ball first and pass second. It is a spread-the-field type of offense we used at Bowling Green University and we carried with us to Utah.

I am going to talk briefly about philosophy. The spread offense began about seven years ago to become a primary set for a number of universities. I think it is getting harder to move the ball because the defenses are catching up with what is happening. The spread is like the wishbone and West Coast offense. The more the defense sees an offense, the better they are able to defend it.

When we recruit a quarterback, we want a throwing quarterback who can run with the ball. I think people make mistakes when they try to fit personnel into an offense that does not fit his talent. If your quarterback does not fit your offense scheme, you are in the wrong scheme. It is amazing that it may take you two years to finally recruit the A-one quarterback to fit your offense, and that is just before you get fired. In college football, if you do not turn the program in two years, you are gone.

We adapted our offense to fit our quarterback's talents. When we were at Bowling Green, we had a non-athletic quarterback. That year we sneaked up on people in the Mid-American Conference and the Big Twelve Conference. People in the MAC had not seen the spread offense. We beat the hell out of Missouri, and I am still trying to figure out how we did it. We finally recruited a great running back, moved him to quarterback, and the offense blossomed.

When we recruit a quarterback, we look at the tape. I want to see the ten or twenty plays on the tape, where there is no chance for the play to be successful. When I find the quarterback who found a way to make those plays gain yardage, that is the quarterback I want.

When I went to Notre Dame, we were an I formation team. We could beat teams we are better than. We could beat Rutgers and Navy because we could run the ball right at them. If you cannot run the ball, you are in trouble in the I formation. That is why we went to a shotgun formation.

When I came to Utah, we had three dropback quarterbacks who were very non-athletic players. Do not run a West Coast offense if you do not have West Coast quarterbacks. Do not run a spread offense unless you have a runner that can throw. Our coaching staff did a tremendous job of adapting the offense to fit what the quarterbacks could do.

They did some neat things to take the ball out of the quarterback's hand. That is hard to do in the spread offense. Not one play exists in the spread offense where the quarterback just hands the ball off and gets out of the way. Every snap in the spread offense, the quarterback has to be a decision maker, an athlete, and a smart signal caller.

When you run the spread offense, you have to equate numbers to run the ball. We want to avoid the bad play by using an audible. We spent four to five months this year studying the offense, and we are going out next year and studying with other teams. Our quarterback is a good thrower. It is the first time in nineteen years of coaching I have had a legit thrower who can run the football.

In the spread offense, we force the defense to defend the field. The purpose of the game is not to get 22 people inside the hash marks of the field. We want to spread the field, create mismatches, and force the defense to defend the field.

We are going to run the football. To do that, we equate numbers so we do not end up running into unblocked defenders.

We put the ball in the hands of our playmakers. Identify your playmakers and find ways to get the ball into their hands. If you have to direct snap the ball to them, get the ball in their hands.

We played California this year and the score was see-sawing back and forth. In the third quarter, we hit a lull and could not move the ball. We went two straight series with three-and-out results. We put one of our best wide receivers in the backfield and direct snapped the ball to him three plays in a row. We went right down the field. It changed the tempo of the game. It was not plays we made up because we had them in the offense. However, it was a way to get the ball in the hands of our playmakers.

This offense is hard to prepare for in two days. If you do not see this offense often, it is hard to prepare the defense in the limited time before the game to handle everything the offense does. You have basically two days to get the game plan in and tweak it to what you do well.

The worst thing that happened to us this year occurred after we received our bowl bid. We won the conference and everyone was excited about playing in the bowl. I watched the TCU-Southern Mississippi game on TV because we played the winner in the bowl game. I was pulling for TCU because of the defense Southern Mississippi ran.

Southern Miss had one of the best defenses in the country, but they ran that wild three-three defense. At one time during the bowl game, they had ten people standing up at the line of scrimmage. When we played BYU, they ran the same type of defense, and it was really confusing to our kids. We want to do the same thing with our offense.

Every year I ask defensive coordinators what they hate to see the offense run. I want to know what gives them knots in their stomach. The first thing they always mention is option football. All the stunts a defensive team likes to run are not good against an option. Man coverage is not good against option football teams. Option football teams force defense to be very vanilla in what they run. We are going to be an option football team.

The second thing that defenses do not like to see is the empty set in the backfield. We have an empty set package. Defenses do not like to play teams that unbalance their sets. We are very seldom in a double slot formation. We line up in the trips set because it allows us to better identify what the defense is doing. We want to be an offense that makes it hard for the defense to prepare.

In the spread offense, we create mismatches with the defense. Our best receivers are our inside receivers in our sets. We run the ball at the defense, which requires the defense to play linebackers. When they play linebackers, we force them into coverages which are mismatches for them. Our inside slot in our trips set has caught close to 100 catches the last three years. That is the position that defenses have to stop. The second receiver on the team is the split end or the one receiver in the three-by-one set.

If you come to Utah and watch our staff work, you will be impressed. I think Pete Carroll is a fantastic coach. He knows football, but if he did not, he still would be a good coach because he is so enthusiastic. If you ever hear him at a clinic, he is so upbeat and enthusiastic that you are ready to play when he finishes talking. I think every coach in America is a great X's and O's coach. Knowing those types of things does not win games.

Being energetic in practice is the way I want my coaches. We only have the players for two hours a day, and I want my coaches to be able to give them two hours of work and enthusiasm. At our practices, you will see coaches that are fresh and energized, coaching their tails off. They are chasing players down the field and coaching like their hair is on fire. If that is not the way they want to coach, I am going to fire them because they are cheating their players. Next year we will win because of the attitude we have right now.

I am going to give you a very simplistic explanation of how we equate numbers in our running. One-high to us means there is a single safety between the hash marks more than 10 yards deep. Two-high means two safeties in the middle of the field on the hash marks more than 10 yards deep. No-deep means the defense is playing zero or man coverage with no one in the middle of the field.

If the defense has one safety in the middle of the field against a double slot set, we say that equates to an equal set and we run the ball (see Diagram #1). The thinking is that the defense is covering your set with a three-deep and four-under zone scheme or a man-to-man with a free safety. That means inside the tackle box, the defense has six players. Since we have five offensive blockers and the quarterback's read counts as a blocker, we are equal in number and run the ball.

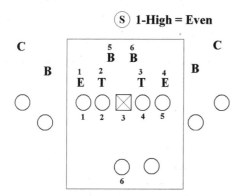

Diagram #1. One-high

If the defense has two high safeties in the middle of the field, that equates to a plus one in our counting (see Diagram #2). The defense is playing with five men in the tackle box, which gives us a one-man advantage in the number of blockers compared to the number of defenders. We run the football.

The last look, which we will see more and more until we get more speed at wide receivers, is no safety in the middle of the field (see Diagram #3). That means the defense has dropped the safety into the box and is playing man-to-man with no free safety. The defense has seven men in the box, and we have only six blockers. That is a minus one and we have to run a speed option or throw the ball.

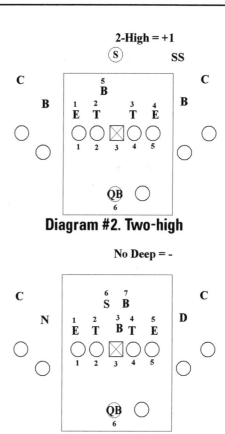

Diagram #2. Two-high

Diagram #3. No-deep

The play I am going to show you is called 14-15 read (see Diagram #4). We run this play 17 to 25 times a game. The 14 play is run right, and the 15 play is run left. It is like the wishbone, which can be run from a multitude of sets. This play is a zone play. The blocking assignments for the onside guard and tackle is what we call Tag. When we give a tag call, the tackle and guard are working together on the block.

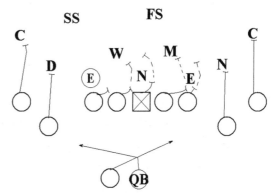

Diagram #4. 14-15 read odd

In the odd front defense, the guard is uncovered. The tackle and guard are zone stepping and reading the hip of the 5 technique. The guard's aiming point is the inside hip of the 5 technique. He steps to the hip and gets his outside hand on the defensive end. If the hip comes to the guard, he takes the block over using two hands, and the tackle goes up to the linebacker. If the hip stays outside, he works up on the linebacker.

If the center has a shade to the playside, he calls "Scoop." (see Diagram #5). That tells the guard he needs help. The guard now calls "Badger," which tells the tackle he is by himself. The backside guard and tackle are working a tag scheme on the backside.

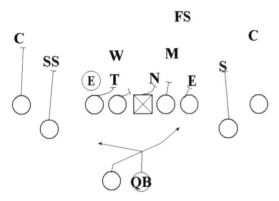

Diagram #5. 14-15 read even

The running back is aligned at five yards from the line of scrimmage behind the offensive guard. The quarterback's hands are at 5 yards, and his heels are at 5.5 yards. The running back is responsible for the mesh. The quarterback is keying the backside hand-off key, which is the first man outside the backside tackle. The running back cannot get in a hurry getting to the hand-off position. He takes a crossover step, which is described as a slow, slow step. The next two steps are called quick, quick steps. He cannot get in a hurry pressing the ball to the line of scrimmage. When he turns up, he does not cut until he reaches the heels of the offensive linemen. At that point, he runs to daylight.

In a double slot, the slot back to the backside has a keep block. He is playing for the quarterback to bring the ball back to him. He is blocking on the inside number of the walk-away player aligned on him. If that defender runs away from him, he does not chase him. He waits for him to come back, and then he seals him inside. To the front side the slot

back is blocking the support, which is the defender's head up to the inside.

If we go to the trips set, nothing changes in the box. The inside slot blocks the MDM, or most dangerous man. This play can be a great misdirection play. The quarterback reads the backside end. If the end is chasing the ball down the line of scrimmage, the quarterback pulls the ball and runs off the slot back's block. The threat of the quarterback running the ball to the backside slows down the inside linebackers.

I want to show you something that we did to take the ball out of the quarterback's hand. This play did not depend on the quarterback making a great run. It is a play called 14-15 triple (see Diagram #6). We are running a triple option depending on the read of the quarterback. The offensive line is zone blocking on a track. They are blocking the inside zone and nothing else. We are counting the men outside the tackle. The number one man is the hand-off key. The number two man is the pitch key, and the number three man is the wide receiver's block.

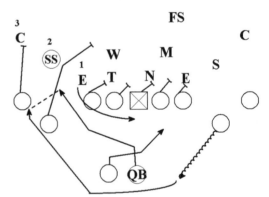

Diagram #6. 14-15 triple

The pitch man is the slot back coming back in motion behind the quarterback in the shotgun set. He is in the position of an I-back when the ball is snapped. The quarterback runs a 14 read play. If there is any doubt of what to do, the quarterback leaves the ball with the running back. If he keeps the ball, he is pitching off the run support to the weakside. This is an excellent play and an easy read on the pitch man. He attacks the inside number of the pitch man as fast as he can. The slot back is five yards outside the quarterback and one yard behind him.

The next play I am going to give you is called 14-15 read option (see Diagram #7). On this play, we are not motioning anyone. We are running the 14 zone play again with the read on the backside defensive end. If the quarterback pulls the ball, he runs the triple option off the run support and pitches to the backside slot back. The slot back is two yards off the ball in his alignment. As the quarterback is making his ride on the running back, the slot is taking three steps backward. He shuffles to get timed up on the quarterback. He is in the pitch relationship of five and one yard from the quarterback.

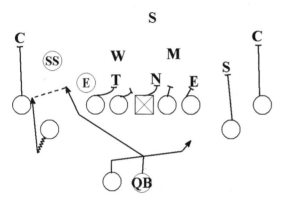

Diagram #7. 14-15 read option

This play is called 6-7 shovel option (see Diagram #8). This play actually started at Notre Dame. We ran the play at Syracuse when I was there. At Syracuse, we ran it from a two back set. We block this play as an off-tackle power play. We are blocking gaps in the offensive line and pulling the backside guard through the hole. It used to be that if you ran the shovel pass and the defender dropped to the inside, the quarterback was screwed. This play gives the quarterback something to do with the ball.

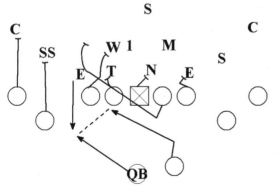

Diagram #8. 6-7 shovel option

The 7 shovel option is run to the left. The running back aligns to the right behind the outside hip of the guard. He is five yards off the line of scrimmage. The quarterback is in the shotgun set with his hands at five yards. His heels are at 5.5 yards. The quarterback runs the speed option down the line of scrimmage toward the read key. He is attacking the outside number of the read key.

If the defender attacks the quarterback, he gives ground and shovels the ball back inside to the running back. The quarterback has to go hard toward the defensive end to make the defense commit one way or the other. If he is lazy, the defensive end can hang in the middle, and he can play both the quarterback and the shovel back. The pulling guard leads up inside on the linebacker.

If the defender does not attack the quarterback and falls back inside on the running back, the quarterback continues to run the option and brings the ball to the pitch key (see Diagram #9). He is running the read option with the slot back as the pitch man. The slot back is reading the key defender so he knows whether to block or become the pitch back.

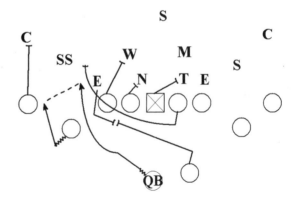

Diagram #9. 7 shovel option

The thing that people have to consider if you are thinking about installing some of these ideas in your offense is the center snap. We had a center at Bowling Green University that was so good he led the quarterback in the direction he was going. The snap is a blind snap and is a dead type of snap. We do not spin the ball. That is one aspect of the play that can destroy the timing of the play quickly.

If we get into the trips set and bring motion by the inside slot toward the quarterback, it looks like the triple option toward the motion (see Diagram #10). We snap the ball and run the shovel option back to where the motion came from with the outside slot back as the pitch man.

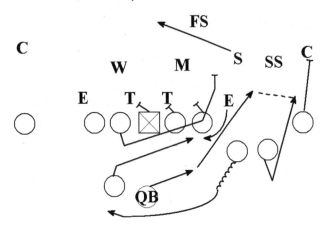

Diagram #10. 6 shovel - motion

If we get in the empty set, we can still run these plays using motion. When we go empty, we like a two-by-three formation. The formation is a double set one way, and a trip set the other. We can run any of these plays using motion and achieve the same results. Nothing gets changed for anyone in the offense. The backs in our sets are interchangeable in the running game. They know how to run the read option as the pitch man. By using multiple formations and motion, you can run the same plays with different looks for the defense.

This year we were not as physical on the offensive line as we will be next year. This year we really played with offensive linemen that were not very skilled. They worked hard and improved as the year went along. We will be better next year. I appreciate your attention, and thanks for coming.

PLAY-ACTION PASSING GAME

University of Miami, OH

I want to cover our philosophy before I get into the meat and potatoes of my topic. When people see us play for the first time, they think we are predominantly a spread offense. If you had looked at our offense three years ago, we were a spread offensive team. In the past three years, we have developed our running game. This year we started using a two tight end set, which really helped our running game.

If you can run the football effectively, it only stands to reason that the play-action pass off those runs will be good. We didn't have a legitimate fullback on the team this year. We had signed those types of personnel, but they went down with injuries, and we couldn't replace them. That is why we got into the two tight end set.

We felt like we had to use more play-action passes this year. We had improved our running game and needed to take advantage of that. The first two years I was here, we were primarily a spread offense with a high percentage passing attack. If you are in the spread offense all the time, the defense will let the offense nickel and dime them with the short passing game, but they are not going to give up many big plays.

We were a high percentage team, but we had to really work to get a big play. When you are in four wide receivers all the time, you are not going to get a whole lot of 1-on-1 coverages. We had two problems that we needed to solve. We needed to run the ball better and come up with some big plays in the passing game. When we went to the two tight ends set, it helped us run the ball and got some 1-on-1 match ups in the passing game.

The one point that you should get from this lecture is to have a play-action pass off each running play you have. We had two different pass protections off the power pass. We had two or three different play-actions off the zone play.

To run a play-action passing game, the offense has to make each pass look like a run. A big difference exists between doing it and selling it. The play-action pass starts with the offensive line. If they are going to keep their pads low on running plays, they have to do the same thing on play-action passes.

If the first thing the linemen do is pop straight up and show their pads, your play-action series will not be very successful. Defensive coaches work hard with their defenders recognizing the pass set of the offensive linemen. The pass protection has to look as much as possible like the run.

The play-action pass seems to slow down the pass rush of the defense. If you are good at play-action, the linebackers will be stepping up when they should be dropping. It slows everyone on the defense down.

What we were looking for this year was a better opportunity for 1-on-1 match-ups. We were so effective at running the ball this year; the defense had to load the box with eight or nine defenders. When that happens, we get what we are looking for in pass coverage. The receiver could catch the ball and have only one man to beat.

Last year we started to get a ton of different kinds of blitzes. We were getting zone blitzes and a great number of safety blitzes. We felt like we needed a gap protection that would pick up the blitzes no matter where they came from.

We went to Oklahoma to see what they were doing with their protection. They used a gap protection that fit into their one back set. We needed to run our protection out of all our formations that could protect against all kinds of blitzes and was simple to run.

The first one I'm going to show you is our gap protection from our wing formation. This is the primary set we use to run the power play. We could put the B back in the wing set, motion him across the set, and bring him back, or we could line him up in the slot and motion him across the set. The protection I'm going to show you is called gap left (see Diagram #1).

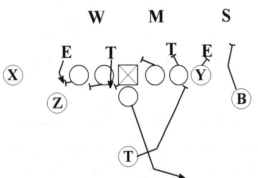

Diagram #1. Gap protection left

Starting with the left tackle, all the offensive linemen blocked the gap to the left side. The left tackle was responsible for the backside C gap. The left guard took the backside B gap. The center turned into the backside A gap. The right guard blocked the front side A gap, and the right tackle blocked the front side B gap. We told our tight end he was responsible for the defensive end. Most of the time, the end was aligned in a 7 technique on his inside shoulder, or he was in a 6 technique on his nose. The B back had the first blocking assignment outside the tight end. If he was in motion, he came off the tight end's butt and blocked the first thing coming from the outside.

The running back took a slide step like he was running the power play and was responsible for the front side C gap. The running back was trying to sell the 26 power play. If no one came in the C –gap, he scanned inside and outside. Where the running back looked first came from our scouting report. If a team liked to bring two defenders off the edge, he scanned outside first.

The quarterback was responsible for the fake. He opened out like he was going to run the 26 power, made a good fake, and set up five to seven yards deep.

We run four different routes off this action. The formation we ran was a pro set with a wing. The first route I'm going to show you is a post-corner route (see Diagram #2). The Z and X receivers ran the post-corner. They exploded off the ball for five steps. They planted and took the pattern three steps to the post before breaking back to the corner.

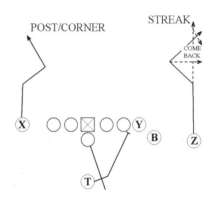

Diagram #2. Combination routes

They were reading the leverage of the corner. If the corner was inside and trailing the receiver, he took it deep. If the corner was off the receiver and over the top, the receiver brought the patter back like an out cut.

The second route we run depends on the strength of the quarterback's arm. We run a 20-yard comeback pattern (see Diagram #2). The quarterback makes a great fake, sets up at five yards, and lets the ball go. This year, we started running this pattern at 15 yards, but expanded it to 20 yards because of the strength of the quarterback's arm. We ran the pattern on both sides and the quarterback could throw either way he felt comfortable. Obviously, it was a longer throw into the field, but if that was the best match-up, that is where the ball went.

The next pattern we threw off this pattern was the take-off (see Diagram #2). The receivers took off, and we went for the home run.

The last pattern we run off this set was what we called a skin route (see Diagram #2). That comes from the type of pass that the Washington Redskins used to run when Joe Gibbs was there the first time. We got some big plays on this route. We called the play X-skin (see Diagram #3). The X-receiver ran a deep post. He was trying to run the free safety out of the play. The corner would be playing him, and we hoped the free safety would feel threatened to the post and pick him up also.

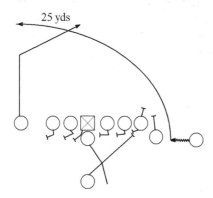

Diagram #3. X-skin

The Z-receiver or flanker back came in motion or simply lined up tighter to the formation and ran a deep crossing route. We wanted him to get behind all the linebackers and start climbing to a depth of about 25 yards approaching the opposite sideline. The quarterback made the play fake and keyed the free safety. If the free safety hung in the middle, we hit the post behind him. If the free safety jumped the post pattern, we hit the deep cross.

If we ran the play the other way, we called "Z-skin." The flanker ran the post route, and the X-receiver ran the climb route. We didn't like to run it that way because the cross became a longer pattern. We liked the cross going into the boundary.

The other formation we used the gap protection on was the twins formation (see Diagram #4). That put the X and Z receivers on the same side, with the two tight ends to the other side in a wing set. Teams played us two ways in this formation. They either played us in zone coverage or they flipped both corners to the same side and played man-to-man. I liked to work against man coverage in this set.

The gap protection is the same (see Diagram #4). We are protecting left. We do this because we had a right-handed quarterback and we wanted to

protect his back. The responsibility is the same. The left tackle has the C gap rusher. In this defense, he will probably get some help from the guard because he is protecting the B gap and no one is aligned in that gap. Everyone else is blocking their gaps. The tight end is blocking the man aligned on him or to his inside. The B back has the first threat outside, and the running back has the C gap.

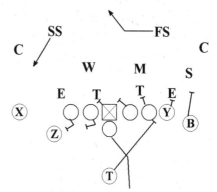

Diagram #4. Twins set/gap protection

The running back goes the opposite of the protection. If we are gap protecting left, the running back is protecting right. If we gap protect right, the running back is protecting left. For a right-handed quarterback, the fake going left and throwing back right is more difficult. Instead of him faking left and trying to open back up to the right, we roll him that way. It makes an easier transition.

When we come out in our twin set, the defense we see the most is cover 3. In a cover 3, the strong safety is rolling down to the twin set. The pattern we like to run against this defense is the curl-flat route (see Diagram #5). The quarterback runs a good fake, sets up, reads the strong safety, and delivers the ball.

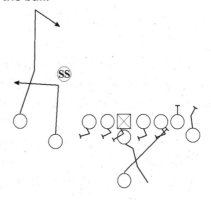

Diagram #5. Curl-flat vs. zone

If the coverage is man coverage, we like to run the double post, particularly in the red zone. If we have both corners flipped over to play man or some kind of man-free coverage, we like this pattern (see Diagram #6). The receivers are running a five step hard breaking post pattern. We are looking for the outside post receiver. That is the area where the receiver has more separation and more room to work. If the defense is using a man-free principle, the first post usually takes up the free safety, leaving the second post open.

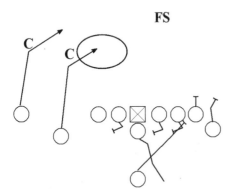

Diagram #6. Double post vs. man

The next pass I want to talk about is the power pass (see Diagram #7). This pass fakes the power running play. The majority of the protection scheme is gap left protection. The center, guards, and tackles are gap protecting left. I will draw this set up out of the twins formation. The B back is sitting in the slot toward the twins side and coming in motion toward the tight end. The tight end and the B back have free releases in this play with no blocking assignment.

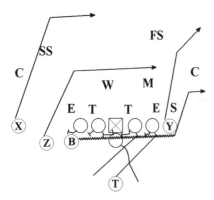

Diagram #7. Power pass

The running back has a blocking assignment and is not responsible for faking the run. The quarter-back does all the faking. The running back takes a slid step and is responsible for the first threat outside the offensive tackle's outside leg. If the tackle has a 5 technique lined up on him, he is the responsibility of the running back if he comes outside. We ask the running back to cut his outside leg. If the defender slants inside, he is the offensive tackle's man.

The quarterback knows that any defender coming outside of the running back's block is hot. The quarterback doesn't know what the Sam linebacker is going to do. If the Sam linebacker comes, the quarterback is going to hit the B back in the flat.

The tight end runs a six-step corner route. He releases drives upfield about six steps and sticks the pattern to the corner. Some people pull the guard like the power play. I don't like to do that because that leaves a gap free on the backside, and the quarterback is setting up to throw the ball. If he were rolling that way, I might pull the guard.

On this play, we are reading in a hurry. If the B back is open, we hit him right now. After that, we look for the tight end on the corner. The third read is the backside receiver coming on the crossing pattern.

The backside receivers are dragging across the formation. We want them coming across into the quarterback's vision. The Z-receiver is running a 10-yard drag and the X-receiver is deep down the middle. We are reading the play side only.

We had a big tendency to throw this pass to the right every time. It is really hard for the quarterback to throw hot going left. The mechanics are much more difficult to execute. We can tag the play and make adjustments to it. If we find the free safety jumping the tight end, we can call "X-post" and try to get over the top and down the middle. We did that against Bowling Green in the MAC conference championship game.

We have two types of zone post patterns we run. When we run one of these patterns, we are looking to go over the top and score. We run eight yards down the field and really stick the cut. Even in college, a lot of receivers don't understand the post cut. They are going to get the ball if the safety comes up. However, they are not beating the safety. They still have to beat the corner. The receiver sees the safety coming up and takes off to the post. He doesn't run a good route, and the corner simply runs right with him. The route looks like a straight arrow or banana route, and the corner is right with them.

The receiver has to stick the corner to leave him behind and to his outside. He doesn't have to beat the safety; he has to beat the corner. The other post we run is a five step skinny post. That ball is thrown on a line and between people, not over them.

I want to talk about the boot game next. I'll show you the bootleg from the shotgun. A couple of years ago when we were putting the bootleg pass in, we tinkered with some things. We were trying to decide who to pull on the bootleg. Most people pull the guard on the bootleg, but we were having trouble with penetration, especially from the shotgun. If we got a 3 technique to the side of the pulling guard, the center had to block back on him. Sometimes that 3 technique got penetration before the center could get to him.

What we decided to do was pull the uncovered lineman. It was either going to be the center or the guard, based on the defensive front. In the defense I am putting up, we would pull the center because he is the uncovered lineman. It is easier to pull the center from the shotgun set. We had a very athletic center this year who could snap with the quarterback underneath him and still pull.

We are going to run the bootleg to the right (see Diagram #8_. We try to make the play look like the inside zone play left. The offensive line is blocking back one gap to the left. The defensive front is going to be in a 3 and 9 technique to the tight end side. To the twin side, we have a 1 and 5 technique. The front side tackle is blocking the B –gap, and the guard is blocking back on the 1 technique. The tackle is protecting the gap in case the 1 technique should fight across the guard's face or if the linebacker blitzes the gap. Once he secures the gap and no

threat exists, he expands back because the quarterback is coming that way. The center is uncovered and will do the pulling. He is trying to get some depth and log the defensive end inside.

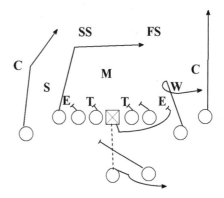

Diagram #8. Bootleg right

The running back is set to the right of the quarterback. We want him to keep his alignment wide. His inside foot should be on the inside foot of the tackle. He is faking the zone play left. The quarterback sits down and rides the running back. That lets the puller get out in front and lets the defensive end squeeze further to the inside. The better and longer the ride of the running back, the better chance we have of getting outside with the quarterback. If the quarterback is too fast, he will beat the puller out. The defensive end will jump upfield, and the quarterback will have to stop and turn up inside.

The running back replaces the puller after he makes his fake. He knows if the uncovered lineman is pulling. If the center is pulling, the running back hits the front side and blocks back. He knows if the defensive lineman is shading on his side, the center is pulling. If the shade is on the other side, the guard is pulling. The frontside tackle becomes the secondary seal man because he is expanding outside and looking inside for a rerouted lineman or linebacker. He has to make sure he doesn't work downfield.

We are in a two by two set. That means we have two receivers to each side. We could be in a two tight ends and two wide outs set, or a twin set on one side and a tight end flanker set the other way. The number one receiver to the side of the bootleg runs a streak, which is a take-off route. If he has a press corner or cover 2 look, we want the receiver to release outside. If he has a soft corner, he releases right through him. We want the corner to pay attention to the receiver and not look in the backfield.

If the corner is soft and the receiver runs real wide, the corner is not going to turn and run with the receiver. He is going to look in the backfield and see the bootleg coming. We want to run right through the corner's heels and make him retreat.

The number two receiver is going to run a snag route. He will have a defender inside him. If we were running the zone play, the receiver would block him. He comes down on the defender for three steps, pivots, and runs to the flat.

On the backside, the number two receiver is running a 10-yard drag pattern. The number one receiver is running a deep cross pattern.

Those are our route rules on any bootleg or naked with a two by two set. The quarterback's first read is the quick snag route. If it is there, we take it right away. This works particularly well against teams with aggressive linebackers.

The X-end needs to align near the numbers. The inside receiver needs to be working the hash mark area. We probably want the inside receiver to get inside the hash marks on his first three steps. We do not want a wide throw on this play. If cover 2 is being played, we don't want the ball to get out into the roll corner's area. We want the ball thrown around the hash marks.

The tight end's release depends on the alignment of the defender lined up on him. If he gets a defender head-up to inside on him, he steps like he is running the zone play, takes an outside release, works his way up the field, and runs the cross. We don't want him to get across the field too fast. The quarterback is buying time with his ride, and the tight end does the same thing. If he gets across too quickly, he overruns the snag route. If he has a 9 technique on him, he does primarily the same thing except he is releasing inside the defender. He wants to work up to a depth of 10 yards before he comes across. He wants to in the quarterback's eyesight.

He doesn't want to be ahead of the quarterback, but more importantly, he must not be behind him.

I'll show you another one from the double slot formation (see Diagram #9). This time we run the bootleg left. The two frontside receivers run the streak and snag. The number two receiver to the backside runs a 10-yard crossing route, and the number one receiver runs a deep crossing route.

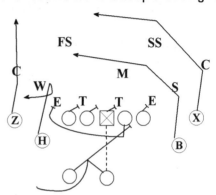

Diagram #9. Boot double slot

Two years ago we were a heavy bootleg team. We started to get a lot of blitzes, especially from the field side. This became one of our big plays. We used to bootleg a lot out of the three by one set because we ran a lot of zone plays from that set (see Diagram #10). We ended up sprint out with this set this year. When we bootlegged out of a three by one set we tagged the routes because we had three receivers in the pattern. Most of the time we ran a flood type of pattern. The outside receiver ran a streak, the middle receiver ran an out pattern, and the inside receiver ran the snag route. There was only one receiver to the backside, and he ran the 10-yard cross. We looked for the snag first, the sideline cut second, and the crossing route third.

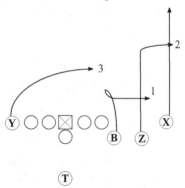

Diagram #10. Three by one boot

Another combination we used in the three by one set was a curl-flat type of play. The outside receiver ran a curl route, the middle receiver ran a wheel route, and the inside receiver ran the flat route (see Diagram #11). I told the quarterback to read the flat pattern off the linebacker first, and the wheel route by the middle receiver second. That was in case the corner jumped on the curl. The curl pattern was going to be run late, which gave the wheel time to get deep. When we ran the curl route, we actually snagged it to the sideline.

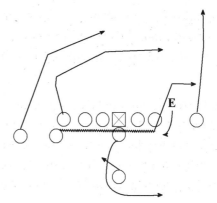

Diagram #12. Naked

We are going to turn the defensive end to the side of the naked loose. We do that on the zone play also. However we liked to bring the B back in motion across the set and block the backside end on the zone play. That keeps the end from running the zone play down and gives the running back a cutback lane. We do the same thing when we run the naked play. We bring the B back in motion. We snap the ball when the B-back is on the inside leg of the offensive tackle.

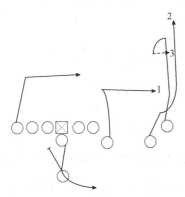

Diagram #11. Curl-wheel-flat

The reason we ran these plays was to move the pocket for the quarterback. I didn't like the idea of setting the quarterback at the same release point all the time. We liked to bootleg from the shotgun because the quarterback was deeper, and if he got pressure he could make a play.

The next series we run is the naked series (see Diagram #12). The difference between the naked and bootleg is the pulling lineman. On the bootleg we pulled someone, while on the naked we didn't. We ran most of our naked plays from a two tight end formation. We ran the bootleg off the counter and zone running plays. The naked plays were all run from a zone action.

The rules for the receivers were the same for the naked as they were for the bootleg. The two by two routes were the same and the three by one routes were tagged. The naked fake was an outside zone play. The running back was aiming for the outside leg of the tackle instead of the inside leg. The linemen were turning their pads and really expanding to the outside. The front side tackle was squeezing the B gap like he did on the bootleg.

The B back tried to make the plays look alike. What he wanted to do was encourage the end to fight across the block to get inside. That meant we were taking him on square, but thinking of getting to his outside shoulder. He couldn't be inside out on his path when we ran the zone play and square when we ran the naked. Defensive ends will pick that up and jump outside on the naked. The B back had a rule we called chip or chop. If the B back engaged the end, he wanted to chip on him for a count of two, throw him inside, and release to the flat. If the defensive end were to fly down inside and disappear, the B –back, to time up the play, would chop his feet for two seconds before releasing to the flat. The B back can't chase the defensive end to the inside if he is on a stunt. If he tries to do that, he will never get out on his route. This set with the motion ends up being a two by two set and the two by two rules apply.

The outside receiver runs the streak. The B back runs the flat route. The backside receivers run the 10-yard cross and the deep cross. The quarterback reads flat, streak, and cross in that progression. We tell the quarterback, after he fakes the running back, to take a step or two deeper before he tries to get outside. That keeps him from being too flat and gives him some depth. If there was an outside blitz man, the quarterback was responsible for that man.

We threw the ball about 535 times this year. You are going to move the chains with the dropback pass. But you are going to get the big plays off the play-action pass. The more you can run the ball, the better the play-action will be. When you can run the football is when you get your home run balls in the passing game.

The previous two years, when we were a true spread offense, we threw 25 touchdowns both years. That was a lot for a 12-game schedule. This year, with the improved running game and the style we played, we threw 38 touchdowns.

These are some of the things that got us to where we are today. The running game and the play passing worked extremely well for us this year. I'll be around for a few more minutes if anyone has any questions. Thank you very much.

GOAL LINE DEFENSE

Syracuse University

It is nice to be here. I am going to talk about our goal line defense. I want to cover a point I think is critical in defensive football. When you teach defensive football, you have to teach your players to take on a blocker.

Defensive football requires a player to defeat the player he is playing against. Everyone wants to run up the field and sack the quarterback. We are in an era of what I call contemporary offense. All the offenses today are in some kind of spread offense, with three and four wide receivers.

However, sooner or later, those teams have to get tough. They have to put their hat on someone and play physical football. The first part of my lecture is going to be about teaching players to take on blockers.

In coaching this technique, I use a progression to teach the skill. It does not matter whether you are coaching at the Pop Warner level or at Syracuse University, the teaching is the same.

Players must be taught to hit in a way that gives them confidence in what they are doing. When they begin to play aggressively, they will have the tools to handle those collisions.

A football player needs a number of tools. The player has to understand that the game of football is played in a five-yard box. The coach has the job of teaching the players how to play within that five-yard box.

This time of year is a great time for coaches because we are trying to get better as coaches and teachers. I am going to talk about quick hands as the first point in my lecture. The skill is accomplished in a speed and hand placement drill. The skill does not initially require a hard hit on the opponent. When the player becomes more confident and understands what the coach wants, he will become more physical. Upper-body violence in football is important, but you are not going to get that the first day you start working on these drills.

For a defensive player to play well, he has to understand leverage. Defensive players are never going to defeat a block or have any degree of success if they do not understand leverage. We have a noseguard that can bench-press 600 pounds, but if he is not in the appropriate leverage position, he gets beat. Leverage is not about strength.

Your players have to understand fit and finish refers to defeating or executing a block. They have to understand how the fit position works. You teach your players the fit position for the various blocks in a progression fashion. When you teach players skills, you start in the final or contact position and work backwards in steps. You do not start apart and work together in a teaching progression.

When teaching, the coach must have an approach to stance and footwork. You have to teach players the footwork to get into the fit. You cannot expect your players to know what you want done.

The final skill that has to be taught is to read and to react. That is the culminating activity of the drill. The read and react drill is the last activity of the day, where you put the skills together and allow your players to play the game. When you get to this part of the progressions, you allow the players to play apart and watch them react together.

What I am going to do for the next few minutes is to put on the tape of the drills and explain them. I am going to coach you off the film. The first drill we teach our players in our progression is called the quick hands drill (see Diagram #1). The players' position is not important because all the players in our program do these drills.

Diagram #1. Quick hands drill

I want you to notice the players in this film are not wearing shoulder pads or helmets. You can teach this drill without those items. In my opinion, you are better off if you start the progression without pads. The drill is a six-point stance for the defender. The blocker is in a two-point stance facing the defender about arm's length apart.

The defender reacts with his hands as quickly as he can. He punches into the offensive blocker's body with the heels of his hands. The objective of the drill is to develop speed and placement of the defender's hands. We want the hands placed within the framework of the blocker's body, with the target inside the blocker's hands and above the defender's own shoulders. That allows you to teach hand placement and the concept of leverage on the body.

The offensive blocker is instructed to put his hands outside on the defender, since it is a defensive drill. That allows the defender to get his hands inside on the blocker and hit the target. You can work on this drill in the off-season on a mat in the weight room.

We do this drill in multiples of three. The coach calls, "Hit." The defender strikes the offensive player with the heels of his hands on the target. The defender resets and the coach calls "Hit" again. The defender repeats the drill and resets. On the third rep, the defender hits, locks out his elbows, and rolls his back as far as he can. The lockout position and the rolling of the hips puts the defender in a leverage position.

The steer drill is all about leverage (see Diagram #2). This is a continuation drill from the quick hands drill. We have the blocker and defender facing each other, with the defender in a two- or three-point stance. The blocker has been instructed to allow the defender to get his punch and hands in a proper placement, with his hands above his shoulders. This puts the defender in a good leverage position on the blocker.

C

Diagram #2. Steer drill

The defender fits into the blocker. The blocker tries to turn the defender to the left or right. The defender wants to keep his shoulders and hips square. When he feels the blocker trying to turn him, he locks his elbow out hard on the side toward the movement. He tries to keep his shoulders square, his hips in relative position to the blocker, and his hands above his shoulders.

The blocker tries to turn the defender the other way. The defender tries to maintain the same leverage position without his hips getting outside of the blockers. The problem with today's teaching is that defenders are taught to get upfield as quickly as they can and sack the quarterback. The defender ends up running around the blocker when the ball is being run at him. That is a move you do not want in a goal line defense.

At some point in the game, your players have to learn they have to take the blocker on and whip him. This drill is designed to make the defender understand that if his hips get outside the blocker's hips, he is done because he loses his leverage.

If you watch, some players will lose their leverage. When that happens they restart the lockout. That is the same movement as the clean in a weightlifting exercise. The player drops his hips and punches hard with the outside hand to the side of the movement. When the defender locks out his elbow, he does not want to get overextended with his arms. If he does, he has no leverage. He has to keep his hips under his body.

We do not call this drill a push-pull drill, but we are pushing on the outside shoulder to keep from getting turned. The pull comes later as the defender is trying to get off the block.

We do the fit and finish drill as the next part of the teaching progression. We fit the defender into the block of the offensive blocker. We teach reaction to the drive, reach, and cut-off blocks. We put the defender in an outside technique on the blocker and give the defender a cut-off block to defend.

The defender wants to keep his shoulders square on the blocker and constrict or squeeze the inside gap. He uses the blocker's body to fill the gap. The defender's gap is outside the block, but he wants to tighten the inside gap. That is the reaction we teach on the cut-off block.

The reach block is the next block we play. We put the defender and blocker in the fit position and let the defender react to the blocker. We do not want him to give ground east and west on a reach block. We coach the defender to knock the blocker back toward the goal line. We get in the appropriate leverage position and try to put the blocker's butt back in the end zone.

In these drills we are giving the defender the feel of different types of blocks. The defender is learning how his leverage should feel in those blocks.

You can see how we are teaching these skills by using the progression of the drills. (All the drills we have done so far have not involved moving into the blocker. We have to put the proper footwork into the drill. In this drill we are going to put together the punch to the target, hand placement, leverage, and a fit with the proper footwork (see Diagram #3). In the film I have an outside linebacker, but it could be any defender in a stance because they use the same technique.

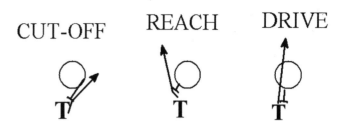

Diagram #3. Footwork drill

We are concerned with the philosophy of the footwork of the defender. If the blocker's helmet goes to the outside of the defender, I want him to step with his outside foot. If the helmet of the blocker goes to the inside, the defender steps with his inside foot. If the blocker steps straight at the defender, he takes a bucket-step by moving both feet. I want to see the hands go to the appropriate target with the appropriate leverage.

The defender has been told what block is coming and is not going to be surprised. We are working on is the footwork. We are not working on reaction to the block. A young player has to learn the appropriate footwork before he can work on read and reaction.

The first block we see in the film is the drive block. The defender wants to bucket-step by dropping both feet. He punches and gets both hands inside the framework of the blocker. He is working his hands above his shoulders. He has outside gap responsibility but gets a turnout block or cut-off block from the blocker. He wants to work the steer drill with the blocker and squeezes the inside gap by using the blocker's body to close the hole.

In this drill, we are also teaching stance. If it were a defensive lineman in a three-point stance, his first step would be with his back foot to the appropriate angle.

The next block we work in the drill is the reach block. The defender knows the reach block is coming. He is stepping with his outside foot to stay within the framework of the blocker. He is reacting to the attempt of the blocker to turn him inside. He is punching with his hands and pushing hard with the outside hand to keep the blocker from getting leverage. He is maintaining leverage and keeping his outside gap responsibility.

After we work on the footwork with a particular block, we go to the culminating activity. This is the drill where everything we have learned is put together. It is the read and react drill. This drill is just like the footwork drill, except the defender does not know what block is coming. The coach stands behind the defender and tells the blocker what block to use.

The defender has been through the progression of how to play the blocks. We are not in pads, so we are not challenging the courage of the defender. I have seen more young players ruined because coaches think they have to challenge their courage. They want to find out how tough they are. When you teach the players how to do the drills, you will find out they are much tougher when they know what they are doing. If a player is unsure and not confident in what he is doing, he will play timid and soft.

As you do these drills, the more the players understand and the more violence they get in their play. Do not force the drill into a challenge of the defender's courage until he understands the skills and knows what you want from him.

The key to the success of the drill is the offensive player. When we do these drills, so much of the time we are working within our position groups. The players within that group have to help the defender to improve on his technique. He cannot try to make it hard on the defender. We have plenty of time to make it a competitive drill during the season.

Players must work together and take care of each other. When it is his turn to play the blocker, he wants to make sure he gives the defender a good look. He wants to make the defender better through his play. That is a critical point to impress upon everyone working in the drills. That is the progression we teach our players to take on blockers.

I want to show you another drill that I think is a great drill. We did this drill at Penn State and I have always done this drill wherever I coached.

This is an off-season drill so we are not wearing pads. We have one defender in a stance facing three offensive blockers (see Diagram #4). The coach stands behind the defender. He points to one of the offensive blockers and he attacks the defender. The defender has to react to his movement. He works the progression of the read and react drill. He is working punch, hand placement, leverage, and footwork. He gets back into his stance and the coach points to another blocker. The drill is done in rapid succession to get as many reps as possible.

Diagram #4. 3-on-1

If the outside blocker attacks the defender, the defender plays that as a down block. He steps to the block, punches his hands to the target, and squeezes outside on the blocker. He is working with his hands above his shoulders and working to get square on the blocker. If the middle blocker comes at him, he plays a drive block and uses the techniques to play that block. If the inside blocker attacks him, he plays that block like a cut-off block, steers the blocker, and squeezes inside.

Next I want to go into our goal line defense. I am going to talk about our goal line defense in regard to having tight ends in the game. We play our goal line defense from the five-yard line into the end zone. The formations I am going to use are tight formations (see Diagram #5).

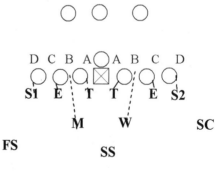

Diagram #5. Goal line alignment

On the goal line, we play a 6-2 leverage defense. The two inside tackles are responsible for the A gaps. Their man-on keys are the offensive guards. The Mack and Will inside linebackers have the B gaps. The defensive ends are C gap players and have outside leverage. We play two Sam linebackers and take a defensive back out of the game. They are responsible for the D gaps.

In our secondary, we play with a strong and free safety. They stay in the game and we bring in our next best safety. He is called the safety-corner. We are playing a zone concept. In this defense, the two Sam linebackers are coverage people. The two inside linebacker are in coverage unless they get full flow by the backs in the backfield.

If the Mack or Will linebacker gets full flow by all backs, he is running through a gap and playing upfield. The backside linebacker on full flow away from him is the middle hook player. If there is split flow, both linebackers are in coverage.

If the backs give a full flow left, the Mack linebacker is running through his gap, and we are going to roll the coverage to that direction. If there is full flow going right, the Will linebacker is going, and the coverage rolls to the right. We call the coverage Key, versus a balanced three back set (see Diagram #6). We are going to key the coverage based on the flow of the backs. If the flow is to the right, the safety on that side is coming in support, and the middle safety is coming over the top to that side. The backside safety comes to the middle. On flow the other way, it would be just the opposite.

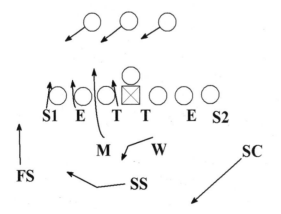

Diagram #6. Key coverage

If the set is an unbalanced set, we predetermine the coverage. If the offensive set is a power-I formation to the left, the coverage is predetermined to the left. That means the free safety is the support, the strong safety is in front half player, and the safety-corner is in back half player. If the formation is unbalanced to the right, we predetermine the coverage right.

If the formation sets the coverage in one direction and motions to an unbalanced set to the opposite side, we check the coverage to that side. They are keying the coverage to the strength of the formation.

The free safety is keying the tight end's block on the Sam linebacker (see Diagram #7). If the tight end tries to reach or drive block on the Sam linebacker, the Sam linebacker plays backer support. The Sam linebacker works for support and has the pitch man on an option play his way. The free safety is filling inside the Sam linebacker and has the quarterback on the option. If the tight end blocks down on our defensive end or Mack linebacker, the Sam linebacker is going to spill everything outside, and the safety is going to support. If a speed option is being run at him, he takes the quarterback. We call that support read support because the safety is reading the tight end.

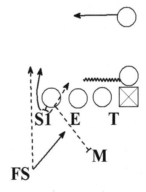

Diagram #7. Backer-read support

If we are in a predetermined rotation left, the Sam linebacker does not have to support. The free safety is the support and can play tighter to the line of scrimmage. To the backside away from the call, we are playing read support. If there is motion and the coverage was checked right, the safety-corner has the support and the free safety plays read support on the backside.

This is what we call an outside leverage defense. If the offense is going to beat the defense, there is only on place the ball is going. The ball is going in the B gap. We have our two biggest and strongest people in the A gaps. The guy playing left tackle benches 600 pounds, and the guy playing the right tackle benches 575 pounds. The offense should not be able to run the ball in there. Those are our two biggest players on the defense.

If the offense tries to run the ball in the A gap, they are going to have to double-team the player in the gap. If that happens, the backside linebacker has to fill that gap.

A formation we see in the goal line situation is the three tight end set, with the third tight end in the wing position outside one of the tight ends. With our coverage predetermined to the left, our free safety is in a support mode (see Diagram #8). Our safeties are keying the course of the ball to the tight end. The free safety is rolled up in support and is reading the course of the ball to the tight end. The middle safety is the strong safety, and he is reading the course of the ball to the tight end either way the ball moves. The safety-corner is in a read support scheme on the backside.

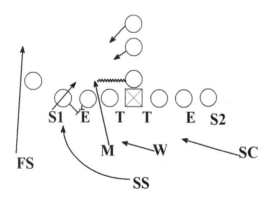

Diagram #8. Outside support

If the ball is on the line toward the left side of the formation, our safeties recognize the possibility of the option. They read the release of the tight end. The free safety takes the pitch man on the option. The strong safety reads the tight end. If there is no release by the tight end, he fills inside the support

of the free safety.

If the ball comes off the line of scrimmage and the fullback is running a tight inside track to the isolation play, the middle safety knows his fit is inside the 5 technique defensive end (see Diagram #9). He has that fill on either side of the formation. The linebacker to that side takes on the fullback and spills the ball to the strong safety. The safeties have a support and a fit in this defense. On an inside run, the middle safety fits inside the 5 technique. The backside linebacker fills over the top as fast as he can. The backside safety takes the backside B gap and plays for the cutback of the running back.

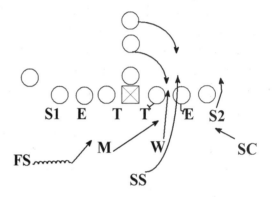

Diagram #9. Isolation fill

The place the offense thinks they can run the ball is the B gap. It looks inviting, but we are getting people into that gap. If the formation key moves from one side to the other, we check the coverage and roll the coverage the other way. No one is affected except the three safeties and the Sam linebacker away from the call. Everyone else is playing the defense the way it was called.

If the ball comes off the line and the path of the fullback is outside the B −gap, the middle safety does not worry about the fit inside the 5-technique (see Diagram #10). We do not need another defender in the B-gap. The strong safety is going to fill on the off-tackle spill. If the fullback is running that type of path generally the tight end is blocking down on the 5-technique or chipping to the linebacker. The Sam linebacker is going to spill everything coming his way, and the support safety to that side is turning everything inside. The middle safety is filling inside the support safety in the off-tackle gap.

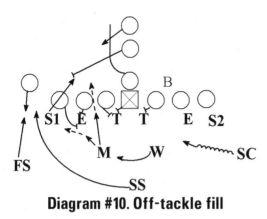

Diagram #10. Off-tackle fill

On the goal line we see a two tight end set with one wide receiver. The best coverage safety in the game has the wide receiver. We can play the wide receiver in four different ways. We can play man-to-man with the strong safety. We can bracket the wide receiver with the inside and outside safeties. In the bracket coverage, the inside safety has all moves made by the receiver inside, and the outside safety has all moves by the receiver to the outside. We can play zone with the strong safety underneath and the free safety over the top. We could take the third safety out of the game and put in our best cover corner.

If our corner can take care of the wide receiver, we have the offense outnumbered in the box ten to eight. If we take two defensive backs out of the box, we still have nine in the box and the offense has nine possible blockers if the quarterback carries the ball (see Diagram #11). Either way we are in good shape in regard to the number of defenders in the box.

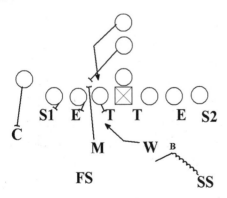

Diagram #11. Isolation play against nine

If we take two defensive backs out to cover on the wide receiver, the linebacker's fill on the isola-

tion play changes. He no longer spills the ball to the outside. He takes the fullback's block on with his inside shoulder and forces the ball carrier inside to the backside linebacker. The backside safety is still filling the B gap to his side for the cutback play.

The formation that gives us some adjustment problems is the two-tight end set with one wide receiver with both the tight ends to the same side in a wing set (see Diagram #12). We kick the coverage toward the wing set. That puts the free safety in support with the strong safety over the tight end. The Sam linebacker to the wide receiver side comes off the line as an invert defender to that side. If the corner needs help, we let the Sam linebacker drive on all inside moves by the wide receiver and let the corner adjust to an outside position. If the corner can clearly play the wide receiver, we do not fool around with the Sam linebacker and align him back inside.

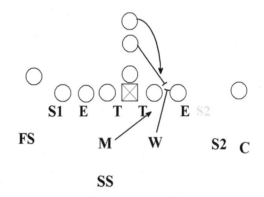

Diagram #12. Two tight end wing

The position of the Sam linebacker tells the Will linebacker where to spill the running back on the inside isolation. If the Sam linebacker is inside, the Will linebacker spills the running back to the Sam linebacker. If Sam linebacker is removed to help with the coverage, the Will linebacker turns the ball back to the backside linebacker. That is not a bad adjustment, and you can still double the outside receiver if you need to. The only difference is you are using a linebacker instead of a safety.

I want to put the film on and show you our goal line defense. The set we are looking at is a two-tight end set with a wing set. That wingback could be a running back, fullback, tight end, or wide receiver. If it is anything except a great receiver, we have a strong safety type in the game. If the player is a great wide receiver, we have our best cover corner in the game.

First, I want to talk about the alignments. Our A gap players are our two tackles. Their man-on keys are the offensive guards. The offensive guards are the men the defensive tackles work on to get their hand and leverage position. The 5 techniques are playing the C –gap, and their man-on keys are the offensive tackles. When we talked about the fit progression in the drill work, those are the techniques these players are going to play on their man-on keys. The tight end - wing is declared to the defense's left; therefore, the coverage is declared left. The free safety has the containment on the outside run and option. He is taking the pitch man on the option.

Since the free safety is the support man, the Sam linebacker to the wing side is aligned heavier on the tight end. The middle safety is reading the course of the ball to the tight end.

To the other side, the Sam linebacker and safety-corner are playing a read support technique. The Sam linebacker loosens slightly in his alignment because he may have to play run support. If the tight end puts his helmet on the Sam linebacker, he takes the support and the pitch on the option. The safety-corner fills inside the Sam linebacker and takes the quarterback on the option.

When the tight end releases off the line of scrimmage the safety-corner takes him, and the Sam linebacker takes the first back out of the backfield, releasing his way. If there is full flow by the backs to the other side, the Sam linebacker drops into coverage looking for the tight end on the drag route coming across the field.

If they throw a pass from this set, the free safety has the flat (see Diagram #13). The Sam linebacker drops into the curl area. The Mack linebacker runs through his gap. The middle safety drops into the deep area at the back of the end zone. The Will

linebacker plays the middle hook area. The backside Sam linebacker drops and looks for the tight end drag coming across the field. The safety-corner plays the tight end deep on the backside. That is our zone concept in the passing game.

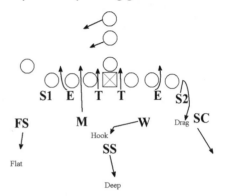

Diagram #13. Zone coverage

If the play-action came away from the formation, the coverage would roll to the other side, and the responsibilities of the defender would reverse. The Will linebacker would run through his gap, and the Mack linebacker would have the middle hook area.

The defense is an outside leverage defense. If the offense is going to beat the defense, they have to beat it in the gaps. This defense is simple and not complex.

The inside linebackers are keying the fullback through to the tailback. However, they must have vision on the course of the ball. We are a fast read team keying on the backs. If the linebacker gets full flow from the backs, he needs to see the guard and feel what is happening up front of him. If we want our 5 techniques to run up field and rush the passer, we give them a rush or a wide go call.

We are all in this game together for the benefit of the kids that play the game. The high school coach is the beacon light for their school and community. We are all supporting the mission of education, which is the development of young people. Do not assume that kids in this day and age know the difference between right and wrong. What football coaches do is underappreciated. You are a great group of men. Keep up the fight.

Brad Paulson

THE NO-HUDDLE OFFENSE

Anderson University

When people talk about the no-huddle offense, most people think of it as a two-minute offense. I am going to talk about the offense we use at Anderson University and what we do with our no-huddle offense.

Last year, we were the number-one passing offense in Division III. We had 383.6 yards per game. Our quarterback threw for 4700 yards. We were seventh in total offense, with 470 yards per game. In our last six games, we averaged 36.5 points per game, with a total of 505 yards per game. We averaged 411 yards passing offense in those last six games.

Let me give you our philosophy on offense. We want to run the complete running and passing game. We want to be fundamentally sound in every phase of the offense. We want to make sure our playmakers tough the ball as much as possible. We do not believe you must get the ball to the split end four times per game, to the tight end three times per game, and to the wide receiver five times per game. We are not going to give the ball to our running backs thirty times per game. We want to get the ball to our playmakers as much as possible. We are unselfish and team oriented. We take what the defense gives us. We want to play with pride and class. We want to be champions on and off the field. We want to get our players involved in our community, and we want a positive impact on the community.

We are a one back spread offense. We like to take large splits with our offensive linemen. We want to score enough points to win. Our goal is to score 40 points per game. We want to score six or seven touchdowns per game. Last year, we average almost 37 points per game.

We do not want any procedure penalties. We always go on one. The defense knows this, and we know it. We eliminate procedure penalties by going on the first count. We want our players to compete in every play. Our receivers and quarterback compete in every drill.

We want to grade out over 90 percent on each play. We all have different grading systems, but that is what we shoot for.

We want to finish in every aspect of the game. Our backs must carry out their fakes, and the receivers must run the proper routes and must be willing to block. We are a big screen and a big draw play team. The players must be unselfish and be willing to block when they do not get the ball. That is a very big part of our offense.

Another goal is to prevent turnovers. We stress ball security in everything we do on offense. We want to prevent negative plays. Our quarterback never calls an audible without checking with us on the sidelines. We want to dominate the short yardage and goal line situations. This is a big key for us. Being a one back spread team, we have a goal line set. We have double tight ends with three backs set to run power football. We use the unbalanced line, and we can play smash mouth football on the goal line. We want our kids to be aggressive in the red zone.

We want ten big plays per game. A big play for us is a 15-yard run and a 25-yard pass play. We want to be 100 percent when we are in the red zone. We ended up with 89 percent scoring in the red zone this year. We want to be successful over 60 percent of the time on third downs. This past year, we were 47 percent successful on third downs. We want to be able to average 4.0 yards per play. If we do not score, our kids are disappointed when they come off the field. We continue to remind them we want to average 4.0 yards per play, and the scoring will come.

We are very simple in our approach to the offense. We believe a confused athlete is a slow athlete. Our base pass package consists of eight to ten plays. We tag a lot of the plays, and most of our formations are very simple. Our kids know what is going on, and they can play fast play aggressive. Our basic run scheme is very simple. We have a draw scheme, a zone scheme, and a counter scheme. That is it on the running game. We spend very little time on our inside game. We work more on pass protection and related schemes. We are very simple as far as the running game is concerned.

Our big thing in practice is the screen scheme. We run the rocket, bubble, hitch, swing, and read screens. I will go over these on tape to give you an idea of what we are doing with the screen game.

The hitch screen has been very good for us. We simply throw the ball out to the open receiver and let him play football in space. The swing screen is for our running back. Our read screens are for our wide receivers and running backs.

People want to know why we use the one–back set. The reason is that it makes the defense cover the entire field. It gets all of our best athletes on the field at the same time. We can create match-up problems with motion and simple formation adjustments. This offense forces the linebackers to play in space. It simplifies our protection schemes. And it simplifies our running game.

Why the no-huddle? It is fun. Our kids like the tempo of the offense. It is fun to practice, fun to run, and fun to watch. Controlling the tempo is the big thing with our offense. You must race up and down the field as fast as you can. When we are in our blazer tempo, you must get the play off in 12 to 14 seconds. Then we have our check tempo and our milk tempo, where we run the clock down within four seconds of the 25-second clock. They must be able to run all three tempos. If they cannot play in all three tempos, they will not play offense for us.

We feel this offense creates stress on the defense. We know it disrupts the substitution patterns. We want to make sure we create stress on the linebackers with our personnel. Our personnel never changes. We do not want to give the defense time to make the substitutions when we get into the red zone. We keep our personnel the same and we want to get the ball snapped at a fast tempo to prevent the defense from getting their special defensive personnel in the game.

Our offense promotes unity. Our secret language is our no-huddle game and our signals. Everyone has to be on the same page. This creates unity for our linemen and for our receivers and backs. We never huddle in practice. We only huddle one time a week. That is in a two-minute situation when we want to talk with our players. We have our two-minute offense built into our no-huddle attack. This offense allow for easy adjustments during the game.

Let me talk about the keys to the no-huddle. We must limit our formations and our motion. We do not want to go into a game with 75 formations. It just confuses the kids. You can't do that.

We make the protection package very simple to call and recognize. Our players create the majority of our signals. I will give them the formations and the protection, and the players call the rest of the plays. I do not care how the players want to call the plays. As long as they know what we are doing, it works fine for us.

We use the signals in every aspect when we are dealing with the offense. During meetings, in walk-through, and in practice we have the kids hold up the signals. They must know the signals. Our kickers know them, the coaches know them, and the players know them. They are very simple.

Once the player has played in our system, he can run the offense without a wristband. We only have about six calls on the wristband. When he gets to the line of scrimmage, he looks at the wristband and calls the play that is signaled in to him. We use the wristband when we are in controlled tempo.

We want to package plays together. We set the run scheme and the passing scheme together. We want to keep things simple. We use the KISS theory. Over time, we give the quarterback more as far as the puzzle is concerned with the no-huddle system. It only takes a few seconds to call a play. With a senior, he can handle a lot more. With a freshman, you have to give him a little at a time until he gets comfortable with the system. If you do that, you will help him out a lot.

If your quarterback is going to be a running quarterback, it is hard to get him off the ground and back to the line to look for the next play. He must look at the signal caller as soon as possible. Our receivers do not quit. Our wide receivers and tight end must look to the sideline right away to see the formation called. They call the formation for us. The tight end will call "Right-Right" or "Left-Left." We do not flip outside wide receivers. We try to get into like formations as much as possible.

We are not concerned with the other team stealing our signals. If the defense calls out "Zone, Zone" our players do not panic. We feel it is easier for us to steal the defensive team's signals than it is to steal our offensive signals. If the defense is watching me give the signals on offense, we are also watching them as they give the defensive signals. It is no big deal to us when it comes to our signals.

We have our automatics ready to call after big plays. We run two automatic plays that we run after a big run or a big pass play. Our kids know the two plays for that week. We really like this in the red zone. We have designed the plays in practice, and our players know what we are going to run.

We have a freeze play ready as well. We run the freeze play with four vertical receivers. We have code names for our freeze play. The first play we run in our summer camp is our freeze play as far as the automatics are concerned. Our players get familiar with the call, and they become comfortable with the call. That is a big key for us.

We want to correlate packages with like terms. For protections we use boys' and girls' names. The linemen are not concerned with all of the information the quarterback is calling out at the line of scrimmage. All they are concerned with is the protection and the running game. That makes it a lot easier for the linemen.

Next we talk about the game plan. We do not want to change the plays between our 20-yard line and our opponent's 30-yard line. We run the same plays out of the same formations and motions each week. We never change those plays. We game plan heavily between the plus 30 and the plus 12-yard lines. We may add a new formation or a new motion in this area. We plan for defensive substitutions and different looks. We look for the defense to be more aggressive in this area.

The big key to the no-huddle Offense is to watch the defensive linemen. Once you see they are tired, you must be ready to jump all over them. Once you jump on them, you must keep on them.

We self-scout for formation and field tendencies. We have a GA break down our last four games each week. We look at our formations and field tendencies to see what we are calling. For example, last year we were calling the "all curls" route on third down and eight to go. So we saw what we were doing and made the changes that helped us later in the year.

We script the opening series. We like to script the first 20 to 25 plays. But because the defenses do some crazy things against you, it is hard to stick to those 20 plays. Our best game of the season was when we were able to run the entire script the first half. We scored seven touchdowns and had 450 yards passing. During the first drive or during the first 15 plays, we want to find out who is the weakest defender. Once we find out that information, we want to be able to take advantage of it.

We have four formations. We have a right and left, which is basically a double set (see Diagram #1). The rip and liz is the X trips set (see Diagram #2). The ram and lion is a Y trip set (see Diagram #3). The rocket and laser are our five wideouts set (see Diagram #4).

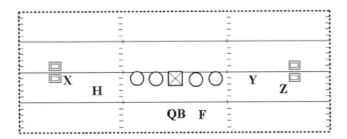

Diagram #1. Right – left formations

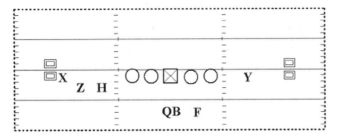

Diagram #2. Rip –liz formations

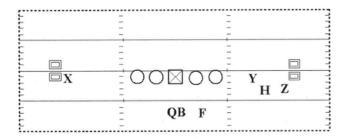

Diagram #3. Ram – lion formations

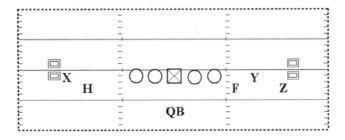

Diagram #4. Rocket – laser formations

Once we get inside the 30-yard line, we give our formations tags. We have a bunch tag. Our Y receiver splits five yards from our tackle. The other receivers split one or two yards off the Y receiver, depending on the play we have called.

If we call a special Tag, it flips the receivers. It brings the X and Z to one side, and the Y and H to the other side. Our Close Tag is our 2 X 2 set. We bring both sides into the bunch set on their side.

Our tight end was a good receiver. He was 6'5" and was a great player for us. At the end of the season, we ran a lot of our Y Tags (see Diagram #5). Our Y tags were simple. We called them A, B, and C.. If the tight end is in the game and it is a regular set, he lines up on the right side next to the tackle. If we give him the A call, he is lined up five yards off the line of scrimmage in the same location, outside the tackle. The B set puts the tight end is a slot set. The C set puts the tight end outside.

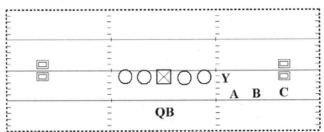

Diagram #5. Formation tags – Y tags

Our shallow package is probably our best package as far as completions are concerned. What we are trying to get a high-low triangle read with our H, Y, and Z receivers (see Diagram #6).

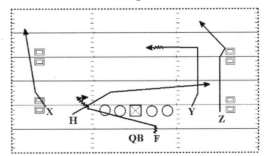

Diagram #6. Shallow package

Our Z runs the deep post route. The Y receiver runs a dig route inside at 12 yards. The X receiver goes on a vertical route. The H back runs the shallow route coming across the field, gaining depth as he clears the linebackers. This is a great call on any down and any distance. If we are not sure what to call, the shallow package is real effective.

We feel this play is a very high-percentage pass. It has big play potential. It is easy to adjust to formations and personnel. It is great against man or zone coverage. It is a good blitz beater. And as I said, it is a safe call on any down-and-distance.

With tags we can run several variations of the play, and that makes it hard to defend. It is a good play anywhere on the field.

Let me go over what we want on the play.

X: Outside release vertical

H: Shallow as possible, 5 yards to opposite sideline; hot receiver. His goal is to run at the butt of the defensive end.

Y: Outside release, push 12 to 14 yards, break under control and turn numbers to the quarterback in first hole. He does not want to spring across the field to try to get open. He pushes outside and sits down at 12 to 14 yards.

Z: Alert TD! Post route 12 to 15 yards. We want him at the top of the numbers.

F: Our running back always goes to the shallow side. Know protection! Run the leak route where H starts from.

QB: Takes a quick five-step drop and reads strong to middle triangle. Progression is Z, Y, H, F.

An adjustment is to send our F back on a release to the flag. Against a single safety defense, we put the F back in the flat and have him turn up and go deep. Now the read is a little different. We want the quarterback to peep at the Z receiver and look for F to Y to H (see Diagram #7).

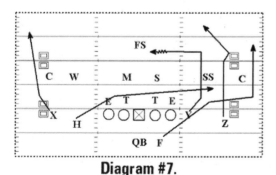

Diagram #7.

Here is the other adjustment on the play. Against the two deep look we want the Z receiver to run the post down the middle. We want the quarterback to look for the safety as soon as he can. We send the F back in the hole inside over the middle (see Diagram #8).

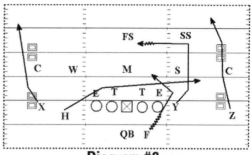

Diagram #8.

We can have the F back check down and come across to the H side and then cut back to the middle (see Diagram #9).

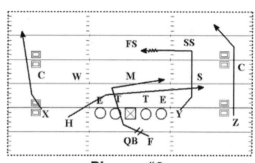

Diagram #9.

Our screens are probably our best package. Our Z receiver is the man we want to get the ball to on our rocket screen. We want him to push upfield two or three steps and belly back one yard behind the line of scrimmage. We are not trying to throw the ball to him quick to get him in the crease. We are trying to run him inside on a crease inside the hash mark (see Diagram #10).

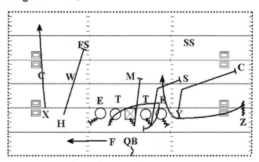

Diagram #10. Rocket screen

Our slot receiver has the first man closest to the play. He has the first threat. If he Sam linebacker attacks, he must block him. He pushes upfield five yards. If Sam attacks, he must take him. The playside tackle invites the defensive man deep, and then he cuts him. He wants to count one thousand one, one thousand two, and cut the man. He wants to make sure he gets the defensive man to get his hands down.

The playside guard sets for two counts and releases for the number two defender. He must read the block of the Y receiver. If the Y receiver does not block the Sam linebacker, the guard picks him up. The center sets for two counts and blocks the first wrong-color jersey playside at the linebacker's depth. The backside guard sets for two counts, wraps around the play, and cuts any one chasing the play. The backside tackle sets his pass block on the outside. The H back goes deep, looking for the free safety. The X receiver goes vertical, taking the corner deep with him. The backside players must do their jobs or the play will not work.

The play is designed to get four yards. It is a good play in that it slows the rush down. We work on the screen plays every day. They are a big key for us.

I want to show you the cutups of these plays. If you would like to know how we call our plays, drop me a note or give me a call and I would be more than happy to give them to you. I appreciate your attention.

PLAYER DEVELOPMENT AND MOTIVATION

University of Missouri

Thank you for being here. I appreciate that introduction. I have not been introduced like this for a long time. I am getting so old not many people talk about my college playing days.

My background is with former Coach Don James. He is my mentor. Don James came to Kent State University just after the May 4 campus killings. We were the first group back on campus after that episode. I was a sophomore that year. He went on to build a winner at Kent State. Later we won nine and only lost two games and we played in the Tangerine Bowl that year.

Later Don James was named the head coach at the University of Washington in Seattle. They had not won many games before he went to Washington. I was fortunate to work for him at Washington. We went to 11 Bowl Games in 12 years. We went to three Rose Bowls and the Orange Bowl. They won the National Championship the year after I left Washington. The point I am making is this. The same program that we used at Kent State in 1970 and 1971 was the same program used at the University of Washington. It was done with a system and a plan.

In 1990, I was fortunate enough to become the head coach at the University of Toledo. The same program that worked at Kent State and Washington was the program that I installed at the University of Toledo. We struggled the first two years, but in the last eight years we averaged over eight wins per year. We were nationally ranked the last six years.

It was speculated that I was going to be moving to a big-time football school. I decided I would not move just to be moving. I wanted to go where I could be involved in building a national program. I was for-tunate enough to get the job at the Missouri three years ago.

We have a plan for everything we do in our football program. We have a plan for absolutely everything we do in our program. The foundation is the things I learned from Don James.

When I go to clinics, I try to cover things that I think will apply to any program. I could talk about X's and O's but some of you would not be interested in what we are doing at Missouri. But we have a certain way we do things that may be of interest to everyone here tonight. So, I am going to talk to you about the things we do to build our program.

We use a systems approach in our program. We have different systems in our program. We tell our coaches and players that we want to be the very best in the country and in everything that we do in our program. My job as the head coach is to make sure we are on the right track and that we are improving each year.

In my first year at Missouri, we ended up 4-7. It was one of the worst years of my life. The second year at Missouri we were 5-7. We lost four games in the last two minutes of each game. But we were not good enough to win those games. We stayed with our program and the basic foundation of what we started. We do not change our philosophy just because things are not going well. In fact, this is when I get more committed. I tell our players the program is not going to change. We let them know we are going to change the people within the program.

This year we were 8-4 and lost to Arkansas in the Independence Bowl. We did make progress. We have most of our team back next year. We do have a pretty good quarterback. Most people know about him. I will let you know he was awful until I started coaching him. I'm kidding. His name is Brad Smith, and he is from Youngstown, Ohio.

I am going to show you how we go about developing our players within our program and the things we do to make our program better.

In all the locker rooms and in the coaching offices we have a simple slogan:

- TEAM IS THE BOTTOM LINE!
- Be enthusiastic!
- Be a six-second competitor!
- Know your assignment!
- Play tough and physical!

You must be able to do these four things to be a good football player. It does not take any ability to have enthusiasm. A six-second competitor to us is this: When the ball is snapped and until the whistle blows to end the play, we want the players to go as fast and as hard as they can. Can you train players to play harder? Yes, we think you can train players to play harder. Watch the films. Most players start slow and most of them do not finish well. They may just be three-second players. Build them up to four-second players, then five seconds, and then take them to the next level as six-second competitors. This is just playing hard, going as fast as your body will go, and training your players to do this. You must have a plan to do this. I will show you how we teach that in our program.

It takes an ability to know what you are doing. Know your assignment. This year we added the fourth aspect of playing tough and physical. We need to be physical and tough to play against teams like Nebraska, Oklahoma, and Kansas State. If we want to win against those teams, we must be able to play physical, and we must be tough.

We grade our players in everything they do. The four points are listed in the corner of the grade sheet for a scrimmage or a game. We ask, "Did you play with enthusiasm during the game?" We ask them if they were Six-second competitors. They should not have any plays where they did not give it their best effort. We ask, "Did you have any make any mental errors? Did you play physical?" If you do those four things, which take no ability at all, it is amazing how much better a football team you will have. Your kids can play hard and they can play hard all of the time. Guess what? You train them to play hard. This is the team bottom line for us.

I will talk about player development as we go through this lecture. We talk about the following items:

- Strength improvement!
- Speed improvement!
- Quickness improvement!
- Mental toughness!

Next I want to talk about measurable probabilities improvement. We talk about these points:

- Win the kicking game!
- Be the least penalized team!
- Win the turnover margin!

These are the things we feel we must get on our side to win games. I learned these things from Don James. First, is to win the kicking game. If you can win the kicking game, you dramatically increase your chances to win the game. You do not want your team to be the worst-penalized team in the conference. If you have 100 yards in penalties each game, that is Missouri beating Missouri. This is a matter of discipline. Can you become the least penalized team if you are disciplined? Yes, you can! You can control all of these points.

Win the turnover margin controls more football games than any other single factor. Last year we were 10th in the nation in turnover margin. In our second year at Missouri, we were fifteenth in the nation in turnover margin. In our first year at Missouri we were 70th in turnover margin. No other statistic will improve your chances to win football games more than winning the turnover margin. This past year, we only had four fumbles. The year before we had three fumbles. We have turned the ball over the least number of times of anyone in Division I. We were sixth in the nation in rushing this past year. So you can see that we do run the football.

How do we accomplish this? We have a plan. We stress these points in our practice so we can do the same in the games. I am not talking about one offensive play at this time, but if I can get those three points on our side, or on Missouri's side, we increase our chances for success and the chance to win games.

Without changing your personnel, if you can get these things on your side, you will be a better team. You must coach these things in practice. We stress these points daily in our offense and our defense.

Our next point is to develop athletes. We want to change the players and how they think:

- Self-starter
- Leadership
- Competitor

I left Toledo with a 10-1 record and went to Missouri. When I first got to the University of Missouri I called my wife, Vicky after our first workout. I said, "Vicky, we are really bad!" She said, "Gary that is the reason they hired you." I got mad and hung up on her. I want love and compassion. She really knows how to get me going!

The first thing we told them when we got to Missouri was that we did not want players with excuses. No excuse! You can not have an excuse habit and a success habit. That will never work. When we got to Missouri, the players had excuses for everything. They had excuses for missing class, missing study table, and every other thing you could think of. Now, they do not have excuses for anything. Our players have a great attitude. If a player does not have a good attitude, he will be in the position coach's office or in my office. If a player is having a tough day and he goes into the locker room with a sorry mood, it will have an effect on everyone. That is a bad attitude to me. That affects the football team. It is important to change how our players think.

When you have adversity on your team, lighting will strike. In my first year at Missouri we had a tough time. We had a plan every ten minutes where we made sure we let the players know they had to think positive at all times. We had a coach that would remind the players to think positive every ten minutes that first year. We wanted to control the situation the best way we could, and the best possible advice we could give the players was to think positive.

Our next area is skill and fundamental development. That is the reason most of you are here tonight. You want your players to be a better fundamental football team. The players must be able to master the positions they play. Coaches must master their positions. If we can do all of the things we have discussed, we will increase our chances for success. My job is to make sure we affect attitudes and that we get player development. We have a plan of how we are going to become a better football team. We are going to make our players stronger, faster, and quicker mentally.

I want to talk about our program goals and what we try to do with our players as far as player development is concerned. We are trying to enhance our performance. In our off-season, we have from January until the players report in August to make the team better. Some teams are going to do a better job than others. Some teams will make their players stronger. It does not matter about the ability, because we all know the better the athlete, the better they will be. I do know if you can make a player stronger and he feels he is faster and he feels he is tougher, guess what? You are going to be a better football team before you ever snap a football or throw a pass or run a play.

Our player development program goals are simple:

- Enhance football performance!
- Reduce injury!
- Increase Confidence!

In our program, we raise the players' self-esteem. They know they are stronger, faster, and quicker.

I want to define some terms at this point. The first is mental toughness. Unless you are mentally tough you do not win football games. We worked out at 6:00 AM on Thursday. We have a program where we work on mental toughness. We train our players to be mentally tougher.

You can make players stronger and faster. You can make your players quicker. You can teach them to change direction, which is agility. That means they must be able to change directions as fast as they can. You can teach your players to do it better than they have ever done it before.

We work on explosiveness. Obviously, power comes with all of this. We are working to develop all of these things in our winter program. We will be able to see the improvement, and we will be able to measure the improvement. We want them to be able to see the results. We are looking a winning edge in doing these things. The thing we are looking for is a change of attitude. We want to change the confidence level of the players. We want the players to feel good about what they are doing. If they feel good about themselves, they will play better.

One of the greatest things that motivate our players is the evaluation process. We start by evaluating individual player development. We measure position player improvement. Each player in our program must get better in our program. Every player must know his role in getting stronger and quicker in our program. We set goals for each position. We are very goal-oriented. We stress offensive and defensive improvement, and we stress team improvement.

To evaluate what you do is as critical as anything you do in your program. You cannot get to the top or to wherever you want to go unless you evaluate what you are doing. Players must know when they are getting critiqued it will make them a better football player, and it will make us a better team.

We are a goal- and achievement- oriented football team. This is what we do. We set academic goals. We have what we call Game Day in the weight room. I will cover this later. Players are testing in the weight room on designated dates to

achieve their PR or personal record. They set goals, and then we test them to see that they obtain those goals. We test them on everything they do in our program. Then we reset goals and test them again. In five weeks, we will test our players. That is our Game Day in the weight room. It is organized with a computer, and it is easy to set the goals.

We set goals in a football game, and then we are tested. That is what we do in our winter program. We set goals four times per year with everything we do in the winter program. The key is this. I do not care what you test at today. I want to make sure that the next time you are tested, you are better. Progress is the key. This is true in everything we do.

Here is our lifting segment and our Game Day in the weight room. Game Day to us is when we go in and test the athletes. We put up big signs in front of the weight room: "Tomorrow is Game Day in the Weight Room." We have this organized five weeks down the road. They know when this date will come up.

We work for five weeks in the winter program. Then we have spring practice the first of March. We lift weights for five weeks. We do three lifts per week. We test 40-yard sprints on Fridays for five straight weeks. The players must run two 40-yard sprints. Some players want to run more than two sprints. At the same time we have a quickness drill going on, and we have a jumping contest going on.

When we get into spring football, we go for two lifts per week for five weeks. We do not have Game Day on Friday now, because we are just in a maintenance mode at this point. We want to make sure we maintain our strength and do not go backwards.

After spring practice we have three lifts per week for four weeks. And them in May we have another Game Day in the weight room. They know what to expect, and they know they must get better. In the summer, we practice for four days for seven weeks. We get three weeks in June, three weeks in July, and one week in August. We have another Game Day in August in our weight room. Our players must be accountable. They know they are going to be tested.

In the two-a-day practices we do two lifts per week. If our players are not playing a lot, we may give them three lifts. At the end of the season, we have Game Day in the weight room in early December.

The personal record or PR is a big thing in our program. They hear us talking about their PR all of the time. The players achieve a PR in everything they do. They are tested in each testing segment. I want to see them gain in each area. We post all of this info so the team can see the improvement of each player. Any time a player wants to go for his PR during a workout, he can ask the coach to test him at that time. He does not have to wait until Game Day in the weight room to improve his PR. The object of Game Day in the weight room is to set up a Game Day environment. You can PR any time you want to try to gain your best lift. In Game Day, we want the players to get their minds right and get after it. We make it a big deal. Get in the arena and make something good happen! When a player reaches his PR we make it a big deal. We have several players that will go over and give him a high-five. They make the guy feel like a million dollars. His self-esteem is going to go up a little higher. We do that for the great players and the average players as well. We have a coach that yells out the player's name that PRs, and the entire weight room will start clapping and yelling. It is a big deal at Missouri.

Here are the tests we use at Missouri to test strength. We do the bench press – 5 reps max estimated. We do squats – 5 reps max estimated. We do 225 reps as our total number. Then we do the hang clean – 5 reps max estimated. We do not go all the way down on this test. This is what we do strengthwise in our program.

In our explosive test, we work on the vertical jump and the standing long jump. These two tests are what we use to measure explosiveness. When we started doing these drills, our players would come in on Friday, they would do one vertical jump and one standing long jump, and then they would leave the locker room. Now they will stay there and work out until they PR in everything. They want to

PR in everything we are working on. They want their teammates to PR in everything. We want to get a certain number of positions to PR in all of the drills, and we want a certain percentage of the team to PR in all drills.

The next area we do is the quickness and agility test. We have them run the I test (see Diagram #1). They line up on a straight line and start in the middle of the line. They go to the end of the line and touch their hand and foot on the line and then come back to the other side and touch again. We time those runs to let the players know how fast they are going. We want them to know if they are getting quicker. This makes the players feel better about themselves. After four years in our program, they will become a lot quicker.

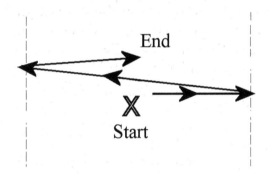

Diagram #1. I test

The other thing we do is the Three Cone Test (see Diagram #2). It is the NFL-type drill that the do at the Combine camps. It really tests the change of direction. It is a timed test. You go from cone to cone changing directions.

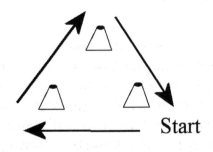

Diagram #2. Three-cone test

That is how we test quickness. As our players become quicker, they grade out better in those areas.

The speed test is the 40-yard Dash. That is it. We have our PR boards set up. We have the PR boards out every day when we are testing. We post the results in the locker room, and the players see all the results the next day. This is a big deal for us. You can use all of these ideas if you want, but if you do not use the numbers to enhance your program so the players feel better about themselves, it will not matter. We keep our PR boards in the position coach's office.

Basically this is what we have on the personal record board. We have the player's name, height, weight, body fat, and the best results of the player for bench, 225 clean, squat, vertical jump, standing long jump, I test, three-cone test, and 40-yard dash. The boards are hung in the position coach's office.

Also we have what we call the All Big 12 Board. When we got to Missouri we did the tests, and the top players on our boards were not very good. They were pitiful. They felt good about what their performance, but they were sub par. So we set the standard for what we think an All Big 12 player at each position would test out on each of the areas. We do not stress height in this area. The important things we are stressing are the tests. We set a bar for the players to see how they measure up with the other players in the Big Twelve. We want to put the standard up high. This shows the players where we want them to go. You cannot be weak, slow, and not possess quickness but still win. It just does not happen.

We feel it is important to let the players know they are developing, and that they are becoming stronger, faster, and quicker. When they can see improvement in those areas, they become a better football team and you become a better football coach.

After each Game Day we have a team meeting. I have graphs that I have prepared on the test results. I show them the graphs. Here are the areas we cover in those team meetings after Game Days. First is the percentage of PR's we had that day. Second is the number of improvements. Then I show them the graphs of improvements. I may say some-

thing like this. "Ok, guys, we had 78 percent of the team that did their PRs in the bench press in this five-week period." I may ask them how many of them ran the 40yard sprint in 4.8 or better. Then I may ask how many ran 4.7 or 4.6 or better in the 40-yard sprint. Then I go to the next test to see how we did. This is a big deal, and we want to get the entire team involved.

I make it a point to go over the number of players that have improved in our program. I will tell them we have 17 players that have reached a certain goal. I may tell them where we were at the same time period last year so they can see how much better we are in certain areas. This information is a great team motivator.

It is very important that you have accuracy in all of your testing. You do not want to play games with the players on the tests. I show the players how we have improved in the three years we have been at Missouri. I know where we are at Missouri in terms of our player's abilities. They can see we are getting better when we can show them the graphs from year to year.

Our winter program is probably the best thing we do at Missouri. We call it our Winning Edge Program. We go two days per week, on Tuesday and Thursday mornings from 6:00 AM until 7:15 AM. Each of the three segments is 17 minutes long. We did these same segments with Don James in 1972 and with Jack Lambert when we were at Kent State. I hated the morning workouts. However I knew this was the thing that helped us of all of the things we do. The entire football team does the workout in one hour and fifteen minutes. We do the workouts at 6:00 AM because our players do not like to get up that early. We want them to sacrifice to become better football players. We had some problems with this in my first year at Missouri. Last year, we did not have any scholarship players miss any of those workouts, and no one was late for any of those workouts.

In our Winning Edge Program, we have three stations going on at the same time. We have 90 players divided up, with 30 players in each group.

We split each group in this period, and they divide the time on the first station when we do agilities. In this session, we get in lines. We have them do carioca, backward runs, change of direction, cone drills, and rack drills. We are working on staying low. Also, we run step over bags drills. You can come up with any drill you want, but the main thing is to work on agilities. It is a 17-minute period for each group. These drills are going to help them with the I test and the three-cone test.

A second group does a change of direction station while the first group is running agilities. It is football. It is bending the knees and changing directions.

Then we go to our second station, which is running. We have the players work on basic running drills. We teach them the basic fundamentals of running. We teach our players how to run. We stress hands and knee drive, body lean, and other fundamentals of running. We do not sprint in this drill. We go about three quarters speed in the drill. We stress the importance of getting a good start. We teach them the sprinter's stance so they can achieve the best time possible in the 40-yard sprint.

The third station is the mat drills. If you read Bobby Bowden's book The Bowden Way, you will find out Bobby was an assistant coached along with Don James at Florida State in the late 1950s. They still do the mat drills at Florida State. Coach Bowden has a page in his books about the mat drills.

This may be the best thing we do in our football program to make our players better. We use the wrestling mats. We have 30 players in three lines, with ten players in each line. We have a coach out in front of the first three players. The first thing we do is the seat Roll. The coach calls out, "Break down." The first three guys in line break down. If one of the three does not break down in unison with the other two, they will back off and repeat the drill. We have them break down and work their feet. After a short time they will be released and the next three step up ready to go.

After they break down we have them do a seat roll, then a forward roll, and when they come up,

they must sprint to the other end of the mat. They may have to sprint right or left to the other end as fast as they can. It is very intense. The coaches are really into it. If one player does not give it their all, we are on them about it. They never walk off the mat. Our players do the drills until they do it right. We may do several drills during this session. If one player does not do the drill right, the three have to do the drill over again. You can cut the intensity level with a knife. This is where we teach the players to be mentally tough and to become six-second players.

After 17 minutes, each group rotates. All drills have specific commands. We want them to feel they have accomplished something they thought they could not do. This is how they build self-esteem.

We insist the players do the drills the right way, or they do them over. Then we carry that over to the football field. We are very much disciplined and we want things done right. It is done right at full speed, or we have them do it over.

We have a 10-minute warm-up session at the beginning of the workout, and then we have three 17-minute periods. That is basically the amount of time it takes us to complete the program. The players are never allowed to put their hands on their knees. It does not matter how tired they get, they do not put their hands on the knees. We feel this shows the opponents you are weak. When we first started this program, we had to tell the players to get their hands up above their head when they get winded. Now they take pride in showing they can take the workout without being exhausted. We may be tired, but we do not want everyone to know we are tired. We feel this is important because it changes the players' attitude. This develops pride in who they are and what they stand for. The basic thing about this program is that we want the players to do things fast, and we want them to do it right.

My basic job it to make sure we do everything right in our program. We want our team to practice better than anyone else in the country.

If you believe in what you are doing, you do not have to change a lot of the things you are doing. The first thing a lot of coaches do when things start getting tough is to change everything. Our philosophy is to find a philosophy, and we stick with the system. We want to change the behavior of the players to fit the system. When the behavior changes, we become a better football team. The players will have a lot more respect for who you are, what you expect, and what you are trying to accomplish.

Our big thing with our staff is attention to detail. We have had the same staff together for three years. When we get back to start working on next year, we stress attention to detail in everything we do. We must coach better, teach better, and we must be more demanding. We must look at the details of things. It is the small things in a football game that is going to make a difference in winning or losing.

I tell my staff they must be role models. The players will watch everything a coach does. They know how you work and how you teach. By doing this, it will help the players become better people, or it is going to go the other way.

Today coaches have tremendous influence on players. In fact, coaches have more influence on kids now than ever before. As we all know, it is not cool to be the person that stands up to do what is right all of the time in the society we live in today. I suggest you use this opportunity to help young players to be better players, better students, and better people. Better people and better citizens make better decisions. My hat is off to you. You can have a huge influence on young people in what you do. Do not forget this. Don't say, "I do not want to be a role model." That is your job. They will remember the position coach and the head coach the rest of their lives. They will remember everything about you. If the things you do are not very good,, or if the things are what a good father would do, then you will have a big effect on that individual. Coaches have a big impact on players. Make sure you use this in a positive way. This is important to me and the other coaches in our program. Thank you very much.

THE INDOOR PROGRAM WITH MATS

University of Georgia

Men, it is good to be with you today. I want to start with a few things that will let you know where I am coming from. The main reason they hired me at the University of Georgia is because they thought the Florida State offense was going to come with me. It has not been that way because we are winning a lot of games with defense. I appreciate having the chance to speak to you gentlemen.

I want to talk about our mat drill program. In the mat drill program, we have agility drills, quickness drills, and running and conditioning drills. It is something that is crucial to our program. It is almost the exact replica of what was going on at Florida State for the years I was there.

When I get back tonight we will have our first workout in the off-season program. I guess when you think about life as a college coach at Georgia, it is a year-round job. We finished the bowl game the first of January, had to finish our recruiting by the first of February, and now we are getting ready to start our off-season program. Next month, we have to get ready to start spring practice.

Our strength and conditioning coach has spent the month of January and part of February getting our team prepared to survive these drills. You cannot start this program without some kind of conditioning to get ready for it.

Normally we would do this drill at 5:45 A.M., but we changed this year for the very first time to 8:00 P.M. The reason we are going at night is because we changed our study hall to 6:45 in the morning. We have a new seven-million dollar academic building. The problem is all the athletes at Georgia use this building at night. There are too many distractions in the study hall at night. In the mornings, we can keep everything quiet and orderly. By having a football player only study hall in the mornings, we have the whole building to ourselves. We know the players are up, dressed properly, and prepared for the day.

There are a number of reasons for having the mat drills. The first thing we want to do is establish control. It is important to establish who is in control at all levels. We have 130 players, counting walk-ons, and they have to know who is in control of our program. I have seen some programs where the players are in control. When that happens in a program, it is the beginning of the end. The program is set up so the players do what we say or they walk out of the room. If that player walks out the door, he is off the team.

This program teaches the players to respond to commands. This is where the players become used to responding to what the coach wants done. It is like the military, with the recruits going through boot camp. The recruits get used to taking commands, and that is what you want them to do.

To get through this program the players have to be mentally tough. You are going to find out in a hurry who is going to quit on you. We do not want anyone to quit, but football is not an easy game. Football is not for everyone. If it were, everyone would be out on the field playing. It takes a special person to play, and it takes mental and physical toughness. The attitude that is developed in this program will help the player when the game is on the line.

An aggressive program like this helps you find the leaders of the team. It takes leaders to bring the team along in a hard, exhausting program. Someone has to say, "Follow me."

It helps you find out who is with you and who is against you. It helps the coaches find out who believes in what the coaches are doing, and who is going to resist what is being taught. When I got to Georgia the first time, I got to work with the players on the mat program. We found our leaders in a hurry.

This is a source of discipline for the program. If a players needs discipline for missing class, study hall, or any other issue that needs to be dealt with, this is the arena that is used. We bring them in early, and they have a pre-mat program of about 20 minutes to go through before the regular mat drill starts. The mat drill lasts about an hour. Players have a tendency to do what they are supposed to during mat drill period. If there are issues to deal with in this new time frame, we will have a post-mat period for those problems.

The mat drill creates team unity. When I came to Georgia the administration wanted to know how I was going to build team unity. I told them we were going to work hard together. Everyone in the mat drill is treated the same. There is no first, second, third, or fourth team. We line our players up according to class and by linemen, big skilled, and skill positions. When guys work hard and they work hard together, that creates the unity you are looking for.

This program builds the overall football conditioning that it takes to play the game. In football, there is a burst of 6 to 7 seconds on each play where the player goes extremely hard. He goes back to the huddle for a short rest, and he does it again. That is the way the mat drill program is set up.

These drills require a player to get into a fundamental football position. I think that has been taught since the beginning of this sport. They learn how to get into a football position and stay in a football position.

This program improves the players' quickness and agility. There is no doubt that those things are accomplished in this program. When we go to our running station, those skills will help them to improve their forty times and overall sprinting form.

The last thing is called finish the drill. That has become a battle cry, so to speak, in our program. We used this term at Florida State and it started in the mat program. What is means is to finish the drill as hard and as fast as you started the drill. We start every mat drill with a "slam and go." We make a big dive onto the mat, pop to our feet, and do the drill. The last things the players do in the drill is a "slam and go" before they sprint off the mat. We want the finish of the drill as intense and as fast as the beginning.

The first year I was at Georgia, we played Tennessee in their home stadium. It looked like Georgia was going to win the game, but we gave up the ball. They threw a screen pass and scored with about 45 seconds to go in the game. It looked like they might win the game. We drove the ball down the field in the closing seconds and had a first-and-goal from their 6-yard line. We hit the fullback down the middle on the last play of the game to win the game.

The locker room scene was pandemonium. I was trying to think of something to say when a player said, "Coach, we finished the drill!" He was right. That was what all that pain and suffering in the mat drill had done. It taught us to fight for the full 60 minutes and finish as hard as you started. Georgia had not beaten Tennessee at home in more 20 years.

That is true in games, academics, and true in life. If we teach them not to quit, that is the best way to finish the drill.

Mat Drill 2004 will begin for us at 8:00 tonight. We start out with all our players on the wrestling mat in a seated position, with their legs crossed and their elbows on their knees. We will have them seated in rows and columns which are as straight as an arrow. That may sound a little overboard, but it is not to us. We want them to know from the beginning that we are serious about this program. They sit there at attention and no one says a word. When the whistle is blown, they pop into position, and not a sound is uttered. Everyone will be there on time, and no one will be late. That includes players or coaches. At that time, we make general announcements, and then I give the motivation speech. I think it is important for the players to know why we are going to go through these mat drills.

By 8:15, we start the drills. We divide our team into three groups. We have a linemen group, which is all offensive and defensive linemen. Our big skill group is what it says; they are bigger players like linebackers, fullbacks, and quarterbacks. The skilled players are wide receivers defensive backs and running backs. We spread the punters and kickers into the groups that we need to balance.

We have three periods that last about 20 minutes apiece. The first period is the Mat Drill. The coaches that run that drill are Coach Neil Callaway, the offensive line coach, Coach Rodney Garner, the defensive line coach, Coach Brian VanGorder, the linebacker coach, and Coach Dave Van Halanger, the strength and conditioning coach. Three of the four coaches are really tough. We have the offensive line, defensives line, and linebacker coaches that know how to get after people and are very demanding.

We have a coaching staff of nine or ten coaches, and each one of them has a different personality. Those personalities make a difference on each of these drills. You want the toughest, hard-nosed coaches handling the mat. That is the centerpiece of the whole program, and it has to be done properly.

The first drill we do in the mat drill is the 2-point wave drill. The drills we do are nothing new to football. Everyone has done the drill for years. What is important about these drill is we make them do the drill exactly as we say do it. We line our first group up across the end of the mat. Generally we have five players going at once. The second group has to be directly behind the front group. We have commands that instruct what that first group is going to do.

The first command is "Ready." On that command, the first line gets into a fundamental football position. They snap to it as quickly as they can. The second command is "Feet." On that command, the first line starts to buzz their feet as fast as they can. The third command is "Go." When they hear

that command, they dive out on the mat in a layout position and land on their chests. As soon as they hit the mat, they are up in a fundamental football position, pumping their feet. As soon as the command "Go" is given, the second line pops up on the mat in a ready position. If someone in that group does not do the ready position right, the first group comes back to the ready position and starts over. At that point, you have to have ten guys doing the drill right, or they start over.

In the two-point wave, the coach gives the players direction by hand signals. He moves them left, right, up, and back. The players are shuffling their feet but not crossing over. When the coach says, "Slam," the players drop on their chest, pop up, and sprint to the end of the mat. At the end of the mat is a second coach. The players get shoulder to shoulder and pump their feet in a fundamental football position. We want their heads up, backs flat, and knees bent. When the coach is ready, he claps his hands and they sprint off the mat.

All five of those players have to do the drill right, or they come back and repeat it. We have one coach doing the drill, one coach at the end of the mat, and one coach making sure they sprint off the mat. If any of the three coaches does not like what went on in the drill, he sends the players back to do it again. As the players come off the mat, if the coach sends them to right side of the mat, they are done; if he sends them left they must repeat the drill.

At the end of the day, we grade each player. We grade them A, B, C, D, and F. The highest grades move up to the front line. Everyone tries to get in the first line because the players in those groups generally do the drills correctly and will not have to repeat a drill.

The next drill is a two-point seat roll drill. The drill is done exactly like the first drill except instead of doing a two-point wave drill, they are doing a two-point seat roll.

The second group should be in the "Ready" position when the first group pops up on the mat. The only time the "Ready" call will be made is with the first group. The coach repeats the "feet" and "go" part of the drill. When the players get to their feet, they do a seat roll. They are not rolling on their back or doing wide rolls. They are doing tight, consistent seat rolls.

The next drill is a four-point wave drill. It is the same drill through the "Feet" and "Go" part. When the players pop off the mat, they are on all fours with their feet moving. The coach gives them directions, and they do the same thing as the other two drills.

The fourth drill in the mat drill is the four-point seat roll. Everything is repeated like the first three drills, except the players execute the seat from the four-point stance.

The problem players have is getting into the great fundamental football position. They want to get their base too wide. We want the feet up under the armpits with the knees in a good bent position, ready to strike again.

We have another drill, which we call front to back. I have been at Georgia three years, and we have not gotten to that drill yet. It takes a great group to do it correctly. After the layout, the players get to their feet. The coach calls "Down," and the players hit their chests, roll their feet to the right, hit the blades, and get up. We run out of time before we generally get to this part of the drill.

While the mat drill is going on, we have the other two groups working at their stations. When we reach the end of the period, we take a break for water. We want to keep our players working at a high rate, but we want to keep them safe. It is a short 2 to 3 minute break.

The next phase is the quickness phase. The coaches we have working in this drill are Coach Mike Bobo, the coach for quarterbacks, Coach Dave Johnson, the coach for tight ends, Coach Willie Martinez, the coach for defensive backs, and Coach Jon Fabris, the coach for defensive ends.

The first drill in the quickness phase is the shuffle drill. This is a side shuffle drill, with the player going from side to side and touching a taped X on the sideline. The group is a three man group in a vertical line, one behind one the other. They are aligned on three dots, which gives them spacing. The coach calls "Feet-Go." On the command "Feet," the group starts to buzz their feet. On the command "Go," the three move forward onto the shuffle board and prepares to do the drill. Also on the command "Go," the first group moves up, and the second group fills the spots on the three dots in a fundamental position.

In the shuffle drill, the coach gives the group a direction, and they shuffle to that sideline, bending sideways to touch the X, with their hand and their foot on the line (see Diagram #1). As soon as they touch, they shuffle back to the middle line and wait for the next direction. They continue going right or left to the sideline until the coach calls them out. At that point, they sprint out the end of the drill to the next coach at the end of the room. They keep their feet moving at all times and never cross their feet as they go from middle to sideline.

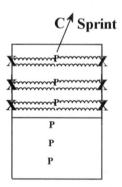

Diagram #1. Shuffle drill

The next drill is the shuttle run. It is similar the shuffle drill (see Diagram #2). The structure is the same as to the positioning of the players. The coach calls "Feet," which starts the feet buzzing. The "Go" call brings the group forward, pumping their feet. The coach will give them a direction. They turn, run to the sideline in that direction, and touch the X on that line. When they touch the line and change direction, going the other way, they cannot turn their back to the coach. They must be facing him at all times. As quickly as they can, they run to the other sideline, touching the X on that line, and return to the middle, facing the coach, and start buzzing their feet. On his command, they sprint out of the drill to the coach at the end of the room.

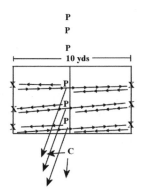

Diagram #2. Shuttle drill

The next drill is called the pens drill. It is a chute that forces the players get down lower than a regular stance (see Diagram #3). It is 12 to 15 feet long, 3.5 feet high, and 5 feet wide. The players start off at one end and come down the chute using super-accelerated footwork. They are lifting the feet only a few inches off the ground. We do this drill in three phases. The first time the players come down the chute straight. Once they reach the end of the chute, they sprint forward out of the chute past a cone set, which is five yards past the chute. The second time they come down the chute, we put flat bags in the chute and make them weave through the bags (see Diagram #4). The third time they come down the chute, they turn parallel to the sides of the chute and step over the bags. Each time they come out of the chute, they sprint past the cone.

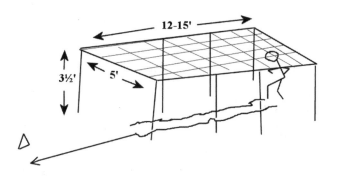

Diagram #3. Pens

The third station we use in our quickness phase is the running ropes drill. We only use two commands in this section. The first man gets a "Ready"

call that puts him in the fundamental position. The second command is "Go," which starts the player in the rope drill. When we say, "Go," the first step taken by the player should be in the first hole of the ropes. If he takes a false step he has to start over. On the command "Go," the second man gets in his ready position.

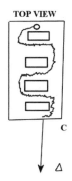

Diagram #4. Pens weave

The first rope drill is to hit every hole in the ropes. Once they come to the end of the ropes, they have to sprint out of the ropes past the cone.

The second drill is to hit every other hole in the rope. When the player enters the ropes, he hits the first hole with his first foot and ever other hole thereafter. If they start low, make the players stay low. The first thing most of them want to do is stand up when they start the drill. Each time they come out of the ropes, they should drop their pads and sprint out past the cones.

In the next drill, they turn sideways in the ropes. On the command "Go," they step in the rope with their first step. The second step is in the same hole. They go all the way down one side of the ropes, hitting every hole. Do not let them turn the shoulder until they are out of the ropes. When they take their last step in the ropes, they turn their shoulder and burst past the cone.

The crossover step, hitting ever other hole, is the last drill in the running rope drill. It is hard to keep the pads down and get the knees up to run this drill. We do not ask our linemen to do this one for obvious reasons. We do not want them to get a twisted ankle doing this drill.

The last phase of our program is the sprinting station. Coach John Eason, wide receiver, and Coach Ken Rucker, running backs, handle this part of the program. We do this part of the program on the basketball court. We start under one basket. The commands are "Ready," "Feet," and "Go." The first run is a high knee bounding movement. It is a high knee lift with an exaggerated spring off the opposite foot and exaggerated arm movement.

The second drill is done with a 10=foot piece of rope. The two coaches stretch the rope across the first group. The commands are given and the players begin rapid foot and knee lifts. They start to move forward slowly, staying behind the rope but keeping the knees and feet moving quickly. When the coaches raise the rope they accelerate to mid-court and stride to the end of the court.

The last drill is simply a stance and start drill. Using a good stance, the players explode out of their stance, run full speed to half court, and coast to the end of the court.

When we finish our workout it will be around 9:15 P.M. We call the players and they get back on the mat the way they started the evening. The coaches of each phase of the workout come to the mat and call out the players who were outstanding in their drill. If any player is mentioned in two drills, they are finished for the evening. They are recognized as the best that evening. Everyone else has to do what we call the flip drill.

The flip drill is a series of movements that each player must do on the whistle. These things must be done by the group together. When the first whistle blows, everyone claps. On the next whistle everyone gets in a fundamental football position. On the next whistle, they go to a four-point position. On the next whistle, they get into a push-up position. On the next whistle, the players go to their bellies. On the next whistle, they flip to their backs. They all have to flip right or left depending on what

they were told. Once they get to the back, each whistle works back to the clap. They flip back to the belly, push-ups, four points, football position, and finally, clap.

If someone messes up, we do the drill over. However, if a player gets called out, he is out of the flip drill. It is not easy to do this drill, as it is the last drill, when everyone is tired.

After the drill we grade every player at every station. We have a sheet with everyone's name on the list, with the date going across the chart. We call the players' names and the coaches give their grades. We take an average for all the drills, and that is the grade for the player. We have their names on a magnetic board. When we get their grades, we put them in the group according to the grades they have. Those who get A's are on the first row in their workout group. We line each player up according to the grade he gets.

Anyone who grades out an A or A- is recognized before the next workout with a black T-shirt with "Big Dog" on the shirt. Everyone else will be in gray T-shirts. It is a pride thing, and players get to keep the shirt. If a player grades all A's, he gets to take the day off. After that, we go over comments and suggestions for each group to help them improve their grades.

If you are planning on doing something like this, please do not forget safety. Make sure you give them water breaks. Basically, you should use common sense when doing a program like this.

Players that do the drill perfectly but have to repeat the drill because someone in his group did it wrong have to be watched. A lot of front runners that fold up when adversity hits. Even though it was not his fault, if he does the drill again and again perfectly, he is the guy you want to lead your team. If a player's performance is affected because someone else is causing him to work, he needs to improve his mental toughness.

PLAYS FOR SPECIAL SITUATIONS

Oregon State University

It is nice to be back in the area. It has been 1986 since I have been here. I really enjoy the business of coaching. I appreciate what you guys do for all the kids that are playing this great sport. I enjoy being around high school coaches.

I have coached in small colleges and in the Canadian Football League. I worked in the predecessor of the World Football League in Europe, and with the San Antonio Riders of the WLAF, which lasted for two years. I coached in the PAC-10 at Southern California for a while, and then went to Oregon State. From there I went to the San Diego Charges for four years and back to Oregon State.

Oregon State is in Corvallis, and that is my hometown. It is a good situation, and I am very fortunate to be there. I coached at a small college in Oregon, Winfield College. It still has the record for the longest consecutive winning season in college football today. For 48 years, Winfield College has had a winning record.

The things that go into being on a football team are invaluable in a young man's life. There are so many guys who get a chance to play high school, college, and pro football, and what that means to them down the road is invaluable. We all battle the same issues. We all have to make sure our players are going to school and doing the right things. There are a million things out there now for kids to get involved with. There is no better leader for young people today than the high school football coach. I appreciate you guys and understand what you are going through.

I am going to talk about why we have a particular play in our offense. We as coaches compile a huge notebook of plays. After we work hard on getting all our ideas together and come up with the finished product, it always occurs to us that we need one more play.

Football is a game of situations. That affects directly what plays you call in a football game. Your play calling comes from the repertoire of plays that you have in your playbook. It all relates back to a game of situations.

When I worked for John Robinson at Southern California, he was the best advocate for kids that I have ever been around. He always described himself as an idea man. Someone else would have to take care of the details, but John had the ideas. He talked more about how to practice than anyone else I have ever been. The situation that we called first-and-ten, he refereed to as normal.

There are all kinds of situation within a football game. There are red zone situations, and within those situations are additional phases. We divide the red zone into about five different areas. I thought at one time we should make our notebook a notebook of situations and slide our plays into each section.

At Oregon State last year, we went back to scratch. I had been here before, but it had been several years ago. I liked the idea of the whole staff putting things together. When we talked about a play, we slid it into a situation. We ended up with a master sheet of plays and made that into our notebook. That master sheet carried us through the entire year.

What you put into that master sheet is going to be who you are and what you are good at doing. Trying to put a new pass pattern in during the sixth week of the season is almost useless. To get the reps done and have it game-ready will take three weeks. What you practice in the spring, fall, and off-season is what your identity is going to be.

The hardest thing in coaching is being selective as to what you teach. It takes time to decide what you want your players to do. When we sat down to talk about our running game, we thought we wanted to teach the zone play. We added some other elements to make us versatile. We run a little power pitch play, and a draw play. We do not have a two back offense but we can use our H back and run the lead scheme. That was going to be our run offense.

From there, we put in the run-action and play-action passes to fit those runs. We called run-action passes the ones that looked like runs. If the protection looked like pass-action but the backfield action looked like run, we called that play-action.

The dropback passing game was divided into a lot of different sections. All those things fit into the game. The players have to make them come alive and know them like the backs of their hands. This talk is going to be about why we have those particular plays within our notebook.

We had a good year at Oregon State and ended up 8-5. If we had controlled the turnover ratio, we would have been better. We were productive and led the PAC-10 in total offense. We were first in red zone play, second in third down efficiency, and first in passing offense. We were a productive offense, but we have to cut down on turnovers and improve in the kicking game.

We are going to build a pattern around a route. We will talk about why we put in a route and how we teach it. After that, we will talk about pass patterns that have the same concepts. The quarterback does not have to learn anything new, and the receivers will have to make minor adjustments. The base pattern will have complementary routes to it.

We will talk about protecting pass patterns within a few formations. Defenses have to defend personnel and the field; however, the number-one thing they have to do is line up against those formations. When the offense lines up in a formation, they have to be balanced.

We package our pass patterns by formations. We will show you a running play, drop-back pass, play-action pass, and a run-action pass, all from the same formation. Our offense is not rocket science.

We package pass patterns by field position. We have pass patterns for what we call the alumni zone. Those are the deep patterns you throw after you cross the 50-yard line to please the fans.

We practice our red zone plays every day. We start at the 40-yard line, which is the alumni zone, with a series of about six plays. We move into to the high red zone, which is from the 30- to the 15-yard line, and throw two passes in that area. We move into the 15- to the 5-yard line area and throw two passes in that area. Finally we get to the goal line and run two plays from the five-yard line. We let one group take the ball down the field, moving into each zone situation.

We package by down-and-distance plays that we want to run. In a third-and-eight or third-and-fifteen, you have to have a play to call in those situations.

When I was at Southern California, I ran this pattern. It is the pattern we build our routes around. Nothing is amazing about the route; what's more important is the purpose behind the pattern. We talk about the intent of the route. On every pass pattern, our quarterback will tell you what the intent of the pattern is. The pattern I have been talking about is what we call the trailer route. It is run from a trips set (see Diagram #1). The flanker or Z back runs a 12-yard trailer route. That is a hook-looking pattern, which we call a hinge. The pattern when thrown is delivered back into the sideline. The slot or R back runs a dig route at 14 yards over the middle. The tight end or Y receiver runs a drag to the opposite hook. The one back runs a check down pattern at three yards over the tight end's position. The split end or X end runs a 12-yard comeback out route.

On this route, the intent is the X-end pattern. We have always put our best receiver at the X-end position. At Southern California, Keyshawn

Johnson was our X-end. We started the pattern wanting to throw the out to Keyshawn. From there, we had to build complementary routes around that one route.

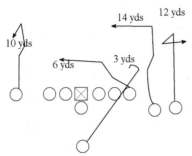

Diagram #1. Trailer route

Whenever you run a pass pattern, the number one thing is protection. In this protection, we are going to slide away from the tight end (see Diagram #2). The center, left guard, and left tackle are blocking back. The right guard and tackle are blocking man-on-man, and the running back is double-reading both frontside linebackers. If both linebackers come on a blitz, we read hot to the tight end.

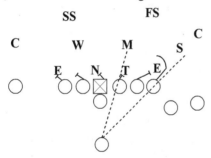

Diagram #2. Slide protection

When we built this pattern at Southern Cal, we had some things in mind for the dig route of the R back. We felt like that route was going to be a factor on certain coverages. We have experimented with the pattern. Our coaching staff is not a big proponent on conversion routes. We do not run patterns off the reaction of defenders. We run the routes that are in the pattern as fast and as precise as we can, but we do not run another pattern because a defender did something.

We do not like to throw the ball into the wide field on a sideline cut. Too many things can go wrong in running the pattern. The ball can be late, the defensive back can get a good jump, or the pass may not be run at the right distance. You are going to be good at what you invest your time in.

When we drill the pattern, we start out with the receivers standing at the end of their routes. We call it a spot drill (see Diagram #3). The receivers are two steps from the completion of their patterns. The quarterback drops back and throws the out cut to the X-end. The coach is watching his drop and footwork and making sure he throws the ball on time. The only reason the quarterback holds the ball is man-to-man coverage on a receiver. That takes a little bit different timing.

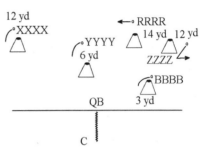

Diagram #3. Spot drill

On the next throw, we give the quarterback a different coverage. We tell him the corner has rolled up on the out route of the X-end. He goes to his next read in the progression, which is the hinge route of the Z back. The progression goes to the dig route over the top to the R back. After that, he goes to the back check down over the tight end position. Finally, he throws to the tight end on the hot read.

In each situation, the quarterback has to use the footwork to change from one receiver to another. After he goes through his progression, we interject a new set of coverages for him to think about. If the coverage is man-to-man, we feel we should win on the out route. That is what we teach the quarterback. Sometimes we do not win on the out and the quarterback has to go on with his progression of reads.

The quarterback has to make that decision. He is the decision maker. That trait is the top priority in a quarterback. In succession, he goes back and throws the ball to each receiver. In each throw he drops, goes through his reads, sets his feet, and delivers the ball. That is what he does in the spot drill.

As the quarterback drops, we call out the coverages. When he hears the coverage, he goes to his second progression, which is the dig route. When all is said and done, the intent of the pass is to throw the out pattern. If it is open, we are throwing the ball to the out. This pattern is all about timing.

There are so many factors that fit into a completed pass. The first thing is the proper split of the receiver. The second thing is the drop of the quarterback. The depth of the patter must be correct for the timing to be there. The steps of the quarterback as he gathers and prepares to throw are a big factor. Probably the most important factor in the throw is the coverage.

The quarterback knows that if the first receiver is not open, he has a progression to go through. He can always get back to the check down route to the back.

The next part of the drill is to bring the receiver back to the line of scrimmage and run the route against air. The quarterback and receiver are working on the timing of the route. There is no defender and no rush. The quarterback and receiver are playing catch. The receivers is running a 12-yard pattern and coming back out.

I always keep tabs on how we are doing as far as our completions. That is telling in deciding which passes to throw. If you cannot complete a high percentage against air, you should not expect to complete them in a game, when there is rush and coverage. The way a quarterback gets better is repetition. We work daily on these throws.

The thing we like about the trailer route is it is good in a number of situations. It is a good third down and first down pass. The trailer route is thrown out of the three-by-one formation, which we call trio. We like to have a balance in the throws to the receivers in the trio set. However, we make no bones about the X-receiver being our primary receiver. If he is open, he gets the ball. Our X-receiver this year caught 78 passes.

All the other receivers in the trio formation are on the other side. The defense has to make a deci-

sion on how they want to play the X-receiver. They know we are going there first with the pass. If the defense does not double cover him, the ball is going there on the out cut. If the defense double covers the X receiver, they have less coverage on the 3 receiver side.

Designs of the routes in the trips set have to be such that it takes advantage of a coverage that is committed to stopping the X receiver. The simplicity of the pattern is to put one guy to one side and see how the defense is going to cover him.

We cannot work with our players at this time of year other than strength and conditioning. We cannot go out with them with a ball and do anything. They can do it on their own, and we can legally film what they are doing. I watched them throwing the other day, and they were throwing the companion route to the trailer route. I will show that to you in the film later. The route is called a follow. It is the one route that protects the trailer route.

The change-up in the pattern is the receivers, not the route. The R back runs the dig route in the trailer scheme (see Diagram #4). Instead of running the dig he runs the crossing route underneath and the tight end runs the dig route.

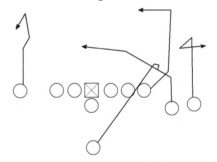

Diagram #4. Follow

After we have thrown the pattern in the spot drill and on air, we take the next step and put defenders in the drill. It is not a coverage scheme, it is one-on-one coverage. In that type of coverage, we win those match-ups. We play a lot of press coverage as part of our defensive scheme, so our receivers work against our defensive backs. They get excellent work against good people.

Any time the receivers run the out against press

coverage, it is important that they get a good push upfield. They get their shoulders upfield and break the route downhill back to the sideline. The quarterback delivers the ball in a place where the receiver can catch the ball and get away from the defender. The out cut should be thrown low and outside to the sideline.

After we work the patterns against single-man coverage, we put the pattern into the coverage scheme. We work against the secondary shell.

Seven years ago, the first time I was at Oregon State, I was totally embarrassed by our lack of efficiency in calling the game, managing the time clock, and signaling plays into the game. We went back and tried to condense everything we did as far as the terminology we used in play calling. It took us forever to get the plays signaled into the game. The next year we started out with a four-word rule in play calling. Our play call for this play was "Explode-trips-left-blue-trailer." Explode is the shift, trips-left is the formation, blue is the protection, and trailer is the play. If we wanted protection the other way, we'd call red. We use Atlantic and Pacific, or Jersey and Cal protection. Jersey is in the east, and California is in the west. The Atlantic is on the East Coast, and the Pacific is on the West Coast. Those are protections that relate to east and west. On a map east is to the right side of the map, and west is to the left side of the map. All the terms we use for protection relate to right and left. Blue is left, and red is right in our protection scheme. If we want to slide the protection left we call blue, Pacific, California, or west.

All that vocabulary works into the two-minute drill or maybe a no-huddle scheme. For a right call in the protection, we call red, Atlantic, Jersey, or east. We made our whole offense two-minute ready.

The secondary skeleton drill is the next progression to teaching the trailer route (see Diagram #5). When the quarterback comes to the line of scrimmage, the first thing he does in his pre-snap routine is look at the X-receivers. He looks at the safety next and gets a presnap read. He deduces the

safety is not going to help the corner on his coverage. When he snaps the ball, he confirms his observation and sees the X-end is 1-on-1. That is the intent of the play, and that is where the ball is delivered.

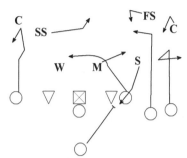

Diagram #5. Skeleton pass drill

You can see on the film how the rest of the route took place. The tight end was open and looking for the ball. The dig route was covered well, and the back did not get out because the defense blitzed a linebacker. The defense should not be blitzing during this drill. That does not help our offense practice.

This next part of the progression came from John Robinson. It is a half line skeleton drill (Diagram 6). We have the center, right guard, and right tackle, along with the quarterback and receivers. We run the trailer route again, except now we see pass rushers in the drill. We put the 1-on-1 blocker on pass rushers. The quarterback has to read the secondary and throw the ball against the rush. That adds one more ingredient into the development of the quarterback.

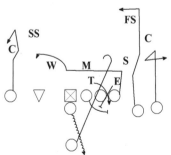

Diagram #6. Half line skeleton

The next progression in our drill work is to put the route into our team drill. We are going 11-on-11 and getting the full picture of throwing in gamelike conditions. The quarterback gets the full look at the pass with all the distractions. If we look at the pattern to the trips side, the defense has outnumbered the receivers five to three. You can see the intent of the secondary was to stop the route inside the hash marks.

The next play, the quarterback reads a two safety look (see Diagram #7). He suspects the safety is going to help the corner. When he snaps the ball, he sees the corner sit on the out. He turns back to the frontside and throws the dig route between the two high safeties, which is open.

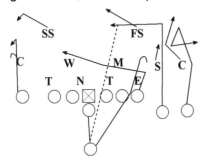

Diagram #7. Trailer vs 2 deep

The next play, the quarterback reads the blitz and gets the ball to the tight end on the hot route. It is not a big play, but it is not a negative play or a sack. The quarterback wants to get rid of the ball. That is the timing we have been working on in the other drills.

Our quarterback got better as the year went on. His best games were the last two he played. He is returning next year and should have a good year.

We like the out route, but we want to change up the pattern. We do not want to have the same thing every time. We want to keep concepts in place for the quarterback. The patterns end up in the same place, with different people running them. In the follow route, the R back and tight end will exchange patterns. The tight end comes out to run the dig route, and the R back cuts underneath the tight end's pattern on the way to the other side of the formation.

We use the bunch formation to run some of our favorite patterns. We run a lot of the rub patterns that everyone runs from that formation. When the defense sees the bunch formation, they have special coverages to handle that formation. If they are ganging up on the bunch set, that means the out pattern is probably being ignored.

Another adjustment we can use with this pattern is the screen. The trailer screen has become a good play for us (see Diagram #8). We run everything the same. The back starts his check down like he always does. He sets up behind the line, and we throw the screen pass. The quarterback has to sell the downfield pass before he delivers the screen pass. To run a screen, everyone has to be a good actor and not get in a hurry to run the play. Screens are safe passes that can end up in big gains.

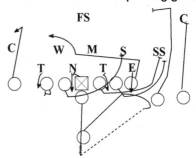

Diagram #8. Trailer screen

We can set the running back away from the formation and slide the protection the other way (see Diagram #9). The back checks the linebacker on that side, slips out, and runs a crossing pattern to get to his check down position. That puts him crossing under the tight end, which gives a different look. The receivers still ends up in the same place.

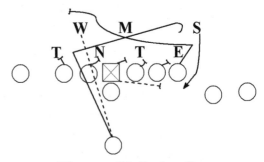

Diagram #9. Red trailer

We do other patterns for the X-receiver besides the out pattern. This pattern, at the beginning, looks like the trailer route, except we call this one blade (see Diagram #10). The tight end is coming across like he has always done. The Z back is running the hinge route, and the back is still doing his check down. The R —back, instead of running a dig, runs his pattern up the seam. The X receiver comes down to his 12-yard break point. Instead of running the out, he runs into the middle of the field between the linebackers.

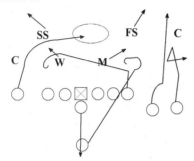

Diagram #10. Blue blade

That is a complement route to the trailer route. The blade route is not a dig route. It is more of a bend route into the middle. The intent of the pattern is the blade route, but the eyes of the quarterback go to the seam route first. He is looking to the seam first, and if it is open, he throws the ball there. The blade pattern is taking shape while the quarterback is looking at the seam. Looking at the seam serves two purposes. The quarterback, besides looking to see if the seam route is open, is faking with his eyes. Defensive backs are coached to read the quarterback's eyes. Again, the intent is to come back to the blade, but the quarterback does not look back until he is ready to throw.

Eyes are huge in route running. If you have a hook in our scheme, you need a hook-and-go. We have the out-and-up as part of our package.

When we think about passing, we think about situations. Taking shots at big plays takes more time and requires more protection. When you try to stretch people downfield, it affects your protection. The longer the quarterback holds the ball, the more solid the protection has to be.

We want to match the protection to the patterns we throw. On the stud route, everyone is releasing and the ball is coming out fast (see Diagram #11). We align in a double formation, with a twin look to the left and a tight end and flanker to the right. The Z back runs the top off the pattern. He is clearing to open up space for the back and tight

end. The back is shooting into the flat. The tight end is running a kind of trail out pattern. The twin set on the backside is running a double slant.

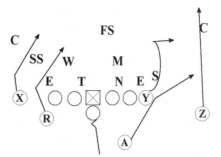

Diagram #11. Stud

The intent of the pattern is to hit the back in the flat. However, on the play in the film, the corner jumps the back quick. The tight end comes wide open. The beauty of this pattern is the double slant to the backside. If the defense decides to blitz and voids the middle, the slant by the slot could break for a touchdown. Everyone can get the ball on this play, but the intent of the play is to hit the back in the flat.

The quarterback has to have enough repetition in the plays to know where to go with the ball. If the intent is covered, he has to know where to go to find an open receiver. He does that by throwing the pattern over and over.

If the back has a flat route, he has an angle route (see Diagram #12). This is a simple pass, but there is no back protection. The quarterback has to get the ball out of his hands in a hurry. We should not get in sacks if we can block the A and B gaps. Anything coming off the outside should be handled by the quarterback throwing the ball. The tight end is running his pattern to look like the out. When he gets to the break point, he fakes the out and takes his pattern down the seam. The back takes off to the flat. On his third step, he plants and angles back to the inside.

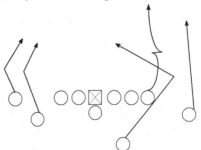

Diagram #12. Angle

The more people that can catch the ball in your passing game, the better off you are. Our back caught 500 yards of passing yardage. The tight end caught 49 balls. We also had two 1000-yard receivers.

One of our 1000-yard receivers was a high school walk-on from a local school in Portland. He was in the program for a couple of years. At my first spring practice last year, I could not have picked him out. I did not know who he was. He came to the fall camp, and we put him in the number two slot behind the X receiver. Needless to say, he made a bunch of plays. We gave him a scholarship and moved him to the other side to give him a chance to play. To make a long story short, he averaged 23 yards a catch.

The longer the ball has to be thrown, the longer the quarterback has to hold it. That increases your chance of sacks. The longer the ball is in the air, the chance for incompletions increases.

This next pattern is the stick pattern. It is run like the stud, but with different people running the pattern (see Diagram #13). We are running the Z back in motion back inside. He is running the out pattern. The tight end is running the flat route. These patterns are high-percentage throws and require little protection.

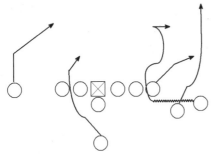

Diagram #13. Stick

This next section is all about balance. We stack our receiver on the outside. The first thing we do is run two corners (see Diagram #14). We run a deep corner, and we run a short corner. If the defenders lay off the short corner, we throw it. If they jump the short corner, we have a chance to throw the

deep corner. The short corner is a speed corner. He runs it off his fourth inside step. When we run this pattern, we protect it. We leave the tight end and back in to protect. We have seven-man protection. The protections we run put the tight end in one direction, and the running back the other.

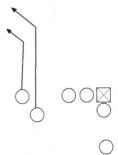

Diagram #14. Stack double corner

The pass is a seven-step drop and takes time to throw. We do not want to be in too wide a split when we run the double corner. When we get in the stack formation, the defenders start to play the double corner moves. To counter that move, we run the double post route (see Diagram #15). When they begin to come off the line, they can twist their releases. When defenders try to play the patterns with an inside outside bracket, it does not work too well.

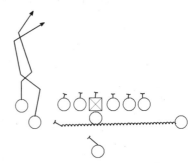

Diagram #15. Stack double post

When we first started to run the stack, the first pattern we ran was the post and corner with the receivers crossing their patterns. From there, we developed into the other combinations.

I really appreciate your attention, and it has been my pleasure to be here. I am glad to be in Colorado today.

WINNING CONCEPTS AND FIRE ZONE BLITZ

Louisiana State University

It is nice to be here. Some of you may not know that I grew up just down the road from Pittsburgh, in West Virginia, at Monongah, which is close to Fairmont, which is close to Morgantown. The big thing for me when I was a kid was to go to see the Pittsburgh Pirates play baseball in old Forbes Field. My fondest memories of Three Rivers Stadium go back to the time when I was the defensive coordinator of the Cleveland Browns of the NFL. In 1994, we lost five games, and three of those games were to the Steelers. Two of those loses were in Three Rivers Stadium. I was glad to see that place come down.

A lot of the values and ideas I am going to talk to you about came from people in this area. This has been a good coaching area. Also, I will talk about our fire zone coverage and the different zone concepts we use. If I get time, I will go over some of our eight-man front schemes.

From my standpoint, I still consider myself a position coach. I still coach the secondary and help with the game plan on defense. Also, I work with special teams. I like to speak at clinics, I like to talk to coaches, and I like to help people in our profession.

Two years ago, we had what many people considered the number-one recruiting class in the country. This year, several people rated our group of recruits the second-best class. USC had the best group of recruits, according to the experts. Some of you may want to know our secret. We have never done anything that would draw a lot of attention to the incoming prospects. We have been fortunate in getting good football players at LSU.

I have had a wonderful experience this past football season. I am sure some of you here have had similar experiences in coaching. Regardless of the level you coach, if you won a championship, it is a special accomplishment. One of the topics I like to talk about is how to coach players in this day and age. This past year, we had a great group of athletes. On the team that beat Oklahoma in the National Championship Game were 45 players that made All-SEC Honor Roll, which means they had a 3.0 GPA or better.

I have coached at three places where we won the National Championship. I was an assistant at Ohio State in 1968 and at Michigan State in 1965. The championship team pictures were hung on the wall of the football offices. At LSU, the 1958 championship team picture was hung on the wall. There is one common dominator those teams had. If you study the pictures and get to know the people that are in those pictures, you will find that a tremendous number of the players in those pictures went on to success. Were they successful because they won the National Championship, or did they win the National Championship because of the kind of character and attitude they had to be successful? I think it was the latter point. This is the tough thing we have to deal with today in working with the players. We must make sure they have the right attitude today. It is different than it was twenty years ago. Today you can tell them to jump, and they do not ask how high you want them to jump. It is not like it used to be.

As a coach, I seem to do a better job of building character and good attitudes in players in terms of how to compete and how to be successful. I think it all starts with how you approach this subject. Most teams I have been associated with, the coach sets the team goals. In our case last year, not one of those goals had anything to do with winning a game.

Not one! Most of the time, team goals include being in the top twenty-five in the polls, being conference champs, and being national champs.

This year our team had five goals. The first goal was to be a Team. Together, everyone accomplishes more. They wanted to establish trust. They wanted to trust in each other. The second goal was to do something every day that had a positive effect on someone on the team. The third goal was to be responsible for your own self-determination. This simply meant, don't blame someone else. Individual responsibility leads to success as a team. The fourth goal was to outwork your opponent every-day. Work to dominate your opponent. The last goal was simply this: to be a Champion on and off the field. We have not had a player's rep for the last three years at LSU. Our players have been doing very well academically. Again, our players made these five goals. I do not think we had better players than some of our opponents. But the team chemistry, togetherness, character, the way they competed, and their resilience were all big in the accomplish-ments of our team. I could give you a lot of examples where we could have taken the easy way out and given up. They had tremendous resilience.

Nothing ever bothered them as competitors. A good competitor should never show his frustra-tions on the field. As coaches, what do we do when someone makes a mistake? The best time to teach someone is to correct them when they make a mis-take. Coaches show their frustrations in correcting the players, and so they think they should show their frustrations on the field. What they are doing is to let the opponents know they have them frus-trated. The opponents think "I have him now." How we approach players is really important in this respect.

Players today want immediate self-gratifica-tion. Not many players are willing to go through the process necessary to be good. Not many of them are used to working for what they want. I can assure you it is more important than ever to be a coach in today's society. For some of the young peo-ple, the only discipline they get is from the coach. The young players do not learn the lessons we teach them in football. Football is a team sport. Competition can bring out the best in the individual. Football is a team sports, and it is the best game there is.

There are two great baseball players from Michigan State, Kirk Gibson and Steve Garvey. They both will probably end up in the Hall of Fame. If you walked into a room and I were present with them, the first thing they would tell you was that they played football. They played baseball for over fif-teen years in the Major League, but they will tell you they played football before they talk about baseball. Coaches can teach special values in the game of football.

It is not natural to be a champion. Psychologic-ally, we are all put here to survive. We are all put here to be average. If we make an A on an exam, the tendency is to let up and not work as hard the next time. It is not natural to work hard. What we do in football is to try to get a lot of players to play together to win a championship. This is just not nat-ural. It is special when you can get it done.

Everyone has heard the expression "There is no 'I' in team." What I like to use with our players is this: "There is an 'I' in win! It stands for individual respon-sibility. Everyone has an individual responsibility."

Last year in the spring, all I heard about our team was that we had lost all of our leaders. "You have no leadership on your team." I started thinking about this and I realized that we had lost some great play-ers and great leaders. It was true; we did not have many established big-time players coming back this past year. I started working on this and asked myself, "Why do we need great leaders if we have individual responsibility?" If everyone on the team has individual responsibility on the team, why do we need great leaders? Why should anyone depend on someone else to do what they are supposed to do?" I took the opposite approach to the situation.

I asked myself, "Do we need sheep dogs because the sheep need to be led?" or did we have players that could accept individual responsibility to be as good as they could be? We had very few leaders on our team, but we had very few players that were not good leaders. They were all responsible for what they were supposed to do.

I like to talk about the three I's in individual responsibility.

Intelligence: Play smart. Be smart in what you do.

Intensity: Play hard!

Immediacy: Have a sense of urgency about what you do all of the time.

This is a very simple approach, but it worked out very well for our team this past year.

There is a saying that we like to stress to our players. "What you do speaks so loudly, I can't hear what you say." Nike has a slogan "Just do it!" That is a good slogan for football.

Coaches have a hard time with all of this, as well as the players. I have one coach that is hard on the players. He is nasty at times with them. I told him one day, "Coach, you could not play for your own team. The way you criticize the players you coach, and what you expect from them, you would have a hard time playing for yourself."

If you allow the players to get by with not doing things right, it is the coaches' fault. We often say, "If you are not coaching it, you are allowing it to happen." You either coach them and allow them to get by with loafing, or you are coaching them and not allowing them to loaf.

Commitment is a real important word in what we do. Having people take individual responsibility for what they do is a tremendous commitment. Knowing what you want to accomplish and having a commitment to that goal is one of the most important single items in being successful. You do not always get what you want in this world, but you almost always get what you deserve. You are going to get out of things what you put into it. As the saying goes, "You reap what you sow." Farmers used to say that all of the time. Everyone has to understand they have to make a commitment to a standard of excellence for the team to be successful.

I have one special story I tell my players to illustrate this commitment. Jaromir Jagr was a hockey player in the National Hockey League. He wore number 68 as his jersey number. He played on the Czechoslovakian Olympic hockey team in the 1984 Olympics Games. His team ended up in the finals playing the Russians for the gold medal. In 1968, the Russians had invaded Czechoslovakia. His grandfather and many other Czechs were killed in that encounter. That is why he wore the number 68. It is a constant reminder of that fateful year. His coach came into the locker room to get the team ready before the gold medal game and asked Jaromir if he was ready to play. To which Jaromir replied, "I've been ready to play this game all my life!" He said his commitment as a hockey player was to beat the Russians in the Olympics for all the people they killed, including his grandfather in 1968. That was Jaromir's commitment.

The moral of this story this year for our team was this, "What is your 68?" It was interesting to go around to our players and remind them everyone needs to have a "68"-type commitment to a standard of excellence. They have to be willing to put in the work, to invest time into it, and to be persistent. They must be able to learn from their mistakes, and they must be able to overcome adversity. In the game of football as in the game of life, you cannot have a great victory unless you have some adversity. You must have adversity to overcome because that is what makes it a great victory. Let me give you an example of what I am talking about.

In 1981, I was coaching at Ohio State. We had won seven and lost two and were getting ready to play a great Michigan team in the last game of the season. When you have lost two games at Ohio State, people are not very happy. Michigan had one of the best teams in history. They had five All-Americans on the team. We were a 17-point underdog during the week of the game. The Ohio State people were very disappointed in the season we had had and were not looking forward to going to Michigan to play that last game.

Our team practiced poorly all week. Our coaches did not have the right kind of enthusiasm for a big game. The bottom line was this. The coaches and players just did not think we could win the game at Michigan. We were all getting criticized by the media and the fans. We were more concerned with how the outcome of the game would affect us as individuals. Everyone felt we were going to Ann Arbor on Saturday to get our tails beat.

Woody Hayes had left Ohio State after the 1979 season. He did not come back to visit the team in 1980. But the day before we left for Michigan in 1981, he came back to talk with the team. It was the first time he had addressed the team since he left in 1979. Woody Hayes stood before the team, and this is what he told them:"There can be no great victory without adversity. When you have a big challenge such as this, it is a great opportunity for a great victory." He turned everything around, from the negative to the positive, to motivate the team. He made the game an opportunity. He mentioned all of the obstacles we were to face at Michigan, including that it would be cold, it would be snowing, and we would have to play with 106,000 people pulling against us. He related all of our obstacles for the Michigan game to the War in the Pacific in World War II. The victory in the Pacific was considered one of the greatest victories in the history of mankind. Why was that such a great victory for the US? It was because of Pearl Harbor. We had lost our Pacific fleet. Rebuilding the Pacific fleet and taking the fight to the Japanese made it one of the greatest victories of all time. It was the adversity experienced and overcome and the positive attitude of the American people that contributed to the victory.

The speech by Woody Hayes that day was the greatest speech I have every heard. I have never forgotten that speech and the effect it had on me and the Ohio State team. We all know we get criticized when we lose a game. But you cannot fear losing. You have to play the game because you have opportunities to determine the outcome of the contest. If you are prepared, you have a good chance to succeed. Sometimes it works out and sometimes it doesn't.

Believing in yourself and having confidence is all part of the commitment to knowing what you want to accomplish and knowing how important the goal is. We all have limitations. I have them. I never thought I would be the head coach of a National Championship team. In 1987, I was an assistant coach at Michigan State. The head coaching job came open at Kent State. I am a graduate of Kent State, so I applied for the head job. I did not get the job, and I was crushed. I thought I would never get a head job. But do you know what? As the saying goes, "Sometimes the deals you make are the ones you don't make." I feel if I had gotten that Kent State job in 1987, I would have never gotten the chance to be the head coach of a National Championship team at LSU. Things happen in funny ways. You never know how things are going to work out. Things will work out if you have the right attitude, do things the right way, and invest your time in the right way.

Your character is a combination of your thoughts, habits, and priorities on a day-to-day basis. This determines the choices you make. The choices you make determine what you are. It can make you lazy, or it can make you a hard worker. It can make you a good guy or a bad guy.

Discipline is doing what you are supposed to do when you are supposed to do something. This is all what we need as coaches. You must have commitments to something. Everyone has a commitment. It was like Harrison Ford in the movie, The Fugitive, when he was being chased by Tommy Lee Jones down the drainage pipe. When he got to the end of the pipe, he turned and told Tommy Lee Jones he didn't kill his wife. Tommy Lee Jones told him he didn't care. He was a marshal and was committed to catching him. He didn't care whether he was guilty or innocent. Having a commitment is the only way you can get people to work and invest their time to be successful.

If you are going to build a team, you must have three things. You must have a good product, you must know your competition, and you must get people that will play together and good coaches that will work together. Division within will kill any organization quicker than anything.

What is a good product? If I ask you for the mission statement for your team, could you tell me? I can tell you what our mission statement is. Everything we do revolves around our mission statement.

We are going to create an atmosphere and environment where players have a chance to be successful. It is people first in our program. Because they are in our program, they are going to be better people and they are going to have more success in their life because they are in our program. It is because of the leadership we provide and the character and attitude we try to build in them that they will have a more successful life.

The second thing we provide is an opportunity for them to get an education, and they are going to go to school. If they do not go to school, they are not going to play. Getting an education is the most important thing our players are going to do.

The third thing we provide is for the players the opportunity to become the best football players they can be. The important thing is that every player has an opportunity to play on a National Championship team.

The fourth point is for us to help them with their career once they leave us. We owe them that much. We are not doing our players any favors when we do not make them go to school and get that education. Not many players go to the NFL. And those that do go to the NFL only last a few years.

We tell all of our players this is the kind of player we want at LSU: "We are going to be a team that plays with intangibles all of the time. It takes no ability to give effort and to play with toughness. You must be responsible to know what you must do, and you must do your job." There is one point we stress for all of this to happen. It has nothing to do with the vertical jump. You must be in great condition to do these things.

We have a fourth-quarter program at LSU. We have a slogan that we stress. Commitment, effort, toughness, and discipline make Tiger pride! All of our players know this slogan and what it stands for. We are branding our product all of the time. Players believe in this. When we go into the fourth quarter, they believe in those things.

The goals the players set for themselves this year reflect the things we stress in our fourth quarter. This is really what we want. It is not the accomplishments. The goal is just a road map and an organizational tool. It helps keep you in the right direction. This is what we want on the team.

Knowing the competition is important. Most of you use a computer to break down the films today. I am probably the only guy in this room that cannot use a laptop and a computer. I had to bring my wife on this trip to learn how to work the laptop. I still have a lot of work to do to get it right. All of the young coaches on my staff have laptops. They cannot coach without laptops. Things have come a long way since I started coaching. We used to cut up the films after we got them back from being developed. It took a lot of time to do all of the cut-ups. Now it is done a lot faster and a lot more accurately. Everyone has a way to do the films.

People ask me how it feels to be the highest-paid college coach in the country. I tell them it is no different than it was when I was making eight thousand dollars a year. It is no different today than it was before. The thing I am stressing is this: you must know yourself as well. You must know your opponent, don't get me wrong. You can underestimate a team or you can overestimate a team. The fact is, when you prepare your team you must know your team. We do not know much about the other team. We stress our strengths and weaknesses. We have a slogan that we use to get the point across to them: "We create what we do!" Nothing the other team will do causes us to win or lose the game. It is all about what we do that really counts. We create what we do by how we execute and how we play together. It comes down to the effort and the intangibles and the toughness of the players. That is how it is.

Knowing yourself is important. Knowing your strengths and weaknesses is important. You must play to your strengths. There are so many coaches that have a system, and they coach the system. I was guilty of this for fifteen years in college and pro football. All players are different. You must coach each player in what they can do best. That is what the coaches do in pro football. I learned that in working with defensive backs in pro football.

You must look beyond just knowing your team. You must look at each player and his strengths and weaknesses. Who is our go-to guy? Everyone works on their weaknesses, but you must play to your strengths. Sometimes you must change what you do to achieve these things. You must feature your best players.

When I was in high school, I was the starting quarterback as a sophomore. We needed to win our last game to get to the state playoffs. It came down to the last play of the game. We had the ball down on the goal line and called time out. We had time for one play. I went to the sideline hoping the coach would call the play. Instead he asked me what I though would work. I told him I was not sure. He told me we had an All-American halfback and our tight end had started for three years. He told me, "I do not care which play you run as long as one of those two players get their hands on the ball on the last play." We ran a play-action pass play. I faked the sweep to the great running back and threw the ball to the tight end in the end zone, and we won the game. My coach told me I should have learned a good lesson from that game. He said, "In tight situations don't think of plays, think of players first."

In the team situation, it gets to be a different problem. How can you have a team when no one takes responsibility for what happens? You must respect all of the players on the team. Here is what we tell our players related to the team: "When you do something on of off the field, you do it for everyone on the team." If they respect everyone on the team, they will not want to hurt them. Everyone on the team has an individual responsibility to uphold his end of the deal.

When you win the National Championship, everyone wants to get in on the glory. Everyone wants credit for doing their part. They want eighty percent of the credit but they only want to do twenty percent of the work. It is tough to make sure everyone feels they are getting enough credit

for the success of the team. Every individual is responsible. That is why I say there is an "I" in win.

We say a player is an impact player if his play has an effect on the whole team. When you approach it that way, you are actually building the players up. You are building team chemistry when you do that.

Everyone talks about fire zones. I am going to talk about what we do, and you can determine the stunts you want to use. I did not invent this defensive concept. I learned this defense from someone else or got beat in it so much I changed to this, and it worked better. It was because of trial and error that we came into this defense. I will give you six or seven principles of fire zone blitzes.

First of all, no matter what the fire zone call is, we always have a corner, a middle of the field safety, and another corner. We are going to have a wall to flat player a hook to number three player, and a wall to flat player. That is how we present this to the players (see Diagram #1).

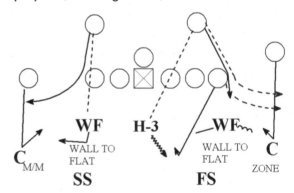

Diagram #1

We have a rule for two backs and one back in the offensive set. If the two receivers in the backfield are on opposite sides of the football, it is a pro set. If they are on the same side of the ball, it is a slot set. That is as complicated as it gets for me.

If the offense is in a pro formation and you are on the tight end flanker side, you are going to play zone as the corner. If he plays the zone in the corner, he is going to read the three step drop and read the number two receiver. If the receiver is in the seam, he is going to get depth and go to the divider. What is the seam of the field? On high school fields, it is the hash marks. If a receiver is going vertical on the hash marks, the corner has to play zone coverage on the number two receiver.

If the number two man is not on running the vertical seam, he must squeeze the number one receiver and play man-to-man on him because no one else is coming into his zone. That is a basic three-deep principle. The corner is playing zone.

If one receiver is on the side, the corner is going to play man-to-man. We play bump-and-run. We do not believe in allowing the receiver to run off the ball. Teams will say they do not want to play bump-and-run because they do not have good defensive backs. I have been teaching this coverage for thirty-three years. If you play back off the receivers, they will complete every pass unless the quarterback cannot throw the ball. If you play bump-and-run, you can deny at least half of the passes and make them throw the ball into a small area when they do throw the ball against the bump-and-run.

If we get two backs in the backfield with a slot on one side and a tight end on the other side, the corner on the tight side is playing zone coverage. If there is only one man to that side, the corner will play man-to-man. We still have our two wall to flat players underneath (see Diagram #2).

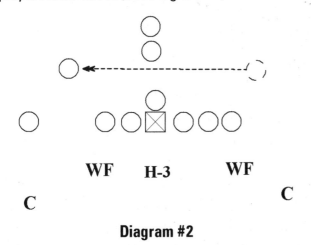

Diagram #2

When we get two back slot set, we make a safety call. A safety call puts the slot side backer outside, and we move the H man over to that side.

We actually play quarters on the slot side. I call this coverage box. Why do I call it a box? The W/F has the outside flat, the H-3 has the area toward the slot, the corner has deep outside, and the man in the middle of the field plays quarters. On the backside, the W/F plays short and the corner plays deep.

If the offense goes to a one back set, we apply our principles. We play zone on the two-man side and man-to-man on the one-man side. If we have a one back set and two open backs, we are going to make a man call. If only one man is playing in a flanker position, we are still playing zone on that side (see Diagram #3). We do have an exception to this rule. If we are in our nickel package, we can make a call and play zone on both sides if we have a defensive back in the W/F position. The reason we do not call the zone is because the W/F can be a defensive end or a lineman. It is a man call and a zone call.

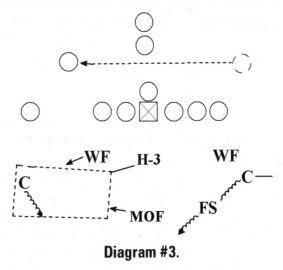

Diagram #3.

Any time we get a three man bunch route, we can bail ourselves out with a man or zone call by making a safety call. Bud Carson made it real simple. He said if the offense is spread out, you play them in man coverage (see Diagram #4). When the offense is bunched up, you are better off playing them in a zone look. The safety call means the W/F is going to get outside to take the flat, and the H-3 is going to slide over and take the inside short area. The corner is going to take outside deep. The free safety is going to move over to the formation and take inside and up.

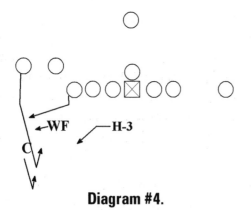

Diagram #4.

If we have a split end and two backs in the backfield, the backside corner can make a man call. We have X short and we think he is going to run across the field. We make a two call, the H-3 takes the man coming inside, and the W/F takes the man going outside to the flat. We make a simple call, with the W/F taking the outside man and the H-3 taking the inside man.

If we face a team that runs four wide receivers, we have a man call on both sides (see Diagram #5). The defensive W/F always thinks he has wall to flat unless he gets a call to change the defense. If we make a "buster" call, it means the W/F has the back man-to-man. We have man calls to both sides of the field.

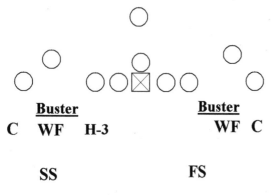

Diagram #5.

If we get any kind of trip formations, we play in-and-out on the number two and the number three receiver. The way we coach in-and-out is, the receivers must cross within the first five yards down the field for us to play in-and-out. If we are playing a man on the slot man, how does he know where to line up? He goes by the seam. If the receiver is outside the seam, he is going to line up inside

the receiver. He is at seven yards, and he is squeezing the man as he gets depth.

If the receiver is inside the seam, the W/F plays outside the man. He is going to squeeze him as he gets depth. The W/F plays the outside man, and the H-3 plays the inside man on the two and three receivers.

You must be able to count to five to play this coverage. That is because they have five players that can go out for a pass. If the receivers are spread out, we do not play in-and-out. We play man-to-man. If they are bunched, we play in-and-out.

We can set the defense up to attack the backside. If the offense is split backs, we can bring four men to the backside. The center blocks to the tight end side of the formation. We can bring the four men to the back side and get to the quarterback. This is what I tell our backs when we are blitzing.

They never make a play on the ball when we are blitzing. We never let the receiver run after catching the ball when we are blitzing. We never get the ball thrown over our heads when we are blitzing. If we can accomplish those three things, we will be the best blitz team in football (see Diagram #6).

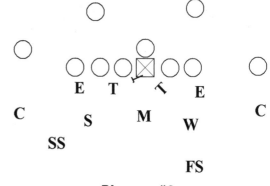

Diagram #6.

We have to put our blitzes into categories. If it is a bird cover, we cover the same way. The corners have the two wide receivers. The safeties have the tight end and the H-back. It does not matter how we are blitzing, that is our bird coverage. It can be hawk, eagle, or falcon. We have all of the calls for bird. You name the birds, and we have them. The coverage in the secondary is all the same.

If we get a snake blitz such as cobra or viper, it is a key blitz. We have eight defenders coming, and the offense can only block seven of them. You have a back to the field side. If the offense motions and goes to a one back set, we are checking the defense, and we go to another call. We check to plumber, miner, or workman. Those are workman terms, and that means we are in the same coverage as the bird coverage. If the offense goes to a one back set, the defensive back is not going to blitz now.

All fire zone blitz plays for us are places. For example we would call "South, Sarasota, Frisco, Seattle, and Split Neck, New Mexico." We can call Florida or California and it means the same to us. When a player hears this call, he knows it is fire zone coverage for him. Again, this is not for the players. It is for the coaches because they need the organization.

I have enjoyed the football part of the lecture, but my time is up. I want to wish the best of luck to all of you next year.

THE FIVE- AND SIX-MAN PASS PROTECTION PACKAGE

Tulane University

I really appreciate you being here this morning. When I got here last night, it was minus 7 degrees. I knew it was cold up here, but not this cold. Sitting in this room right now. it is colder than it was in New Orleans when I left yesterday. You can imagine what I felt like last night waiting for my ride from the airport.

It is good to be here this morning, and I am going to talk about our five and six man pass protections. When I first got to Tulane, I found a type of offensive linemen like I have never coached before. I had just come from the University of Georgia, and the five guys I coached there are in the NFL. I came into a situation at Tulane where we didn't have five guys who would be in backup positions at Georgia. I struggled with that for a little while.

I decided I was going to call every contact I knew and ask them what the most important aspect in college football was today. I talked to NFL guys all the way down to high school coaches. I talked to everyone in between those two groups that I possibly could. The common denominator in all that conversation was protection. That topic existed in every successful coach's agenda. That is where I have set my focus the past couple of years.

I am going to give some credit to myself, our University, and our program. I know you don't hear a lot about Tulane up here. Two years ago, we had a first-round draft choice at quarterback who signed with the Washington Redskins. This year we will have another first- or second-round pick, depending on how well he does at the combines. That is coming from a school which is not known for putting out NFL players. Tulane is known for putting out graduates in the professions.

As coaches, we spend too much time trying to find the magic play. We spend too much time trying to out-scheme and outsmart the opponent instead of working on the fundamentals of the game. My philosophy in the passing game goes back to protection. If you can protect the quarterback when you have to throw the ball, you are going to be successful.

When you listen to coaches talking about playing the Super Bowl, they all have one thing in common. They all talk about getting to the quarterback with the pass rush. I am not going to talk about mismatches today. I'm not going to talk about the defender coming off the edge that no one can block. I am going to talk about match-ups. I am going to tell you how to get five and six man protection done. It is very simple to do.

When we started to build our offensive line, we took our best player and put him at left tackle. We took the worst of our five offensive linemen and put him at center. From there, we filled in between the best and the worst with players of varying skills.

In our protection schemes, we are always trying to build the scheme so we will have a free player. I know most of you in here coach both offense and defense. You know the offensive line is the last stop before the bus stop. If you can't play in the offensive line, there is no place to play. The best players on the team are on the other side of the ball. As offensive coaches we are asking the worst athletes on the team to block the best athletes on the team. How smart are we as offensive coaches?

We are asking these guys to block the best players on the team and they can't do it. They couldn't block them in a phone booth. But we ask them to do it and then get mad at them when they can't. What we have to do is give them some help. What we try to do is free someone up to help in the mismatches on the line.

In our rules for the offensive line, we have two basic formulas. We tell our offensive linemen that the defensive front is either even or odd. People think there is more to the offensive line than that. Well, there is, but there really isn't. The defense can only put eleven players on the field. They can only line up in an even or odd front.

The first question people ask is, what about the shade defenses that are so predominant in college football today? They look even and odd at the same time. If our guards are covered, the defense is even. If the guards are uncovered, the defense is odd. The offensive linemen have a problem when one guard is covered and one is uncovered. Is that defense an even/odd defense?

The answer to that question is no. We split the offensive line and talk about even and odd to each side. When we apply the rules for five and six man protection, we are going to apply it to the right side of the line and the left side of the line. Two calls will be made for the offensive line. If the right guard is covered by a lineman or walked up linebacker, he calls even. The right guard and right tackle block even rules. If he calls even, we block even rules although the defensive line stems to another position. His call has nothing to do with the scheme that the left guard and tackle are working. If the defense is aligned in a 3 technique and 5 technique to the right side and a 5 technique and 9 technique to the left side, the right side will block even rules and the left side will block odd rules.

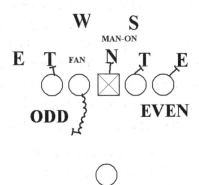

Diagram #1. Odd and even

I don't have time to coach my offensive linemen to block all the defenses there are in football today.

We can't teach them to block a 4-3 defense on first down, an under front on second down, and a 4-6 front on third down. They block rules, not defenses.

The center has his set of rules. He is the worst player, but he is the smartest player. He has some additional things to know in a protection scheme. The center's rules are the same in the five and six man protection. If it is an odd defense, he blocks the man that is covering him, which we call man on. If it is an even defense, he blocks to the call side. The call side is the formation call made in the huddle. The call side means he blocks the linebacker to that side. In the 4-3 defense, he is not covered, but has a linebacker aligned on him. His rule is man on.

The center's rule is not a constant rule. If the defense changes, so does his rule. If he has a nose-guard, he is blocking an odd rule. However, if the nose stems to the guard, his rule becomes even. His rule is not hard and fast because he is the only one affected by the rule. The hardest thing the center has to do is apply the rule to the direction call he heard in the huddle. If the call is right in the huddle, he has to apply that rule when the defense is jumping all over the place.

We play teams that move or stem their fronts. If the guard comes to the line of scrimmage, he has to make his call as to where the defender aligns. If the defensive tackle aligns in a 2 technique on him, he makes an even call. The offensive guard knows the snap count and has the advantage of knowing how much time he has before the ball is snapped. If the defensive tackle stems to a shade technique on the center, the guard knows whether he can change the call or not. If he can change his call to odd, he does. If he doesn't have enough time, he lives with the even call.

When you are watching a game and you see a defender come clean with no one attempting to block him, that is a communication problem. If we can't change the call, we live with it. That is not the way we want the play to come off, but at least we are not turning a defender loose unblocked. The scheme is still sound, but the angles are different and harder to execute.

When you have an experienced offensive line, you can handle the stems of the defense and not make too many mistakes in calls. This will be the third year we have had our offensive line together. We think this spring we will be able to handle stems and twists of the defensive line. It takes continuity of coaching to build a cohesive line. When defensive changes occur that quickly and we can still protect, we have come a long way. If we can protect the quarterback, the receiver will beat the defensive back. The stemming defense is one advantage the defense has on the offensive line. If we can hold up against that, we can protect.

Let's look at the odd front to start with. We have five offensive linemen and the quarterback aligned in the shotgun. There are seven defenders in the box. That means I have five receivers aligned somewhere in an offensive formation. The defense is going to have to cover them with some kind of scheme. This is how we begin to coach our quarterback. If we have five receivers, the defense is going to commit at least five defenders to cover them. If we have six-man protection, the defense has to have at least four defenders committed to coverage.

When we protect with five men, we want the quarterback in the shotgun set. We don't want him under the center. In the shotgun, the quarterback can get the ball off when he sees the defense blitzing more defenders than we can protect. Never put him under the center in a five man protection if you can prevent it. You can show your quarterback in practice that he has time to get off the throw with an unblocked blitzer coming off the edge. He may get hit, but he will not be sacked.

In the true odd front, where the center has a noseguard and both of the offensive guards are uncovered, the entire offensive line will be blocking odd rules. In our five-man protection, we want to block the five most dangerous defenders. That sounds good, but the five most dangerous defenders can change as quickly as I talked about them.

We want to figure out who the defense wants to get to the quarterback. We have to know who the cover defenders are in the defense and who the

rushers are. The defender who leads them in sacks is obviously a blitzer. We want to know all we can about their defense. With the ability of the linebackers to play half in the box and half out and the ability of the defensive outside linebacker to drop in coverage, it is hard to figure out who the five most dangerous defenders are.

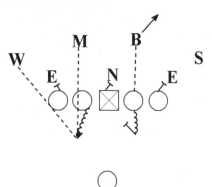

Diagram #2. Odd defense

If everything is balanced in the defense, we are going to start with our rules taking care of the quarterback's blind side. If you have a right-handed quarterback, it is the left side, and just the opposite for a left-handed quarterback. That being the case, we are going to declare the three down linemen, the Mike linebacker, and the Will linebacker as the five most dangerous defenders. We will double fan and protect the left side of the defense. The center blocks the noseguard, and the tackles block the defensive tackles. The left guard is double reading the Mike and Will linebackers. If the Mike linebacker drops and the Will linebacker runs a blitz, the left guard steps out on the Will linebacker.

The quick throw by the quarterback is tied into our five man protection. We run a series of quick patterns with a designated hot receiver as part of our protection. The quarterback has someone that he can get the ball to. The defense can always bring one more defender than the offense can block. We can block ten, but the defense can bring eleven. The designated wide receiver must have a quick read and quick route. The quarterback has to know who that receiver is and how to find him.

The next question we have to answer is, how are we going to help the center in five man protection? He is the worst lineman, and has to snap the ball and block a nose guard. When Buddy Ryan was the defensive coordinator for the Chicago Bears, he created havoc in the league with his defense. He did it by covering both the guards and making the center block 1-on-1 with a nose guard. That created a mismatch with the center, and the guards could not help him. The center is on an island. We try to give our center help on every play (see Diagram #3). The guard that is double reading is the one who is designated to help the center. He is reading linebackers. If nothing happens, he helps the center. The guards are getting depth off the line of scrimmage already. He is falling back inside to help the center if his linebacker doesn't come.

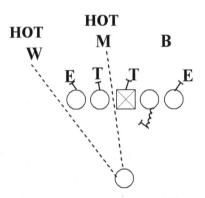

Diagram #3. Help the center.

The uncovered lineman or one covered by a linebacker has to get depth off the line of scrimmage as quickly as he can. If the linebacker walks up on him, he still is retreating and getting depth off the line. If the offensive lineman can only get a piece of the defenders, we have five receivers who are going to beat the defense. All we need is a little time to find them. We ran 26 plays last year in five man protection that went for 35 yards or more.

In the six man protection everything is the same for the offensive line. We still have the quick throw for the quarterback, and we are still protecting his blind side. The most important thing is having the receiver and quarterback on the same page on the quick throws. We don't throw to a position. We designate a certain receiver to be the hot receiver. He is the one who has to see the blitzes and break off the right pattern. The quarterback is going to throw the

ball to him regardless of where he lines up. He could be the inside receiver or the outside receiver. He could be by himself or a middle receiver. That keeps the defense from getting a fix on him.

In the six man protection, I will set up the defense with an even side and an odd side. On the even side, the guard calls even and he and the tackle block the number one and number two men on the line of scrimmage. On the odd side we have to decide what we are going to do. We have to decide who is going to be the most dangerous men to this side. We have to know the personnel and what they do in the defense. If the man outside the tackle is the rush end, we are going to fan the protection to him and block the first down defender on the line of scrimmage with the guard, and the second defender on the line of scrimmage with the tackle. But blocking that situation in that manner causes me a problem. That leaves the center on that island blocking a nose tackle, and I don't like to do that. The even side rules are the same as the odd side rules on five or six man protection.

The next question we have to answer in the six man protection is where to put the sixth protector. That is the same situation as your receiver's routes. You can run any routes that you want as long as you have the hot route for the quarterback. The same thing holds true for the sixth protector. You can put him anywhere you want. You can put him anywhere you want within the box and not affect any of the other protectors in their scheme or the quarterback.

We insert the sixth protector according to the scouting report (see Diagram #4). I don't like to fan the front, and I want to give the center help. The sixth protector for a given week could be an additional tight end to the left side of the formation. That allows the guard to help the center. We may not use a tight end in that position. We could put another tackle in that position and still run our offense. Of course, that tackle would not be eligible as a pass receiver, but I can still run all my running game toward him or away from him without a problem. I could line that tackle up on the wing if I wanted to. I could line him up in the backfield if I wanted. We do not limit ourselves in relationship to the sixth protector.

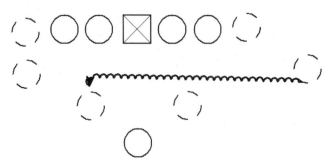

Diagram #4. Alignment of the sixth man

When you put the sixth protector into the protection scheme, the five core linemen's rules don't change. They block their odd or even rules on the five and six man protection. When we put the sixth protector in the scheme, we tell him who to block. We assign him a man to block on each scheme. The sixth protector could be a tight end, a fullback, a running back, an extra lineman, or a wide receiver that motions into the box to block the edge. We are not limited by who we choice to use.

We see different variations of defense, but the defenses are either odd or even. The defense can overload the offense with additional defenders in the box, but we are still counting odd or even alignments, and the quarterback is taking care of the overloads. If my sixth-best offensive lineman is my replacement at right guard, and my tenth-best lineman is my replacement at left guard, when the left guard goes down with an injury, I am going to replace him with my sixth-best lineman. Even though he has been practicing at right guard, I can get him ready to play left guard because the rules do not change from the right side to the left side. I have the ability to interchange linemen without confusing them as to their pass protection. When you start moving linemen around in your offense line, protection is the area of concern. It is not a problem for our group. One thing about offensive linemen that is constant. They are the smartest people on the football field.

In our huddle call for each of our formation, we have a right and left call. That is telling the center which way he blocks on the even fronts. When we come to the line of scrimmage and the center reads an even front, he knows he is blocking to the right side because that was the huddle call. The sixth protector will always go opposite the call side. His alignment doesn't matter. We will tell him where we want him to align, but that point is not important. When we face a 40 defense, the center, right guard, and right tackle are assigned to block the defensive tackle, end, and linebacker to the right (see Diagram #5). The left guard, left tackle, and the sixth protector are assigned to block the defensive end, tackle, and linebacker to the left.

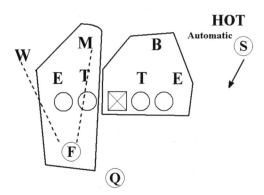

Diagram #5. Six man protection vs. forty

In the six man protection the sixth protector double reads the inside and outside linebackers to his side. The quarterback knows what his protection is doing. If both linebackers come off the backside, the quarterback knows he is throwing hot. If they bring one linebacker off the backside, he is protected. If neither linebacker comes, we have an extra blocker on that side.

On the call side, if the fourth man comes, the quarterback is throwing hot. If no one else on the call side rushes except the fourth rusher, the quarterback is throwing hot. He is going to the hot throw without hesitation. He knows we can only protect against six, and the fourth rusher from that side makes seven.

We know through our scouting report what the defense is trying to do. If we feel they are going to attack us from the backside, we have the ability to put the center on the weak side (see Diagram #6). We can do it in the course of a game if we feel we need to.

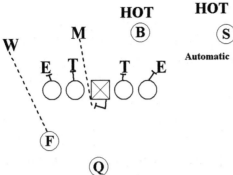

Diagram #6. Center adjustment

In closing there are five things that you should remember from this lecture:

1) Get help for your center.

2) Block odd or even rules.

3) Have a hot read and a hot route.

4) Plug your sixth protector any where you need him.

5) Run any combination pass routes you want.

If you can do those thing and train the quarterback to see the blitzes, you will be able to throw the ball when you have to throw it. Remember not to be too critical of the offensive linemen in pass protection. They are inferior talents trying to block the most talented players on the opponent's team.

Guys, I appreciate you all having me here. I can see why you have great football in this part of the country. Another person who would come out on a day like today to learn some football is dedicated to the sport. I guarantee it was tough for me to come out in this snowstorm.

I wish you the best of luck in the coming years. If you are every in New Orleans, except for Mardi Gras, please stop by and see us. If you come during Mardi Gras, I won't be in the office. Again, good luck to all of you, and if you come our way please stop in. Thank you.

BASIC QUARTERBACK FUNDAMENTALS

University of Alabama

First I want to let you know I am a little nervous today. It is only 60 miles from my home, so my wife decided to come with me today. She said she would go shopping while I could go to the clinic for the lecture. She has been out all day shopping, and I can assure you, that is why I am nervous.

I want to thank Nike and Rush Probst for having me on this clinic. It is an opportunity to get together and talk football. Hopefully, all of us will get better at what we are doing so we can help the kids get better. That has been one of the big things for me in coming from 15 years of experience in the NFL.

My first year in college coaching has been exciting in the personal relationships with individuals. In the NFL, you really do not have that individual relationship. I hate to say it, but in the NFL you have to treat the players as numbers. In college football, you get to know the parents of the players. In the NFL, you only see the players after their senior year, and that is only for about six weeks in training camp. A lot of the athletes are cut and they move on. You may never see them again. At the college level, we have so much more invested already in our recent recruiting class. I know a lot of their parents, and I know a lot of their coaches. So I am looking forward to working with the college players, parents, and coaches.

A lot of people outside of Alabama just do not realize what football means to people of this state. I thought I knew what football was all about when I came up here out of high school to play at the University of Alabama. After I got here, I found out I really did not know the true meaning of football to the people of this state.

What I would like to do now is to talk about basic quarterback fundamentals. I found my 1985 playbook about coaching the quarterback. These things were given to me by the head coach of the Miami Dolphins when I was in the eighth grade. I guess the thinking was this material would help me to get ahead of the game. These are things I was taught in high school and the same things I was taught in college. Also, I got the same information in my only year in the NFL.

I have told quarterbacks that I have coached the same information that was given to me by my dad when I was in the eighth grade. What I am saying is this: the method does not change, regardless of the level you are coaching. The basic fundamentals stay the same. We preach about all of the fundamentals, and we stress doing the little things right and being detailed. There are so many things involved with the quarterback position. It may be the mechanics, the fundamentals, the intangibles, the leadership, the way you must set examples and yet be your own self. You have to know how all of your teammates are going to look at you during crunch time and how you must respond. The quarterback must make quick decisions in three seconds.

I think the quarterback is a unique position. I am a little biased, of course. I am going to share some of these thoughts with you today. I will start with real basic fundamentals. After that, I will try to get into some of the intangibles. I want to stress gaining confidence for the quarterback, earning the respect of teammates, finding the winning edge, and doing what it takes to win. Some of this will sound a little repetitive. But again, that is the way we teach these fundamentals. The more the players can hear this information, the better chance they have of doing good things on Friday night and Saturday.

After we finish the fundamental session, I have some drills that I want to show you and I want to describe to you how they apply. If we have time, I will talk about some other things on tapes that involve other coaching points.

First, we start with the stance for the quarterback. With the quarterback under the center, we want the feet parallel, with a slight stager. Some coaches stress the stagger more than we do. We only want the opposite foot from the throwing hand to be slightly staggered. This is especially true when we are dropping back to throw the ball. At times, when you are handing the ball off, you may stagger the feet the other way. The thing we stress is getting the weight on the pivot foot so we can get an advantage without giving it away.

We want the knees slightly bent. The weight is over the instep, with the body slightly leaning forward. Any mechanics we teach, we want to really stress these points in the spring, more so than in the fall. We want our quarterback to be comfortable in his stance so he can look at the defense and study his keys. We do not want him worried about his stance in taking the snap.

The hands should be firmly pressed under the center's crotch. Basically, we want the quarterback to give the center a target to bring the ball up to on the snap. The second point is to have good hand pressure on the center's crotch so the ball does not come out when the center snaps the ball. We tell the quarterback to put his hands under the center's crotch, knuckles deep, and to apply pressure.

We want him to bend the elbows of the throwing hand slightly. We want the opposite thumb to be on the thumb of the throwing hand. The opposite thumb is where we want the pressure on the center's crotch. If the snap comes up a little deep and you have pressure on the crotch with the opposite hand, you have a chance of getting the snap so it does not split your hands.

The ball must fit into the crease of the throwing hand. We want the quarterback to trap the ball with the off hand. Once the ball is secure in the hands, we want to stomach the ball. In other words, we want him to "seed" the ball into his stomach. When he is handing off, he does not want the ball hanging outside of his body, or down low where he has to raise it up to get it to the ballcarrier. We want to make sure he gets the ball into his stomach as soon as he gets the snap.

Next we move to the pivot foot. It starts with the head and shoulders first. He must twist his body to look at the handoff spot. If he is handing the ball off, he must lock the ball into the mesh area. He must pivot on the foot with a little pressure on that foot. He comes out to the handoff area and he must look the ball into the handoff spot.

After the handoff, he fakes as if he has the ball, using proper footwork. The point we want to make here is this: we do not want the quarterback to get too excited about faking until he gets the ball handed off to the ballcarrier.

The handoff is the responsibility of the quarterback. For whatever reason, if the quarterback can not make the handoff, he tucks the ball and follows the back through the hole of the play called. He does not want to shovel the ball to the runner, and he does not want to be late getting the ball to the ballcarrier. If he misses the handoff, he follows the back into the hole and continues upfield. We do not want him to make the play worse by trying to get the ball to the ballcarrier when he is late or the back is too wide.

We use two types of fakes with the quarterback. First, we use a fake by showing the ball with two hands. If a quarterback is left- or right-handed, we do not ask him to take his throwing hand off the football. If we are going toward his throwing hand, he can give a one-hand fake with the open hand. He can give the open-hand fake and hide the ball on his hip.

If he is going away from his throwing hand, he will always use a two-hand ball fake and then set up in the pocket. We are never going to make an open-hand fake with our throwing hand. The reason for that is simple. If there is pressure and the throwing hand is late getting on the ball, the ball could come out and result in a fumble.

Next we move to the drop, where the quarterback gets to the passing spot. We use crossover footwork on the drop. It is a comfortable drop from the center to the set-up spot. Some coaches stress for the quarterback to keep the ball up near the open ear as they retreat on the drop. I am more interested in the quarterback being comfortable on the drop as far as the position of the ball is concerned. We do not want the ball down around the belt on the drop. As long as it is between the letters and the ear hole on the helmet, that is fine with me. It depends on the quarterback. He can use the momentum of the ball swinging back and forth as he sets up. That is what we teach them.

We talk about keeping the shoulders at a 45-degree angle on the drop. Not many quarterbacks can drop back where they can keep the shoulders straight down the field on the crossover dropback.

We use three drops. We do a three-step drop, a five-step drop, and a seven-step drop. We take the drop and set up, ready to throw.

There are a couple of ways we teach our quarterbacks as far as setting up. All of this is based on timing. On the three-step drop, the quarterback is going to take the third step, transfer his weight, and then thrown the ball. His action is not a hitch step.

On the five-step drop, we call it a quick five-step drop. Again, there is no hitch in the drop. He transfers his weight and throws the ball. When he does this, he must be under control. If he is taking five steps back, and his momentum and his weight are still on the back foot, it is going to be hard to transfer the weight in the throwing motion. It will be difficult to get much on the football He may be able to get something on the football, but he probably will not be accurate. The key is to keep the feet underneath you, transfer the weight on the fifth step, and then throw the football. This is one way we teach the five-step drop. This is used on a shorter route. These routes are very similar to the routes used on a three-step drop passing route.

Then we teach the five-step drop, which is a hitch and throw. The quarterback takes the five-step drop, takes a hitch step, and then throws the football. This is what most of our routes are set up on.

There will be some times when the quarterback has to hitch twice. Most times for us, the double hitch is on a seven-step drop. We try to time everything on the steps the quarterback has to drop to the pocket. Every now and then, it takes a little longer to run the route, or the defense is playing bump-and-run coverage and it takes a little more time to run the route. That forces the quarterback to take two hitches. He takes seven steps, hitch, hitch, and then throws.

On all the drops, we continue to stress the fundamentals. We check the feet to make sure he is balanced in his stance so he can make an accurate throw.

The last point here is play-action footwork. Basically, we are using the action on the running play. We want to get the feet and hips set up to throw the ball. He must get his feet set, and he must get the hips turned toward the target. These are the things we talk about in setting up before we throw the football.

Next is the throwing motion. I am no guru on throwing motion. I had the worst throwing motion in the world. But these are things that I have learned from people I had respect for when I was growing up around some good programs. These things made sense to me.

First is the motion of opening up the opposite hip. To do this, you must open up your opposite foot. A drill we use for this is having the quarterback drop on a line or yard strip with a receiver 10 yards away on that same line. The quarterback drops, and as he is ready to throw, we ask him to open his opposite foot This will help open the opposite hip, which will give him the power to get the ball to the receiver, and this will help him with the velocity on the throw.

If the quarterback is on the line and the receiver is on the line, the quarterback does not want to open the opposite foot too much. If he does, he will start throwing the ball across his body. He should open the foot on the line toward the receiver.

When the quarterback releases the football, the thumb on the throwing hand should be pointing toward the ground as the ball comes off the hand. He must snap the wrist to get the rotation on the ball. It is almost like throwing a screwball in baseball. You can take films of the quarterbacks and look at the thumb as they release the football. The thumb should be pointing down. To me this makes sense.

We teach our quarterbacks to visualize a four-pane window frame to throw the ball into on the pass pattern (see Diagram #1). He wants to release the ball through a window frame. That large window is divided into four panes. For a right-handed quarterback he wants to aim for the pane on the upper right-hand side of the window. This will give him the best chance to be accurate, and this also gives him a better chance for a higher release. We do not feel the low release is that bad, but we just feel the higher release gives the quarterback the best chance for accuracy and the opportunity to get more velocity on the ball.

Window Pane

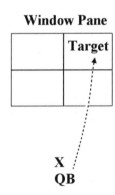

Diagram #1. Window frame

The next point is the transferring of the weight from the throwing foot to the front foot. We have talked about setting up. We want to get the weight transferred from the back foot to the front foot. As far as the timing of it, some quarterbacks get the weight transferred too early, and that makes the arm come around too late. That is when the ball sails on them. Some quarterbacks have the arm going forward before they get the foot transferred. That is when the ball goes down low on them. The weight movement must transfer first, and the arm must come right behind it. Again, the key is to get the weight transferred.

Now, I know there are some guys that can throw the ball off the back foot. A good example would be Brett Favre. Dan Marino and Jeff George were other quarterbacks that could throw off the back foot effectively. I do not see a lot of quarterbacks that can do this effectively. But as these guys released the ball, you could see the shoulder come forward as they came through the throw.

The last thing in this progression is the rotation that I talked about earlier. It starts with opening the foot and opening up the hips. Then the quarterback must rotate his shoulders. It is almost like a baseball player. The batter is sitting there, waiting on the pitch, and he is coiled. As the pitch comes to him, he uncoils. The quarterback wants the same type of motion. Dan Marino was one of the best ever at this.

Those are basic fundamentals that I have carried with me throughout my coaching career, and when I played quarterback. Again, this is technique. These things may be boring to quarterbacks but we still work hard on them in spring practice. We feel this is very important, and we start with page one of the fundamentals. We go through this each year. It may be boring to the older quarterbacks, but it is important enough that they can still pick up some important points.

Next I want to talk about some intangibles related to playing quarterback. I have been building on this for the last few years. These are little things that I think are important to quarterbacks. First is gaining confidence. The quarterback must know the play and the formation. He must know what to do. He must go into the huddle with confidence. The players can see if the quarterback has confidence or not when they get into the huddle. The players know if the quarterback knows what he is doing. At that position, he better know what he is doing. He better know what is going on before he gets into the huddle if he wants to be the leader.

The quarterback must step into the huddle and he must speak clearly. He must never assume the other players can hear him. For the college players, it is the freshmen coming into fall camp that have a problem with this. When I was coaching in the NFL it was the rookie quarterbacks that had this problem. They are real quiet and talk in a low whisper.

When the quarterback steps into that huddle, he must realize the wide receivers are winded from running the previous play, the linemen are breathing hard for an all-out effort, and he must speak up so they can hear him. He must be very precise in his annunciating, and he cannot take for granted what he is saying. He must be loud and clear.

When the quarterback gets to the line of scrimmage, it is the same thing. If he calls an audible, he must make sure he calls it loud and clear, and he must make sure everyone hears the calls. He cannot allow a penalty to occur because he was not loud enough on the audible.

He must always be himself. He cannot be a phony. The only way he can be himself is by knowing what to do as the quarterback. If he is not a rah-rah type player and all of a sudden he starts the rah-rah stuff, the players will see through this. He must show the team he knows what to do and he is in control. The quarterback must take charge in the huddle. He must demand respect in the huddle. To do this he must be able to perform.

We talk about leadership by the quarterback. To me, leadership is not getting on another player in the huddle. He cannot give the left tackle the devil because the quarterback got sacked by the defensive man the tackle was supposed to block. Leadership is not getting on a receiver in the huddle because he dropped a pass that could have been caught. To me, leadership is when the quarterback goes to the guard that was offside the play before and his head is down, and he tells him to forget that play and get ready for the next play. That, to me, is leadership. This will command more respect from teammates.

The quarterback is going to make mistakes as much as other players make mistakes. If he throws an interception, what can the quarterback expect the teammates to say to him if he is getting on them every time they make a mistake?

We want the quarterback to concentrate to avoid the silly mistakes. He can not be so concerned about the other positions that he makes a silly mistake. It may just be going the wrong way, but that is something that will not happen if he is concentrating.

He must always be positive in his support and in his commands. This is the same area I have just talked about. He does not have to get on the players. He should let the coaches get on the players. As the quarterback, he has a chance to be real positive in and out of the huddle and on the sidelines.

The quarterback must never criticize a player on or off the field. In college it is a little more involved with the media. In the NFL, it is a lot more involved with the media. There is always going to be a time when someone is going to say to the quarterback, "That receiver should have caught that pass. If he had caught that pass, you guys would have won the game." The media will bait you. This could even be your own teammates. This type of talk can spread. If you do get a chance to knock a player, don't do it. Leave the criticism up to the coaches. If you do not have anything good to say about another player, don't say anything.

The quarterback must be willing to take the responsibility for a poor play. If it is an interception and it is close as far as who was at fault, the quarterback must step up and say, "It was my fault, coach." If the ball does not hit the bottom hand and the snap is fumbled, he must step up and say, "It is my fault." He must take the blame for the snap even if the center did not get the ball up. This will go a long way in working with the centers. They know when the ball does not get up and they know when it is their fault. That goes a long way with them.

He must congratulate a teammate on a good play. So many times the quarterback will throw a touchdown pass and then just walk off to the sideline. He may come off the field with his fist high in the air and he may have a smile on his face. The rest of the team is down in the end zone congratulating the receiver that scored the touchdown. We want our quarterback to get his butt down to the end zone and congratulate his teammates.

He must congratulate his teammate when he makes a big block that leads to a big play. Again, it is showing leadership, and it is going to help him down the road.

The quarterback must never make excuses. This is the same thing we have just talked about. The last thing a coach wants to hear is a bunch of excuses. In the NFL, it is hard to change those kinds of players. They want to make excuses for everything. The coaches and the teammates do not want to hear excuses.

The quarterback must execute his position with precision on every play. It is obvious that his teammates are watching him on every move. He can not gain respect if the he does not know what to do.

The quarterback must do all of the little things. He must set the pace for the team. He must carry out all of his fakes on all plays. He must do the little things, such as changing up the snap count when necessary. These are little things that can help the quarterback gain the respect of his teammates.

I want to talk a few minutes about gaining an edge as a quarterback. He can watch film to see what the defense likes to do. Today, we are all seeing a lot more defenses than we use to see. By studying the film, he can pick up keys that will help him later in the game.

A key point here is for the quarterback to watch some film on his own. When the quarterback watches the film with the coaches, he is listening to the coaches. He watches what the coach is watching. If the quarterback can watch the film on his own, he can pick up some points without having to listen to the coaches.

Today we see all kinds of different coverages. We can pick those things up on the film. We know the safeties' alignment will always tell us what the coverage is going to be. These are things high school quarterbacks can view on their own. The more they can do this without the coach having to tell them, the better a quarterback they are going to be. If they only watch film when we tell them to look at them, they may be ok, but they will never be as good as they can be without doing those little extra things on their own.

Moving to the mechanical aspects, the quarterbacks can work on the things that give them the hardest time. It may be the drop, getting away from the line of scrimmage, or handing the ball off; they can work on their weaknesses. We all know we are only as good as our weakest part of our game. They must work on the mechanics so they do not have to think about them on Friday night. If they work on these points through the week, they should come natural to them in the games.

Here are some mental things we stress with our quarterbacks:

- Know the outlet receiver on every play.

- Be deceptive on the play fakes.

- Be prepared to mix up the snap count.

- Think about one play at a time. This is true on a good play and a bad play.

- Take what the defense gives you. As the saying goes, "You can't go broke taking a profit."

- Keep the chains moving by making first downs. Live to play another down.

- Be aware of all situations on the field. Be aware of the two minute situations.

- Know when not to take a sack.

- Be prepared to do extra study on your own.

- Have fun every day in practice. Go out with the attitude you are going to get better each day. See how many players will follow that lead.

Now I want to go to the drill tape to show these fundamentals. After the drills, we review these drills with our players to show them how the drills apply to the game.

I want to thank your for your attention. Good luck to everyone.

EFFECTIVE USE OF THE BOOTLEG PASS

Yale University

I want to thank Nike for giving me the opportunity to speak today. I need to validate why I should be talking to you about football. We were a high-powered offense this year. We were second in the country in total offense, and our quarterback was number one in the country in total offense. It takes very talented players to do that. We have good players playing for us. We have a good coaching staff that tweaks our system from year to year to make the scheme work with the talent we have.

Yale is not a scholarship program, so we cannot go out every year to find the kid that fits our position needs. This year we had a great tight end and had to find ways to get him the ball. He will be drafted by the NFL. He is 6-7 and weights 265 pounds. He caught 71 passes this year. One of the ways to get him the ball was the bootleg pass, which I am going to talk about today. The two things I want to talk about are the bootleg and the waggle.

The quarterback in our offense has to be an intelligent player. He has to make the right decisions and not make stupid plays. People think we run a very high-risk offense. We threw the ball almost 400 times this year. We run 50 percent of our offense from the shotgun set.

We had the lowest number of turnovers in the country. We threw seven interceptions and lost four fumbles. What we do on offense is very simple, but we do it from a lot of formations and motions. We want to make people adjust to what we are doing.

We averaged 35 points a game. We averaged 480 yards of total offense per game. We threw for 307 yards and ran for 173 yards per game. We averaged 80 plays a game. We protect the football and do not turn it over. We keep the drives going because we average 46 percent on our third down plays. That is a tremendous conversion rate for third downs. To pick up those third downs, you have to have kids who are playmakers. You have to identify them and get them the ball.

Our quarterback is a big play football player. He had 3460 yards of total offense. He threw for 2990 yards, and ran for 450. We completed 230 passes this year, and our wide receivers and tight ends caught 219 of them. Our backs only caught 11 balls this year. Our receivers are our best skill players, and we want to put the ball in their hands. We have two excellent tailbacks. Between the two of them, they rushed for 1200 yards this year. The tailback position is going to get the ball 20 to 25 times a game.

To have a good pass offense, you have to be consistent. We completed 60 percent of our passes. We threw the ball 385 times this year and completed 230 of those throws. That means we are throwing the ball more than 40 times a game.

If you want to be a passing offense, you have to be productive. We threw from 3000 yards this year. I think that is being very productive.

To be effective on offense you have to get the ball into the end zone. The offense has to score. It does not matter what kinds of numbers and statistic you have, if the ball does not get into the end zone, you will not win. That is what happened in our Harvard game this year. We had 553 yards of total offense against Harvard and never got into the end zone. We were the number-one team in the red zone this year. We got in the red zone three times in that game and did not score. We lost the game because we did not score.

We threw the ball this year for 23 touchdowns and had 7 interceptions. The play-action pass is 25 percent of our passing game. That means 75 percent of our passing game was from behind the center in some kind of five-step passing game. We played six teams that ran a 4-4 defense. They were eight-men fronts before we even snapped the ball. Most of the teams we play are eight-men fronts after we snap the football, with a safety rolling into the box.

We have committed ourselves to having a versatile quarterback who can move out of the pocket and run with the ball. Two years ago, we had a 6-5 quarterback who could really throw the ball, but he had no mobility at all. We had trouble when teams blitzed us. To make matters worse, he did not read the hot patterns very well. Now that we have a mobile quarterback, most of those problems have disappeared.

If your offense can run the option play, the defensive secondary will be limited in the amount of man-to-man schemes they can run against you. That is why we run a little option play as part of our offense. Last year, Harvard played 50 percent of the snaps against us in a man-under coverage. This year, they did not play one snap of man-under coverage. They could not defend the quarterback running the option play with all their defensive backs chasing a receiver in man coverage.

We run the option two or three times a game. We run it quite a bit in long yardage situations. That is why our third down conversion rate was so high. We ran the option when people expected us to throw the ball. We restricted what defenses could do against us because of the multiplicity of the offense.

On the bootleg, we had 25 completions for 37 attempts, or 68 percent. The waggle was 19 completions for 33 attempts, or 58 percent, and all the other play passes we were 15 for 28, or 54 percent. We had a tight end who was first team All-American. The bootleg is the easiest way to get the ball to the tight end.

I first taught this play and put it into our offense more than 20 years ago. I got it from the Washington Redskins. Joe Gibbs was the head coach, and Joe Bugel was his line coach. They were one of the first pro teams to experiment with moving the pocket for the quarterback. Joe Theisman was the quarterback. They ran the counter tray with the bootleg off that play. It is funny because 20 years later, Washington has the same two guys, with a new coaching staff, making their second appearance at the reins.

When we first put the bootleg in, we protected the quarterback every time we ran the play. Twenty years ago, we did that 99 percent of the time. Today we never protect the quarterback on the bootleg. We still have the protection in our playbook, but we did not run one snap of a protected bootleg this year.

Twenty years ago the play was a two-back play. Today almost every play comes from the one-back set or shotgun set. We did not run the shotgun 20 years ago. We want to keep the play simple but multiple. We want to run it from any formation we have in the offense.

I call the plays, but our quarterback coach keeps track of what I am doing. I have never asked him for a game report, but every Sunday he puts a report on my desk. It has a breakdown of the plays we ran in practice on Tuesday, Wednesday, and Thursday, and a breakdown of the plays we ran in the game. It also has the percentages of the plays that we ran in practice that we actually ran in the game.

On Tuesday we probably have seven or eight bootlegs in the game plan. By the time we get to Saturday, we have only one or two we actually are planning to use in the game. Today, I am going to show you 10 to 15 combinations of bootlegs that we could run from various formations. We have a rule that anything that is brought up after 10:00 P.M. Sunday night is probably ridiculous and will not be considered for the game plan. In the last three years, we have gotten better at eliminating those types of plays before they get to practice. We want to practice plays we are actually going to run in the game.

You cannot put a play in on Tuesday, run it twice in practice, and expect it to succeed. You will see a reverse pass on the film I am going to show you. We have a ten-minute period on Tuesday where we run bootlegs, waggles, screens, and junk. We run as many plays in that period as we can run. On Tuesday, we run the plays against the opposing defense. We run the reverse pass during this period, but it is not in the game plan. We practiced it during that week, but we will not use it in the game plan until we have thrown it enough in practice to make it look smooth.

Wednesday and Thursday, we run these passes against air. We are trying to get timing and spacing on the plays. We are going to practice the reverse pass in that period also. We will run the reverse pass several weeks before we will consider using it as part of the game plan.

When people watch us practice, they cannot believe we run the football as well as we do. Our starting quarterback throws the football for about 90 percent of the practice time. There is probably ten minutes in our practice when the quarterback is not throwing the ball in one way or another. We spend about five minutes working on running the football. When you throw the football as many times as we throw it, you have to spend a ton of time working on it. Our commitment is to throwing the football.

On every bootleg play we are going to have a takeoff pattern by the outside receiver to that side. We are going to have a five-yard slide pattern and a ten-yard drag pattern. The spacing on the patterns will be the same for every bootleg. When people look at this pass they think it is really simple, and it is. However, you have to spend time working on the play to get the timing exact.

We installed our entire offense in three days during preseason. In preseason, we teach this play from a two-back set. If we run the bootleg weak, the split end runs the takeoff. The slide pattern from a two-back formation is always run from the backfield. The slide pattern is a flat route that is never run deeper than five yards. If the receiver runs the pattern at three yards, that is fine. It is really a misnomer to call the last pattern a drag. The drag could come off the front side. The drag pattern is

run at 10 yards. We tell the receiver running the drag pattern we never want the pattern under 10 yards. If he gets slightly deeper, that is acceptable.

If we run the bootleg to either side out of the two-back set, the outside receiver runs the take-off, the back out of the backfield runs the slide pattern, and the next receiver toward the call side runs the drag. That rule is true for any formation we run.

If we are in a one-back set, it doesn't matter what kind of formation we run, the patterns are the same. If we are in a double wing set and run the bootleg to the left, the first receiver on the left side runs the takeoff. The second receiver on the left runs the slide, and the third receiver from the other side runs the drag. If we were in a three-by-one formation running the bootleg into the 1 receiver side, the 1 receiver runs the takeoff. The inside slot back runs the slide pattern, and the outside slot back runs the drag.

We have two clarifications to the rule. If we run a bootleg into a three wide receiver side from a one-back set, the two outside receivers are counted as one pattern. They both run vertical patterns. They can run a takeoff, or they can cross their patterns and get deep. The inside slot runs the slide, and the backside receiver runs the drag. If we are in a twin set with a two-back set, the twin set is counted as one pattern. It is a very simple concept. We can run the play from any formation you can draw up.

We can run the bootleg from any running play we have. This year, about 75 percent of our bootlegs came from the counter play out of the shotgun set. Our number-one running play from the shotgun set was the counter play. We had about four different ways we ran that play. Obviously the number-one play-action pass was the bootleg off that fake.

Before I show you the plays, let me go over the coaching points for the receivers. The outside receiver is the least likely receiver to get the ball. His job is to clear the area and run people off. He has to take an outside release even if he has to run out of bounds. If the corner is in press coverage on top of the receiver, he never comes inside the corner.

The rule for the slide receiver is that he never gets into a position where the slide pattern and the drag pattern are in a stack. That means you have two receivers at different levels running the same pattern. If the window is closed for the low receiver, it is closed for the high receiver also. You would not think that would be a problem, but it could be if the tight end has trouble getting off the line of scrimmage.

If the tight end is the slide receiver, he fakes a block before he comes out on the slide pattern. Since we had a good tight end, defenses would try to double-team him and keep him from getting off the line of scrimmage. The drag man in a wide receiver position generally has no trouble getting off the line of scrimmage. He has to be aware of what is happening to the tight end. If he sees the tight end having trouble getting off the line, he has to throttle down his pattern to stay out of the stacked receiver position. We played two senior tight ends this year, and they were very good at seeing those things happening.

You could see the drag receiver throttling his pattern down to let the slide receiver get out in front of him. You could see the windows opening behind the slide receiver.

The rule for the drag receiver is to get into vision of the quarterback. That sounds like a contradiction from the previous point. The drag has to get to his depth and get across the field before he worries about the slide receiver. If he does not get into the vision of the quarterback, he will never get the ball.

If the takeoff pattern gets the ball, it is generally a call from the press box. When we read the patterns in the bootleg, we read low to high in our progression. That is why it is a 68 percent completion pass. There are a couple of deep patterns thrown on the tape, but those plays were sent in from the sideline and the quarterback was told to look deep first. We threw one pass against Columbia. They had a tough press corner and a two-deep safety. The two-deep safety was hung up on the run, and we hit the take-off behind him.

I do not feel the quarterback can look deep first. If he does, his percentage of completion will come down drastically. He is going to get the slide almost every time if he wants it. This is an extremely high-percentage pass.

The first formation is the two-back set with the bootleg going weak (see Diagram #1). This is how we teach the play when we start out in the fall. The split end runs the takeoff. The fullback runs the slide from the backfield, and the tight end runs the drag. The flanker back clears down the middle and holds people in coverage. We get some defenders that will jump the tight end with the safety and leave the backside of the field open. If we threw the ball to that receiver, it would be called from the press box.

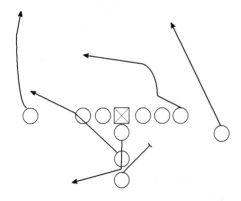

Diagram #1. Pro set, two backs weak

From the pro set, we can run the bootleg to the strongside (see Diagram #2). The flanker runs the takeoff. The fullback runs the slide pattern from the backfield. He runs the slide pattern, which is a hard arrow pattern into the flat. The tight end runs the drag, but he is on the strongside. The pattern

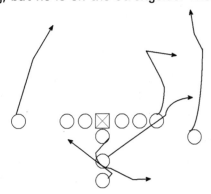

Diagram #2. Pro set, two back strong

looks like an out cut for the tight end. He has an immediate vertical release up the field to get the separation between the slide receiver and his pattern.

The next set is a twin formation with the two-back set (see Diagram #3). This is the two receiver rule. We have two outside receivers, and they count as one pattern. In Diagram #3, I have them running a deep crossing pattern. The fullback runs the slide, and the tight end runs the drag. Against 4-4 defensive teams, the tight end has a problem getting a release over the top of the inside leverage end that is playing on him. In the 4-4 defense, the inside linebacker has a better opportunity to find the tight end coming across. The tight end has to get the release and get across the inside linebacker without getting knocked off. Against a three-man front or 50 look, the release is much easier. He has to locate the inside linebacker and avoid him. It does not matter whether he goes under or over the linebacker. He does not want a collision with the linebacker.

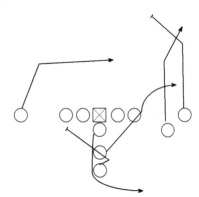

Diagram #3. Twin set, two-back strong

The quarterback is faking a counter play as he comes out. We are pulling the guard and tackle off the backside as part of the fake. The fullback is coming off the pulling tackle's butt to get into the flat. The quarterback fakes the counter to the running back, brings the ball out. and looks low to high.

If we run the same formation and run the bootleg weak, the rules are the same (see Diagram #4). The tight end runs the takeoff. The fullback runs the slide from the backfield and the slot back runs the drag. If you have a team that has trouble covering in the second level, this is a great way to run this

play. The slot receiver can get across the field unmolested, and carry his speed with him. If you can hit him with the ball, he generally can turn it up for a big gain.

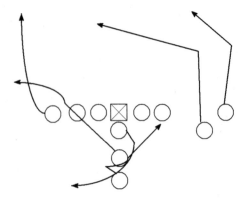

Diagram #4. Twin set, two-back weak

Our number-one set this year was the one-back with two tight ends formation (see Diagram #5). We had two excellent tight ends on our football team this year. In this set we are two tight ends and two wide receivers in a balanced set. We use one-back rules to find out which receivers run the patterns. In this set, if we are running the play to the right, the wide receiver runs the takeoff. The tight end to that side runs the slide pattern, and the backside tight end runs the drag.

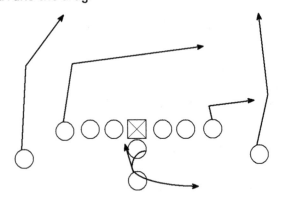

Diagram #5. 2 TE, 2 WR one-back

The most difficult pattern to time up is the slide pattern. If the tight end releases immediately, he will be out of bounds before the quarterback gets ready to throw. Generally, we run the zone play fake with this bootleg. The tight end fakes his zone block before he releases to the flat. You have to convince him that the longer he blocks, the wider he comes open. The tight end has to block the zone play. He will have no problem releasing if he blocks the run. The defensive end does not want to get tangled up with him and will try to get away from him. He cannot make the pass look any different than the zone running play.

The 4-4 teams we play do not like this next set (see Diagram #6). We get in a twin set with our wide receivers, and a wing set with the second tight end away from the twins. We have a ton of success with this formation against the 4-4 teams. Applying the rules, the second tight end runs the takeoff. The tight end runs the slide, and the slot receiver runs the drag.

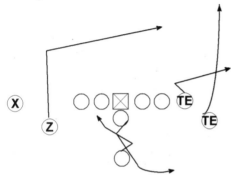

Diagram #6. Twin set wing

On the tape, you will see this set. We use our fullback in the wing set also. The 4-4 teams play the wing man-to-man with the linebacker and bring the corner down on our tight end. On play-action passes they get confused and let the wing get deep on them. The quarterback actually hits the drag, but you can see the wing running up the sideline absolutely wide open.

You have to have good people in the press box. With the tight end we had this year, teams loaded up to stop him. By loading up on him, they gave us something else. We have to be smart enough to find the weakness in the coverage. We did that several times this year. I can show you some of those things in the film.

The next set is a tight slot to the split end side (see Diagram #7). This could be the second tight end or a fullback. He has to make the play look like a run. He cannot release until he blocks. The first time the receiver runs this pattern from this formation, he is always too quick and gets too wide.

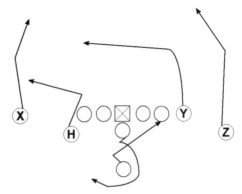

Diagram #7. Weak tight slot

People do not believe how many times we run the bootleg into the boundary. It is a good play to that side, but the timing is critical. If the slide receiver gets in a hurry, the play is no good. The bootleg does not have to be a middle of the field or wide side of the field play.

I will show you a few trip-set formations (see Diagram #8). The rules are always the same. The tight end runs the takeoff. The inside slot runs the slide pattern, and he has to bust his butt to get across that formation to the other side. The outside slot runs the drag. In this situation, it is easy to get your slide and drag receivers stacked as they come across the field. You have to get the drag receiver following the slide receiver. The Z-back has an easier release and can run his pattern so much faster than the slide pattern. He has to be careful any time we are in a trips formation.

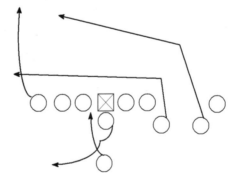

Diagram #8. Trips weak

This is the last diagram I will show you before we see the film (see Diagram #9). This is a bootleg toward the trips set. In this case, we apply the two-receiver rule. The X-end and Z-back count as one receiver. They run the takeoff. The inside slot runs the slide pattern, and the tight end runs the drag.

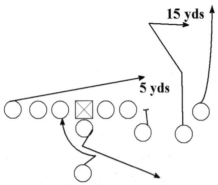

15 yds

5 yds

Diagram #9. Waggle, takeoff, out, slide

Next I will show you the waggle on the film and tell you what we do. We have two combinations we run with the waggle pattern. The first combination is a take-off, a deep out, and a slide pattern. We run the deep out at 15 yards. We also like to run the out and up from this play. We run the play with the trips look, but the inside slot does not release. He secures the corner so the quarterback can get outside.

The second combination we run with the waggle is a comeback, a deep flag, and a cross (see Diagram #10). The deep comeback is run at 16 yards coming back to 14 yards. When we throw the waggle routes, we are looking high to low.

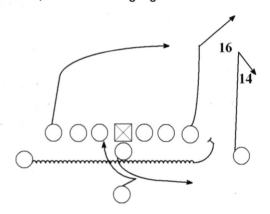

16

14

Diagram #10. Waggle comeback, flag, cross

I appreciate your attention.

THE SHALLOW CROSS PASSING GAME

Purdue University

As a head coach, you have multiple opportunities to go out and speak. When you speak at banquets you want to be a gracious person and say how it is nice to be here. When I speak at banquets and my wife is not in the audience, I tell them it is nice to be here because I finally will get a good meal. Obviously if she is present I cannot get away with that.

As I look out over the audience, I see eight or nine guys that share the same barber that I have. When you have a hairline like mine, you learn how to defend yourself. I have all the comebacks for guys with receding hairlines. I am giving you permission to use my favorite comeback. My wife refers to me as a solar powered sex machine.

When we went to Purdue from Wyoming seven years ago, we were a big bubble screen team. Eight years ago, the only school I saw running the bubble screen was the University of Idaho. I had not seen anyone else running it. We stole it from Idaho and put it into our scheme.

We put the scheme in at Purdue and ran it extensively over the last few years. People are beginning to defend us better. I do not know how we are winning football games. Our receivers have gotten smaller and slower. We are not as good now as we were in the past at running the bubble screen.

We have evolved to some other parts of our offense called the shallow cross pass series. That is what I am going to talk about this evening. It is a route that has been very good to us. I say this with tongue in cheek, but it surprises me that we are not able to go out each year and recruit three great wide receivers.

It totally mystifies me that a school like Purdue, which throws the ball as much as we do, has trouble recruiting receivers. We have signed some receivers that can catch the ball, but we are so lacking in speed. We are taking advantage of the things we do to move the ball at the college level. We have very average wide receivers. If you fit into that category, maybe you can use some of the things I am going to talk about tonight.

We have done these things for the last 14 years. Our tight end is called the Y receiver. The split end is the X receiver. The flanker back is called the Z receiver. The slot back in our offense is the A back. The running back or fullback is called the F back. If we have a second tight end on the field, we refer to him as the U end. All these things give you reference points to identify the players when you look at the diagrams.

My introduction to this offense occurred in 1987 when I went to the University of Wyoming as an assistant. When I went there, I did not know anything about the one-back offense. In 1987 no one in the country was running an empty set in the backfield. It was the first time I had seen this offense, and it was a shock to me. Coach Dennis Erickson was the coach at Wyoming. That was before he went to Washington State and on to Miami of Florida. When he left Wyoming, he left his playbook behind.

In the Big Ten, they refer to this offense as garbage. The evolution of the offense is interesting. When we came to the Big Ten in 1997, Jim Wacker had coached at Minnesota in the Big Ten. He was no longer coaching at Minnesota, but had run some one-back offense when he was in the league. Jim Wacker left Minnesota, and Glenn Mason came in. They went to the power football game. We were the only team in the Big Ten running this offense.

The first year we played Penn State at Purdue. I had not met St. Joseph Paterno before. I met him prior to the game. As we were talking before the game, he grabbed me by the arm as asked me if we were going to put our players all over the field and run that stuff against him. I told him I called it sissy ball and that no real man would run this stuff. Unfortunately, that is all we have right now, so we are going to run it.

I knew I was in trouble when he told me I was a breath of fresh air to the league. They pounded us 37-13 that day and ran up 600 yards of total offense. We were out of the field trying to throw the bubble screen.

Purdue is a great engineering school. I coach at Purdue, and I am not a computer guy. I had a guy ask me the other day what I thought about computers. I told him one day I hoped to be smart enough to turn one on. Purdue is a high-tech school. It is the largest engineering school in the United States. Purdue has more employees in the NASA space program than any other school. You cannot be at Purdue and not be involved in technology, and that means PowerPoint.

Last year, our offensive statistics were not very good. Our quarterback has a big-league arm and is coming back next year. He threw for a lot of yardage this year, but not many touchdowns. Our passing attempts were down this year, but our completion rate was up. The thing I liked the best about this year was we only hit the open linebacker seven times.

I am going to talk about five different ways in which Purdue uses the shallow cross route. Some of this will apply to the two-minute situation, but most of it can be used at any time.

Our passing series are 60's, 70's, and 90's. The 60 series is our five-man protection scheme. The 70 series is our six- and seven-man protection schemes. The 90 series is our quick package.

There are three reasons we like the shallow cross. The shallow cross is a curl-flat read involving the tight end, wide receiver, and back. The shallow cross starts out as a hot read in our 60's package.

The second thing is our shallow cross-dig combination. We generally run that combination out of an empty formation. The thing we like about the empty formation is it gives us the chance to throw a high-low read on the linebackers.

The last thing is our shallow cross against the soft corner. With the advent of the zone pressure schemes that are becoming popular in college, it gives us a way to throw the ball against the soft corner into the boundary.

We like the series out of the heavy package. The heavy package is our ace formation. In that formation, we have two tight ends, two wide receivers, and one running back. The pattern reads of the quarterback make him stay to the playside on most of these patterns.

A normal grouping for us is a double set. That type of set has three wide receivers, one tight end, and one running back. A double set is the Z back and Y end to one side, and the A back and X end to the other.

We also like the shallow cross from a four wide receiver grouping. That grouping is called our light formation. Everything we do comes from personnel grouping. That is how we make our calls from the sidelines. We yell out the grouping we want on the field.

The first shallow cross is run from the normal grouping with the quarterback in a shotgun set. This play is a five-man protection, which makes it a 60 series play. In this set, the first thing the quarterback is looking for is the tight end on the cross. The second option is the Z back on a curl pattern over the tight end alignment. The third thing he looks for is the fullback running a flare to stretch and widen the flat defender.

The huddle call is "Doubles-left, gun, red, 60 Z-X-Dig." The doubles left is the formation call with the tight end and Z back left. The gun call means the quarterback is in the shotgun series. Red tells the offensive line that the tight end and fullback are in the pattern and not blocking in the protection scheme. Red tells the line the play is a red-alert protection. The 60-protection is the five-man protection for the line. The quarterback knows he has five-man protection and has to throw hot off blitzing linebackers. The zero in the number 60 relates to the pattern being run. The 0 pattern is the 10 to 12 yard curl route. The 60Z tell the fullback he aligns left toward the call. If the play was a 60X the fullback aligns on the other side and swings toward the X end.

In the 60Z pattern, the flanker runs a 10 to 12 yard curl route over the alignment of the tight end (see Diagram #1). The tight end runs a 6 to 8 yard cross route. The fullback runs a swing toward the curl route. The backside A back runs a go route down the field. The backside X end runs a 14 to 16 yard dig route.

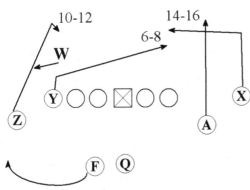

Diagram #1. Double left 60Z

The quarterback's read is tight end, curl, swing, and dig. That is the order he reads the pattern. When the quarterback is in the shotgun, he is about five yards from the line of scrimmage. He catches the ball and takes a three step drop. He is looking for the tight end first. If the linebackers are in zone coverage and have split to go to their zones, he hits the tight end.

If the linebackers are walling off the tight end, the quarterback looks at the flat defender. If he is dropping under the curl route by the Z back, the quarterback throws the ball to the swing pattern. If the flat defender is covering the swing, he throws the ball to the curl.

The backside patterns are the ones the quarterback very seldom throws. We have hit the go pattern for a touchdown more than one time last year,

but we are not looking to throw the ball that way. Frankly, it was pure luck that we did it. We mention the dig route in our progression of reads, but we are not going to get there with the ball.

The next set we use is the light package. That is our four wide receiver package. In this set, we take our tight end off the field and replace him with another wide receiver. If we did not take him off the field, he would be detached from the line in a slot position. This formation has been a good formation for us and is the primary formation in the two-minute drill.

The formation is a twins right. The X and A receivers are to the left of the formation, and the Z back and H receiver are to the other side. The tight end alignment is always to the direction call (see Diagram #2). The pattern is 60 X-Z-dig. The X end is running the curl, the A back is running the cross, and the Z back is running the dig route on the backside. The fullback aligns to the call side and runs the swing.

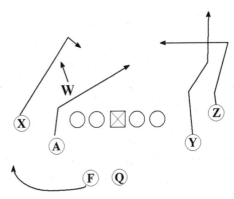

Diagram #2. Twins 60 X-Z-dig

The quarterback is looking to throw the cross route to the A back in his first read. The quarterback is reading the flat defender in the next progression. He throws the ball to the curl route or to the swing pattern. We call the backside patterns, but we are not looking to throw that direction.

This throw is a high-percentage throw. We prefer to throw it on first down. In the two-minute game, this pattern will be the first pattern you see. It is a good third down throw in the two-minute game, particularly after you move into the four-down zone. In the two-minute game, we set the formation into the boundary. If the defense plays soft on the curl, you can throw the ball to the swing route. Since it is a third down, if the F back cannot make the first down, he runs out of bounds to stop the clock.

The next thing is the shallow cross against the soft corner read (see Diagram #3). The formation is a light package twin set right. We call "74 Y-cross X-dig." The 70 protection means the fullback stays in and blocks. The call gives us a six-man protection. We call Y-cross because we want to make sure everyone knows who is running the cross. Since we are in the light package, there is no Y receiver on the field. We replace him with a wide receiver, but his letter stays in the formation. The four pattern is a smash route for the callside receiver. The smash route is a modern football term for the 4 to 6 yard hitch or stop route. On the backside, we run the dig and a smash for the outside receiver.

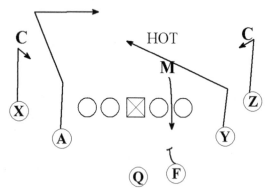

Diagram #3. Twins 74 Y-cross

The next formation is a heavy grouping. We throw the shallow cross out of that formation with an empty set in the backfield. In the heavy grouping, we leave both tight ends on the field. The Y end is the regular tight end. The U end is the second tight end or a receiving tight end. We like this set because we are looking for the mismatch. When we use this formation, the defense cannot substitute their nickel and dime package. It dictates that the defense play with their normal personnel on the field.

We call this formation pig. That is a crazy name, and people want to know why we named the formation pig. Before we came to Purdue, we were at the University of Wyoming. That conference was called

the crazy WAC when I was in it. New Mexico played in the WAC conference. They are called the Lobos. We used a unique formation against them and we called it a Lobo formation. The term Lobo is now part of our terminology. Our offensive coordinator is Jim Chaney. He comes from the great state of Missouri. He grew up on a pig farm. In this formation we had the U end out flanking our X receiver. After arguing for about an hour, I told them to come up with a name for it. From all that discussion, we now have a pig formation as part of our offense.

In the pig formation, the U end is opposite the call outside the alignment of the X-receiver. He is off the line of scrimmage, and the X receiver is on the line. To the other side, we have the Y end wide on the line of scrimmage and the Z back in the wide slot. The F back is outside the Y end off the line of scrimmage. This is an empty set. The call is "Pig-right, gun, 64Z-cross."

The U end and F back run the smash route as the widest receivers in the formation (see Diagram #4). The Y end runs a fade route down the field. The Z back runs the cross, and the X receiver runs the dig route. The complimentary route opposite the cross is always the dig.

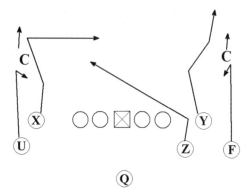

Diagram #4. Pig 64 Z-cross

Two years ago we played Michigan State on their home field. It was fourth-and-four on their 30-yard line. Our starting quarterback got hurt on the third down play and had to leave the game. We were down by six points, and we had less than a minute to go in the game. Our backup quarterback went into the game. The huddle call was 64 Z-cross. We wanted him to throw one of the smash routes and pick up the first down. He threw the fade for a touchdown and we won the game. That was the only pass he threw the entire game. Anything can happen in the game of football.

The first thing the quarterback wants to do is throw the smash route against any soft corner on either side. If the quarterback comes off the smash, he reads the cross to the dig route. He reads low to high in his read. The cross is at 6 yards, and the dig is at 12 yards.

A thought process should go through the quarterback's head. We are looking for the easy completion. If the coverage has a soft corner, we want to take advantage of it. We throw that pattern because it is a high-percentage throw and a way to get the ball to the outside receiver.

At Purdue we throw a lot of inside breaking routes. Our two best receivers are our inside receivers. Our slot receivers are catching about 80 percent of all passes thrown at Purdue. We wanted to get the ball to the outside receiver, and this was a way to do it.

We feel this is a way to attack zone pressure. What ends up happening in those kinds of defense situations is that a defensive end will be matched up on the swing pattern going into the boundary. That puts a defensive end on a skilled running back. We think we can make hay out of that match-up.

We can throw the ball against a cover 3 defense because the corners are soft. Against a man-free coverage, we feel the corner is going to be soft. We feel like this offense has big play potential to it. If defenses are going to sit on the smash, we go up on top with the fade route.

This year our statistics were average, but our points were good. We were fortunate to play Georgia in the bowl game. In that game we threw the shallow cross 12 times in the fourth quarter and scored some points. We ended up losing the game in overtime, but we played well.

I am going to the film and show you some of the things I talked about. The first thing we see is the heavy group with two tight ends, two wide

receivers, and one back. The play is the right 60Z-X-dig (see Diagram #5). The quarterback is under the center. If he is under the center, he takes a five-step drop. The Y and Z align to the right, and the U and X align to the left. The Y runs the cross, the Z runs the curl, the U runs the go, and the X runs the dig route.

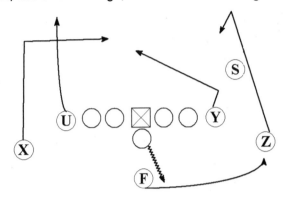

Diagram #5. Heavy 60Z-X-dig

If the quarterback reads a blitz coming inside, he throws the cross right away. If it is a zone he works shallow cross, to curl, to the flat pattern.

One thing we can do with our heavy package on the field is the following (see Diagram #6). We go to the twin look, with the tight end outside and the wide receivers inside. When the defense adjusts, they cover our slot receivers with linebackers and our tight end receivers with corners. That puts their linebackers in a mismatch on the wide receivers. We ran the 74 X cross. The tight ends run the smash patterns, and the wide receivers run the cross and dig routes. That is an example of mismatching the personnel.

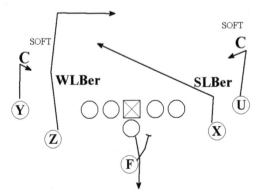

Diagram #6. Heavy twins 74 X cross

We have our big tight ends on the corners running smash routes. That is a tall order: to have a nonphysical corner that is playing soft come up and take on a tight end. In a mismatch situation, if you have speed at the receiver, you have a chance to split defenders and take the play a long way. Working the cross to the dig with two wide receivers is a good combination.

I learned a long time ago that if you split someone out, someone will cover him. We could split an offensive tackle out and some defensive back would cover him.

In our pass protection, we can block man protection or slide protection. The quarterback knows the protection scheme each time, so he can pick up his hot reads (see Diagram #7). If we are sliding the protection right and the outside linebacker on the right is coming on a blitz, the quarterback knows he will be picked up unless both linebackers on that side blitz. In that case, the outside linebacker comes free.

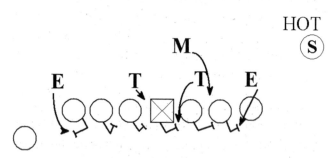

Diagram #7. Slide protection

In a slide protection, the quarterback knows that most of his hot reads will come from the outside. In man protection, his hot reads are probably going to be inside. However, he knows the schemes and generally can pick up the blitzes and throw accordingly. All of our protections are color coded. Our yellow protection tells the tight end to stay in and block. The tight end is the Y—receiver; therefore, the word yellow starts with Y and that designates his protection.

Red protection means red alert to the offensive linemen. The lineman has no help and is on an island. Our white protection means the fullback stays in and blocks the weakside of the formation. This protection gets its name because weakside and white both start with W.

That is our shallow cross package. We run the cross with a good combination pattern behind it. The reads are simple, and you can do them out of multiple formations. We stopped throwing the bubble screen because of our talent level. We went to this type of offense because the patterns were safe and the passing game was high percentage.

My wife and I bought a cabin in Buffalo, Wyoming. I should have stuck a stick of dynamite in it and blown it up. Nevertheless, the wife finally remodeled the cabin. We have a one-bedroom cabin with an outhouse. However, the gate is always open and the coffee pot is always on. There isn't but one Tiller there, and that is me. You can come by and draw plays on napkins and drink beers right out of the stream. Those mountain streams are where we keep the beer so it is always cold. I am not there very often, but I am there for a couple of weeks in July. You are certainly welcome, and see you all.

DEVELOPING A HARD-NOSED DEFENSE

University of Georgia

It is good to be here representing the University of Georgia. Football has always been a player's game and it always will be. I see great coaching jobs done every day, but the talent just does not match up to the competition, and because of that programs struggle. Success in a football program is all about players.

The game of football has changed so much, it is really unbelievable. Many reasons exist for that happening. The distractions that exist outside of football are always going to be there, and they are probably going to get worse. We as coaches have to decide if that is acceptable, or if are there other ways to combat those distractions.

I am going to show you some things that are very general in regards to our defense. After that I am going to show a video of some things that we do at Georgia to emphasize toughness. Obviously motivation is a big part of being tough.

I think motivation to me is more about the players' success than anything else. I think that it is more important now than it used to be. When you teach a scheme or a fundamental to a player, he is not going to be motivated if he does not have success in the scheme, and certainly in the fundamentals you are teaching. I have seen this for the past three years at Georgia. When the freshmen come into camp, they have a problem picking up and doing fundamentals drills for the first time. In fact they are resistant in their practice of fundamentals.

The moment the player has some success with what the coach is teaching is the time he begins to trust the coach. When the player becomes more successful, you are starting to get a motivated player. That is the challenge facing all coaches in college and high school football. Football clinics are great for coaches. Too many times the coaches come to clinics looking for schemes instead of what motivates players to play in those schemes.

A scheme will work if it is sound. However, you will not be successful unless you find motivated players to play in that scheme. It has never been what the coach knows that wins games. It is what he can teach and what his players know that win games.

Along with motivation in teaching, we have to keep our ideas simple. Simplicity is the key to success. You need to say the same thing over and over until players know what you are talking about. There is nothing greater than a player that wants to please his coach.

If you want to teach toughness as part of your program, you have to be tough year-round. One of the reasons we are good at Georgia is because we practice tough.

I am a big time believer in a blueprint. Philosophy and objectives are the blueprint within your defense. Your philosophy is the thing that is going to make your defense successful. Once you come up your philosophy, you have to stick with it. You are going to be good at the things you emphasize. Sometimes we get so carried away with preparation for the game that we forget to emphasize the very thing that makes us successful.

If you do not emphasis tackling, you are not going to be a good defense. If you do not tackle well, you will have no way to stop the run. To tackle well, you must tackle every day in practice and practice the fundamentals of tackling.

We have philosophies and objectives, but you must have a method to accomplish those things. One of the methods of achieving your goals and objectives is creating turnovers. I believe to be a good defense, you have to emphasize turning the ball over. We practice taking the ball away. We drill punching the ball out in our inside drill. We practice stripping the ball in our defensive shell drill. We have a circuits drill we call county fair, which teaches take-aways. Our players rotate around to different stations taking part in ball take-away drills.

The most important down for the offense is first down. That is the down which is not a situation down. As one of our objectives, we want to stop the first down run. The defense must win on first down and have a method to do that. If the offense is held to under three yards on first down, the second and third downs become situation downs in favor of the defense.

The third down play is the next important down for the defense. We call it the money down. If you do a good job on third down, the defense gets off the field. We drill and practice that down in practice every day. We chart the third down plays. The phrase three-and-out is part of our goal board and has become a catchphrase with our defense. We want the defense talking the same language all the time.

To play good defense, you cannot give up the big play. Allowing a big play has a lot to do with a number of breakdowns within the defense. You cannot overemphasize eliminating the big play. There has to be a mentality on the defense that makes that a big goal for the team

To play sound defense, you must eliminate foolish penalties. Each player has to think about what he does on the football field. Foolish penalties keep offensive drives alive. They give up field position, and they affect the head coach.

One of our primary goals is to score on defense. If the defense has the mentality to do this, the defense will be faster. The secondary will want to play the ball quicker when it is in the air. If the ball is on the ground, our defenders are going to scoop it up and try to score.

We want to score on defense, but when our offense turns the ball over, the defense has to react to the sudden change. The sudden change is a huge momentum builder for someone. If the defense can go out and stop the offense, the advantage goes to the defense. If the ball is turned over in the red zone and their offense gets no points, or at the worst, a field goal, the defense has turned the momentum in their favor.

When you play great defense, you must be physical. When you play physical and swarm the football, you can develop that physical toughness that every defense needs. When you show your defense film of swarming defenses that get eight or nine players to the ball, they need to see that. Those types of plays are contagious and spread to all member of the defense.

Within your staff, you will have coaches that the players feel comfortable talking to about some of the problems they may have. Those coaches are the good cops, and there is nothing wrong with that. However, within every staff there have to be bad cops. Those are the coaches that get after players and stay after them. I believe in some way you have to keep the players on edge, where they do not feel too comfortable.

When we grade our films, we use a production chart to assess our players. We give them points for goals accomplished and minus points for things not done. That gives us a production ratio for our player. We can tell if he is being productive on the field for the amount of plays he participates in. One of the minus categories that can really bring the ratio down is called a loaf.

We judge if a player is loafing by a number of criteria. If the player changes speed within the play as he is running to the ball, that is a loaf. If a player is running across the field at three-quarter speed and increases his speed because he sees a missed tackle, that is classified as a change of speed. He should be coming hard all the time. We want to see our players accelerating to the ball.

If a player does not turn and run to the ball, that is a loaf. That situation occurs in the defensive line with the pass rush in most cases. The quarterback will throw the ball, and the pass rusher will not turn and run to the ball.

In the pursuit of the football, if a defender is passed by another player in his position, that is a loaf. We tweaked this reason a bit because we did not think it was fair to consider everyone on the defense. We would expect a defensive back to pass up defensive linemen. What we do not expect is a linebacker to be passed by another linebacker in pursuing the ball.

We do not expect players to never get knocked down. When a player is knocked down, we expect him to get off the ground and pursue the football. We never want a player lying on the ground. We use the same evaluations in practice and in games. If you do not do these things in practice, you will not do them in a game.

We never want to see a defensive player turn down a chance to hit someone. If we have a pile with the running back still up, we want the pursuit to finish the play. I want the defender coming until the whistle blows. If we see players pull up at the end of a play instead of accelerating, that is a loaf.

You cannot be tough only during football season if you expect to build toughness throughout your program. You cannot live soft and play tough.

You have to have a plan to keep your football players tough during the time they are away from the football field. You cannot turn toughness on and off like a water fountain.

As you look at your players that are coming back for next year's team, you are probably very optimistic because of the talent level you have. Good talent just gives you the chance to win. You have to develop a team to win games. These off-season drills are where you begin to build your team for next season. Your talent has to be committed to the team to be good. If your players do not suffer together and sweat together, team unity is not going to happen. That is what our mat drill really does for our players.

We are going to force our players into a situation where some of them think about giving up. That happens during the season in a close physical game going into the fourth quarter. We want to handle that feeling in the off-season so our players can fight through that because of the team.

When we do our mat drill, the emphasis is put on doing it right. If the players do not do the drill right, they have to go back and do it again. We do a better job in our indoor program than anywhere else I have been. Doing the drill right is demanded of the players.

(Editor's note: The mat drills that Coach Vangorder is referring to are covered in Mark Richt's lecture in great detail.)

This next drill is a board drill (see Diagram #1). We use a wide soft board and have a 1-on-1 offense-versus-defense drill. This is not a technique drill. This is a face the issues drill. I will talk about the players' techniques, but I am more interested in seeing who will fight and be tough in this drill. This is a safe drill because it only requires two guys on a board. The offense locks up with the defense and they do not stop until they hear the whistle. This is not a feel-sorry, buddy drill; it is a get-after-them drill.

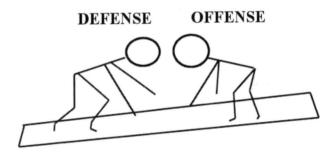

Diagram #1. Board drill

This drill will tell you a lot about the personalities of your players. In this drill, we have to have explosion, lockout, and foot movement. What I am looking for is a player's effort until the end of the drill. The personality of the player will not lie to you in this drill. Doing this drill, you want your players to stay on the board and not drop their heads.

When you do this drill make sure you get your players reps. Do not practice slow because today's players want to practice fast and move.

We have boards all over the field and our players are going at it. If you want tempo in your practice, you cannot have players standing around doing nothing. Your players improve when they can get multiple reps on any skill. The coach has to get the tempo high with plenty of reps for the players. If you move players through the drill rapidly, you can shorten your practices and keep their attention.

We started something in the spring that goes along with our board drill. We call it a spider drill (see Diagram #2). This drill has a degree of techniques and fundamentals, a team issue, and a toughness drill. It is important for teammates to see who the tough players on your team are. You want the team to see what you are seeing. Also, a special emotion exists in team or group drills.

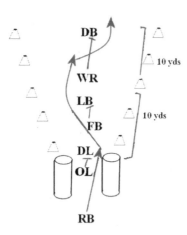

Diagram #2. Spider drill

In this drill, we match O-line with D-line, fullbacks with linebackers, and wide receivers with defensive backs. You include the tight ends with the offensive linemen. We start out the drill with the offensive lineman blocking the defensive lineman. They are playing in an area bordered by two dummies about three yards apart. From there, we proceed down the field, building a chute with cones in a V shape. Ten yards behind the linemen are the fullbacks and linebacker, and ten yards behind them are the wide receivers and defensive backs. We have defenders at three levels, with each level having more distance to cover than the one in front of them. You can set up as many chutes as you need to keep the drill moving.

The running back starts behind the linemen and attacks between the dummies. The defensive lineman has to deliver a blow, shed the blocker, and make a tackle. If the defensive lineman gets off the block, he runs past the running back but does not tackle him. If the running back gets past the level of a defender, we do not allow the defender to chase and tackle the running back from behind. The running back proceeds down the chute to the next set, which is the fullbacks and linebacker. The same thing happens in this grouping, except the linebacker has more space to cover. The third part of the drill is happening at the same time, with the wide receiver stalking the defensive back. This is a live drill with the defensive back coming into the linebacker area if he can get off the block.

The goal line tackle is a drill that emphasizes toughness (see Diagram #3). We put the tackler on the goal line and the ballcarrier on the five-yard line. We put a bag in between them to keep the ball carrier from running straight downhill at the tackle. The bag makes the ballcarrier run on an angle to get to the goal line. The running back can go to either side of the bag he wants, but he must stay inside the cone to score. The cones are five yards apart.

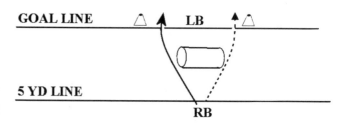

Diagram #3. Goal line tackle

This is a rapid-fire drill, but we are emphasizing a goal line situation. You get to see who will fight in this drill. On the goal line, fundamentals are not as important as desire. The tackle will not be a pretty tackle if the running back knows what he is doing. It will be a fight to keep the ballcarrier out of the end zone. The fundamental we are looking for is foot movement away from the goal line. They have to drive through the ballcarrier and keep the feet moving.

I'm now going to talk about two of our pressure blitzes. These pressures are very simple, and they fit well within our system.

At Georgia we play an eight-man front, and I am very meticulous about our fits being accurate and perfect against the run game. The first thing we are going to do defensively is to stop the run.

Our system is a very simple to teach. I will put up our under front for you to see (see Diagram #4). On this front, we have moved the bubble to the tight end side. Our Sam linebacker is a 9 technique player on the tight end. Our defensive end, called the Buck, plays a 5 technique to the field side. The nose tackle is on an outside shade of the center into the field. The 3 technique tackle is aligned to the boundary, and the F, who is the rush end, is in a 5 technique to the boundary. The Mike linebacker is in a 20 technique alignment on the guard, and the Will linebacker is aligned in a 30 technique stacked behind the tackle.

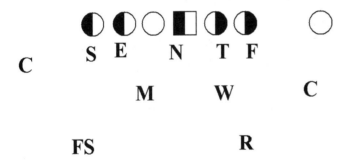

Diagram #4. Under front

We play with a strong safety and free safety in our system. We call the strong safety the Rover. One of these two players is generally going to drop down and be the eighth man in the box. The corners are aligned on the wide receivers to the outside. Most of the time, we drop the free safety down to the bubble side of the defense. He is the defender the offense cannot block.

This type of system allows the linebackers to play fast and get downhill in a hurry. That is where the big hits come from in the defensive scheme. The Mike linebacker on any play run to the weakside is fast fill and flow. He does not have to worry about the cutback seam in the defense. The free safety rolls into the box and has the cutback seam.

We play the under fire defense in first-and-ten running situations (see Diagram #5). If we are going to involve our free safety in our blitz or movement calls, we are going to use some kind of word beginning with "f." If we want to involve the strong safety or Rover, we use some kind of word beginning with "r." The companion stunt we run with the Fire stunt is what we call Rifle.

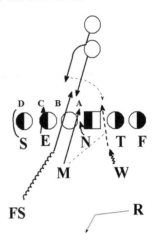

Diagram #5. Under fire run toward Mike

The Fire call brings the free safety down into the B gap to the Mike linebacker's side. If the ball is run at the Mike linebacker on an isolation-type play, the Mike linebacker inside fills on the fullback and bounces the ball to the free safety, who is unblocked. The Will linebacker slows play, watching for the cutback on the backside because there is no place for him to fit to the strongside. If the ball is run at the Will linebacker on an isolation type of play, the Will linebacker sticks the fullback on the outside shoulder and turns the ball back inside to the fast-flowing Mike linebacker.

I do not want to create pressure schemes that are huge changes in teaching for the players. This defense is great against the run and possibly in creating some problems with the pass. If the offense ran the isolation at the free safety, the free safety sticks the fullback with an outside stick and forces the ball back to the Mike linebacker (see Diagram #6). The Will linebacker plays slow and checks for the cutback.

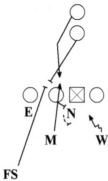
Diagram #6. Under fire run at FS

If the offense gave us a double slot formation, we might make some adjustments on the free safety fill. From the double slot, wing-T offenses like to trap the B gap. We would run a tiger call for our 5 technique Buck end (see Diagram #7). That would drive him inside to take on the trapper. He knows the technique to handle a trap blocker. I do not like to run a free safety through the B gap and let him get trapped. He does not know how to play that block, and he would probably get ear-holed. The stunting end plays inside on the trapper and bounces the ball to the free safety fitting outside of him.

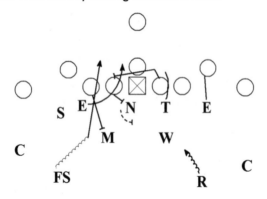
Diagram #7. Under fire tiger

The coverage we play with these types of movements would be fire zone coverage or man coverage. The fire zone coverage is three-under in the short zones and three-deep coverage. If you are playing three-under, we are giving up one underneath zone.

In our defensive philosophy in our regular defense, we are a spill team. We are going to spill everything outside except when we have inside pressure. If we have inside pressure coming, we are going to contain the ball. If the offense runs a power

off-tackle play when the safety spins down, we are not sure what is going to happen to him. In the fire and rifle stunt, the safeties have to work on their timing in the stunt. That means we have to have some idea what the opponent is doing with his cadence. We want the safeties to hit those stunts with speed.

We also coach them on what we call their entry area. We want the safety to know his entry area can change on certain situations. His entry landmark is generally the inside leg of the offensive tackle. The power off-tackle is one of the most difficult fits for the free safety. In the SEC when teams run this play, it is a downhill play (see Diagram 8). It does not hit off tackle. We want the free safety to time up the play so that he fills hard through the B gap and knocks off the backside pulling guard. If the play is not timed correctly, the double-team chip block may pick off the free safety. If that happens, we are in trouble because the backside guard can turn up in the hole on the Mike linebacker, who is fitting over the top of the double team.

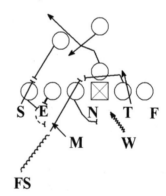
Diagram #8. Power off-tackle

Since we have an inside force, the Sam linebacker runs a contain technique called a cage. He is going to play blocks with his outside arm free and turn the ball back inside. When the Mike linebacker sees the power off-tackle, he has to make sure the free safety gets through the B gap. He screws his position down into what we call a plus 10 technique on the center. He is making room for the free safety to get through the B gap. If the free safety gets through and picks off the pulling guard, the Mike linebacker becomes the unblocked player and pursues from the inside out.

If we did not have a Fire call, we would not have inside pressure (see Diagram #9). The Sam linebacker plays everything differently. He goes back to the regular defensive technique and spills the ball outside. The Mike is in a hole position coming from inside. He has to get over top of the double-team, but stay inside the pulling guard. He knows the free safety is reading the flow and is going outside. The Mike linebacker is inside the pulling guard, and the free safety is outside the pulling guard. Either way, there is only one blocker and someone is going to be free. The only thing that hurts the play is the Mike linebacker overrunning the pulling guard.

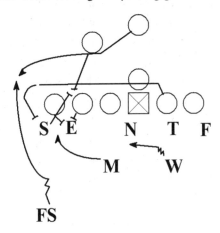

Diagram #9. Power 0 no fire

The companion stunt is called rifle. It is the same movement, except the Rover is coming down into the box and the free safety is going to the middle (see Diagram #10). When we use the rifle, we put a tiger call with it to bring the tackle down inside into the A gap. Since we are spinning the Rover into the box, the linebackers have to adjust their alignments. The Will linebacker is going to a 20 alignment head up the guard, and the Mike linebacker is moving to a 40 head up the tackle, or at least a wide 30 alignment on the outside shoulder of the guard. We stem to these positions so as to not give away what we are doing with the Rover.

If we get the isolation play toward the Mike linebacker, the Mike linebacker fits outside on the block of the fullback, and the Will linebacker plays fast over the double-team, looking for the big hit on the inside of the fullback. The Rover is filling the backside B gap and playing the cutback running lane.

If the ball attacks toward the Will linebacker, the Will linebacker is attacking inside on the fullback and spilling the ball to the Rover back (see Diagram #11). The Mike linebacker plays slow and takes the cutback lane. The rush end has a cage call and plays everything back to the inside.

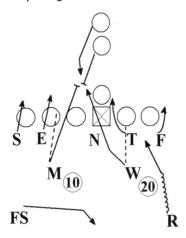

Diagram #10. Rifle run away

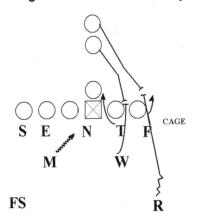

Diagram #11. Rifle run toward

Using field and bench calls will really help the defense with a no-huddle situation or a two-minute defense. It will save you a lot of problems in communication. Our bubble is going to be set to the wide side of the field. That means the free safety, Buck end, nose, and Sam and Mike linebackers are into the wide side of the field. The Will linebacker, tackle, rush end, and Rover are into the boundary on the field. We have boundary and field corners that align into their field and boundary positions and are anchored regardless of motion or formation.

If we give a field call and the offensive comes out in a twins set to the field, we adjust (see Diagram #12). The Sam linebacker walks out on the slot. The buck end is aligned in a 5 technique, and the nose tackle is in a shade on the center into the field. The Mike linebacker and the free safety are into the field. The boundary tackle is in a 3 technique. The rush end has the tight end and aligns in a 6 technique head up the tight end. The boundary corner squirms up and in toward the formation, and the Rover aligns to that side.

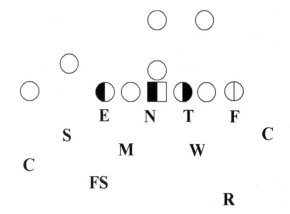

Diagram #12. Field vs. twins

If we want to run fire or rifle we simply add the term to the field call. I have one more to show you before we go to the film. This movement is called hot (see Diagram #13). If we call "field-hot," the boundary side corner is coming hard from the outside. The adjustments and play of the defense are like a rifle stunt with one exception. The rush end is going to become the B gap player on the run and the corner is the C gap player. The Rover is going to sneak out and cover the wideout to the boundary side. The reaction for everyone else in the defense is the same. The Will linebacker on flowaway is a fast player because he has a cutback player behind him. It does not affect the frontside at all.

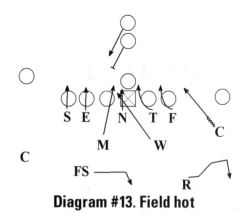

Diagram #13. Field hot

If the call was "under cover 1 hot," we might have to make slight adjustments. The defensive front would be an under call, meaning the bubble would be to the tight end side. Cover 1 is our man coverage scheme, and the hot call is the stunt for the boundary corner. If the offense came out in a twin set onto the field, both corners would be on the field (see Diagram #14). In that case, there would be no boundary corner. The hot call would come from the field, but everything else would be the same.

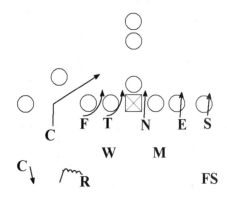

Diagram #14. Cover 1 hot

I hope you got something you can use in your program. I want to say thanks to Ray Lamb. It has been a pleasure.

IMPLEMENTING THE MASTER COACHING PLAN

University of Memphis

It is my pleasure to be here on behalf of Nike and to represent Memphis University. I really don't mind being here on Sunday morning because I know everyone in this room wants to hear what I have to say. You are the die-hards of the clinic. You are the guys who are here to pick up maybe one thing to take back to your programs. I think that is critical right now.

Before we get into football, I want to talk about some of the things I've learned through 23 years of coaching and 10 years of being a head coach. These are some philosophical ideas that I think are more important than X's and O's. These things help you be successful and win football games.

I believe it is harder than it has ever been to be a good coach. I believe kids need us now more than ever before. When you look at what is going on in the world right now, kids need us. In college football, if you look back over the past ten years, the NCAA and college presidents have cut about everything there is to cut out of the sports programs, with the exception of accountability. They have raised the accountability for college coaches.

The head coach has to take the responsibility for the players we recruit, and we can only visit them one time. You would have to be blessed with ESP to meet a recruit one time and know everything about him. We can't do that.

At Memphis we have tried to develop as the most aggressive football team we can be. That aggressive style includes our offense, defense, and the kicking game.

From a philosophical standpoint, we are aggressive in every phase of the game. That is the way we look at it. We are making the defense defend what we do offensively, and we are making the offense condense to handle what we do defensively.

We had a tremendous turnaround this season in our won and loss record. I hired some outstanding assistants. When I hire a coach, I hire a good person and let him work. The thing I have to do is make sure what we are teaching stays simple. You don't outcoach people on Saturday. You have to outcoach them during the week. I know you have heard that before, but we live that philosophy.

I've had players make plays, but we coached those players during the week to make those plays. They are the ones who win games for you. Players on the field making plays win games. We don't outcoach anybody; our players out play the other team's players.

When I am interviewing a coach, the first thing I look for is his ability to communicate. He has to be able to communicate with me, the staff, and the player. The players have to believe in the coach. The coach has to communicate with them. You have to be honest with your players. I have learned through the years that you have to be straight-up with players.

The last thing I look for in a coach is production. I don't care whether our coaches come into the office at six o'clock or nine o'clock. We don't have hours for our assistant coaches. We don't have staff meeting during the season. If the head coach has a staff meeting, he is eating up 30 to 45 minutes of his assistant coaches' time. If I need something, I go to the coordinators and get it done that way. It is important to me that my assistant coaches produce.

The coach I hire has to be a producer. When a coach comes to me on the Friday before signing date, all I want to know is whether we signed the kid he was recruiting. I'm not interested in why we didn't get him. We are a no-nonsense program, from coaches to players.

The most important thing I'm going to say today is have a plan. It doesn't matter if you are the head coach or a graduate assistant; you better have a plan for how you are going to help your players. I have to have a total plan to make sure everyone is on the same page.

That holds true for everyone on staff, dealing with the training room, the equipment room, the weight room, and the academic center. Everybody associated with the program is on the same page as the coaches. We had the same plan two years ago, when we won three games, as we did this year, when we won nine games. However, we had a plan and we stuck to that plan. That is what makes the difference.

I have been in this game for a long time and have had time to develop a plan. When Clemson fired me, I had a whole year to sit out and think about the plan I was working on. I had to tweak some things in my plan. I learned something from my experience at Clemson. At Clemson, I lost sight of the plan and it got away from me.

Once you develop your plan, you have to sell it to your staff. Our staff knows how we are going to win and be successful. The way you win is to get the best players. The team with the best players usually wins the game.

The next thing you have to do is sell your plan to your players. You have to sell it on a daily basis. You have to be committed to the plan.

If you are not committed to your plan, you'll be like I was at Clemson. If you don't stand for something, you'll fall for anything. You will get away from what you really believe in because the pressure can be enormous. If you don't believe in and are totally committed to your plan, you will lose it. When you lose it, you are finished.

We have an off-the-field philosophy that our players live by. The first thing on that list is no drugs.

I do not want them involved in that. I am not naïve enough to think that no one on our football team has ever been involved with marijuana. I'm not an idiot. Drugs are no good for players. I always ask our kids if they want to be successful.

The second hard-and-fast rule is go to school. That is very simple to understand. We only have three rules for our team. When I played college football they gave us a handbook of rules called the Do's and Don'ts. It was about two inches thick. I learn something from that experience. You better keep your rules simple if you want people to follow them. The team has to go by your rules, whatever they are.

If you give them 50 rules to live by, they won't be living by them. When that happens, you don't have any credibility. If school starts at eight o'clock in the morning, this is when we want our players there. We want them in the classroom making progress toward that degree. I have a little group that checks on class attendance. The team calls them the Gestapo.

These are my rules, and they are not negotiable. My players know this. I sit in their homes and ask them what they want to get out of college life. They tell me right there that they want an education. I tell them and their parents that if they are interested in getting an education, you have met the right man. If they come to Memphis, they are going to school every day. I guarantee those parents if they sign with Memphis they are going to graduate with a degree.

If they stay at Memphis for the four years, they will graduate. I tell my coaches when they go to a prospect's school, to look at his grades. I want them to look at the number of tardies and absents that prospect has in school. If a kid won't give you an honest day's work, won't get there on time, or won't go, they can't play in our program. They cannot survive in our program because that is what I believe and that is what I stand for. This is how we win. It is more important than any offensive system.

The third rule is do your best. We want our players going as hard as they can and to do the best they can. It doesn't matter if they can bench 400 or 200 pounds, whether they run 4.4 or 5.0, or whether they are a 4.0 student or a 2.0 student, we want them to do the best they can every time.

If I check a classroom and one of my players is sitting in the back of the room with his hat cocked sideways, and he has no book, no paper, or no pencil, that is not the best he can do.

I believe it wholeheartedly if they do those three things they will graduate from our college. Don't be naïve enough to think you can save them all. There are some who are not going to follow your rules and you are going to have to get rid of them. With all the academic help we have available in schools today, if a player will go to class and try, he will graduate.

At our place, if one guy misses a class or is late for a study hall, all our players get up at 5:30 and do up/downs until they are pretty tired. I am the one who does the drills. I am the one who stood up in front of the group and told them they were going to class. When someone misses a class they have defied my rules, and have told me that they don't believe in my plan. He has told his teammates that they are not important to him.

You will find the older guys getting their buddies up for class. They don't want to do too many of the 5:30 sessions because I am generally peeved when I get there.

Let me tell you what helped us win nine games this past season. Our turf room burned down a year ago before this past season. It was a multipurpose room where we did our indoor workouts. We had just come off a 3-8 season and had a much better team than that. We underachieved badly. It hurts to say that because I am the one responsible, but we underachieved as a football team.

We had to find a way to get mentally and physically tougher as a football team. That was the key to our success last season. What I did was take the players outside and do what we normally did inside. We didn't have any mats, but we still did mat drill. We did them on the ground. The weather was never a factor.

Mother Nature was beautiful for us. The first morning we went out at 5:30 it was 30 degrees and icy on the field. After we stretched, we got in lines and did our dives. I wanted them all wet, muddy, and cold. On the third morning at 5:30 there was two inches of snow on the ground. We did not have one player late. Every one of them was there, and we went on with our off-season program.

That brought our football together. The thing that did it was that there was no moaning and groaning.. We told them we were going to work. We were not tough enough mentally, and we were going to make ourselves tougher. That is what turned our football team around.

Those three philosophies that I just talked about are carved in stone and are not negotiable. The traits that really win for us we don't change. We interweave them throughout our system and scheme. The first trait is toughness. This type of toughness is both mental and physical. I'm not talking about doing something incredible. I am talking about sucking it up and getting the job done.

Players are not as tough today as they were when I played. I know the young guys don't want to hear about us walking sixteen miles to school uphill both ways. I heard it from my dad, and you heard it from yours. Nevertheless, we have to help our players be tougher mentally.

It doesn't matter what you do offensively or defensively, if you are not physical or tough in our game, you can't win. We won three games two years ago because we were a talented football team with not much toughness. If we are going to ask our players to outhit the other team for sixty minutes, we have to be tough enough to do that.

Starting Monday morning we will be outside at 5:30 in the morning going at it. We are not the most physical team in the world, but we are tougher than we were. The players believe they can overcome adversity. When we were 3-3 and we told them we were going to win six games in a row, they believed that. They believe that we will not get beat physically. We may lose by turning the ball over, but we will never be beat physically again. That is what the game of football is all about.

If you have the best players you should win the game. I haven't been fortunate enough everywhere I've coached to have the best players. If you don't have the best players, you can't give up and accept the fact that you are going to lose. How am I going to beat a team when I don't have as good players as he does?

When you don't have the best players, you have to be in better shape. The second trait in our system is conditioning. You have to go harder, longer than the other team.

We want to be in better shape and be in better condition then everybody we play. I don't have to be a great athlete to be in shape. That is why we run a no-huddle offense and do the things we do on defense.

We are so simple in the things we do on offense and defense we can spend time conditioning and still get the reps in. I can't ask our players to out hit a team for sixty minutes and have them wear out halfway through the fourth quarter. That can't happen. If they buy into the physical part of the game, they have to buy into the conditioning.

The third trait we have to have in our system is attitude. I tell our players that coaching football is the best thing I do. We are not going to be miserable doing what we do best. We are not going to dread doing what we do best. I am not going to be miserable on Friday night with my butt so tight I can't sit down. I am going to enjoy Friday night because I like what I do. If you don't enjoy what you do best, you are going to be a miserable person.

On game day, the first thing we want to do is run the ball. To run the ball, you have to be tough and aggressive. Two years ago, we did not run the ball. This year we were better at running the ball. We kept it simple for the offensive line. Our scheme was simple and we are a no-huddle, one-back football team.

On defense we had to stop the run. We were not very good at stopping the run two years ago. We hired Coach Dunn and got really good at stopping the run this year.

The third thing on game day is to be on the plus side in turnovers. The last thing we have to mention is our special teams. We have to get better at that phase of the game. Punting is a big part of your defensive play. Field position is an important point in football, which is directly related to your special teams.

We teach fundamentals to every kid on our football team. I worked for Coach Johnny Majors at Tennessee. Coach Majors was the finest fundamentals football coach I've ever been around. These fundamentals came straight from Johnny Majors.

In our fundamentals, we talk about the target and aiming point. That is a direct reference to the players' eyes. We teach the concept of aim point to every player on our team. It doesn't matter whether the player is on offense or defense. They all have targets and aiming points. The running backs have aiming points. On defense, the linebacker has a landmark he has to hit. All those fundamental skills require the player to use his eyes. He has to be able to see, and he has to put his head and pads in the right place. When he puts his hat in the right place, he gets leverage.

The second fundamental is takeoff. Football is a game of movement. The team that moves the quickest has an advantage. Takeoff is important in every aspect of the offensive and defensive teams.

The third fundamental is body lean, which relates to pad level. Playing with good pad level gives you leverage and lets you play against bigger players.

Aiming points, take-off, and body lean are the whole game of football. If we can do those three things, we can beat you. My team may not be as good as yours, but I can beat you if I can do those three fundamental skills.

John Majors taught us to run behind our pads. He talked about never taking shots on the ball because we ran behind our pads. Our running backs take the shots on their shoulder pads because of their body lean. We just went through our break-downs of our turnovers from last season. All but one of our fumbles came from a helmet on the ball. Our fumbles came from hits right on the ball or the arm carrying the ball. It doesn't matter if the back gained ten extra yards if he gives up the ball.

Our offense started down at Tulane four years ago. The year after I was fired at Clemson, I got the opportunity to be the defensive coordinator at Memphis after I sat out a year. We had a great defense that year. The last game of the year was Tulane down there. We were not having a good year, but our defense was leading the nation in rushing defense and was number two in total defense.

We got to halftime of the game, and Tulane had us down 17-3. I had just made a big speech Friday night about being number two in the nation and had an opportunity to lead the nation in defense. At halftime, we were basically getting it handed to us. They were a no-huddle fast tempo team. Two times in the first half, they ran plays and I didn't have a defense called. I couldn't get matched up in the secondary, and they scored one time because I didn't cover a receiver.

I had never been as frustrated as I was that night. I got in at halftime and ripped our defense. I got after them really hard, but I noticed they wouldn't look at me, which was never the case in any game before this one. I asked our graduate assistant how many plays we played in the first half. He told me the defense played 56 plays. That is almost a total game for our players. We normally play around 70 defensive snaps in a game. They were tired.

We went back out and Tulane scored 27 points with about 450 yards of offense. No one throughout the year had been able to do that. They had us on our heels the whole night, and they had at best, an average offensive line.

After the game I was sitting out in the Super Dome just thinking. I began to give a lot of thought to that kind of offense. To make a long story short, I got named the head coach at Memphis and had to put together the pieces to try to build a program.

I looked at Northwestern and they had beaten Ohio State that year and finished second in the Big Ten. Everybody knows Northwestern doesn't have as good players as Ohio State. I looked at Tulane. They had won 12 games and their coach had replaced me at Clemson.

I hired an offensive coordinator who was a two-back guy like me. I did that on purpose because I wanted to build this offense from the beginning. I wanted someone like me that could take those ideas and build the type of offense we wanted. All the one-back, no-huddle offenses, in their own way, are different. You have to fit the offense to your personnel.

This style of offense already fit the things we believed in. This offense fits the toughness we built into our program. To run this type of offense, you have to be in shape and conditioned to handle it. The offense fits our attitude because it is a fun scheme. You can enjoy what you do.

The only thing I was worried about was the toughness factor. Could we be tough enough in this style of offense to not kill off our defense? I thought I could control that enough as the head coach. I could make sure we were playing sound offensive football and not making stupid mistakes. I felt I could control the urge to go for the first down on four down all the time. That is an absolute disregard for defensive football. We were going to play field position and help our defense on offense.

This offense was perfect for us. The location of Memphis is the thing that made it fit. Memphis is sitting in a place with a little bit of population around us. However, we don't get the big offensive linemen. We get average offensive linemen, but we can get great skill players. For us to go to a two-back set and hammer the ball up inside is not going to be our game. Our offense did fit our philosophy and players.

You have to be able to run the ball. The offensive staff has DMSU written on the sides of all their boards. They don't think I know what that means. It stands for don't make stuff up. We are going to let our players win on game day. We basically have four runs. We have what we call a gut play. It is a zone play. We run it because you have to have a downhill inside running play. That is our number-one running play.

We have the reverse off the gut play. We fake it every time. I didn't grow up on the reverse, but I love the play. I love the theory of using the reverse as the companion play for the inside zone play. That gives us an inside run and an outside run with misdirection mixed into the scheme.

Our third run is the draw play. The reason we run the draw play is the offensive blocking scheme allows the offensive linemen to take the defender anywhere they want to go. We don't come off the ball; we just pop up in pass-protection mode and the defense starts to move for us.

We are always going to have an option in our offensive scheme. That goes back to my defensive upbringing because it is hard for the defense to play option teams. An option team forces the defense to play sound responsibility types of schemes. We run a little speed option. It is designed to pitch the ball. We don't want our quarterback running the ball because he cannot. It is basically a sweep play which does not block the defensive end.

That is our running game. We are going to make this system flexible by using formations and tempo. We are going to run the no-huddle offense and go fast. Then we are going to act like we are going fast and try to trick the defense into jumping offsides. We are going to make the defense go at our pace. We are going to use formations and make the defense adjust to those types of sets. We are not going to make mistakes. We are never going to have a defender who is unblocked. If that does happen it is the coaches' fault.

In the passing game we are more complicated. We lost four out of our five offensive linemen and had fewer sacks this year than we had last year. We threw the ball all over the place this year. You need to run the ball because you need the toughness that it takes to run the ball. You have to run the ball to keep your defense off the field. If you have a six-point lead, it is the offense's job to control the ball.

It is not their job to throw the ball three times, take no time off the clock, punt the ball, and tell the defense to stop the other team. The four-minute offense is more important than the two-minute situation. In the four-minute offense you have the lead and you have to control the ball to win the football game. That comes back to the toughness philosophy we have.

However, if you plan on winning big today, you better throw the football. I knew we couldn't protect in the dropback scheme we ran the year before. I worked eight years at Clemson for Danny Ford and we never threw a dropback pass. We either sprinted out with the ball or play-action passed the ball.

We decided to do the same thing this year. We became a bootleg team. It could help our offensive line because they could simply block down, and we could pull the guard and get on the perimeter. It also helped with blocking the blitz scheme.

We run about three routes. The first pass pattern we run is four verticals. We are going to run this from every formation we have. We want to put pressure on the defensive secondary. We want to be aggressive and throw the deep ball better than anybody in the country. We have a quarterback that can throw the deep ball accurately. I can't stand to see a quarterback overthrow a deep ball. If he underthrows the ball, the receiver is going to catch it about eight out of ten times, and it is hard for the defensive back to defend the underthrown ball.

The second pattern we run is called a smash route. To the two receiver side, the inside receiver runs a corner route and the outside receiver runs a six-yard stop route.

The third pattern we run is an option route. The outside receiver runs a takeoff, and the inside receiver runs the option route. The option gives the inside receiver the option to run a hook in the hole inside or an out if the linebacker is covering him.

Let me tell you how we practice. I don't like a lot of individual meetings. We have offensive meetings and defensive meetings. I want the coordinator putting in the new stuff we are going to use. I don't like all the position coaches putting in their piece of the play. I want one guy to give the whole presentation.

If you have four or five coaches putting in a part of the defense the explanation can get conveyed in different ways. That eliminates all questions, because everyone is going to know what we are doing. It is coming from one mouth how things are supposed to work. That is why I want only the coordinator putting in the new material.

When we go to practice we get 15 to 20 minutes of individual work. After we do our individual period, we go to team drill. We spend one hour in our team period. During that period, most of our offense is run against air. The defense will go team for an hour. We get the reps we need both offensively and defensively.

That is the first thing I said when I started at Memphis. I told people the first thing we have to do is learn how not to lose. People immediately took that to mean we were going to play not to lose instead playing to win. The first thing a team has to learn is not to give the game away through mistakes, busted assignments, turnovers, and penalties.

We don't have all the answers at Memphis. We don't have any more answers, and probably less, than a lot of coaches. We are not as smart as a lot of people out there. However, we know how to keep what we do simple. If you want your players to be aggressive, keep it simple. You can't confuse them. A confused player can't play fast and has no confidence. Let the players play. Don't tie them down with too many plays, and don't outcoach people on Saturday. Outcoach your opponents before you get to game day.

I have enjoyed this. Thank you for your attention.

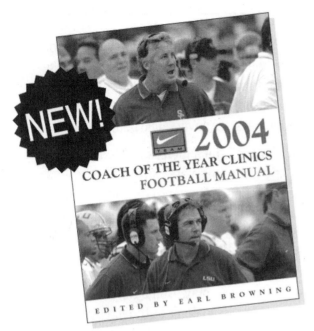

NEW!

2004
COACH OF THE YEAR CLINICS
Football Manual

Featuring lectures from several of America's most renowned coaches. Edited by Earl Browning.

$30.00 • 280 pages • 1-58518-896-4

Also available:

1998	1999	2000	2001	2002	2003

1-58518-214-1	1-58518-154-4	1-58518-298-2	1-58518-485-3	1-58518-644-9	1-58518-856-5
288 pp. • $15.00	271 pp. • $15.00	288 pp. • $20.00	272 pp. • $20.00	288 pp. • $20.00	288 pp. • $25.00

Title	Item #	Price	Qty	Total

Kentucky residents only include tax form 51A-126 or pay 6% sales tax.
Shipping & Handling included in cost.

PLUS	KY Tax 6%		
	TOTAL		

Name _____ Organization/School _____

Address _____

City _____ State _____ ZIP _____ Phone ( ) _____

Method of Payment: ☐ *VISA* ☐ MasterCard ☐ American Express Cards ☐ DISCOVER ☐ Check # _____ ☐ P.O. # _____

Account # ☐☐☐☐ ☐☐☐☐ ☐☐☐☐ ☐☐☐☐ Expiration: _____

Signature: _____ Email Address: _____

Send check, money order, or P.O. form to: **Telecoach, Inc.**
P.O. Box 22185 Louisville KY 40252
or call: (502) 425-2937 or fax: (502) 425-0306

NIKE TEAM